Religion and Politics in the World's Hot Spots

Roy C. Amore
University of Windsor

2016
Sloan Publishing
Cornwall on Hudson, NY 12520

Library of Congress Cataloging-in-Publication Data

Amore, Roy C., 1942-
Religion and politics in the world's hot spots / Roy C. Amore, University of Windsor. -- 1
[edition].
pages cm
ISBN 978-1-59738-049-2
1. Religion and politics. I. Title.
BL65.P7A475 2015
322'.109--dc23
2015024445

Cover photo by
Cover design by K&M Design

Sloan Publishing, LLC
220 Maple Road
Cornwall-on-Hudson, NY 12520

Printed in the United States of America

10 9 8 7 6 5 4 3 2 1

ISBN-10:   1-59738-049-6
ISBN-13:   978-1-59738-049-2

Dedication

This work is dedicated both to the religious persons who have peacefully resisted anti-religious political oppression, and to all the political actors who have peacefully pushed back against overly zealous or violent religious movements. "Blessed are the peacemakers" (Matthew 5.9).

Contents

Preface

I have used drafts of this work in my classes. One day a student I didn't know stopped me on campus to say how much she was enjoying the textbook. I must have looked puzzled, for she quickly explained that her roommate was in my course and "she let me read your book." That has to be a good sign, I thought. My other textbooks do not get passed around like that!

The Ultimate Show-and-Tell teaching. It has been my good fortune to have travelled, as their teacher, with many groups of students to many countries and regions. Almost immediately after our marriage, my wife and I travelled to India with a group of 20 young Canadians. We visited successful NGOs (non-government organizations) focused on sustainable social and economic development projects during the day, and enjoyed Indian food and culture in the evenings. In several later years I was part of a team of professors who led student study trips organized by Eastern Michigan University's *Study Abroad* program. Walking atop the Great Wall with students and then talking to them about who built it, when, why and did it work, is the ultimate in show-and-tell teaching. These great experiences, for my students and myself, suggests the style of learning underlying this book. Throughout its pages are 'travel boxes' by my students, other authors or myself. Readers are invited to imagine they are on a study trip.

The Interface of Religion and Politics. My training was in religious studies, with a specialization in the religions of Asia. After teaching world religions in a religious studies department for years, I was invited to join a political science department. So, for the past two decades my focus has been on the way religions try to shape politics (public policy, laws, elections, leaders, gender norms), and vice-versa. I call this the interface of religion and politics.

The Hot Spots. Religious and political actors and concerns happen everywhere, but in some countries or regions they are so heated that demonstrations, arrests, assassinations or even wars occur. I call such places the Hot Spots of religion and politics.

xiv

I am so grateful to all the students whose questions, interests, misconceptions and wonderful insights have helped give birth to this book. Many students and former students have helped me improve the drafts or provide pictures used in the work. Too many to mention, but I do wish especially to thank former students John Cappucci and Muaamar al-Haddad as well as MITACS research intern Yashasvini Rajeshwar. My wife Michelle Morrison provided great editorial help and encouragement. Finally, Bill Webber of Sloan Publishing has been great to work with.

—Roy C. Amore

Chapter One

The Interface of Religion and Politics

Old Patterns, New Trends

In this chapter you will learn about:

- the twin powers of religion and politics
- traditional patterns of the interface of religion and politics
- some new trends
- some theories about the interface of religion and politics

> *"While most religions preach universal brotherhood, religion has been a source of friction throughout human history."*
>
> —Romesh Thakur[1]
>
> *"In truth, man is incurably foolish. Simple things which the other animals easily learn, he is incapable of learning. Among my experiments was this. In an hour I taught a cat and a dog to be friends. I put them in a cage. In another hour I taught them to be friends with a rabbit. In the course of two days I was able to add a fox, a goose, a squirrel and some doves. Finally a monkey. They lived together in peace; even affectionately.*
>
> *"Next, in another cage I confined an Irish Catholic from Tipperary, and as soon as he seemed tame I added a Scotch Presbyterian from Aberdeen. Next a Turk from Constantinople; a Greek Christian from Crete; an Armenian; a Methodist from the wilds*

---

[1]Romesh Thakur, "Ayodhya and the Politics of India's Secularism: A Double-Standards Discourse," *Asia Survey* (1993: 33, 7): 646.

1

of Arkansas; a Buddhist from China; a Brahman from Benares. Finally, a Salvation Army Colonel from Wapping. Then I stayed away two whole days. When I came back to note results, the cage of Higher Animals was all right, but in the other there was but a chaos of gory odds and ends of turbans and fezzes and plaids and bones and flesh not a specimen left alive. These Reasoning Animals had disagreed on a theological detail and carried the matter to a Higher Court."

—Mark Twain[2]

RELIGION AND POLITICS—WATCH OUT!

I still remember the first time I heard the famous saying that haunts this book. It was when my old high school friend returned home from barber's college. He said the teachers had told him that being a successful barber meant getting repeat business, and doing so was more about becoming friends with the customer than about the haircut itself. He was told to get the customer talking about sports, cars, new gadgets or almost anything. But whatever you do, he was told, **don't ever talk about religion or politics!** Since then I have heard this wise old saying many times. More recently I have had many conversations that went like this: "What are you writing your book on"? "On religion and politics." "Oh no, those are the two topics you're not supposed to discuss, and you are writing on them both! Watch Out."

It is hard enough to have a conversation with someone about religion and still remain friends. Politics as well. But when we deliberately set out to ask tough questions about the interface of religion and politics in the world's hot spots—Watch out, indeed!

Religion and Politics—Should They Ever Mix?

The other famous saying that underlies this book is: **Don't mix religion and politics!** Lots of other questions follow. Would the world be better off if they never mixed? Is that even possible? Are there any places in the world where they do not mix to some extent? Is it always bad when religious leaders try to intervene in politics? Is it always bad when political leaders try to intervene in religious matters? Do they need each other?

Our Journey to the Hot Spots of Religion and Politics

Our mission is to travel around the world to see the hot spots of the interface of religion and politics. In this book the term *interface* refers to the places where religious leaders are trying to influence such things as public policy, government structure, and political party platforms; or where the government or other political actors are trying to influence such things as religious beliefs, practice, or leadership. When finished, we will at least be better informed to answer the proverbial question, should religion and politics mix?

---

[2]http://skeptically.org/logicalthreads/id14.html

We will pretend that we have round-the-world airline tickets that let us travel as much as we like for a year, as long as we go either west to east or east to west. We could start anywhere, but we will follow the sun starting in Japan, the Land of the Rising Sun. Along the way, we will visit China, Thailand, Myanmar, Sri Lanka, Nepal, India, Iran, Iraq, Saudi Arabia, Israel, Palestine, Turkey, Nigeria, and some countries in Europe. We will finish in the United States, where separation of religion and politics is the official position but the political realities are quite different.

On our trip from Japan to the Americas, we will see those hot spots where religion and politics are interfacing—where religion and politics are in each other's face. We will see many varieties of the relationship, from the Chinese model in which the political regime keeps a tight check on religion to the Iranian model in which religious leaders keep a tight check on politics. And there are so many variations between those extremes. We will see that India is a secular state but is embroiled in a struggle between its two main religions, with both wanting to shape public policy. Most tragic are the Middle Eastern countries because the interface of various kinds of religion and politics leads almost daily to military actions, terrorist attacks, and serious strife among religious groups and nations. Or possibly the breakup of nation states.

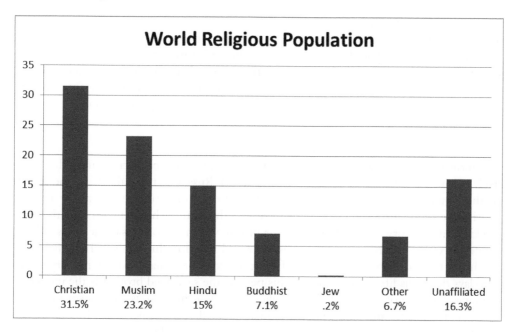

Figure 1 Estimates of percentage of world population for the religions discussed, plus Other & Unaffiliated[3]

[3]Based on figures provided by the Pew Research Center, 2012.

THE TWIN POWERS: TRADITIONAL MODELS OF RELIGIOUS AND POLITICAL AUTHORITY

Historically, humans have organized their social groups in a variety of overlapping ways, including extended families, clans, production guilds, occupational networks, city-states, nations, and empires. But whatever form the socio-political leadership may take, there is usually a religious leader who shares the power structure. Thomas Molnar uses the phrase *"twin powers"* to characterize the traditional relationship between the political and the sacred leadership roles. A brief survey of some traditional societies will show how widespread this power sharing arrangement was around the world.

The Ancient Model: Shaman and Warrior Chief
The oldest model we know anything about involves the dual leadership roles of the warrior chief and the shaman. Our knowledge of the lines of authority in archaic times comes from the oral, story tradition and from anthropological studies of modern shamanic peoples The shaman has authority over social norms, rituals, healing, death, and contacting the spirit realm. The chief has authority over governance and war.

The African Model: Priest and Chief
The precise relationship between the priest and the political leader varies among the hundreds of African peoples, but in general the authority rests with the chief, who is required by custom to consult with the priests for advice on major matters such as controlling the rains, ensuring the seasonal cycles are normal, and making sure that the ancestors or spirits do not cause trouble. The priest is in charge of funerals, as they are most everywhere.

The Indo-European Model: Priest and King
The term Indo-European is used for a language family and ancient civilization that most likely originated somewhere around the steppes of Russia or the Balkans by the fourth or third millennium B.C. and eventually spread throughout Europe and as far East as India.[4] The Indo-European creation myth reveals the relationship between the priest and the king. In the story, a primal sacrifice was held in which a brother sacrificed his twin to create the world. As the one who makes the world function through ritual sacrifices, the brother is the model for priests, who officiate at sacrificial rituals. As the military leader who lays down his life for the good of his people, the sacrificed brother is the model of the king. The role of the royal class families, including the king, is to sponsor sacrifices by hiring the priests and supplying the animals and other items needed. The role of the priests is to have knowledge of the sacred formulas and ritual practices necessary to per-

---

[4]The time, place and culture of the origins of Indo-European civilization are quite controversial. For a good summary of the various theories, see D. Pontikos, "Indo-European Origins in Southeast Europe." http://www.geocities.com/dienekesp2/indoeuropean.

form the sacrifices properly. If this is done, the rains will come, the herds will prosper, and life will be good.

The Han Dynasty and the Chinese Model: Priest and Emperor

The above pattern is found in traditional China as well. The emperor sponsored elaborate sacrifices at a ritual site near the capital, with priests officiating and with all high ranking officials in attendance. For example, during the latter period when the capital was in Beijing, one of the most important ritual functions of the king was to lead the fall and spring sacrifices at the nearby ritual complex housing the Temple of Heaven and the Temple of Harvests. Many animals were sacrificed in connection with these rituals, and the court officials were expected to consume all the meat before sunset. This was said to be a problem because there was so much meat and it was boiled rather than being prepared in a more delicious manner. They coped with this problem by getting their servants to eat the boiled meat.

The Semitic Model: Aaron and Moses

During the Exodus from Egypt, the Hebrew model for the king-priest relationship was established. Moses became the model for the political leader and his brother Aaron became the model for the high priest. The unusual feature of priesthood among the Israelites before Solomon was that God was thought of as making his name, or energy, dwell with the Ark of the Covenant. The Ark was a box for holding the laws issued to Moses, and it was kept in a special tent. Only certain priests were allowed to move the Ark, and even they were not allowed to touch it. To move it they used poles through rings attached to its sides. When Israel went to war, the Ark was carried into the battle, with cries of "Yahweh (God) is a soldier." On one occasion their enemy captured the Ark, but when sickness broke out in their camp, they soon returned it!

King David had the idea of building a proper temple, and his son Solomon was able to build one. After that, the Hebrews thought of their God as dwelling in a fixed place, the temple, and no longer "tenting"; that is, residing wherever the tent was pitched. They also developed the concept that it was not appropriate to sacrifice to God at any other location. Basically, the Jerusalem priesthood gave itself a monopoly over religious rituals. Over time, the number of priests and Levites, assistant priests, grew so large that they only had to report for work during high holidays and a few other weeks a year. Nice work if you could get it, but you could only become a Levite if you were a male born into the tribe of Levi. To become a priest, you had to be a male from the tribe of Levi and the house of Aaron. It was a hereditary rather than recruited priesthood.

When the Christian Jews broke away to form a new religion, they developed a new, recruited priesthood. The main function of the Christian priest was to officiate at the symbolic sacrifice known as the Eucharist or Mass, for it was thought that animal sacrifices were no longer needed after the death of Jesus on the cross. For Christianity's first three centuries, it had no political power, and so the traditional priest-king power sharing arrangement did not apply.

The Islamic Model: Muhammad as Religious and Political Leader

The Islamic model is different. After his migration to Medina, Muhammad was both the political leader and the religious leader, the Messenger of God. Although Islam continued the annual sacrifice of an animal, normally a sheep, a traditional style priesthood was not needed in Islam. A lay leader (Imam) led local prayers, and the interpretation of the Quran was placed in the hands of trained scholars. After the death of Muhammad, the Caliphs (his "successors") assumed his political powers, while the legal scholars took on the role of interpreting the law.

The Twin Powers as Reflected on Flags

One indication that the Twin Powers of religion and politics are intertwined, at least in the sense of national identity, may be seen on flags around the world. Religious symbols occur on the flags of 64 (of 196) nations. As counted by the Pew Research Center, leading the list are 31 nations with Christian symbols and 21 with Islamic ones.

NEW TRENDS: SECULARISM, SOCIAL ACTIVISM AND FUNDAMENTALISM

There are many recent trends in the interface of religion and politics, but here we will focus on three of the more important for our topic: Secularism, **Social Activism** and Fundamentalism. Secularism is important because many of the nations we plan to visit follow it to some degree. Social Activism is important for understanding the interface of liberal religion and politics. Fundamentalism is crucial for our understanding of the way many religious conservatives interface with politics.

Secularism and the Rise of the Secular State

The distinction between secular and religious originated in the terminology used by the Roman Catholic Church for two distinct roles played by its members. Those Catholics who lived "in the world" were "secular" (worldly), whereas those who had chosen to leave the secular life and enter into religious orders were "religious." Those who had taken vows as priests, brothers, or nuns were thereby set apart from those living in a worldly, family way. A secular (lay) person might be very pious or "religious" in the modern sense of the term, but they were still part of the laity rather than part of one of the religious orders.

Historically, most states looked to religious institutions for support and legitimacy. That is, the twin powers of religious and political leaders typically benefited from a system of mutual support in which the government gave protection and financial support to religious institutions, which in turn guided the populace in the view that the ruler had divine authority to govern. But in more modern times secularist views of the state have become widespread. The nineteenth century British thinker George Holyoake, author of

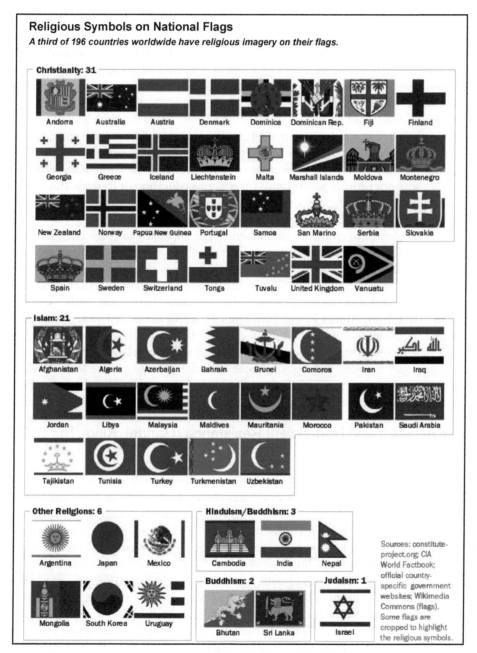

Figure 2 Pew Research Center Graph of National flags with religious symbols.[5]

[5]http://www.pewresearch.org/fact-tank/2014/11/25/64-countries-have-religious-symbols-on-their-national-flags/

The Origin and Nature of Secularism, is sometimes credited with laying the groundwork for a secularist theory of the state, but he was not the first one to argue that a state should avoid direct support for any or all religions. Holyoake held that the state should depend on secular knowledge in established laws of morality. His view of secularism did not intend to limit religious freedom, but he thought that the authority of the state should not rest on the moral dictates of religion.

Secularist states tend to follow some or all of the following principles. They avoid making any one religion the normative religion; that is, they do not have an "established religion." They avoid justifying laws by appealing to scripture or religious doctrine. They may prefer not to have a cleric offer prayers or otherwise act as a leader at public occasions. They may not provide public funds for religious education or festivals. But secularist states often do protect religious freedom and indirectly support religious institutions by allowing for some exemptions from property or income taxes.

Not all secularist governments are the same. The approach to religious organizations or to requests for accommodation varies along a scale from strict secularism to a softer approach. Scholars use various terms for this distinction. For example, Barry Kosmin, who heads the Institute for the Study of Secularism in Society and Culture at Trinity College in Hartford, Connecticut, distinguishes between "hard" and "soft" secularism. Along the same lines, Ahmet Kuru in his book *Secularism and State Policies Toward Religion* distinguishes "passive secularism" and "assertive secularism."[5] By assertive secularism he means a state ideology in which government actively excludes religions from government and public policy matters. But a government following a more passive form of secularism may be content with just maintaining government neutrality with regard to organized religions. We will encounter both types of secularist states as we travel around the world.

Social Activism and Non-violent Resistance (Gandhi, King, The Dalai Lama)

M. K. Gandhi and the Power of Truth
The role of religion in the modern world was changed one night in 1893 when a young Indian lawyer named M. K. Gandhi was thrown off a train in South Africa for insisting that the conductor honor his first-class ticket. He spent the night shivering on the train platform in a high elevation town, Pietermaritzburg. He had plenty of time that night to reflect on the injustice of a political system that classified himself and other persons of Indian origin as "coloured," native South Africans as "blacks," and Europeans as "whites." His confidence in the justness of British law had been shaken by this experience of how unjust discrimination can be tolerated even under the rule of law.

For the next three years Gandhi worked in South Africa for the India community, which included Hindus, Sikhs and Muslims. After a trip back to India, he returned for a

---

[5]Ahmet T. Kuru, *Secularism and State Policies Toward Religion: The United States, France, and Turkey* (Cambridge: Cambridge University Press, 2009), 10–14.

longer stay in South Africa. He led the resistance to a new law requiring all "coloureds" to carry identification papers. Gandhi insisted that the resistance should be non-violent. Even when the police attacked with clubs, the resisters should take the blows and neither strike back nor get angry. In taking this approach he was following a spiritual principle taught by Hinduism and other religions of India. He was also influenced by the Sermon on the Mount in which Jesus had taught that if someone struck you on one cheek, you should not resist but should turn the other cheek. It all came together for Gandhi—the *ahimsa*, non-violence, of Jain and Hindu teachings he learned as a boy and the Sermon on the Mount. He and many other leaders were beaten and jailed, but refused to either turn violent or to cease their resistance. Prime Minister Smuts finally agreed to rescind the worst of the discriminatory apartheid ("apartness") laws.

Upon returning to India with his family, Gandhi travelled around the country to see the conditions of all its regions. He led protests as he wrote about *satyagraha*, the "power of truth," which became a way to sum up his demands for justice through non-violent resistance. *Satya*, "truth" will win out, Gandhi believed. In the short term, a person protesting injustice might be beaten, jailed or killed, but in the long term the power of truth is such that truth will triumph. This is a deeply spiritual concept, but it was not articulated in terms of prayers offered to God or rituals done to bring about the change. Rather, an

Gandhi leading the Salt Satyagraha, the march to the sea to make sea salt in protest over the British ban on Indians making or trading in salt.
Photo: From WikiMedia Commons.

oppressed people should confront their oppressors with the truth, trusting that the power of truth will eventually prevail.

Martin Luther King, Jr. and the Civil Rights Movement
After reading Gandhi's works and writing a paper on his non-violence approach to social justice during graduate study in Boston, the young Baptist pastor Martin Luther King, Jr. returned to his Atlanta home in 1953 and soon found himself caught up in the civil rights struggle touched off when Rosa Parks refused to give up her seat in a Selma bus in 1955. She likely did not know of Gandhi's refusal to give up his first class train seat, but her similar act set off a protest movement in the United States along the lines of the ones Gandhi had led in South Africa.

M. L. King soon emerged as the writer and orator behind the civil rights movement. Adapting the thought of Gandhi to an American Christian setting, King insisted on a non-violent approach. He helped found the Southern Christian Leadership Conference based on the principle of non-violent resistance. But as Gandhi warned, practicing non-violent resistance is no guarantee that the oppressor will not react with violence, and many civil rights activists were beaten, jailed, or killed. King himself was gunned down in Memphis in 1968.

Other Non-violent Protestors
Gandhi's example has inspired many others, including Hindus as well as some Buddhists we will mention later in Chapter 3. The Dalai Lama, another Buddhist we will feature in Chapter 2, has been a strong advocate of non-violent resistance to the oppression of his Tibetan people by the Chinese government. In South Africa, Christian leaders such as Bishop Tutu used non-violent protests in the struggle to overcome apartheid. D. Little's book *Peacemakers in Action* profiles several lesser-known religious peacemakers working toward conflict resolution in war-torn places, including many of the countries we will visit on our trip to the world's hot spots.[6]

Starting in 2007, the United Nations has declared October 2, Gandhi's birthday, as the "International Day of Non-Violence." It is a day to recall and celebrate the spirit of non-violent resistance to social injustice.

Fundamentalism (Twentieth Century Origins)

The first people to be called fundamentalists were ultra-conservative American **Protestants** in the early 1900s. The background was that Christian theological school professors were becoming increasingly divided into two camps. The more liberal camp had several traits in keeping with progressive thinkers of their era. For one, they tended to be open to modern science, and wherever the Bible seemed to be in blatant conflict with science, they tended to look to science for the facts and look to the Bible for the underlying spiritual

---

[6]David Little, *Peacemakers in Action: Profiles in Religious Conflict Resolution.* Cambridge: Cambridge University Press, 2007.

truths. For example, the Bible begins with the well-known story of God creating the world in six days and then resting on the seventh, the Sabbath. Taken literally, this conflicted with science in many ways. Darwin's theory of evolution suggested that the various species had evolved over millions of years, which hardly fit with the idea of God creating all the animals on a single day. So, the more liberal theologians were content to praise God as the Creator while not taking the Biblical account as the literal truth. A related liberal trait was to accept the relatively new approach to Biblical studies known as **Higher Criticism or Literary Criticism**. This approach had been pioneered by German theologians and was making inroads in North America. The basic idea was to use the same literary and critical tools to understand the Bible as scholars would to understand other books. The liberals also tended to downplay the miracles in the Bible, preferring to think that God's will could be worked without violating the laws of nature. The liberal camp got a boost when John D. Rockefeller endowed the Chicago Divinity School, which proceeded to staff itself with liberal minded scholars.

Some of the more conservative Christians were quite alarmed at these liberal developments in science and Biblical interpretation. They saw Darwinian evolution, Biblical Criticism and the rejection of miracles as a direct threat to the basics of Biblical faith. A group of these ultra conservatives met in Niagara in 1910, and arising from that meeting was a list of the "fundamentals of the faith" and then later a series of tracts on the same topic. By 1920 another meeting was held, and a reporter described this new movement as "fundamentalism" due to its adherents' desire to adhere strictly to the fundamentals of the faith as they saw them.

The key traits of these fundamentalist Christians have not changed much since they were formulated in the 1910s and 1920s. The Protestant fundamentalist position is summed up in their phrase, the "**inerrancy of scripture**." The slogan means that the Biblical stories, such as the creation of everything in six days, are to be taken literally. Any scientific claims that there were species of animals that did not exist on earth for millions of years and then came into existence later, therefore has to be wrong. Similarly, any claim that humans evolved billions of years after the creation of the earth must be wrong. The sharp contrast between the fundamentalists' refusal to accept evolution and the scientific claim that humans evolved from primates became the focus of the **Scopes Monkey Trial** that gripped the attention of the United States in the summer of 1925. In that trial, a high school teacher named Scopes was charged with teaching the theory of evolution. Fundamentalist Christians insist that the miracles of the Bible are to be taken as literal facts. Fundamentalists also tend to be social conservatives, feeling that the traditional roles for women were the proper ones and that the male was supposed to be the head of the household.

We will follow the underlying concerns of Christian fundamentalism, including the Scopes Monkey Trial, further in the North American chapter, for the agenda of the Christian Right in America follows almost directly from the agenda of the 1920s fundamentalists. The Scopes trial is long over, but the fight continues within the interface of religion and politics in the United States.

SOME THEORIES RELEVANT TO THE INTERFACE OF RELIGION AND POLITICS

In an attempt to be as scientific as possible about human behavior, social scientists have often developed theories to explain why individuals and social groups behave as they do. A brief introduction to several of the social scientific theories relevant for understanding the interface of religion and politics may be helpful before we start our travels. We will revisit some of these theories in more detail as we travel to the hot spots around the world.

Rational Choice Theory

One well-known theory holds that human behavior can best be understood as a series of "rational choices." The idea is that we humans base our behaviors on our perceptions of what will lead to the best outcomes for ourselves. Rational Choice theory holds that our choices take into consideration what actions will maximize desired effects while minimizing undesirable effects. For example, if we perceive that the goal of being in good shape outweighs the time, effort, or boredom from exercising, then we will take time to jog or work out. If we perceive that attending a religious service is more rewarding that using the time or money in some other way, we will join in religious rituals. Whether consciously or not, people are thought to make their choices rationally, based on their perceptions of the pros and cons of the situation.

Why, for example, do many Tibetans in China remain loyal to the Dalai Lama despite the risks this places upon them? Or why do some Muslims leave the families and friends in the West to join a jihadi group in the Middle East? Why have some Buddhists in Sri Lanka turned violent despite the strong non-violent ethic in Buddhist thought? Are such persons making rational choices? We will want to look for answers to such questions as we travel around the world.

Conflict Theory and Marxism

Whereas Rational Choice theory focuses on individual choices, Conflict Theory pays more attention to the role of conflicting goals among various social classes. It stresses the role of power imbalances in explaining social, religious, or political behavior. For example, class conflict may be used to explain why South Africa followed an Apartheid policy for so long despite world opinion and the norms of democratic societies. Class conflict theory may help us understand why caste discrimination continues in India despite laws to the contrary. Class conflict may also help us understand the political undertones of the increasing conflicts between Sunni and Shi'i Muslims.

The most important conflict theorist is Karl Marx. Writing in the early industrial era when Europe's factory workers, including child laborers, were typically overworked and grossly underpaid, Marx argued that conflict between the ownership classes (the bourgeoisie) and the working classes (the proletariat) was at the heart of social change and revolution.[7] But for Marx, class struggle was a theme running throughout history and not just a creation of the industrial revolution. His reading of history suggested that the social group that controlled wealth and power had always managed to oppress the lower classes, no matter what the economic means of production might have been.

Marx held that the upper class uses religion, among other institutions, to control the masses. This explains his characterization of religion as being the "sigh of the oppressed creature" and as "the opium of the people."[8] That is, working classes could be encouraged to put up with their miserable lot if institutionalized religion encouraged them to work hard and accept their hardships in the expectation of rewards in the afterlife. In this view, religion serves to drug the masses into compliance, especially during times of crisis.

When Russia turned to communism, Marx' critique of religion as a regressive and outdated social force led to denunciation of religion in the Soviet Union and elsewhere as communism spread to China and beyond. In our travels to China we will want to ask how the resurgence of Islam, Buddhism and Christianity is possible in a communist system.

Clash of Civilizations Theory

Rational Choice theory's more individualist approach was broadened into a struggle among social classes by Conflict Theory, but the Clash of Civilizations Theory takes the level of analysis to an even larger social network called civilization. In this context the term *civilization* refers to a cluster of cultures that share something in common. Typically, what they share in common is a religious identity. For example, in the following discussion of Samuel Huntington's thought, six of the seven civilizations he discusses are defined by religion:

Civilization	Religious Identity
Sinic (Chinese)	partly based on Confucian Values
Japanese	based on Shinto, Buddhist and Chinese values
Hindu	Hinduism
Islamic	Islam
Orthodox	Orthodox Christianity
Western	Roman Catholic and Protestant Christianity
Latin American	Roman Catholic and Hispanic values

Huntington's Clash of Civilizations

> *The central theme of this book is that culture and cultural identities, which at the broadest level are civilization identities, are shaping the patterns of cohesion, disintegration, and conflict in the post-Cold War world.*
>
> —Samuel Huntington[9]

---

[7] Marx' main works include *Das Kapital* and *The Communist Manifesto*, co-authored with Friedrich Engels.

[8] Karl Marx, *Critique of Hegel's Philosophy of Right* (CreateSpace Independent Publishing Platform, 2012), 4. This work was written by Marx in 1843.

[9] Huntington's argument first appeared an article in *Foreign Affairs* in 1993 and then in book form in 1996.

Writing shortly after the fall of the Soviet Union in 1991, Samuel Huntington's book *The Clash of Civilizations and the Remaking of World Order* argues that the world order based on the cold war between communists and capitalists has been replaced by a new world order based upon the interests of the world's various civilizations.[10] In part Huntington was reacting to F. Fukuyama's claim that, with the defeat of fascism and the collapse of the Soviet Union, we had entered a time Fukuyama labelled the "end of history" because there was an absence of major competing ideologies. Huntington found this to be naïve. His belief was that new tensions and alignments were arising along civilizational lines.

Although his book is about the whole world, the thrust of Huntington's work was to warn the west about the rise of Islamic militancy backed by the identity of millions of people with roots in the Islamic civilization. He also expressed concern over the possible alignment of China with the Islamic interests, possibly leading to the scenario he calls the "West verses the Rest."

Ali's "Clash of Fundamentalisms"

> *In a clash between a religious fundamentalism—itself the product of modernity—and an imperial fundamentalism determined to "discipline the world," it is necessary to oppose both and create a space in the world of Islam and the West in which freedom of thought and imagination can be defended without fear of persecution or death.*
>
> —Tariq Ali[11]

Tariq Ali is a well-known lecturer and author of both fictional and scholarly books, including *The Clash of Fundamentalisms*. The title is a take-off on Huntington's *Clash of Civilizations*. The difference between the two is that Ali sees the Western approach as a kind of imperialism attempting to impose its will on the rest of the world. It is, he argues, a "fundamentalism" in its own right, although not a religious fundamentalism. Whereas he is also quite critical of militant forms of Islamic fundamentalism, he throws his sharpest verbal barbs at the West, especially at the United States. Writing in the preface to the paperback edition after the American reaction to the events of September 11, 2001 he notes, "My argument that the most dangerous 'fundamentalism' today—the 'mother of all fundamentalisms' is American imperialism—has been amply vindicated over the last eighteen months."[12] He laments that the United States was, at the time, preparing for war against Iraq, seeing it as a blatant example of the very imperialism that he and so much of the rest of the world denounces. The fact that the United States has a military presence in

---

[10]Samuel P. Huntington, *The Clash of Civilizations and the Remaking of World Order* (New York: Simon and Schuster, 1996),

[11]Tariq Ali. *The Clash of Fundamentalisms: Crusades, Jihads and Modernity* (London and New York: Verso, 2002), xi.

[12]*Ibid.* xiii.

most member states of the United Nations furthers his case, he claims. Ali argues that the main motivation for American imperialism is economic.

Ali criticizes Huntington for implying that the Islamic world really is fairly unified, arguing instead that Muslims around the world are not a monolithic political entity, and have not been for centuries.[13]

Rejection of Modernity Theory

Bruce Lawrence on Fundamentalists as Anti-modernity

> *Fundamentalists are not atavistic Luddites opposed to the instrumentalities of modern media, transport, or warfare. Fundamentalists related fully to the infrastructures that have produced the unprecedented options for communication and mobility that today's world offers. Fundamentalists are modern....*
> *Fundamentalists are moderns but they are not modernists....*
> *Fundamentalists oppose modernism and its proponents....*
> *Because modernity is global, so is fundamentalism.... The name in English is linked to turn-of-the-century Protestant Christianity, yet fundamentalism, like other reactions to modernity, has been at once cross-creedal and multicultural. Fundamentalism is as intrinsic and inevitable to Israeli haredim and Sunni or Shi'i Muslims as it is to American Protestants.*
>
> —Bruce Lawrence[14]

The thesis of Bruce Lawrence's book *Defenders of God, The Fundamentalist Revolt Against the Modern Age*s is that religious fundamentalists are those modern persons who reject modernity. By "modernity" he means the secular ideas, values, and forms of government that have arisen out of Western civilization since the Enlightenment. It is important to understand that he is not saying that religious fundamentalists reject modern technology or modern clothing. Rather, they reject the modern concept that ultimate knowledge and authority come from such things as science, democracy, and the rights and norms derived from humanistic values.

Lawrence's book also gives a strong argument for using the term fundamentalism for other religious movements and not just for conservative American Protestants. He finds the following traits held in common by fundamentalists of the three religions he considers: Judaism, Christianity and Islam.

1. Fundamentalist are advocates of a pure minority viewpoint against a sullied majority or dominant group.

---

[13]*Ibid.* 300.

[14]Bruce B. Lawrence. *Defenders of God: The Fundamentalist Revolt Against the Modern Age.* (San Francisco: Harper and Row, 1989).

An Ultra-Orthodox Jew in Antwerp using a cell phone.
Photo: Roy Amore

2. Fundamentalists are oppositional. They do not merely disagree with their enemies, they confront them.

3. Fundamentalists are secondary-level male elites.

4. Fundamentalists generate their own technical vocabulary (i.e., new meanings and jargon).

5. Fundamentalism has historical antecedents, but no ideological precursors.[15]

Malise Ruthven on Family Resemblances among Fundamentalists
Malise Ruthven is another scholar who argues that it is appropriate to use the term fundamentalism for certain forms of other religions as well as Christianity. He notes several traits that the various fundamentalisms have in common. He calls these "family resemblances." They all tend to be missionary, wish to transform society, are anti-secular, are pro-traditional family roles, and advocate for ideological purism.[16]

Terrorism Theory

Another relevant theoretical question concerns why some seemingly devout religious persons turn to violence and terrorism despite the teachings in their religion about peace and harmony.

---

[15]*Ibid.* 100.

[16]Malise Ruthven. *Fundamentalism: A Very Short Introduction,* (Oxford: Oxford University Press, 2007), 1–23.

Juergensmeyer on Why Religions Sometimes Use Terror

> *What puzzles me is... why bad things are done by people who otherwise appear to be good—in cases of religious terrorism, by pious people dedicated to a moral vision of the world. Considering the high-sounding rhetoric with which their purposes are often stated, it is perhaps all the more tragic that the acts of violence meant to achieve them have caused suffering and disruption in many lives....*
>
> *Religion is not innocent. But it does not ordinarily lead to violence. That happens only with the coalescence of a peculiar set of circumstances—political, social, and ideological—when religion becomes fused with violent expressions of social aspirations, personal pride, and movements for political change.*
>
> —Mark Juergensmeyer[17]

Mark Juergensmeyer's book *Terror in the Mind of God* describes the use of terror by various religions in the contemporary era. His book grew out of interviews with terrorists of many religious backgrounds, from Christians who bomb abortion clinics to the World Trade Center bombers. His goal is to understand what goes on in the mind of a religious person who turns to militancy and violence in the name of God.

In the process of describing the use of terror, Juergensmeyer concludes that terrorists often draw upon the image of a cosmic war to justify the use of violence in their struggles against corruption, displacement, or poverty.

Phares's "War of Ideas"

> *Indeed, a War of Ideas is raging, relentlessly, behind the War on Terror. The outcome of the second is ineluctably conditioned by the consequences of the first. For the party that succeeds in convincing the largest numbers on the opposite side will eventually either stretch the war into the future or end it to its advantage. During the fall of 2001, Osama bin Laden said on the* al Jazeera *that as long as he can reach the next generations of Muslims, he will be winning the war against his enemies.*
>
> —Walid Phares[18]

Walid Phares is an expert on Middle Eastern Politics who has a long history of alerting readers to the global conflict between Islamic Jihadis and democracies. He subscribes to a civilization theory similar to Huntington's and wrote about it long before Huntington did. Civilizations "were not referred to for decades, but deep down, they were the real tectonic plates of world politics. After the collapse of the Soviet Union, a new division emerged between those who wanted to reignite the clash, the jihadists, and those who did

---

[17]Mark Juergensmeyer. 2000. *Terror in the Mind of God: The Global Rise of Religious Violence.* Berkeley: University of California Press. 7–10.

[18]Walid Phares. 2008. *The War of Ideas: Jihadism against Democracy.* (New York: Palgrave Macmillan. xx.

not, democracies."[19] Whereas Huntington writes about the whole world with its multiple civilizations, Phares focuses on the particular interpretation of Islamic civilization taken by the Jihadis. He describes them as those Muslims who seek to defeat democracy, at least among Muslim countries, and to replace Islamic nationalism with a unified Islamic state. In effect, the Jihadis seek a new version of the Sunni caliphate or later Ottoman Sultanate that ruled over most Muslims.

Phares asks the question of why clashes of ideas cannot remain just that, without becoming classes of arms.[20] His answer is that sometimes those ideas become ideologies, and ideologies can be such a strong motivator that they take precedence over social, national, or economic interests. He is critical of those who attempt to explain Jihadism in terms of economic factors such as low levels of education, underemployment, or poverty. He is also critical of Marxists who turn to class struggle as an explanation. "Ironically, ideologies may start as an expression of age-old desires, such as lust for territory and domination, but as history evolves, they become self-fueled as a desire in itself, an autonomous wish to accomplish an idea regardless of its irrelevance."[21] His title, "War of Ideas," is meant to stress the role of ideology in the conflict.

Resurgence and Pendulum Swing Theory

The Global Resurgence of Religion and the Transformation of International Relations: The Struggle for the Soul of the Twenty-First Century by Scott Thomas argues that whereas the notion that religion is largely irrelevant to politics was popular in the twentieth century, the recent global resurgence of religion means that the role of religion should not be ignored. He argues that the Treaty of Westphalia in 1648, after the Thirty Years War, disrupted the dominant role of the Catholic Church in Europe and established the nation state as supreme. But now religion is "returning from exile," leading to religious-inspired global terrorism, to faith-based diplomacy, or even to the discussions at the famous annual meetings of financial and political elites at the World Economic Forum in Davos, Switzerland.[22] Thomas' main point is that the rise in levels of religion and spirituality taking place in public life are having an impact on international relations. There is an emerging consensus among scholars that we are in an era of a worldwide resurgence of Islam. We will also discuss the resurgence of religion, especially Christianity, in China.

The "pendulum swing" theory sets the resurgence theory into a broader historical and social context. We all are aware of how trends come and go, and some scholars and financial analysts take cycles very seriously. Gold goes in and out of investor favor, as do certain

---

[19]*Ibid.* xi.

[20]*Ibid.* xiv.

[21]*Ibid.* xv.

[22]Scott M. Thomas. *The Global Resurgence of Religion and the Transformation of International Relations: The Struggle for the Soul of the Twenty-First Century* (New York: Palgrave Macmillan, 2005), 33.

colors, styles of art and music, tastes in food, length of basketball shorts, and so on. The role of religion in political life also swings like a pendulum, in long cycles, according to the pendulum swing theorists. The favorite illustration of the pendulum theory by the late Will Herberg involved the period in American religious-political history between the Great Awakening and the beginning of the Great Revival. The Great Awakening had taken place in New England in the 1730s and 1740s. It was led by Jonathan Edwards, whose sermons went on for hours and may seem boring upon reading today. But in Edwards' day, people had profound spiritual experiences during his sermons and the resulting Great Awakening brought religion into the American political arena in a way that had not been anticipated. The Great Awakening pushed the religion pendulum toward the view that public policy should be informed and guided by a certain religious conviction.

By the 1800s, a few decades following the Great Awakening, the pendulum had swung back to the side that wants religion kept out of political decisions. That is the setting of Herberg's anecdote about a swing in the religion-in-politics pendulum. One state legislature voted to abolish the office of chaplain, on the grounds that it cost money and that such an office was not needed. In the same state later that year, the Great Revival started. As thousands of Midwestern Americans were converted to a fervent form of Protestant Christianity through camp meetings, the pendulum got a big push back to the religion-in-politics view.

By the 1960s, the pendulum had swung far toward the separation-of-religion-and-politics side. So much so that for the first time a Roman Catholic, John Kennedy, could be elected president because most voters thought a candidate's religion was only a personal matter and many Protestants were willing to vote for a Catholic. And politicians worried more about "peacenik hippies" or communists than about the opinion of the clergy. But the farther the pendulum swings to the separation of religion side, the stronger the reaction from the opposing camp. In our North America chapter, we will see how the Christian Right struck back against secularism in politics by forming political activist organizations that networked across many denominations.

Feminist Theory

Traditionally, most societies were dominated by males who shaped laws and religious doctrine to support their dominance. Among other things, Feminist Theory attempts to explain how this system became so entrenched in society, including religion and politics. Feminist activism seeks to correct the power imbalance.

Judith Lorner's book *Gender Inequality: Feminist Theories and Politics* is a helpful source.[23] It contains essays on many varieties of feminist theory relevant to the interface of religion and politics; such as Marxist and Socialist Feminism, Development Feminism and Social Construction Feminism.

---

[23]Judith Lorber, *Gender Inequality: Feminist Theories and Politics* (New York: Oxford University Press, 2011.

As we travel, we will see that despite attempts to reverse male dominance, the imbalance of power persists. The top leaders of the largest religious organizations are all male. In the political realm, the top leaders of communist countries have all been male. But most democratic countries—the United States being a notable exception—have had at least one female leader. Females have been elected to political leadership most often in South Asia, and Europe continues to have female political leaders.

Gender Theory overlaps with several of the other theories. For example, one of the "family resemblances" discussed in Fundamentalist Theory is that fundamentalist movements tend to be very maledominated and to be eager to return to the days of male dominance in the public sphere.

One interesting source for descriptions of the role of women and especially female activists in the Islamic world is Judith Miller's book *God has Ninety-name Names*. We will draw upon that work when we get to Saudi Arabia.

> *We are ready to begin our trip to the hot spots of religion and politics, having had our vaccinations, bought our round-the-world tickets, and loaded our passports with visa stamps. We download the books mentioned above into our notepads or laptops and head for LAX, departing from Los Angeles in route to Beijing, with a stopover in Tokyo.*

FURTHER READING

Books in Our Laptop:

Ali, Tariq. *The Clash of Fundamentalisms: Crusades, Jihads and Modernity.* London and New York: Verso, 2002. Argues that American imperialism is a "fundamentalism" in a sense.

Huntington, Samuel P. The *Clash of Civilizations and the Remaking of World Order.* New York: Simon and Schuster, 2003. Argues that the new world order is based on the tensions among civilizations, which in turn are mainly religion based.

Juergensmeyer, Mark. *Terror in the Mind of God: The Global Rise of Religious Violence.* Berkeley: University of California Press, 2000.

Lawrence, Bruce B. *Defenders of God: The Fundamentalist Revolt Against The Modern Age.* San Francisco: Harper and Row, 1989. Argues that religious fundamentalists are reacting against the values of modernity.

Miller, Judith. *God Has Ninety-nine Names.* New York: Simon and Schuster, 1996. A journalist's keen eye on the Islamic world.

Phares, Walid. *The War of Ideas: Jihadism against Democracy.* New York: Palgrave Macmillan, 2008. The author's sequel to his book *Future Jihad.*

Thomas, Scott M. *The Global Resurgence of Religion and the Transformation of International Relations: The Struggle for the Soul of the Twenty-First Century.* New York: Palgrave Macmillan, 2005. Argues that international relations must take the religion factor into account.

Other Reading:

Hanson, Eric O. *Religion and Politics in the International System Today.* Cambridge: Cambridge University Press, 2006. A survey of religion and politics.

Juergensmeyer, Mark, ed. *Religion in Global Civil Society.* New York: Oxford University Press, 2005.. Essays by various scholars on religion and politics, especially as they relate to globalization.

Little, David. ed. *Peacemakers in Action: Profiles in Conflict Resolution.* Cambridge: Cambridge University Press, 2007. Interesting essays profiling religious peacemakers in many troubled places of the world.

Farhat-Holzman, Laina. *God's Law or Man's Law: The Fundamentalist Challenge to Secular Rule.* New York: Times Publishing Group, 2002. Readable, but hard to find.

Lorber, Judith. *Gender Inequality: Feminist Theories and Politics.* New York: Oxford University Press, 2011. Introduces various feminist theories on the interaction of women and politic policies.

Norris, Pippa, and Ronald Inglehart. *Sacred and Secular: Religion and Politics Worldwide.* Cambridge: Cambridge University Press, 2004. Gives special attention to the role of secularism among contemporary religious movements.

Oxtoby, Willard G., Amore, Roy C. and Hussain, Amir. *A Concise Introduction to World Religion. 3rd* ed. Toronto: Oxford University Press, 2015. Has introductory chapters on the religions we will be encounter in this book.

WEBSITES

www.mkgandhi.org A comprehensive source on Gandhi's life and writings.

www.themonkeytrial.com Gives detailed comments on the trial.

KEY PEOPLE

M. K. Gandhi An Indian lawyer who championed the cause of non-violent resistance to unjust laws and discrimination.

Martin Luther King, Jr. A Baptist minister who applied Gandhi's non-violent approach to the civil rights movement in the United States.

The Dalai Lama The spiritual leader of Tibetan Buddhists who now advocates for social action from his home in exile in India.

Rosa Parks An African American woman who refused to give up her bus seat because she was in an area reserved for whites—an act of protest that touched off the civil rights movement.

GLOSSARY

ahimsa An term for "non-violence," derived from religions in India, which Gandhi and others advocated as an ethic to be following even while resisting unfair laws or practices.

Scopes Monkey Trial A small town trial in 1925 that gained nationwide attention because it featured the conflict between the liberal acceptance of evolution and the conservative rejection of that view based upon the authority of the Bible.

fundamentalism A very conservative form of Protestant Christianity that rejects scientific ideas, public policies, and lifestyles that appear to be in conflict with scripture. Although originally a term applied to the Christian context, it is now often used as a generic term for other very conservative religious movements.

satyagraha "Power of truth," an Indian term used by Gandhi to stress that non-violent civil resistance will win in the end if it has truth on its side.

Social Activism A term for movements, often based in religious convictions, that protest and seek to change social norms or laws that are considered unfair, harmful, or discriminatory.

Chapter Two

China

Government Control over Religion:
Hui and Uyghur Muslims, Tibetans, Christians, Falun Dafa

In this chapter you will learn about:
- the background of Chinese religion and politics
- the anti-religion stance of Marxist Communism
- the relationship between Muslims and the Chinese government
- the Hanification of the Tibetan Autonomous Region
- the rise of Christianity in contemporary China
- the role of religion in China's international relations

"Religion is the opiate of the people." Karl Marx

"We must strive to closely unite religious figures and believers among the masses around the party and government and struggle together with them to build an all-around moderately prosperous society while quickening the pace toward the modernization of socialism." Hu Jintao, Former General Secretary, Communist Party of China[1]

"We must take full advantage of the positive role that religious figures and believers among the masses can play in promoting economic and social development." Jia Qinglin, member of the Politburo's Standing Committee, speaking to government connected religious officials[2]

"China is still one of the worst violators of writers' rights for freedom of expression in the world," she says. *Untouchable subjects include the Tiananmen Square massacre, the Falun Gong movement and Tibetan and*

---

[1]Edward Cody, "China's Leaders Change Tactics Toward Religion," *Washington Post* (January 22, 2008). See www.southcoasttoday.com/apps/pbcs.dll/article?AID=/20080122/NEWS/801220350.
[2]*Ibid.*

Uighur cultural rights. "Any time somebody crosses the line to write about any of these issues," says Field, "they're putting themselves at enormous risk." Ophelia Field, the Acting Director of English PEN's Writers in Prison programme, as quoted by Richard Lea.[3]

STOPOVERS IN JAPAN AND SOUTH KOREA

Buddhism and State Shinto in Japan

We land in Narita Airport, just for a quick stopover, and find it is really easy to get into Japan. The immigration officer stamps a Japan tourist visa into our passport. We board the train for downtown Tokyo, and at first we travel past small towns and tiny farms growing mostly rice. Japan protects its farm land in several ways. Zoning laws keep farm land from being turned into residential or commercial use. The domestic price of rice is kept way above international prices—the USA rice farmers have lobbied to get the USA to pressure Japan to end this policy, but Japan is not about to change it. And farm districts get a disproportionate number of seats in the Japanese Diet, the Parliament. The second thing we notice, as we travel at a good speed through its outskirts, is that Tokyo is huge.

We do not have much time, so we take a quick sightseeing trip around old Tokyo, which used to be called Edo. We see the impressive grounds of Edo Castle, from where the Shoguns long ruled Japan, but the public is allowed in only two days a year.

Tokyo

During the Shogunate period, various Buddhist sects (or schools) had influence, but the **Zen Buddhist** school had the most lasting influence because many Samurai, the knights of old Japan, practiced Zen. They found it helpful in training for battle. By developing the state of "no-mind," they learned to react instantly to the attack of the opponent without being slowed by thinking. To understand this, think of the way in which our hand might instinctively and instantly move off a hot object, even before we consciously realize that the object is hot. The difference may be only a few milliseconds, but if the enemy is swinging a sword at your neck, it could make all the difference in the world to you. The classic book *Zen in the Art of Archery* by Eugen Herrigel gives an autobiographical account of a Westerner who apprenticed under a Zen archery master. The master kept telling him it was not important to hit the target. What was important was to get into an egoless state of mind in which the shooter, the bow, the arrow, and the target were not different. All this was completely puzzling to the student until one magic day when he broke through into the state of no-mind.[3]

---

[3]Eugene Herrigel, *Zen in the Art of Archery* (New York: Pantheon Books, 1953, 1999).

When they were not practicing their martial arts, the Samurai, along with other upper-class Japanese, practiced other Zen activities such as drinking tea in a slow, relaxing, almost ritualistic way—the famous Japanese tea ceremony. They also practiced sitting meditation, *zazen*, like the Zen monks did for much of their days. Other Zen practices ranged from flower arranging to archery.

Kyoto, a Sacred Buddhist Capital

> *We get on the famous bullet train and head south to Kyoto, the second imperial capital of Japan.*

When the capital moved from Nara to Kyoto in 794, the new city was modeled after the Chinese capital at the time, Chang-an, near modern Xi'an. It was laid out in accordance with Chinese *feng shui* principles. The capital was situated so that it would be protected from the Northeast, the direction from which evil energy might come, by Mount Hiei, the location of a famous Buddhist monastery. The original city was laid out following the special numbers 8 and 9, with eight streets and nine avenues. The government had nine departments and eight ranks of officials, and so forth.[4] Religion, if we consider *feng shui* beliefs a "religion," and politics were quite entwined.

> *In Kyoto we visit the famous Zen monasteries, with their rock gardens, or "dry gardens" as the Japanese call them. The rock gardens were constructed by renowned architects as areas for meditation. Meditators sit overlooking the garden, which is designed to resemble the rocks and sand of a sea shore. There is something soothing about a sea shore and the sound of rippling waves. The gardens cannot reproduce the sound of the waves, but the sand is raked in a way to suggest little ripples on water.*

Rock Garden at Zen
Temple, Kyoto.
*Photo:*Roy Amore

Nara. Imitation of Buddha's First Sermon in Deer Park

We take the train to the first capital, Nara, the main goal of our stop in Japan. Here we see an example of the traditional interface of religion and politics. The government buildings and residences of Nara were laid out in conjunction with Buddhist ideals based on Chinese feng shui. The mountains to the Northeast and their monasteries were to protect the city from evil influences. And the main government buildings were situated in a huge park modeled after the Deer Park in India where the Buddha preached his first sermon. We stroll through the park, watching the hundreds of deer, and it seems obvious why the gentle deer became a symbol of the Buddhist path of non-violence and compassion. The male deer are not that gentle, however, and we learn that a festival is held each spring during which the antlers are cut to keep the deer from hurting each other as they fight for mates.

We enter Todaiji, the "Great Eastern Temple," and strain our necks to look up at the enormous Buddha statue in this huge structure, said to be the world's largest wooden building. Todaiji was the headquarters of one of the most powerful Buddhist sects. Here we see both the pro and the con side of the religion and politics interface. On the one hand, Todaiji was a very visible testimony to the harmony of religion and politics. It brought religious influence to the court and vice versa. On the other hand, the close ties between Buddhism and politics later caused the Emperor to move the capital to Kyoto, to escape the influence of powerful Buddhist priests.

In Japan there has been tension between **Shinto** and Buddhism, but for most of Japanese history the two religions traditions coexisted peacefully. It helped that neither Buddhism nor Shinto were exclusivist in their approach. As a generalization, the idea that there can only be one true religion seems to be strongest among monotheistic religions such as Judaism, Islam, and Christianity. East Asians do not buy into the one true god or one true religion concept, and perhaps for that reason have been less inclined to fight wars or form political parties along religious lines. Tour guides in Japan have a hard time answering a typical western tourist question: "Are you Buddhist or Shinto?" The real answer is that most Japanese are both, but answering "both" just leads to a battery of other questions.

It also helped that wherever Buddhism spread, it usually did not denounce local spirits, gods, and goddesses, but allowed traditional spiritual practices to continue. In Southeast Asia and East Asia, local gods and goddesses were often assimilated into Buddhism. That happened in Japan as well, where something called "dual Shinto" arose. It was a form of Shinto, the traditional religion of Japan, which incorporated Buddhist elements. Both Buddhist temples and Shinto shrines were sometimes enclosed in the same compound. A pattern developed in which weddings and some childhood rituals were held at Shinto shrines, whereas funerals, memorials, and other solemn events took place at Buddhist temples, with cemeteries nearby. Japanese will sometimes explain to tourists, "We go to Shinto shrines for happy things and to Buddhist temples for sad things."

The most important interaction of religion and politics in Japan involved the establishment of **State Shinto** at the time of the Meiji Restoration in 1868. The Tokugawa shoguns (military chiefs) had been ruling Japan while the emperors held little power. But the shogunate refused to modernize, and Japan, like China, was falling behind the West and its industrial revolution. The shogunate was overthrown and power was restored to the young Emperor Meiji. To consolidate power, the court started State Shinto, which played up the old mythology claiming that the imperial house was descended from an ancient union between the sun goddess and a man. Hence, the emperor was to be respected as a *kami*, a spirit or god. It was a Japanese version of the old theme of religion providing legitimacy to a ruler, as a divine sovereign. Under the new regime, Japan rapidly modernized and won a war with Russia in 1905. By the 1930s and 1940s it had become the dominant power of the region and was rapidly colonizing Manchuria, parts of China, most Pacific islands of the region, and much of Southeast Asia. The United States set up an oil embargo to slow down this expansion, and the Japanese bombed Pearl Harbor in part to destroy the navy enforcing the embargo. After the Allies defeated Japan, State Shinto was abolished and the emperor was forced to say publicly that he was not a *kami*.

> We head back to Narita airport, leaving time to enjoy the shopping center inside the airport. The Japanese, like other Asians, traditionally built shops and restaurants around bus depots and train stations, and the pattern carries over to airports. There are so many places to eat, but the selection is made easier because Japanese restaurants put very realistic plastic models of their dishes in the window. We select a soba noodle shop so we can try Japan's favorite style, made with buckwheat and wheat flour, before catching a plane to Seoul, the capital of South Korea.

The Koreas: Two Nations, Two Systems

> We make the quick flight to the mainland and find our way to downtown Seoul. The capital bustles with activity, and the big, bright neon signs signal a prosperity that is amazing when we stop to think about how far South Korea has come economically.

In his book *The Four Little Dragons* on the economic rise of South Korea, Taiwan, Hong Kong, and Singapore, Ezra F. Vogel notes that after World War II when the Soviet Union took control of the North and introduced a Soviet-style communist economy, the South started the process of rebuilding and modernizing with almost no factories, infrastructure or workers with technical skills.[5] The North had the initial advantage of having some infrastructure and it got aid from China, but its economy has now been near collapse for

---

[5]Ezra F. Vogel, *The Four Little Dragons: The Spread of Industrialization in East Asia* (Cambridge: Harvard University Press, 1993).

decades. It diverts an enormous percentage of its resources into the military and in showy megaprojects in the capital, while the standard of living of most North Koreans falls farther and farther behind that of South Koreans. The South has been through the Korean Conflict (war betweeen the North and the South 1950–1953), periods of demonstrations, coups, and severe instability, but it has emerged with a stable democracy and an industrial system that now rivals that of Japan. The South now has modernity, with all its creature comforts and technological gadgets, as well as the breakdown in the extended family life and rise of social problems. The North is an impoverished totalitarian state which refuses to follow China's lead toward a free market economy and more relaxed social control.[6]

As for the interface of religion and politics, in South Korea both Buddhism and Christianity have a lot of adherents but they do not interfere in politics very much. In North Korea the authoritarian socialist regime of Kim Jong-un follows a set of principles called *Juche*, "Self Reliance." The Juche term was used by the Kim Il-sung, founder of modern North Korea, to express a strong sense of the independence of the masses as masters of their own destiny. Being self-reliant means not being dependent on foreign military, economic, or other assistance. There is no thought of relying on religion either. Nevertheless, the adoration of Kim Jong-un's father, Kim Jong-il, and grandfather, Kim Il-sung, has taken on some of the characteristics of a state religion.

CHINA

Landing in the Shanghai Pudong International airport, we show the passport visa stamps that we had to get before leaving on this trip. Our bus ride downtown passes some traditional, low-rise housing compounds, but we see that these are rapidly being condemned, leveled, and replaced by luxurious high-rise apartments and shopping complexes. We recall that this has been controversial because families who have lived in their compounds for centuries are being forced to relocate on the outskirts of Shanghai, but even there they can barely afford the housing. When we reach the Bund, the embankment and promenade region downtown, we are amazed to see the contrasting views. Standing on the promenade and looking behind us at the downtown we see the old European-style banks, hotels, and other buildings from the last century, when some claim that Shanghai was the most cosmopolitan city in the world, and was called "Pearl of the Orient" or the "Paris of the East." Looking across Huangpu River we see the colorful, ultramodern high-rise buildings of Pudong, looking like a scene out of The Jetsons.[7] Then we go to the very modern Shanghai Museum, which is shaped like a ding, a traditional style pot, to see displays on all eras of Chinese history and art.[8]

---

[6]Links to contrasting pictures of the Koreas today from *The Guardian:* Tourist pictures of North Korea—http://www.theguardian.com/world/2014/feb/27/view-from-tour-bus-north-korea. Tourist photos of South Korea—http://www.theguardian.com/travel/gallery/2013/feb/22/seoul-life-in-the-megacity-in-pictures

Historically, the relation between religion and politics in China varied greatly from dynasty to dynasty. The First Emperor, Qin Shi Huang (r. 221–210 B.C.), favored the **Legalist** school of thought and ordered Confucian scholars to be buried alive in a mass grave. Subsequent dynasties, fortunately, were more tolerant of rival schools of religious or political thought. The court often favored one of China's religions, but the commoners were usually allowed to practice whatever religion or combination of religions they preferred. After Buddhism had established firm roots in Chinese soil, by the second century, the Chinese culture was characterized by a system of three-teachings (*san jiao*) under which it was acceptable to follow **Daoism**, Buddhism, or **Confucianism**, or some combination of those. Note that the term "teachings" (*jiao*) here is not quite the same as "religion." Confucianism is considered a teaching but not a religion.

Besides the three more organized "teachings," an informal complex of beliefs and rituals made up what scholars call **Chinese Popular Religion** or Folk Religion. Much of Chinese Popular Religion centers on the belief in a large variety of spirits (*shen*) associated with homes as well as natural phenomena such as forests, mountains, rivers, and the sky. Its practice involves the performance of rituals designed to appease the bad spirits and bring the blessing of good spirits. For example, before moving into a new home, traditional Chinese might perform a series of rituals to exorcize bad spirits from the property and then invite good, protective spirits to reside in the home. After doing this, the furniture is carefully placed in the home in accordance with the principles of *feng shui*, the traditional Chinese practice of maximizing the flow of good energies—in this case, the laying out of the home furnishings and arrangement of the living quarters so as to bring health, wealth, and other blessings to the residents. Although important to Chinese family life and ritual life at the court, such religious practices do not play an important role in the Chinese political landscape.

The tradition of religious tolerance in Chinese politics came to an abrupt end with the beginning of Communist rule on October 1, 1949. Since then, China has been characterized by an imbalance of power between religion and politics. The government of China has effectively kept all the traditional religions of China under close surveillance and control, although as we will see there are signs that the Government may be relaxing its control. Despite the official atheist state policy and the fact that nearly all Chinese alive today have been educated in an educational system that views all religion as outmoded, there has been a remarkable resurgence of religious identity and practice in China since the late 1970s.

We will begin with a brief review of the religious and political backgrounds to set the stage for understanding the more recent interactions of religion and politics. Then we will focus on four crucial issues arising from the interaction of religion and politics today. The first three topics center upon the way the government interacts with three of China's religious minorities: **Hui** and **Uyghur** Muslims, **Tibetan** Buddhists, and Protestant and

---

[7]A popular 1960s futuristic cartoon television show. For a picture of Pudong, see https://www.flickr.com/photos/ru_boff/12859350385/.

[8]For a picture of the unusual museum, see http://www.shanghaimuseum.net/en/.

Catholic Christians. Then, the fourth topic investigates the serious accusations **Falun Dafa (Falun Gong)** and the government make about each other. Finally, we will consider what implications of the resurgence of religion in China have for China's international relations and developing economy.

RELIGIOUS BACKGROUND

One important concern for religion and politics in modern China involves the right of China's ethnic minorities to maintain their traditional religion and culture. We will look at three such groups—the Tibetan Buddhists and the Uyghur and Hui Muslims. Their Buddhist or Islamic culture sometimes brings them into conflict with official government policy.

Since 1982, the Constitution of China guarantees freedom of religion and the freedom not to be religious. The Constitution recognizes only five religions: Daoism, Buddhism, Islam, Protestantism, and Catholicism. Note that the list includes three traditions from the outside—Islam and two forms of Christianity, as well as two of the "three-teachings" religions. Buddhism became established in China so long ago that it doesn't seem foreign.

Estimated Numbers of Adherents in China:
Confucians: 6 to 8 million
Daoists: 2.5 to 3.5 million
Buddhists: 200 to 800 million
Muslims: 17 to 18 million
Hui 8 to 9 million
Uyghur 9 to 10 million
Christians: 65 to 70 million

A closely related issue derives from the government policy of only recognizing religious organizations whose leadership follows government directives. As long as their approved status is maintained, some public money is available to support the most important temples, mosques, or churches. The money restriction has impacted Protestant missionizing, and to maintain its "approved" status, the recognized Catholic Church of China must maintain some separation from the pope or Rome. Those Catholics who want to maintain closer ties to Rome have to affiliate with an underground Catholic organization that does not enjoy government approval.

Members of the Chinese Communist Party (CCP) are discouraged from engaging in religious or superstitious practices. Because being a CCP member is required for most senior level governmental and public service positions, this means that overt religious affiliation is not possible for most government officials. The same restriction applies to higher ranking officers in the People's Liberation Army (PLA).

What about new religions or minority populations not on the list of five? How do they gain acceptance in a "five religions" system? So far the government has not provided any mechanism for new or outside religions to gain constitutional status, other than a change in the constitution itself. Jews, Sikhs, and other minority groups without constitutional status are allowed to practice their religions, as long as they are not perceived to be a threat to the current social order or regime. As we will see in the case of Falun Dafa, it is not easy for larger religious movements to stay under the government's radar.

Confucianism

It is debatable whether to classify Confucianism as a religion or not. As we have seen, the Chinese understood it as a moral philosophy (teaching) rather than a religion, and it is not listed among the modern constitution's list of five religions. Early Confucian thinkers such as Confucius and Mengzi were sages, not gods on earth or founders of a religion. However, in later centuries the Chinese built temples at which people came to pay respect to Confucius by lighting incense, bowing, and other behavior typical of religious worship of gods. That is, Confucianism is really a set of teachings about proper social, ritual, and political values and norms, but these values and norms came to be institutionalized in a way that looked a lot like a religion. Strictly speaking, Confucianism is not a religion, but it is usually discussed together with Daoism and Buddhism as the "three religions" of traditional China. That is, outsiders tend to turn "three teachings" into "three religions."

However we categorize it, Confucianism has been very important in shaping the social and political values of China for 2,500 years. For centuries the entrance exam for positions in the civil service was based on a set of books known as the Confucian Classics. An aspirant civil servant had to prove that he (females were not considered eligible) was able to bring the principles taught by Confucius, Mencius and other early thinkers to bear on decisions that might arise in their careers as the administrators (known in the west as Mandarins). There are estimated to be 6 to 8 million Chinese today who would identify themselves as Confucians. Because Chinese culture itself is largely based on Confucian values, the worldwide number of persons influenced by Confucianism is well over a billion.

Kongfuzi (Confucius)

Nanjing, the "Southern Capital" in earlier days, is our next stop. Near the river in an old section we find a Confucius Temple complex that was a training center for young men planning to take the national exams on Confucian texts with the hope of getting a position in the civil service; that is, becoming a Mandarin official. Passing through the three part gate, we visit the temple dedicated to Confucius. The courtyard has statues honoring his key disciples. People pay respect to Confucius by placing lighted incense sticks near a large statue of him in the entrance hall. The classroom building lies behind the temple, and we see one of the small rooms where the students lived and studied. In traditional China a person (if a male) of any social class could rise to a position of great importance in the government. We realize that wasn't the case traditionally in most Western nations.

> *We also visit the nearby Taiping Museum. It exhibits materials from the 1860s peasant Taiping Rebellion against the Imperial forces. In other parts of the old city we see the room where the Chinese Communist Party was founded and the Jade Buddhist temple.*

Confucius lived in northern China around 2,500 hundred years ago, but his precise dates are unknown. He is known to the Chinese as **Kongfuzi**, Master Kong Fu. Like all the important ancient sages, he was given the honorific title "master," zi, after his death. His English name, Confucius, comes from Jesuit missionaries who gave his name a Latin ending. We do not really know much for certain about his life, but a legendary account includes this story about his mother. While she was pregnant, a unicorn delivered a message to his mother saying that the child would be "a king without a kingdom." This was seen as a prophecy of his later status at a sage leader, but not a ruler. He was a precocious child who could read at a very early age. Another story tells how he and his playmates used to dress up as court officials and play at doing court rituals. If true, it gives a foretaste of his later idealization of ritualized behavior and acting as a "gentleman" at all times.

Confucius' first position was as a records keeper for a livestock farm. Then he became a minor official in the civil service, but he seems to have become very critical of the bureaucracy of his day. He was appalled at the way rich men could buy a civil servant position for their sons, since appointments were often made by a bribery system. Later, he would call for a "rectification of names," that is, a radical reform of the system so that those appointed to offices (here called "names") would be right for the position. Confucius wanted appointments made on the basis of qualifications rather than money and social class. The system he criticized had two major problems. The office holders were often not good at their positions, and after getting the office, they took bribes to repay the extended family members who had put up the money to buy their appointment in the first place.

Confucius idealized the philosopher-kings of the early Zhou dynasty (1046–256 B.C.). He thought they were true gentlemen rulers who were above corruption and whose government decisions had the best interests of the people in mind. He also admired them as cultured persons who appreciated music, rituals, and proper personal interactions. But in the later days of the Zhou dynasty when he lived, Confucius thought the political culture had deteriorated such that bribery and incompetence had become the norm, leading to social discord and the loss of moral principles. He taught that social harmony comes only when inferior ranked persons give both respect and obedience to their superiors, while superior ranked persons in turn rule with wisdom and benevolence. This applies, in his thinking, to all the levels of the social hierarchy. Confucian thought expresses this in terms of the "five relationships." The four hierarchical relationships are ruler-subject, father-son, elder brother-younger brother, husband-wife. The fifth is a relationship between equals, called friend to friend. From a modern point of view the absence of sister to sister and the subordination of women seem problematic.

Statue of Confucius in courtyard of Confucius Temple, Nanjing.
Photo: Roy Amore

After leaving his civil service position, Confucius travelled around his home region in northern China, going from village to village recruiting promising young men to be trained by him as potential civil servants. In these middle years of his life, he was an unpaid teacher of public administration. He taught in what the West calls the Socratic Method, asking the students questions and then probing them into deeper and deeper levels of discovery. For example, he would ask students to pretend they had just been made a high official in a certain kingdom, and then ask them what they would try to accomplish first, second, and third. Some students would want to shore up the military first, and then work on feeding the people. Most followed their master's lead and expressed a desire to support high culture after the basics of defence and food were met. One student confessed that when it came time to support culture, he would have to leave that to a real gentleman. These dialogues between the Master and his students are collected under the title "Analects of Confucius," which is available in many English translations.

There was a human side to Confucius as well. One student, when asked what he would do first, was reluctant to give an honest reply. Upon encouragement, he told the Master that on a fine spring day like today, he would just like to go on a picnic in the meadow with his friends. Ah, said the Master, a man after my own heart.

Confucius was a social conservative. Based on a belief that all societies were naturally hierarchical, he laid down principles that he thought should lead to a harmonious and prosperous society. The ruling aristocracy should be recruited from young men with the brightest minds and highest characters. They should rule fairly and in a way that would effortlessly earn the respect of the people. The people themselves should be prepared to obey such leaders faithfully and without complaint. Education of the youth was the key to making this political vision work, he thought.

While still a young and relatively unknown writer, Mao Zedong published an essay in which he attacked the Confucian ideal of the calm and moderate sage. Mao's vision of the new ideal was a militant radical who would fight for the new China like a warrior charging on horseback. This 1917 essay foreshadowed the revolutionary ideology of the mature Mao in the era of the Civil War and the early days of his rule of China.

Donald Munro, a philosopher specializing in China, has called attention to how "Confucian" ideas such as holding up role models, valuing education and idealizing social harmony are still followed, perhaps unconsciously, in Communist China. Although the Chinese Communist state developed under the Soviet model, Chinese cultural values deeply rooted in Confucian thought remain important. Throughout Chinese history, Munro traces the assumption that a change in the educational system will bring about a moral consensus that makes it possible for government to develop a harmonious and prosperous society. This assumption was following in the Maoist period up until the upheaval of the Cultural Revolution in 1966.[9] After the Cultural Revolution ended in 1976, government policy returned to this Confucian principle.

Daoism

Daoism began as a moral or philosophical system, but the thought of the early Daoist sages was later incorporated into a religious system. For this reason, a distinction is usually made between early philosophical Daoism (the era of Laozi—see below—and other early sages) and later Daoist religion. Philosophical Daoism played a large role, along with Confucianism, in shaping the character of Chinese culture. Religious Daoism remains one of the active religious systems of contemporary China.

Laozi
Laozi, or Master Lao, lived approximately 2,500 years ago. He was not a religious figure at all, at least not in the sense typical of monotheistic religions. Actually he was an archivist by day, but in the evening young men would come to his house to hear his wisdom on all sorts of topics including politics, education, social norms, and above all, how to live a life in conformity with the eternal Dao.

According to the story, he resigned his job in a huff one day, got on a water buffalo and proceeded to ride westward out of China. Daoist artists later liked to paint him riding away, toward the west. As he left, he was stopped by a border guard who just happened

---

[9] Munro, Donald J. *The Concept of Man in Early China* (Stanford: Stanford University Press, 1969), 163.

to be one of his disciples. The guard pleaded with Laozi not to leave, reminding him that he had promised to one day put his teachings into writing for his students. Reluctantly, it seems, Laozi paused long enough to write down a small book of poems. In China this book is typically called *Laozi* after its author, but in the West we refer to it by its other title, *Daodejing*, the book (*jing*) about Dao and De. (Another way to spell the title in English is *Tao De Ching*). Whether or not he really dashed off this book in a day or so before leaving China, the *Daodejing* remains one of the world's most influential books.

Laozi opens his book with a now famous disclaimer. He warns that the Dao that can be described is not the eternal Dao. Because

> As you read this chapter, note that the *pinyin* system of English transliteration is used here. Some words may be more familiar to readers in the Wade-Giles system, which is not as common any longer because China has adopted the pinyin system as its official way to transliterate Chinese characters into English. To indicate two sounds not found in the English alphabet, pinyin arbitrarily assigns new sounds to two otherwise unneeded English letters. The letter q is assigned a certain ch sound not normally found in English and x represents a soft sh or tsh sound. So Qing is pronounced somewhat like "ching" and the city Xi'an sounds like "shi-an" or "tshi-an."

the human mind and words are not adequate to describe the mystical Dao force that pervades the universe, Laozi cautions that we must be content with allusions or similes. Whereas most cultures talk of the highest God as "Sky Father" or "Father in Heaven," Laozi prefers feminine imagery. He writes that Dao is the Mother of all things. Whereas most cultures prefer to think of the gods and goddesses as "he" or "she," for Laozi the Dao is more an "it," an energy force. One should not try to become someone one is not, Laozi suggests. The goal is not to become "superior," he writes. The goal is not to become rich, famous, or important. Rather, the goal is to live life in touch with the Dao within, to let the Dao flow through oneself.

Laozi suggests we should be more like water, which seems weak and shapeless, and yet it remains what it is throughout. What appears to be weakness is really great inner strength. To be like water, to maintain your Dao nature even under adversity, you should do things effortlessly, as if you had nothing to do. The Daoist term for this is *wuwei*. Great athletes usually can do this. They perform great feats seemingly without effort. Laozi wants to do everything *wuwei*, without undue thought, reflection or effort. This is the origin of the Zen Buddhist concept of no-mind we find among the Samurai of Japan.

Zhuangzi

Zhuangzi, the second great sage of Daoism, lived about two hundred years after Laozi. His name is better known in the West under the older spelling Chuang Tse or Chuang Tzu. His book, The *Zhuangzi*, adds some new dimensions to Daoist thought. His approach is quite simple. When you are hungry, eat. When you are sleepy, sleep. And whatever you do, be yourself. Live naturally, in harmony with the Dao within and nature without. He is quite critical of the Confucian approach to education. He sees it as an artificial project to turn a person into someone else's ideal model. The people need food, clothing, and

The Jade Emperor in the White Cloud Temple, Shanghai.
Photo: Pierre Bouchard (own work)) [GFDL (http://www.gnu.org/copyleft/fdl.html

shelter. They do not need to be turned into model upper class gentlemen or ladies with formal, ritualized behavior.

One fine spring day Zhuangzi was strolling through the meadow, watching the springtime activity, including the way butterflies flitted about on the breeze, sipping nectar from flowers. He became sleepy, and true to Daoist practice he took a nap. He dreamed he was a butterfly flitting about on the breeze. When he awoke he remembered that it had been quite fun dreaming he was a butterfly riding the breeze. Then he thought, "Wait a minute, how do I know that I'm a not a butterfly dreaming that I am a human?" He realizes there is no sure way to know whether he is a butterfly or a human. He reflects on this paradox for a while, then laughs, realizing it doesn't really matter! Daoists love such paradoxes because they jolt the mind out of its normal confidence and rationality. Here is another Daoist paradox story. While crossing a bridge, one Daoist pauses and looks down at the water rushing under the bridge. For a moment it seems as if the bridge is moving and the water is still. It becomes a moment of awakening. Later, this love of paradox came into the Chan (Zen) school of Buddhism in China.

Daoist Religion

Laozi and Zhuangzi might be called mystics, but they did not start a religion in any sense, which explains why the Chinese call the era of the early Daoist sages, "philosophical Daoism." By the time of the Han Dynasty (206 B.C.–A.D. 220), which roughly corresponds to the era of the Roman Empire and the beginning of Christianity, a Daoist religion arose in China. It had temples, priests, and a pantheon of gods headed by a god of the highest heavens known by several names, but now usually referred to as "The Jade Emperor." The Daoist Religion continues in China today, with around 2 million lay adherents and an estimated 25,000 priests affiliated with either the Perfect Truth sect that maintains Buddhist-style monasteries, or the Heavenly Masters sect that is older and less influenced by Buddhism. The Daoist canon of scriptures has over a thousand books, including those by Laozi and Zhuangzi. Religious Daoism was respected by government officials, but seldom in Chinese history was it the religion favored at court. It was popular with the people, especially artists and other creative individuals.

China expert Kenneth Dean calls attention to the difficulty that Daoism has in conforming to the Chinese state's concept of "religion." The state had adopted the modern and Western definition of religion as an institution with buildings, priests, and devotional activities. To conform to this concept, Daoist schools training priests have stressed the study of Daoist scriptures, as expected of a "religion," while downplaying traditional rituals that might, under government definitions, fall under the label of superstition rather than religion.[10]

Daoist Politics or Lack Thereof

Laozi, Zhuangzi and other early Daoist sages were strong advocates of a political theory that might be termed Minimalism. They thought that the best government was one that interfered least in the lives of the people. They told stories such as this one: Once a man was travelling across China, passing through many small kingdoms. In each one, he asked the peasants along the road, "What is the name of your king?" In most kingdoms, even the most remote peasants knew the name of the king and went on to say that his men came every spring to draft young men for his army or work crews and to take young women to work at his palace, and every fall the king's men came back to take large amounts of the harvest as taxes. Whenever the king rode by, they all had to stop working and bow low to the ground. But in one kingdom, the peasants didn't seem to even know the name of their ruler. Ah, thought the Daoist traveller, now here is a good ruler. He leaves the people alone. In Daoist political thought there is a strong confidence in the basic goodness of humans to govern themselves and an equally strong distrust in institutions and institutionalized behavior.

---

[10]Dean, Kenneth. "Further Partings of the Way: The Chinese State and Daoist Ritual Traditions in Contemporary China," in Ashiwa, Yoshiko and Wank, David L, eds. *Making Religion: Making the State* (Stanford: Stanford University Press, 2009), 179–210.

Buddhism

The exact date of the birth of Gautama the Buddha is disputed, but we can safely say that he lived around 2,500 years ago. He is usually thought of as the founder of Buddhism, but Buddhist tradition sees him as the latest in a long line of Buddhas, fully enlightened teachers, who have appeared on earth to provide a path for overcoming suffering and achieving **nirvana**, ultimate bliss. He travelled throughout northern India and southern Nepal, giving moral instruction and accepting disciples. Those who were willing to leave home, renouncing the householder life, took vows of celibacy and spent their days either as homeless, itinerant monks or nuns, or they lived in monastic communities. During Buddha's lifetime most of the monks travelled from place to place, except during the rainy season when travelling was difficult and one could not walk on the roads without harming insects. After Buddha's death (*parinirvana*) it was more common for monks or nuns to reside in monasteries year round.

Buddhism teaches an "eightfold path" toward enlightenment. Following this path involves continually striving to purify one's mind by such means as discipline, generosity, meditation, and wisdom. The ethical ideal is non-violence (*ahimsa*), which means avoiding harming others, including animals or even insects, as far as is practical. Buddhism spread rapidly throughout the various kingdoms and republics of the Indian subcontinent, and by the late third century B.C. King Ashoka financed the sending of Buddhist missionaries abroad, eastward into Southeast Asia, south into Sri Lanka, westward toward the Greek-speaking world of Alexander's successors, and Northwest along the trade route to Central Asia. Having established a strong Buddhist presence along the caravan cities of Central Asia, Indian monks followed the Silk Road to its Eastern terminus, the old Chinese capital in Xi'an, bringing Buddhism to China by the first century A.D.

Buddhism had arisen in an Indian culture that idealized monastic values, but those values were very foreign and quite immoral to the Chinese. The Chinese especially objected to the Buddhist monastic ideal, according to which their sons were supposed to leave the family compound and go live in monasteries where they would shave their heads and remain celibate. To the Chinese it seemed an insult to one's ancestors to shave one's head, thus altering what the ancestors had given them. If one's son became a monk, he would not be available to help on the farm or care for his parents when they became old. Even worse, by remaining celibate rather than marrying and having sons, the family lineage was endangered because sometime in the future there might not be any male relative alive to do the annual rituals to feed the ancestors. With no supportive family on earth, the ancestors would be hungry and miserable in the afterlife. And daughters were not thought to help on this matter because they would have married into some other family.[11]

[11]See Leon Hurvitz, "The Mind of the Early Chinese Buddhist," in *Developments in Buddhist Thought: Canadian Contributions to Buddhist Studies*, ed. Roy C. Amore (Waterloo: Wilfrid Laurier University Press, 1979), 118.

The Chinese did get used to the strange Indian ways, but Buddhism adapted itself to the Chinese culture by downplaying monasticism and by making Buddhist temples a place to revere one's ancestors. It depicted the Buddha and the Bodhisattvas in a more Chinese way. Monastic robes became more Chinese in style, and the monastery buildings evolved to accommodate Chinese architectural form, usually along the lines of an imperial complex. Buddhism adapted itself to accommodate the Chinese ancestry cult by making the temples a location for a complex of rituals and beliefs surrounding funerals, burials, and memorial rituals. The Chinese culture adopted the Buddhist concept of multiple heavens and hells, the latter being filled with a large variety of elaborately conceived forms of torture according to one's sins—along the lines of Dante's *Inferno.*

Buddhism then took on the role it still has, as one of the main components of Chinese spirituality with Buddhism touching the lives of most Chinese, at least before Mao's version of atheistic communism in 1949. The earliest forms of Buddhism to arrive in China were Hinayana. Mahayana forms of Buddhism arose in India early in the first centuries A.D., and Mahayana established itself as the main form of Buddhism in China. The division of Mahayana Buddhism—known as Pure Land—is the dominant form of Chinese Buddhism. It is a devotional form of Buddhism in which followers put their faith and trust in **Amida**[12] Buddha by chanting "Homage to Amida Buddha." This Buddha is said to have been a prince in old India who took a vow to become a Buddha and to set up a heavenly Pure Land, or Western Paradise, for all of those who turn to him for help. As a theological system, Pure Land Buddhism is curiously similar to Christianity. In both, followers are to put their faith in a savior figure who will help them during this life and after death they will go to be with him in heaven. This is a form of Buddhism that does not require profound textual knowledge or long hours of meditation. Devotional faith is sufficient.[13]

Chan (Zen) and Shaolin

> *After a long bus ride through beautiful mountain scenery we arrive in the town of Shaolin, home to Zen Buddhism and the martial arts. We are in luck because it is early afternoon and the students are practicing their martial arts in the schoolyards. Two boys stop to watch us, then the bigger one catches the other off guard, kicking him really hard. Rather than complaining to the teacher, the smaller boy winches in pain but quickly recovers and kicks back. Boys and girls come from all over China*

---

[12]Amida comes from the Japanese spelling and is usually used in English. The Sanskrit original is Amitabha.

[13]For more detail in Mahayana and other topics on Buddhism see Roy C. Amore and Julia Ching,"The Buddhist Tradition," in *A Concise Introduction to World Religions*, ed. Willard G. Oxtoby and Alan F. Segal (Toronto: Oxford University Press, 2007), 376–439.

[14]See www.shaolin.org/cn/en/. For a picture of the cave www.shaolin.org/cn/templates/EN_T_newS_list/index.aspx?nodeid=316&page=ContentPage&contentid-2123)

and beyond to attend school here, where they have regular lessons in the mornings and martial arts in the afternoons. Many schools have a Buddhist focus, but there are Muslim ones as well. Girls have separate schools. We tour the huge Shaolin Temple, the home temple of Zen in China, and then make the hour-long hike up the mountain to the cave where it is said that Bodhidharma spent his days and nights practicing "wall-gazing"'meditation.

Students at Shaolin posing after a martial arts demonstration.
Photo: Roy Amore

The Indian monk **Bodhidharma** brought the **Chan** (or Zen) school of Buddhism to China in the sixth century. He settled into a cave in the mountains of Shaolin forest, where he meditated intensely in a style called wall-gazing. This introduced the practice of long hours of sitting meditation (*zazen*) into Chan Buddhism. Bodhidharma taught "mind to mind transmission," an approach in which one enlightened person passes along a higher form of consciousness through encounters with students. Later, masters used stories, called *koans*, of such master-student encounters to help new students. *Zazen* and *koans* are important Chan practices. Besides starting the Chan School in China, Bodhidharma is credited with teaching the young monks of the Shaolin monastery in the town below his cave some exercise techniques that developed into the martial arts system of East Asia. He is both the founder of Chan and the founder of Chinese martial arts.

POLITICAL BACKGROUND: FROM THE FIRST EMPEROR TO THE COMMUNIST ERA

Our train arrives in Xi'an, the modern city in Eastern China that lies near the ancient city of Chang-an, the Eastern terminus of the famous Silk Road. For centuries the trade caravans arrived here from the west, through Central Asia, bringing goods from the Middle East, India, and other points. Like most travellers, we take a bus to see the Terracotta Warriors who guarded the tomb of the First Emperor. We visit the archaeological sites where the warriors were found and the museum exhibits where we can get up close to some of the warriors, horses and chariots. Then we stand with others in the middle of a theatre in the round, watching a fascinating video about the life of the First Emperor who had this tomb complex constructed. It ends with a re-enactment of how the terracotta warriors were destroyed after the First Emperor's death, as a protest against his tyrannical rule. Back on the bus, we stop at the site of the First Emperor's actual tomb, which to our surprise is quite a distance from where the terracotta army was located. It seems strange to have the army over a mile away, but maybe that reflects the practice while the Emperor was alive. We buy some fruit and a copy of Mao's Little Red Book *from one of the numerous roadside vendor women.*

The First Emperor

China was governed by kingship until 1911, when the young boy Puyin was overthrown as the last emperor.[15] In ancient China there were earlier dynasties, but in 220 B.C. Qin Shi Huang conquered areas and expanded his territory to cover much of modern China, thus earning the title First Emperor. In his short, ten-year reign as emperor he made major changes in the political system. He undermined the power of the old clan system by drawing new administrative boundaries and systems. His court was staffed by thinkers of the Legalist school, who introduced a strong law code spelling out specific punishments for crimes. Their thought was influenced by the teachings of Master Mo, or Mozi (ca. 470–391 B.C.). Mo was a pragmatist or utilitarian who had little use for occupations that did not produce material benefits for the people. He was also an egalitarian who had foreseen the need for creating a legal system that would be uniformly applied to all persons, independently from the personal whims of a particular administrator. The legalists took these ideas and invented a system of government based upon a rule of law. Their idea was that to create a fair and uniform law code, there needed to be one set of standards throughout the Empire. This law code was rigorously and brutally imposed, with the public being forced to watch the administration of severe punishments, included numerous capital deaths, as deterrents to others. To further the ideal of creating uniformity within the state,

---

[15]The movie *The Last Emperor* depicts the life of the young Puyin.

Soldiers of the terracotta army guarding Qin Shi Huang's tomb.
Photo: Roy Amore

the regime adopted a uniform set of weights and measures, a standardized writing system that underlies the one still in use, and a standardized system of thought, including political theory and religious concepts. But the attempt to standardize political philosophy and culture brought them infamy. Under their guidance, the Emperor ordered the burning of Confucian books and had Confucian scholars buried alive. After his death, the Chinese rebelled against this tyrannical regime, but kept many of his reforms. Today he is credited with doing a lot of construction on the Great Wall, but he is best known for his tomb guarded by armies of life-sized terracotta warriors and horses.

Han Dynasty and Han Chinese

The Qin dynasty was soon replaced by the **Han** Dynasty (206 B.C.–A.D. 220). Its four hundred year reign forms the classical period of China. Rather than attempting to force one system of thought upon everyone, as the Legalists had, the Han dynasty advocated the three teachings system (*san jiao*) mentioned earlier. Known as the Han synthesis, this approach created a government policy that tolerated a variety of religious and philosophical thought. The ethnic Chinese call themselves Han, in the sense of being descendants of the classical Chinese people. The issues of this chapter mainly deal with the government's relationships with the ethnic minorities, the non-Han people of China, and with a policy known by its critics as "Hanification."

Foreign Dynasties

Two of the dynasties that ruled China were of foreign origin. The Mongols ruled in the thirteenth and fourteenth centuries as the Yuan Dynasty. And the Manchurians ruled from 1644 to 1911 as the Qing Dynasty. In between China was ruled by the Ming Dynasty (1368–1644), which undertook land reform, revived agriculture, and developed an impressive naval power. Despite the progress, China was starting to fall behind Europe in manufacturing and technology.

During the 1800s the Qing Dynasty let China continue to fall behind the West. The court took the attitude that China was the most civilized country in the world and did not need any goods from abroad. The European trading powers reacted with **Gunboat Diplomacy**. This term refers to bringing gunboats up the rivers to the major cities and then threatening to fire into the cities to force the Chinese to sign agreements opening up ports to the foreign traders. Chinese call these the "unequal treaties" because they were not entered into voluntarily by equal partners. In the nineteenth century, in the era when the Meiji Restoration was modernizing Japan, the Qing court went in the opposite direction. China had only an old style army and practically no navy, although in a previous period it had perhaps the best navy in the world.

Mandarin System of Civil Service
From the Han days until the Republic (1912–1949), China was usually administered by a recruited class of civil servants known in the West as **Mandarin**. Bright young boys would study in special training schools or under private tutors for years and then take the civil service qualifying exams based mainly on Confucian (or later, on neo-Confucian) works. The exams were open to boys from any region or social class, but the rich families had some advantage because they could afford the best private tutors. Once appointed, an official could work his way up through the nine ranks. The top officials served at the palace. Each morning the emperor held court, receiving reports from the officials and taking decisions. This Mandarin system made Confucian thought extremely important for determining public policy.

The Republic period started in 1911 when the weakened and unpopular Qing dynasty was overthrown by a small group inspired by Dr. **Sun Yat-sen**, a Christian who had gone to an Anglican school in Hawaii. But the Republic's ideals were soon thwarted by regional warlords who had military might on their side. China degenerated into a prolonged **Civil War**, starting in 1927, between the Nationalist Party, known as the **Guomintang**, led by **Chiang Kai-shek**, and the Communists, led later by **Mao Zedong**. Because of its anti-Communist stance and its pro-Christian leader, the west, especially the United States, backed the Guomintang. The Communist Party (CCP) was funded and guided from Russia. An invasion by Japan worsened matters greatly. At first the communist forces were on the run. When they were driven out of their stronghold, Shanghai, a large number of communists first fled southward, where they were joined by Mao Zedong and his followers. Several communist Red Army contingents and supporters joined the march to safety.

The main group worked its way toward the relative safety of the Northwest frontier. Along the way, many died, but they also gained many peasant supporters because they promised "land to the cultivators." This promise meant a revolutionary shift of land ownership from large landowners to peasant cultivators. Their famous **Long March** ended when the few who survived found sanctuary in the far northwest, where many had to live in caves. Through promising land to the peasants, they gradually gained control of rural areas. They gained strength as the Nationalists lost support. By fall 1949 they were able to take control of the capital. On October 1, 1949 Mao stood in front of the Imperial city in Beijing, overlooking Tiananmen Square, and proclaimed the new era of the People's Republic of China. China, he said, had stood up. Meanwhile, Chiang Kai-shek and several elite families had escaped to Taiwan, where they intended to regroup and retake the mainland. But that did not happen.

Communist Period (1949–)

The new Maoist government inherited many problems. China was poor, overpopulated, not industrialized, and surrounded by hostile powers. China had been experiencing hyperinflation that had impoverished millions, and Mao did well to get the inflation under control. At first the policy was to leave religions alone, to die on their own, but during the Anti-Rightist Campaign of 1957, any person or group thought not to hold to ideological purity came under heavy criticism. Religion practitioners became suspect. The Anti-Rightist Campaign was quickly followed by Mao's plan to rapidly industrialize, called the **Great Leap Forward** (1958–1960). In an attempt to close the industrial gap with the West, especially in steel production, and to become more efficient in agricultural production, rural Chinese were forced to form communes in which they shared a common kitchen as well as farm implements and work. The combination of communal living, where private religious activities were not possible, and the bias against anything other than increasing production output, was another setback for religion in China. Despite its goal of increasing agricultural output, the Great Leap Forward made the serious mistake of undermining agriculture for the sake of industrial production, especially of steel. Prolonged drought made matters worse. Millions starved, and the plan was abandoned. Mao's leadership gave way to that of more pragmatic leaders who slowly began to improve the economy. The open practice of religion again became more tolerated, until the onset of the Cultural Revolution.

Anti-Religion and the Destruction of the "Four Olds" During the Cultural Revolution
Mao's distrust of religion came from two sources. Ideologically he had become a Marxist, which meant among other things that he believed the only way forward was by class revolution and that religion was part of the old, classed society and therefore part of the problem. Personally, he did not practice religion and considered it to be outmoded superstition. Although Mao was quite willing to use force to defeat the upper-class elements, he was more reluctant to attack religion, preferring to let it fade away on its own. At least,

that was the case from 1949 until the mid-1960s, when he made a last effort to transform Chinese society.

Through Mao's wife and the other three members of what came to be known as the **Gang of Four**, China was led into the **Cultural Revolution** (1966–76). The Cultural Revolution was really an attack on traditional culture—its ideas, buildings, art, leaders, books, and everything else that the bands of students called the **Red Guards** took to represent old cultural values. These gangs of youth became a law unto themselves in many regions. They enforced Mao's injunction to "Destroy the **Four Olds**," which he defined as "old customs, old culture, old habits and old ideas." Religion, art, and other traditional things were to be eradicated and replaced by Mao's thought. To educate the new generation on Mao's teach-

> ## How the Jade Buddha Temple Survived the Cultural Revolution
>
> Since its construction almost a century ago the Jade Buddha temple in Shanghai has seen the highs and lows of the interface of religion and politics in Shanghai. It was built after a monk returned from a trip to Burma (Myanmar) with two large Buddha images made of Jade.
>
> The Shanghai temple survived the sweep against Communists in 1927, the Japanese invasion (1937–1945), the civil war, and the early days of Communist rule. But surviving the Cultural Revolution was more challenging, as many temples had already come under attack. When someone warned the abbot of the Jade Buddha Temple that his temple was to be the target of that evening's Red Guard activity, the desperate abbot had Mao posters pasted over the temple gate, which consisted of two swinging doors hinged at the sides. When the Red Guards arrived, they didn't dare deface the Mao pictures by opening the doors, so they only shouted denunciations from outside the gate. The historic Jade Buddha and its precious contents were spared.

ings, a collection of his sayings known as the **Little Red Book** was distributed widely. Memorizing the sayings of that Little Red Book formed the main part of the curriculum of the school system during the period of the Cultural Revolution, and everyone was expected to own a copy and read it frequently. Mao's picture, which could be seen everywhere, was an important component of what historians of this period have dubbed "**The Cult of Mao**."

Since religion was a prime example of old culture, all religious buildings and institutions came under the wrath of the Red Guards. Their destructive attacks targeted not only the traditional religions of China (Daoism, Buddhism and Confucianism, and Popular Religion, but also the more recently imported traditions such Christianity, Judaism, Islam and others. The slogans of the revolution included "beating down foreign religion" and "beating down Jesus following." The storied Jade Buddha Temple (see the inset box) that was sparred is one of the rare exceptions. It took almost ten years for the anti-religious Cultural Revolution to fade away, but following the end of the Cultural Revolution in 1976 the official government policy toward religions began to relax. People slowly began to find their way back to the Buddhist and Daoist temples, the mosques and the churches. After the death of Mao, China has benefited by the leadership of more pragmatic men who have adopted measures intended to bring the economy into a pattern of sustainable growth. As a result of these economic and administrative reforms, China slowly started on the road toward its current status as an emerging economic superpower, with the potential to become a military superpower. There are problems, however. The Han Chinese in the cities are prospering as never before, while most of the Han people in rural areas and the ethnic minorities are only marginally more prosperous.

The post-Cultural Revolution constitutions of 1975 and 1982 guaranteed the right to practice religion or to be atheist, as encouraged by CCP and the educational system. By the 1980s China's religions were gaining in popularity. More and more Han Chinese who were not party members or government employees felt free to openly practice a religion. Despite the fact that most had been educated into communist ideology, a religious revival began in the 1980s and it continues to gain momentum. The resurgence of religion causes an ideological problem for the Marxist government. In communist theory once socialism has replaced capitalism, people collectively own the means of production and no longer feel alienated from their labor. Although Marx did not envision a need for a strong central government in the coming socialist era, in later communist state theory the era of religious allegiance to God or institutional religions was said to have ended, for now the people should have loyalty to the state and no need for religion.

A 1982 document entitled "The Basic Viewpoint on the Religious Question during Our Country's Socialist Period"[16] expressed the policy framework under which religion and socialism have co-existed in the post-Cultural Revolution period. The document reaffirms that, according to socialist theory, religion will eventually disappear, but it is to be tolerated during this stage of history as a help toward the economic goal of constructing a modern socialist state and economy. The quotes from Hu Jintao and Jia Qinglin at the beginning of this chapter reflect this policy—religion is to be encouraged because it will help move China toward economic prosperity.

The post-Cultural Revolution policy of tolerating but not encouraging religions continued until 2008, when government rhetoric about religions became more accepting. As reflected in the quotes at the beginning of this chapter, the government is experimenting with moving in the direction of using religious values as a means to promote social harmony, but always under government authority. Hu Jintao, the highest ranking leader at the time, called upon the party officials to "closely unite religious figures and believers… around the party and government and struggle together with them to build an all-around moderately prosperous society while quickening the pace toward the modernization of socialism."[17] The economic benefits to China that might be achieved by bringing religious

---

[16]The People's Republic of China: Document 19. See http://www.religlaw.org/content/religlaw/documents/doc19relig1982.htm

[17]Edward Cody, "China's Leaders Change Tactics Toward Religion," *Washington Post* (January 22, 2008).

leaders into the socialist fold were stressed by another high official, Jia Qinglin, while speaking to religious leaders. He wanted to take advantage of "the positive role that religious figures and believers among the masses can play in promoting economic and social development."[18] That is, religions and their leaders should serve the state.

State Registration and the Special Case of Chinese Popular Religion

The government does keep a very tight control over organized religion through the State Administration for Religious Affairs. The most important administrative means of control is the constitutional recognition of only five religions. To be officially recognized, all religious organizations must apply to the local subdivision of the State Administration for Religious Affairs. Once registered, the leaders of each religious association take the responsibility to communicate government policy to its members and to report on its activities to the state. For Daoist or Buddhist temples, as well as mosques and churches, the approval is based on their being affiliated with one of the five official religions. But the registration process is problematic for most local temples, which are really part of Chinese Popular Religion rather than any of the five official religions. All temples, no matter how small, are administered by a temple organization committee, and the burden of getting the temple registered falls upon them. They must put together an application that successfully argues either that the local temple is affiliated, however loosely, with Buddhism or Daoism, or that the activities carried out by the temple are charitable and religious rather than superstitious in nature.

The distinction between "religion" and "superstition" is a crucial one in the government's eyes. The category *religion* (*zongjiao*) includes all of the institutions and activities of the five official religions, and is protected by the constitution, whereas *superstition* is officially banned. However, most of the activities of the local temples would, if carefully scrutinized, fall under the "superstition" label. These activities include fortune telling, operatic performances honoring folk deities, psychic healing, and festivals. The local temples do not have a professional priest, as would a Daoist or Buddhist temple. The financial support of these temples comes mainly from donations made by people who come to the temple, light incense sticks in honor of the deity and pray for a favor—usually something very tangible such as help overcoming a medical problem, help with getting a promotion, or help in a family matter. As part of the request, the person promises to pay some amount of money, depending upon their means and the severity of the request. Later, if the prayer is granted the person returns, usually during the time of the temple's festival, to make the "incense donation" as promised. During the Cultural Revolution such activities had to be done in secret, if at all. But since then the officials of the State Administration for Religious Affairs have permitted the local temples to grow in number and expand in scope. The officials register the temples, turning a blind eye to the "superstitious" activities that are openly practiced there. Chinese Popular Religion has thus enjoyed a great resurgence despite being officially rejected.

---

[18]*Ibid.*

Anthropologist Adam Yuet Chau's study of the Black Dragon King Temple in northern China reveals several characteristics of the relationship of the state and local temples.[19] He explains that the local officials are not well paid and that their pay is often delayed for weeks or months. Also, as members of the local community, they may take pride in seeing a local temple thrive and hold festivals. A cooperative arrangement is therefore established in which the local officials allow the festival to take place—overlooking the fact that its activities fall under the banned "superstition" category—while themselves profiting from the festivals in various ways. For example, members of the security forces may be paid for keeping the peace during the festival. And local revenues are enhanced when people from nearby areas attend the festival. As well, the festival organizers ask local officials to be present on stage, and shower them with gifts and expressions of gratitude.

The cooperative way that local temples and officials often relate is just one reason why anthropologist Yoshiko Ashiwa and sociologist David Wank argue that the relationship between the state and religion in China should be seen as one of multiple actors (business persons, state officials, priests, festival organizers, adherents) and multiple processes, rather than a simple, dichotomous state-religion polarity.[20] They call our attention to the fact that the concept *religion* is not fixed or definitive but has evolved over time. In the case of China, the vague distinction drawn between religion and superstition serves to make the point that in the "religion-state" dichotomy it is not clear what all "religion" covers. Nor should one hold a simplistic notion of the "state" in China, for the motives and behaviors of officials may vary regionally and among the various levels of government.

The official five must have their leaders approved by the government, and leaders who challenge the government's policies can be dismissed. The leaders must affirm loyalty to the government, and we will see the problem this causes for Roman Catholics who want to affirm a loyalty to the papacy. We will see that many Christians meet in house churches, which are not part of the officially registered Christian church system.

Policy Toward Minorities[21]
Another lingering problem faced by the government is to develop good policies concerning the **minority peoples**. The government recognizes 55 minorities. They are very diverse culturally, linguistically and economically. The minorities constitute about 8 percent of the total population, but that is over 100 million people. Some are tribal groups living in the mountains of the south. Others are nomads in the north. Many minorities follow a different religion than the Han Chinese and include various tribal religions, Hinayana

---

[19]Adam Yuet Chau, "The Politics of Legitimation and the Revival of Popular Religion in Shaanbei, North-Central China (Black Dragon Temple)," *Modern China*, Vol 31(2) (April 2005), 236–278.

[20]Ashiwa, Yoshiko, and Wank, David L. 2009. Stanford: Stanford University Press. 3–4.

[21]For an interactive map of China's minorities, visit http://www.nytimes.com/interactive/2009/07/10/world/20090711-xinjiang.html?_r=0

and Tibetan Buddhists, and there are ten Muslim minority groups. We will discuss the two most important Muslim groups, and then consider the Tibetan Buddhists.

Under Mao's leadership, the government attempted to assimilate the minorities into Han culture as quickly as possible. They were educated in Chinese rather than their native languages, and they were governed by Han officials rather than traditional elders. China historian Thomas David DuBois draws attention to the way in which China's policy toward its minorities followed the lead of Soviet model in the 1950s.[22] Soviet Communism had defined the nature of a socialist state. Both the USSR and China had to govern a vast territory embracing diverse ethnic and religious groups dwelling on lands rich in valuable natural resources. He notes that prior to the 1949 advent of a socialist state in China, the Soviets had gone back and forth between the two extremes of either repressing ethnic identity in the name of national unity, or promoting the concept of a cultural federalism which allows for religion under the larger concept of the state. Mao learned from the Soviet mistakes in being too zealous in repressing ethnicity, and followed instead the emerging, 1950s concept of a people's state in which the ethnic minorities were happy members. Public displays of minorities in their ethnic dress were encouraged at games and celebrations. Religion was seen as an integral part of ethnic identity and was permitted, but only under ethnic leaders who supported the socialist state and its ideals.

June Dreyer, a political scientist and China specialist, mentions several reasons why the Chinese paid so much attention to the minorities.[23] One was territory. The Han areas were mostly overpopulated, whereas the minority areas were sparsely populated because they tended to live in areas other than the fertile rice or wheat areas farmed by the Han. So, the government planned to move Han Chinese into the minority areas as a solution to Han overpopulation. This policy has led to the "Hanification of Tibet" discussed below. A second reason was strategic. Many of the minorities lived on the borders, near perceived enemies of China. This applied especially to two of our focus issues, for the Tibetans had close ties with India and the Uyghurs with parts of the former Soviet Union. A third reason is that many of the minority regions are rich in natural resources. The Tibetan region is the source of two major river systems flowing down from the Himalayas. It also contains large reserves of natural gas and oil as well as having great potential for geothermal and solar power production. The Xinjiang region, homeland to the Uyghur minority, has gold, precious stones, and valuable minerals in its mountains and oil under its valleys, as reflected in the saying "treasure on every mountain, oil in every basin."[24] A fourth reason was for propaganda purposes. Mao was eager to show that his version of communism would work to bring prosperity and socialist development to the backward minorities. For

---

[22]Thomas David DeBois. 2010. "Religion and the Chinese state: three crises and a solution" *Australian Journal of International Affairs*, Vol. 64, Issue 3 (2010): 348–352.

[23]June Teufel Dreyer, *China's Political System: Modernization and Tradition* (New York: Pearson Longman. 6th ed., 2008), 277–278.

[24]http://www.aboutxinjiang.com/topic/content/2008-01/11/content_2389669.htm.

example, the government-controlled media played up how happy the Tibetans were to be liberated from feudalism. Finally, another reason that is very important more recently is tourism. The government has learned that significant revenue can be generated by tourists, especially in the case of Tibet.[25]

With this background, we turn to the issues involving Muslim and Buddhist minorities.

ISSUE 1. HUI AND UYGHUR MUSLIMS VS. THE HAN MAJORITY

The Hui Minority

Although considered one of the minority groups, the Hui are more assimilated into Han society than most other minorities. However, they follow an Islamic culture and marry within their own Hui communities. They are the descendants of Muslims who came as traders from Persia and Central Asia, and intermixed with the Han Chinese who were converted to Islam. They look like Han Chinese and speak Chinese in the dialect of their region. Their version of Chinese contains a lot of Persian and Arabic loan words, however, that Han Chinese might not understand. There are Hui in many cities, and some have migrated into Central Asia and states of the former Soviet Union, where they are called Dungan. The need to be close to mosques and Islamic halal butcher shops leads them to live in close proximity, so there are usually Hui Muslim quarters in Chinese cities. Non-Hui mingle with them freely, and their restaurants featuring Hui cuisine are frequented by all. But many Hui live in rural areas. A common Hui family name is Ma, a shortened form of Muhammad. Their background as a trading class is reflected in some of their occupations, such as engaging in modern style trading or being in the restaurant or hotel business.

Estimates of Hui population in China range from 8 to 10 million. They are predominantly Sunni[26] and follow the Hanafi form of Shariah, Islamic law. Many are not affiliated with any outside Islamic movements, but approximately one fourth identify with the Yihewani (from Arabic Ikhwan, "brother-hood"), a Chinese version of the Muslim Brotherhood started in the late nineteenth century by a Chinese who had been educated in Mecca. Another quarter of the Hui population identifies with some form of the more mystical Sufi Islam.[27]

The Hui communities have been a part of China for so long that they are accepted, and for the most part have not made demands on the political system. As one of the five officially recognized religions, they are under the watchful eyes of Chinese officials, which ensures that they do not openly criticize the government.

---

[25]June Teufel Dreyer, *China's Political System: Modernization and Tradition* (New York: Pearson, 5th ed., 2006), 279.

[26]See the chapter on Saudi Arabia for a discussion of the Sunni and Shi'i division.

[27]Dru C.Gladney, "Islam," *Journal of Asian Studies*, Vol. 54, No.2 (May 1995), 372.

Street scene in the Hui Muslim quarter of Lhasa. Note the white hats and the mosque visible in the background.
Photo: M. Morrison

The Grand Mosque in Xi'an provides an example of government support for the Hui as one of the official five religions. The Great Mosque has been there since the days that Hui Muslim traders settled in Chang-an (old Xi'an), at the end of the famous Silk Road across stretching across Central Asia and on to India and the Middle East. The mosque is enormous and is laid out in the Chinese imperial style, like the imperial palace. Most religious structures in China follow this architectural norm. The large central courtyard contains rock pillars with messages celebrating the money donated for restoring and improving the mosque by emperors of several dynasties, including the Tang, Ming, and Qing. Regardless of the religious leaning of the dynasty, it seems that funds flowed to the main mosque in Xi'an. A new monument and sign calls attention to the way the current communist government is continuing this pattern. The government also charges a sizable entrance fee for visiting tourists, so the money spent on renovations is being offset by entrance fees.

Panthay Rebellion and other Hui Incidents in Yunnan
Although the Hui relations with the government are generally good, there have been occasional protests and outbreaks of violence both before and after communist rule. The

Panthay Rebellion (1856–1873) in Yunnan Province was the most deadly of the conflicts between the Hui and government. Panthay is an old name for the Hui. The rebellion started in part as a conflict among tin miners during a time of general Hui and regional discontent with the Qing rulers, who subsequently ordered the massacre of all the Hui in Yunnan. The Hui fought back, and made allies of other Yunnan minorities and some Han of the region. They declared a separate state, but after 18 years of war the Qing re-established control of the region.[28] We will see that discontent with the Qing led to the Taiping Rebellion in this same era.

Serious trouble again erupted in Yunnan Province in the 1970s. It had started in 1968, during the early days of the Cultural Revolution, when a government "propaganda team" came to the town of Shadian to enforce the anti-religion dictates of the time. The members of the team stayed at the local mosque and defiled it by eating pork and throwing the bones into the well used to wash before prayers. By 1973, a local Hui leader appealed to Beijing to have the government officials removed from the mosque so that normal prayers could be restored. Beijing refused, and things became worse. By 1975 the People's Liberation Army arrived, surrounded the town and eventually attempted to enter. The PLA was kept out by a local Hui militia. In a brutal response, the PLA launched an attack on Shadian with bombs, flame-throwers, and other serious weapons. The town was left in ruins, and over one thousand Hui were killed in Shadian and nearby villages.[29] The government blamed the Hui for being counter-revolutionary, which is ironic because they were revolting against the suppression of their religion by the government.

Another clash between the government and the Hui erupted in 1992 in Pingyuan, a town in Yunnan Province near the border with Vietnam and Laos. At the time, some Hui may have earned their living through the drug trade from nearby opium poppy-growing areas. Army troops and other police forces entered the town and arrested many on charges of trafficking in drugs and guns, accusing them of being a part of an organized drug transport operation moving drugs from Southeast Asia to Hong Kong and beyond. When some Hui resisted with gunfire, the army retreated and kept the town surrounded for days. Finally the army entered the town again, arresting over four hundred people on drug and related charges. The government said that this was not a crackdown on a minority or a religion, but on a criminal drug ring. China historian David Atwill points out that there is widespread poverty in the region and that trade of drugs and other goods from Southeast Asia is the traditional occupation here. He also notes that whereas the government usually bans media coverage of such operations, it arranged for this one to be covered.[30] Presumably the government felt that media coverage would substantiate its claim that it was arresting drug traffickers who happened to be mostly Muslim, rather than repressing

---

[28]David B. Atwill, "Blinkered Visions: Islamic Identity, Hui Ethnicity, and the Panthay Rebellion in Southwest China, 1856–1873," *The Journal of Asian Studies*, Vol. 62, No. 4 (Nov., 2003), 1079–1108.

[29]David B. Atwill, "Ethno-religious Violence in China," in James K. Wellman, ed., *Belief and Bloodshed: Religion and Violence across Time and Tradition* (Lanham, Md.:Rowman and Littlefield, 2007), 123.

[30]*Ibid.*, 124.

Muslims as such. But one unfortunate effect of the media coverage was to leave the false impression among some Han Chinese that many Hui were drug smugglers.

The Uyghur Minority

There are many spellings of Uyghur in use in English. We are following the one used by the Uyghur American Association[31] and the World Uyghur Congress.[32] The government of China uses Uygur, and some others use Uighur or Uigur. The Uyghur Muslims are a Turkish minority whose homeland is in the Xinjiang region in the far northwest of China. The Uyghurs' habit of wearing turbans and their Turkish language and culture set them apart from the Hui, who tend to be much more loyal to Han China.[33] That is, the Uyghur are not so assimilated into the Han culture as the Hui. Based on his interviews, B. Kaltman reports that most Uyghur hardly know when the main Chinese holidays are, and do not even celebrate National Day, at least not those living outside the major Han cities such as Beijing.[34] They are a Turkic people who speak an old dialect of Turkish, but many now also speak Mandarin Chinese as well.

The Uyghur did not migrate from Turkey; rather, long ago some Turkic-speaking Uyghurs moved west from Xinjiang into Anatolia. When they later gained control, the region was named Turkey after them. The 1990 census reported 8.4 million Uyghurs in China.

During the Qing Dynasty the government military used Uyghurs because they were good at soldiering. Uyghur culture respected the profession, whereas the Han traditionally looked down soldiering as a profession. This Uyghur soldiering tradition adds to the worries of the current government.

Soon after 1949, China created five Autonomous Regions for its minorities, including Xinjiang as a **Uyghur Autonomous Region** and the **Tibetan Autonomous Region (TAR)** for the Tibetan minority. This policy sounded good in theory. The minorities could keep their language and culture, and they would be given preferential standing when government positions opened up in their region. All they had to do was not rock the socialist boat, so to speak. Yet in practice the minorities had very little autonomy. Their culture was undermined, or even trashed during the Cultural Revolution. Han officials were strictly in charge and often showed distain for local leaders and customs. After 1971, when the worst of the Cultural Revolution was over, China moved to a more multicultural policy and things improved for both the Uyghur and Tibetan regions. Yet both were still subject to ruthless repressions, however, at the slightest hint of objection to government policy.

---

[31]See www.uyghuramerican.org.

[32]See www.uyghurcongress.org.

[33]"The Hui: China's Most Loyal Muslims," originally published in the *Asian Wall Street Journal*, and now available online at CPAmedia, http://www.cpamedia.com/politics/hui_muslims_in_china/.

[34]Blaine Kaltman, *Under the Heel of the Dragon: Islam, Racism, Crime, and the Uyghur in China, Ohio RIS Global Series,* (Athens: Center for International Studies, 2007), 59.

One of the worst times for Uyghur relations with the central government occurred in 1989 in and around Urumqi in Xinjiang.

Uyghur Separatism and ETIM

There are active Uyghur movements advocating for either more autonomy within or separation from China. This worries the Chinese government. The most militant one has been the East Turkistan Islamic Movement, or **ETIM**. Its founder was killed by the Pakistan army in 2003, and Pakistan has cooperated with China in its efforts to suppress ETIM. China, the United States, the United Nations, and some other countries have put ETIM on their lists of terrorist groups. It wants independence for Xinjiang Province, which it calls East Turkistan, but it likely dreams of a larger Turkistan embracing much of the territory that used to be called Western Turkistan. This means that ETIM is feared by Tajikistan, Turkmenistan and other states carved out of the former Soviet Union. The government of China blames several terrorist attacks on ETIM.

Several of the United States detainees at Guantanamo were Uyghurs, and the main allegation against most of them seems to have been that they were associated with ETIM, which some associated with Al-Qaeda or the Taliban. When five Uyghur detainees were released, there was a problem about where to send them. The United States refused to take them in, and the fear was they would be tortured or killed if they were returned to China. Finally a home was found for them in Albania.

The execution of Uyghur activist Ismail Samed in 2007 for the crime of "trying to split the motherland" and alleged involvement with ETIM was highly criticized by the human rights group Amnesty International, which feared that a confession had been obtained by torture and that the trial was not a fair one.[35]

In 2004 a group of Uyghurs living outside China formed the East Turkistan Government in Exile. A Uyghur named Anwar Yusuf Turani (who lives in America) was elected the exile government's Prime Minister. Their goal is to reverse what they see as the occupation of East Turkistan by China.[36]

Chinese policy in Xinjiang has sometimes seemed ill-advised. For example, during Ramadan, teachers have sometimes been instructed to make sure Uyghur students ate their lunches. The official reason was that the students needed the nourishment, but it was a very thinly disguised attempt to keep young Uyghurs from observing the **Ramadan** fast. And the policy of encouraging Uyghurs to break the fast was also extended to adults working in government offices, which got international attention before the 2008 Olympics. Free lunches were offered, including a choice of Chinese or Uyghur food, to government employees in Xinjiang. The government's motive was not stated, but critics said the free lunches were meant to test if the workers were more loyal to the government or to their religious practice. This seems credible because some Uyghur government

---

[35]Jonathan Wells, "Execution of Chinese Muslim Condemned," *Guardian Unlimited* (February 9, 2007). See http://www.guardian.co.uk/china/story/0,,2009574,00.html.

[36]For their declaration, see http://www.eastturkistangovernmentinexile.us/about_us.html.

employees have been asked to sign pledges, called "letters of responsibility," affirming that they would not keep the Ramadan fast, say the daily prayers, or otherwise participate in religious activities.[37]

A new round of controversial restrictions on Uyghurs started in 2012, with government denunciation of men who wear overly long beards or women who cover their hair with veils. After a terrorist attack in the southern city of Kunming in the spring of 2014, the enforcement of the restrictions was stepped up by the introduction of cash rewards for citizens who came forth to report on restricted activities ranging from wearing long beards to plotting against the government.

Some alleged terrorists incidents in Xinjiang may not be that at all. For example, in April 2013 the Chinese press denounced East Turkestan terrorists after a confrontation between armed Uyghur civilians and the police lead to 21 deaths. But the World Uyghur Congress claimed that the confrontation was an angry reaction to a previous incident in which Chinese officials killed a young Uyghur man during an inspection raid.

The fact that Xinjiang province, home of the Uyghurs, also contains as much as one third of China's oil reserves means, in practical terms, that China would never give up control of the region without a fight. In the Uyghur case, as in the Tibetan one discussed next, the issue is the extent to which the Uyghurs will have enough real autonomy to follow their cultural and religious preferences. The choices range from separation from China to almost total assimilation into greater China. The government is encouraging Han Chinese to settle in traditional Uyghur areas, to tip the area toward a pro-China stance. This is similar to the "Hanification" of Tibet.

ISSUE 2. "HANIFICATION" OF TIBETAN CULTURE

Our train trip from Beijing to Lhasa takes 48 hours! It is a nice modern train, but our small compartment sleeps six and there is no door. It turns out to be a crowded but fascinating trip. As we enter the Tibetan high plateau someone yells "yak, yak, yak" and we all rush to the windows to see our first of many herds of yak. The elevation is quite high here, but fortunately this is a specially built train that has oxygen inside the cars, with oxygen masks available under the seat if needed. To stretch our legs, we step onto the platform at a station at very high altitude. We quickly get light-headed and welcome the return to the oxygenated air of the train. When we depart at the new Lhasa train station, we again feel light-headed. It will take a few days to adjust to the altitude. At first, some of us feel nauseous and get out of breath just from walking. It is worth it to see Lhasa, with its Muslim quarter, Buddhist pilgrimage circuit, ancient temples, the Potala Palace, and numerous monasteries. For many of us, the high points will be the many things of interest inside the Potala Palace

---

[37]"Ramadan Lunches for China's Muslims," *Radio Free Asia* (24 September 2008). www.rfa.org/english/news/uyghur/ramadan-09242008063029.html.

and the warm welcome and geniune spirituality of the Buddhist nuns during their morning chanting service. On our free time, we enjoy Tibetetan food and tea on the rooftop terrace of a restaurant overlooking the surrounding Himalaya mountains.

Tibetans are an ethnic group adapted physically and culturally to the high altitudes of their homeland, the Tibetan plateau of the Himalayan region. The Tibetan language is part of a language family that includes the Burmese, Khmer, and Mon language groups of Southeast Asia. A Buddhist monk named Padmasambhava, usually referred to by his title Guru Rinpoche ("Precious Teacher"), successfully introduced the Vajrayana (tantric) school of Buddhism to the region in the eighth century, and most Tibeans to this day are Vajrayana Buddhists. However, some follow an older religion of the region known as Bon, or a mixture of Bon and Buddhism. There are estimated to be around 5.5 million Tibetans living in China today, with about 45 percent of those living in the Tibetan Autonomous Region (TAR). Since 1959, many Tibetans have migrated to India or beyond India to avoid living under Chinese control.

Tibetan pilgrims walking the sacred Barkhor Kora, a pilgrimage circuit in Lhasa.
Photo: Roy Amore

The tension between the Tibetan Buddhist religion and Chinese politics is quite similar to the Uyghur case. When Mao took control of China in 1949 he made it a top priority to "reunite the Motherland." That policy included taking control of Tibet. Since the 1600s Tibet had been ruled by a series of monks with the title **Dalai Lama**, "Ocean of Wisdom." This system was started in the period of the Mongol Empire. The Mongols ruled China directly, but they ruled Tibet indirectly through a Dalai Lama. So, besides being the head of the Gelugpa Sect of Tibetan Buddhists, each Dalai Lama also ruled Tibet from the Potala Palace, the famous multi-storied complex of buildings built along one of the hills overlooking Lhasa. According to Tibetan Buddhist belief, each Dalai Lama is a reincarnation of the previous one and also an earthly incarnation of the Bodhisattva of

Compassion, Avalokiteshvara. A bodhisattva is a human who has made great progress on the path to nirvana but has postponed final nirvana to help others.

The Dalai Lama

The current, fourteenth Dalai Lama was chosen by a committee of senior monks after one of them had dreamed of an unusual house and temple. The dream led them to locate a two-year-old boy, the right age given the amount of time since the death of the previous Dalai Lama. That boy then passed tests involving identification of objects favored by the thirteenth Dalai Lama and was approved by a trance medium.[38]

Bilateral relations between India and China were quite tense in the early Maoist years. The period just before and after India's independence in 1947 coincided with the final years of China's civil war. India, like the Western countries, backed the Nationalists rather than the Communists who won in 1949. Also, during the British rule and after independence, Indian policy recognized Tibetan autonomy. China was especially angered when India invited both China and Tibet to a conference on Asia. These and other factors such

The Potala Palace in Lhasa. The red palace is the sacred area and the white palace was the residence of the Dali Llama and seat of the government.
Photo: M. Mortson

---

[38]For a short sketch of his life see "The Dalai Lama's Biography" at http://www.tibet.com/DL/biography.html.

as a China/India border dispute may have encouraged China to assert its control of Tibet as soon as possible.[39]

Although the fourteenth Dalai Lama was only 15 years old, the Tibetans performed a ceremony making him the Head of State in 1950. Mao had just taken control of most of China the year before. Having now finished consolidating control of all of China, Mao was turning his attention on Tibet. The Dalai Lama had talks with Mao in Beijing in 1954, but Mao insisted on taking over Tibet. The Dalai Lama then met with Prime Minister Nehru of India in 1956, and in 1959 Tibetans took to the streets of Lhasa to affirm their independence. Then this Tibetan National Uprising was crushed by the People's Liberation Army, China accomplished its goal of "reuniting Tibet to the Motherland" ten years after the founding of the communist government. It then set up the Tibetan Autonomous Region, which consists of four provinces but is not as large in total as the former Tibet.

The Dalai Lama and many Tibetans escaped, setting up a government-in-exile in Dharamsala, in the hills of northwest India near the border. It greatly angered China that India allowed this to happen.

Hanification

Soon after 1959 the **Hanification** of the TAR began. The term is used by outsiders to describe the process of making the population, government, educational system, buildings, and everything else in the TAR more Han and therefore less Tibetan. Han Chinese have been given tax and other incentives to settle in Tibet. This was not an easy sell by the government, however, because the Han tend to think it is very unhealthy to live on the Tibetan plateau.

Towns have been given new Chinese names. Signs must be in Chinese, but Tibetan shops and restaurants are allowed to add Tibetan in smaller letters. The situation is somewhat like that of Quebec, where signs may have English in addition to French, but the English must be smaller. Han teachers run the schools, government committees, police, courts, and other public institutions. Tibetans are more and more being reduced to the status of ethnics living in a foreign place. The opening of the new rail line from Beijing to Lhasa in 2007 brings more Han settlers and tourists than ever.

Most Tibetan monasteries were destroyed before or during the Cultural Revolution, and the monks and nuns were forced to return to lay life. Tibetans allege that the nuns were often raped by Han soldiers. Since Cultural Revolution ended in 1976, a few of the major monasteries have been partially rebuilt and the number of monks and nuns is increasing. But the government keeps a very tight control over the monasteries. For example, a government official oversees all policy matters as well as much of the day-to-day operations at important Buddhist temples such as Jokhang in Lhasa. Even the major monasteries in and near Lhasa have been subject to severe restrictions imposed by govern-

---

[39]Yun-yuan Yang, "Controversies over Tibet: China versus India, 1947–49," in *The China Quarterly*, No. 111 (Sept. 1987), 407–420.

ment officials. Some monasteries, which function as the training centers for young monks, have been closed for extended periods of time, and then reopened under strict conditions. The government still fears what it calls the Dalai Lama separatist faction, and it therefore sees the monasteries as a threat to its control of TAR. The government has put money into restoring some of the major tourist attractions such the Jokhang Temple and the Potala Palace, but as with the Grand Mosque in Xi'an, it profits from the admission fees.

The history of the Jokhang Temple exposes a stark contrast between the relation of religion and politics at the time of its construction and now. It was built 1300 years ago by the powerful king Gampo to house a Buddha image which his Nepali bride brought with her to the marriage. This explains why the temple, and many other old buildings in Lhasa, are in a Nepali style. Her Nepali Buddha image is on the main altar. Around the four sides of the temple are images of famous Tibetan teachers and small shrines to various Buddhas and Bodhisattvas. King Gampo also married a Han princess from a part of China that he had brought into his kingdom. He built another temple in the style of her region of China. By marrying a Nepali and a Chinese princess, and by building Nepali and Chinese style temples in the capital, King Gampo embraced religious diversity and used it to solidify his ethnically diverse Kingdom.

The forced closing of the large monasteries here during the Cultural Revolution and its aftermath is ironic, given the history of the great monastic universities. For these universities became world-class Buddhist training centers after the rise of Islamic control of northwest India brought persecution and the closure of monasteries there in the tenth century. Many of India's finest Buddhist professors fled to Lhasa to escape Muslim persecution. A millennium later, the monasteries here were closed, this time motivated not by a rival religion but by Marxist and revolutionary fervor.

An interesting silver lining for Tibetan Buddhism in this otherwise dark cloud is that the Dalai Lama has become a well-known figure and the most important Buddhist leader in the world. He received the Nobel Peace Prize in 1989 based upon his tireless efforts to find a solution to the suffering of his people in a non-violent way. When asked how he feels about the rape and torture of Tibetans by the Chinese army, he has surprised many audiences by saying that he feels sorry for the Chinese! After all, he explains, it is very painful to a person to be asked to carry out torture on innocent persons.

As a highly visible symbol of the new, secular regime in Lhasa, the government has built a very modern monument in a park opposite the Potala Palace. The modernistic government structure makes a statement over against the seat of traditional Tibetan autonomy. The 2000 government census reported that 92.7 percent of the population of the TAR were Tibetans, but the figures for areas that used to be in Tibet but lie outside the TAR show that the Han now outnumber Tibetans in some of those areas. In the future, if China becomes more democratic, the Tibetans will likely find themselves a political minority within many parts of their former territory. The only good news for Tibetans is that the Hanification of Tibet is now complete enough that the government has been able to relax some of its restrictions.

We might say that the Han have done to the Tibetans what Europeans did to the native people of North America. Encroach on their territory, assimilate them, destroy their culture, and reduce them to small areas (reservations) of population.

The Fiction and the Protests

Within China, the government has been remarkably successful in maintaining the fiction that the Tibetans are happy under Chinese rule. Unless they travel abroad for study of their own political history, few Han Chinese ever become aware of the suffering of the Tibetans and their culture. Given the government blockage of Internet access to websites critical of the government, Chinese cannot access pro-Tibet sites such as freetibet.org or even articles in online encyclopaedias.

From time to time, Western tourists or performers make some act of protest, but these attempts do not get coverage in China's tightly controlled media. For example in 2008 the singer Bjork, while ending her Shanghai concert with the song "Declare Independence," inserted the words "Tibet, Tibet." This got international coverage and the video clip was posted on freetibet.org, but most Chinese never learned of the protest.

As had been done in past years, demonstrations were staged in the spring of 2008 to mark the anniversary of the 1959 uprising against the Chinese takeover of Tibet. Monks in the three main monasteries of Lhasa staged demonstrations that were surprisingly strong, given the massive presence of military police on duty around the monasteries and in the old, downtown area of Lhasa. Some shops were burned, some monks staged hunger protests, and others did their best to mount public demonstrations. Monks were arrested for demonstrating, which led to larger demonstrations of monks calling for the release of the arrested monks.

Being especially sensitive to such protests during a period when international attention was focused on China as host of the 2008 Olympics, the government reacted decisively. It banned foreign press from TAR, and the domestic press blamed the trouble on what it labeled the "Dalai Lama clique." Given the insistence on non-violence in Buddhism and the Dalai Lama's special stress on that ethic, most Tibetans were inclined toward non-harmful forms of protest, but a few turned their frustration upon themselves. Two monks tried, unsuccessfully, to commit suicide by slashing their wrists. When the police brutally suppressed those demonstrations, lay Tibetans got involved. They acted on their pent up frustration at the Hanification of their cities and culture by burning Han-owned shops. They looted the goods and burned them in bonfires in the street. They stoned police cars and in some cases threw stones at Han Chinese. Such acts of violence are quite against the teachings of the Dalai Lama, and he threatened to resign if violence did not cease. It did, and the demonstrations ended well before the Olympics began. Later, the government courts imposed harsh sentences on the protesters, giving the leaders sentences of life in prison.

The Tibetan Buddhists living in exile in northern India also staged a protest, and the demonstrations spread to other towns in the TAR and to other places in the world with sizable Tibetan communities, such as Nepal. But most Han Chinese inside China were unaware of the underlying causes of the protest. The government again reported that the problem was caused by outside agitators who were a part of the "Dalai Lama clique," and most Han had little grounds for questioning this. Whereas international sources were reporting over eighty fatalities, the Chinese media reported that "at least" ten persons were killed, and focused on the violence of the Tibetans rather than the underlying causes of the anger.[40]

The Dalai Lama, from his headquarters in India, called for an investigation of the events by some respected international organization, but the government of China refused to consider having any outside agency investigate its internal affairs. The government of China continues to threaten trade reprisals against any foreign officials who meet with the Dalai Lama. In the context of the 2008 protests, one government official stated that the Dalai Lama is a "political refugee engaged in activities of splitting China under the camouflage of religion."[41]

Besides functioning as spiritual leader of the Gelugpa Sect of Buddhism, the Dalai Lama continued, with the help of another monk who functioned as Prime Minister, as the head of the Tibetan government in exile until March 2011. At that time the Dalai Lama shocked his followers and others by resigning as secular head of the government in exile. There should be, he stated, an election in which Tibetans everywhere would vote for a secular leader of the government. So, with Tibetans from over 30 nations, except China, voting in April 2011, a young Harvard Law graduate named Lobsang Sangay was elected as Tibetan Prime Minister.

The Chinese attempt to control Tibetan Buddhism will most likely lead to a major confrontation when it is time to select a new Dalai Lama after the passing of the current one. A spokesperson for the Chinese government has already made it clear that the tradition of the Tibetan people choosing the successor must be maintained. On the surface this may seem to be a strange position for the government to take, but the real meaning is likely to be that China wants to have the selection process carried out within China, where it can oversee the selection and make sure that the advisors to the young boy selected are loyal to China. There will likely be one Dalai Lama selected within China, under government control, and another selected by the Tibetans in exile, under the control of the leading monks at their headquarters in Dharamsala, India. There is precedence for this. There is another very high ranking monk who holds the title Panchen Lama and whose role is to help select and then teach doctrine to a new Dalai Lama. When the previous Panchen Lama died in 1989, there were two selection processes: one led by the Dalai Lama and the other led by Tibetans in China under government supervision. The one recognized by China was then relocated to Beijing where he could be kept under close control. The fate of the other one is not known.

---

[40]For quotations on the contrasting view of Tibetans and the Chinese government, see *BBC News* for May 21, 2008. http://news.bbc.co.uk/2/hi/asia-pacific/7410745.stm.

[41]From an *AP News* report. See apnews.excite.com/article/20080320/D8VH52280.html

ISSUE 3. ROMAN CATHOLICISM AND EVANGELICAL PROTESTANTISM AS UNDERGROUND CHURCHES

Although **Roman Catholic** and **Protestant** Christians each enjoy the status of being one of China's five officially recognized religions, they both face problems. To better understand these problems, we should review the history of Christianity in China.

Nestorian Christians, followers of the Assyrian Church of the East, followed the Silk Road to old Xi'an, starting from the seventh century. Their community lasted for centuries, but has long since died out.

The first wave of Roman Catholic missions was led by Italian Franciscans, who came to Beijing just before 1300 and had some success during the next century. The Jesuits came next, in the 1600s, led by Matteo Ricci. As a strategy they decided to focus on the Mandarin class, believing that if the elite were converted, the masses might follow. They had some success, and the Qing government drew upon their Western knowledge. There were periods of persecution against Christian missionaries, but lasting conversions as well, and a minority of Han Catholics today are descendants of these early Roman Catholics.

Protestant missionaries did not arrive until the early 1800s, but have made up for lost time, spreading from the trading port cities inland. Protestants started clinics and schools open to both boys and girls of all social classes. They introduced Western concepts during a time when the Qing leaders were resisting modernization. Protestant missionaries and their converts came under suspicion or persecution because they were working in an era when the Chinese greatly resented Western interference. Western ships were causing trouble by bringing opium to China. China resisted, setting off the "Opium Wars" starting in 1839. When China tried to close their ports to Western trade, the Western powers forced treaties to open the ports. The West practiced its Gunboat Diplomacy, arriving with their superior ships and forcing Chinese concessions and reparations. In this mid-nineteenth century period, Christians in China were blamed for the expansionist and bullying tactics of the European sea-trading nations.[42]

Taiping Rebellion

Protestant Christianity took on a political form in southern China in the 1850s. Hong Xiuguan, a man who had tried and failed the civil service exam three times, began to have mystical experiences, in part under the influence of Protestant mission teachings. He announced that he was called to lead the Chinese by the same god as in Christianity, but he used an old Chinese name for this god, and called his movement *Taiping Kingdom*, meaning Heavenly Peace or Great Peace. The **Taiping Rebellion** against the Imperial authority and army quickly gained a large number of followers in southern China and undertook to remake society along lines thought to have been revealed to Hong. He con-

---

[42]Aikman, David. *Jesus in Beijing: How Christianity is Transforming China and Changing the Global Balance of Power* (Washington D.C.: Regnery Press, 2006). 36.

fiscated large land holdings and put his followers to working them, but under oppressive conditions.

His followers formed armies. One army under the command of a brilliant general with the title Loyal Prince succeeded in capturing many cities. At first Hong had the support and encouragement of Protestant missionaries. He thought the West, being Christian, would recognize and assist his new government as the Taiping Rebellion fought bloody battles against the Qing Imperial forces. Yet his claim to be the Younger Brother of Jesus and some other extreme acts convinced the West to side with the Qing, who then suppressed the rebellion. It was at the time the world's most costly war in terms of lives lost on both sides.

Two Forms of Roman Catholicism

When the revival of Roman Catholicism was well underway in the mid-1950s, some Roman Catholic leaders looked for ways to meet the demands of the new Communist government while remaining faithful Catholics. This led to the formation of the Chinese Catholic Patriotic Association (CCPA) in 1957, which was then recognized by the government as the registered Catholic organization. There are estimated to be 5 million Catholics affiliated with the CCPA. As with other recognized religious organizations, the government has the final say in the appointment of the association's leaders. Its leaders were made to officially renounce the authority of the pope and any pronouncements issued from the Vatican subsequent to the forming of modern China in 1949. All Chinese are supposed to be loyal above all to the state, which is referred to as "the people," and not to a foreign entity such as the papacy. Sociologist and China expert Richard Madsen points out, that because the Catholic Church is an authoritarian, hierarchical organization like the Chinese Communist Party, the party is suspicious of Catholics.[43]

Many Catholics wished to remain obedient to the Vatican, and therefore refused to associate with the CCPA leadership. Since 1957 the number of these unregistered Catholics has grown, and their numbers are now estimated at 8 million.

The underground Catholic Church in China has its own bishops, who remain in contact with the papacy through clandestine means. Its members are referred to as "unregistered" or "illegal" by the government, but may better be referred to as "underground" Catholics. Having an underground Catholic organization with secret contact with the Vatican and the support of Catholics worldwide is not a good arrangement for either the Vatican or the government. Beginning in 2004 there has been an increasing spirit of cooperation between the two. An effort is being made to appoint new bishops jointly, and to bring some of the underground bishops into the recognized CCPA association. By 2008 there were signs that the government was ready to move toward a rapprochement with the Vatican. During that year, the Vatican sent a delegation to Beijing for secret talks

---

[43]Richard Madsen, *China's Catholics: Tragedy and Hope in an Emerging Civil Society.* Berkeley and Los Angeles: University of California Press, 1998.

about improved relations, and another round of talks was held in 2009. But nothing substantial emerged from these promising meetings, and a setback occurred in late 2010 on the occasion of the convening of the congress of China's officially recognized Catholic leaders. It convenes every five years to review its constitutions, elect new leaders and set its mission strategy. A Vatican communication dated December 17, 2010, a few days after the congress met, criticized the government of China for violating religious freedom by intervening in religious affairs. An official speaking on behalf of China's State Administration for Religious Affairs (SARA) in turn criticized the Vatican for interfering in Chinese affairs and for making imprudent comments. The official argued that the congress does not deal with doctrine, with the implication that its undertakings should not be a matter of concern to the Vatican. The spokesperson reiterated the longstanding Chinese policy that all religious organizations in China must be self-governing. The implication was that the congress has the right to elect its leaders without the approval of the Vatican. Note that in this instance the Government of China was arguing in favor of free elections, in contrast to the Vatican's insistence on its right to appoint Catholic leaders.[44]

Two Forms of Protestants

The Three-Self Church
The main issue for Protestants is that the government no longer allows foreign missionaries or funding. The government-recognized umbrella organization for Protestants is the Three-Self Church, or Three-Self Patriotic Movement (TSPM). The meaning behind this name is that its members are required to follow three principles affirming their independence from foreign influence. The TSPM is to be self-governing (no control from foreign mission offices), self-supporting (no foreign money) and self-propagating (no foreign missionaries). Whether despite these restrictions or because of them, the movement continues to grow rapidly. In 1980 the China Christian Council was formed as the umbrella Protestant group reporting to the government. It works with the Three-Self Church in China and is a member of the World Christian Council internationally.

As with the other registered religions, the state attempts to control the ideological bent of the religious leaders through "patriotic education," by requiring that training in government policies be a part of the seminary curriculum. The government may also refuse admission to seminary applicants who might hold views contrary to those of the government. This attempt to control the political ideology of Protestant pastors comes at a price. It means that potential seminarians who reject a "patriotic education" tend to avoid the registered seminaries and instead train to be leaders in the unregistered, house churches. Another restriction is that the government forbids baptizing persons under 18 years of age. Besides the obvious interference with a constitutionally protected religion's

---

[44]"China rejects Vatican's criticism as very imprudent," China Daily. 22 Dec. 2010.
www.chinadial.com/cn/china/2010-12/11/_content_11741 752.htm .

right to set its own rules on its initiation ritual, this has the practical effect of reducing the official number of Three-Self members because the youth are not counted.

House Churches

> Fortunately we have been invited to attend a House Church service. Although the service is in Chinese, it is easy for anyone familiar with a Christian worship service to recognize the prayer of invocation, the Old and New Testament readings, the hymns with familiar tunes, the fervent, evangelical sermon and the deeply emotional experience of the congregation. The service is in the main room of a family home, but its existence doesn't seem to be very secretive. But someone tells us that in the past that was not the case. And the participants fear there may again be a crackdown on their meetings, as there has been in other provinces.

Similar to the split between registered and unregistered Catholics, Chinese Protestants are divided between those affiliated with the TSPM and the many other Protestant groups known collectively as "House Christians." But unlike the two forms of Catholicism, the Protestant division has pre-1949 roots. The divide between liberal and evangelical Protestants in the United States was spread to China by missionaries as early as the 1920s. The evangelical style of Christianity stressed the need for a profound sense of renewal or rebirth and the need to adhere strictly to Biblical teachings. The liberal style was not so insistent on a profound personal conversion experience, and thought that Christ called Christians to help shape their social world as well as their personal lives. The majority of the house church Protestants in China, estimated to number as many as 140 million in 2014, are affiliated with one or more of the house church networks.[45] Their churches are unregistered and therefore considered illegal by the government. They meet in homes or compound courtyards to "read bible," pray, and sing hymns. They are proud that their house churches resemble the earliest forms of Christianity as depicted in the Acts of the Apostles of the New Testament. Not only do they gather in smalls groups in private homes, but some stress sharing and simple living, as did the early Christians. Yalin Xin notes that they do not put as much stress on the difference between clergy and laity as do most modern churches.

With an estimated 20 million followers in 2005 and a pattern of rapid growth, the Word of Life (WOL) movement is the largest of the House Church networks.[46] It was founded in Henan Province in the 1970s by Peter Xu. The WOL is evangelical and stresses the need for repentance and a profound experience of being reborn in Christ. Its mem-

---

[45]The estimate of 140 million comes from www.billionbibles.org It starts with the estimated number of Three-Self Protestants and guesses there are four times as many house church members. For an older and more modest estimate, see Xin, Yalin. 2009. *Inside China's House Church Network: The Word of Life Movement and Its Renewing Dynamic.* Lexington: Emeth Press, 21.

[46]*Ibid.*, 20.

bers literally meet in private houses or apartments. It is missionary and has expanded its following beyond Henan and is now active in most provinces.

During the Cultural Revolution and even during the following decade, several individuals active in the house church movement were harassed, fined, or "re-educated" by local officials, but more recently government officials have mostly turned a blind eye to the movement. Maybe this is because it is so diverse and therefore is not seen as a threat to start any mass rebellion against the government or the party. Yalin Xin, a participant-observer of the house church movement, reports that in recent years the meetings of the house churches do not have to be in secret. Everyone living in the apartment building or on the block knows when and where the Christians meet. As long as the number of worshippers does not get too large or the meetings draw too much publicity, the local police ignore them. The police do sometimes intervene in meetings where leaders are being trained or especially if a foreign missionary is in attendance.[47]

Beginning in 2012 there have been periodic government crackdowns on churches in some provinces. For example, in February 2014 a party official in Zhejiang Province complained that too many prominent crosses were visible on churches near main highways. This led to police raids in which crosses were torn down from churches. The members of one congregation staged a prayer sit-in in an effort to protect their church's cross and their right to exist. Some of these are large, very visible churches that are registered with the government, but are not part of the Three-Self Patriotic Movement. The government's demand is that the large, prominent crosses on the church exterior be replaced with a smaller cross inside the building. The congregations are trying to resist this demand.[48]

Estimates of the total number of Christians in China vary greatly. On the low end, the Chinese government, basing its numbers only on Catholics and Protestants in registered organizations, reports 20 million Christians. High end estimates range as much as 200 million. The Pew forum gave a moderate estimate of 67 million in 2011. Estimates based on surveys of Chinese who admit to being Christian put the number in the 35 to 45 million range, but this approach may not be counting those who do not want to risk identifying publicly as Christians. Writing for the Christian Century periodical, Philip Jenkins, after considering these various estimates, settles on a mid-range estimate of 65 to 75 million Christians. As he points out, this amounts to almost 5 percent of the total population, about the same percentage as the Muslim population in many Western countries.[49]

It also should be noted that many Han Chinese outside mainland China have converted to Christianity, and therefore many mainland families have Christian relatives abroad.

---

[47]*Ibid.,* 33.

[48]"Why Chinese Christians are camping out to save their church and cross from demolition." *The Washington Post* (April 4, 2014). http://www.washingtonpost.com/blogs/worldviews/wp/2014/04/04/why-chinese-christians-are-camping-out-to-save-their-church-and-cross-from-demolition/.

[49]Jenkins, Philip. 8/10/2010. "Who's counting China?" in *Christian Century.* Vol. 127, Issue 16, 45–46.

ISSUE 4. FALUN DAFA AS A BANNED ORGANIZATION

So far we have considered the tensions between the government and four of the officially recognized religions of China: Islam, Buddhism, Catholicism and Protestantism. Now we turn to an unrecognised movement that has gone from being ignored to being banned and severely persecuted.

Falun Dafa, "Great Law of the Wheel of Law," is also known as Falun Gong, "Practice of the Wheel of Law." It arose out of the Qigong tradition. The term *qi*, or *chi* in the older transliteration system, refers to unseen energies flowing through the body. *Qigong* refers to various techniques of breathing and bodily movements designed to free the body so that the energies may flow properly, thus promoting healing, health and long life. Utiraruto Otehode's history of *qigong* in modern China reveals the way that the understanding of *qigong* has shifted in modern China. To make it more acceptable to the modern state, *qigong* practitioners have minimized its connections to Daoism or Buddhism and instead emphasised its role as a means toward health. Furthermore, by claiming that it has roots in peasant culture, it was made more acceptable to the communist state. By this means *qigong* was institutionalized in the 1950s as a national medical heritage, as a component of the state's national medical system. But from the mid-1990s, the understanding has broadened and *qigong* is now accepted as a sport as well. Although official categorizations of qigong have shifted, two things have not— the state continues to control *qigong* and the people continue to practice it because they think it produces results.[50]

Although Western science has never accepted that such energies are real, Chinese and other East Asian cultures have evolved techniques and eating patterns based upon these ideas. And even sceptics have trouble explaining why acupuncturists are able to anesthetise persons by putting pins in various parts (energy points) of the patient's body.

Logo of Falun Dafa, from its website, en.www.falundafa.org/introduction.html.

---

[50]Otehode, Utiraruto. "The Creation and Reemergence of Qigong in China," in Yoshiko Ashiwa and David L. Wank, eds. *Making Religion: Making the State.* (Stanford: Stanford University Press, 2009). 241–265.

A man named **Li Hongzhi** introduced a form of *qigong* in 1992 called Falun Dafa. The term Falun, *Wheel of Law*, comes from Buddhism, and Li incorporated several other Buddhist elements into his teachings, including the swastika, one of the auspicious symbols in Buddhism. Although his teachings of compassion and self-development are based on Buddhist principles and he uses Buddhist symbols and terms, Falun Dafa is not recognized by Buddhists as part of their tradition. More importantly, the government of China does not see it as a form of Buddhism.

Beijing Demonstration and Banning

From 1992 until 1999 Falun Dafa grew rapidly. For most Chinese it was just a new variation on an old system of healing practices. Only 2 to 3 percent of Chinese are members of the Communist Party, and the total party membership in 1999 was just over 63 million. It is estimated that there were 50 to 70 million Falun Dafa members by 1999, which means that Falun Dafa practitioners may have outnumbered the Communist Party in 1999. And to make matters more frightening for the party, Falun Dafa was very popular among a lot of younger party members and their children. When some senior party officials expressed alarm over Falun Dafa in 1998 and early 1999, the leaders of Falun Dafa made a fateful decision. They organized a silent demonstration which brought ten thousand or more members to Beijing to assemble in the area where top government officials live and work. The intent was to show that Falun Dafa was just a spiritual exercise group and not any political threat to the government or the social order. It had the opposite effect. The government was alarmed by the presence of so large a protest gathering in the heart of Beijing's center of government, not far from Tiananmen Square, the seat of many historic events, including Mao's founding of the new State in 1949 and the massacre of protesting students in 1989.

The government talked the Falun Dafa leaders into sending the demonstrators back home. Then three months later the government banned the organization, on the grounds that Falun Dafa was bad for the people. The government alleged that Falun Dafa discouraged followers from going to regular doctors, that its practice led to insanity and depression, that it was really an unregistered religion, and that it was intent upon overthrowing the Communist Party. Falun Dafa members all over China were arrested, fired, imprisoned, sent to prison camps or killed. The denunciation was followed by repeated media coverage of former Falun Dafa practitioners denouncing the organization and making statements corroborating the government's accusations. As a result of the media coverage, most mainland Chinese believe the government's claim that Falun Dafa is poison. When a Falun Dafa practitioner tried to commit suicide along with her daughter at Tiananmen Square in 2001, pictures of her badly burned daughter reinforced the government's image of the movement as an evil cult.[51] Falun Dafa teachings prohibit suicide, so there is some question about the incident.

---

[51] To read the report of the incident in *The China Daily* (the government's English language newspaper), see http://www.facts.org.cn/Feature/tsi/3/200708/t60809.htm.

Li Hongzhi had escaped China before the crackdown and now lives in New York City. The movement has spread worldwide. From that base it has mounted a campaign of severe criticism of the Chinese government. The movement has published brief points critical of the CCP called "Nine Commentaries on the Communist Party" and claims that over 90 million Chinese have signed a pledge denouncing the CCP.[52] Besides its general criticism of communist rule, according to Falun Dafa the government holds many members in long-term work prisons that amount to slave labor camps. Falun Dafa further claims that some of the goods sold in the West are manufactured in these prison camps. The Falun Dafa Information Center group claims that organs are involuntarily removed from Falun Dafa prisoners to be used as transplant organs.[53] The Falun Dafa news outlet *Epoch Times* reports that a new case of a practitioner dying in custody in China is reported every three days on average. Outside organizations such as Amnesty International have lent some credence to these accusations. In 2006 The Coalition to Investigate the Persecution of the Falun Gong in China (CIPFG) requested David Matas, an international human rights lawyer in the United States, and David Kilgour, a former Member of Parliament in Canada, to investigate the allegations of human organ harvesting from Falun Dafa practitioners in China. Their report concluded that that the allegations are true. "We believe that there has been and continues today to be large scale organ seizures from unwilling Falun Gong practitioners. We have concluded that the government of China and its agencies in numerous parts of the country, in particular hospitals but also detention centers and "people's courts," since 1999 have put to death a large but unknown number of Falun Gong prisoners of conscience. Their vital organs, including kidneys, livers, corneas and hearts, were seized involuntarily for sale at high prices, sometimes to foreigners...."[54]

Control of the Media

One of the reasons China blocks so many Internet sites is that the government fears the spread of the criticisms made by Falun Dafa. Through websites and its e-news outlet, *Epoch Times*, Falun Dafa has been effective at getting its message spread worldwide. If these criticisms concerning alleged organ harvesting, slave labor, torture, and killing were to become widely known among the Chinese, the government might be put on the defensive. China blocks the Internet by holding the service providers responsible for policing the use of its connections. One cannot access links dealing with Tibetan, Uyghur, Falun Dafa or other such groups critical of the government. China also keeps tight control over TV, radio, and print media. Blog sites have been harder to control, but a series of arrests and convictions have slowed down the activity of dissidents.

---

[52]http://ninecommentaries.com.

[53]See faluninfo.net.

[54]http://organharvestinvestigation.net/report0701/report200070131.htm#_Toc160145104. Also see David Matas and David Kilgour, *Bloody Harvest: Organ Harvesting of Falun Gong Practitioners in China* (Woodstock, Ontario: Seraphim Books, 2009).

Ironically, Falun Dafa is not banned in Hong Kong, even though China administers it as a "Special Administrative Region." Despite China's more tolerant approach to Falun Dafa in Hong Kong, when Falun Dafa wanted to hold demonstrations there on the occasion of the tenth anniversary of China's takeover, Beijing successfully blocked the worldwide gathering by refusing to grant visas to foreign Falun Dafa members. Falun Dafa has regularly staffed protest booths near the mainland's Liaison Office. The booths feature pictures alleged to be of torture and involuntary organ donors in China. A Hong Kong court ruled in 2004 that this ongoing protest was legal. Starting in 2013, a group called the Hong Kong Youth Care Association (HKYCA) has employed tactics to counter the protest booths. The mainland government maintains an organization known as the 610 Office dedicated to suppressing Falun Dafa, and it is alleged to be funding the HKYCA.[55] All of this has brought media attention to Falun Dafa in Hong Kong, making Falun Dafa something of a poster child for mainland interference in Hong Kong. July 1 each year marks the anniversary of the 1989 British "handover" of Hong Kong to China, and this date has become an occasion for pro-democracy gatherings and marches in Hong Kong. When an unusually large number of Hong Kong citizens participated in a pro-democracy 2014 march, the marching music was provided by Falun Dafa members.[56]

Is Falun Dafa a religion or not? Its leaders insist that it is not. This makes sense in that they dare not call it a religion without further jeopardizing their underground practitioners in China. Whether or not we classify it as a religion or just a quasi-religious spiritual practice, it is embroiled in one of the worst relations with politics to be found anywhere today.

OVERVIEW AND THEORETICAL DISCUSSION

Our first two issues considered the way the government of China has dealt with its Muslim and Tibetan Buddhist minorities. Although the Hui Muslims have been fairly well integrated into the larger Han society, the Uyghur Muslims and the Tibetan Buddhists have quite a strained relationship with the Han-dominated government. After the Communist takeover of China, the government asserted its authority over all the minority peoples, setting up special administrative units called "Autonomous Regions" for the Tibetans and the Uyghurs. However, there was very little local autonomy for either group. Han Chinese officials maintained strict control over all matters of concern to the government. Religious institutions not adhering to government control were closed or curtailed. Religious leaders were arrested or forced to resume lay life. Government policy has been to encourage

---

[55]"Hong Kong Protest Overwhelms Communist Party Group Sent to Silence Falun Gong." August 23, 2013. http://fofg.org/2013/08/hong-kong-protest-overwhelms-communist-party-group-sent-to-silence-falun-gong/.

[56]"Hong Kong Democracy Protest: Thousands March Through City." July 1, 2014, in *Wall Street Journal*. http://online.wsj.com/articles/hong-kong-democracy-rally-city-prepares-for-record-march-1404192707?mod=World_newsreel_3.

Han Chinese to move to the autonomous regions, and now the Tibetans are becoming an underclass in the Tibetan Autonomous Region.

The situation with China's Christian minority is not so grave, but there are concerns. Many Protestants have gotten around the restrictions placed on them by meeting in private homes. The House Church movement has been quite significant, and now that the number of Chinese involved has grown substantially, the government is looking for ways to gain more control over unregistered churches.

The CCP's religious restrictions on its membership are also softening. The Global Security Organization claims that in some regions of China as many as 25 percent of CCP members practice some religion, with Buddhism and folk religion being reported as the most common ones practiced.[57]

Marxist Theory vs. Human Spirituality in China

The interface of religion and politics in China has been a strained one since the beginning of the People's Republic in 1949. Mao's mother was a devout Buddhist and he once told his staff "because my mother believed in Buddha, so did I."[58] But by the time he was a teenager, Mao turned away from his Buddhist roots, believing all forms of religion to be useless superstition. Later, he embraced an international communist movement with roots in a Marxism that saw religion as an outmoded system used by the capitalist class to keep the workers content with their miserable lot. Although practicing a religion was discouraged and doing so would harm one's chances of success, religion was not brutally suppressed in the early Maoist era. Mao felt that "it was the peasants who made the idols, and when the time comes they will cast the idols aside with their own hands; there is no need for anyone else to do it for them prematurely."[59] The Cultural Revolution of the late 1960s, however, was a nightmare for all religions in China, and was especially brutal on two of the minority religions considered in this chapter, Islam and Tibetan Buddhism.

Despite the Marxist denunciation of religion and Mao's plan to just let religions die a natural death as outmoded superstitions, we have seen that religious practice is making a dramatic resurgence in China. The reasons for this may vary by social group. For minorities such as the Uyghurs and Tibetans, religious identity is part of their ethnic identity, in contrast to the dominant Han culture. The more a minority feels threatened, the more likely many of its members are to assert their religion, language, and culture. There is, therefore, a political dimension to their religious practice. But there is no threat to the culture or identity of the Han majority, so why are they returning to Buddhism or converting to Christianity? The answer may be that despite Mao's expectations, spirituality is so deeply rooted in human nature and practice that it has not died a natural death even

---

[57]http://www.globalsecurity.org/military/world/china/ccp.htm.

[58]Jung Chang and Jon Halliday, *Mao: The Unknown Story* (New York: Alfred A. Knopf, 2005), 5.

[59]Cited from DuBois, Thomas David, "Religion and the Chinese state: Three crises and a solution," *Australian Journal of International Affairs*, Vol. 64, Issue 3 (June 2010).

among a Chinese population that has been educated in a non-religious curriculum and lived its whole life under a regime that considers religion outmoded and useless. Now that something approaching religious freedom has become government policy, China is beginning to conform to a more typically religious profile—some people are very religious, some are very secular, and many are somewhere in between.

The Resurgence of Religion in China and the Pendulum Theory
Sociologist of Religion Will Herberg's pendulum theory of religion—that on a time scale of decades, religious zeal in a particular culture swings back and forth from the secular to the strongly religious like a slowly moving pendulum—seems to fit in the case of China. For decades the pendulum had been swinging toward the secular side. Organized religions had already been rather weak before 1949, and since the Maoist Revolution all Chinese have been educated into an official atheism that denigrates religion. The Chinese were aware that the most desirable employment positions and members in the CCP were not open to those who were openly religious. The period of the Cultural Revolution beginning in the mid-1960s, with its wholesale destruction of religious property and harassment of leaders, marked the extreme movement of the pendulum to the left, the secular side. Since the mid-1970s the pendulum is swinging back to the religion side, and with increasing momentum. Religious institutions and open religious identity are making a comeback in China. Buddhist, Muslim, and Christian practitioners are on the increase. The majority of Christians are part of the underground House Church movement, but Buddhists and Muslims are able to be more open with their religious practice. China may now have more Buddhists and more Daoists than any nation in the world, and the numbers of its Christian and Muslim populations also place China high in the world rankings.

Religious Impact on International Relations

We have seen that after the death of Mao in 1976 and the demise of the Cultural Revolution, the government has removed some of its restrictions on religion. Besides any internal reasons there may be for this change, there are motivations arising from China's goals in international relations. After China adopted a broader statement on the rights of officially sanctioned groups, including religious groups, in 2005, the United States government removed China from its list of human rights offenders.

One major driver of China's foreign policy is the need to secure the natural resources to fuel China's growing economy. To supply its rapidly growing domestic market as well as continue to grow its export market, Chinese industry needs to import huge amounts of oil and mineral resources. China was a net exporter of crude oil through early 1990s. But the quickly rising domestic demand for fuel, plastics, and other petroleum usages combined with the rapid increase of goods manufactured with petroleum has turned China into a net importer of crude oil. By 1990 China accounted for almost one third of the world's increasing petroleum demands, and by 2009 China had passed Japan to become the second greatest oil importer, behind only the United States. And then China passed the United States as the world's largest net importer of petroleum and other liquid fuels in March 2014.[60] China also imports increasingly large amounts of liquefied natural gas, which may be shipped from afar, as well as natural gas, which it has to import by pipeline from nearby regions such as Southeast and Central Asia, as well as from Russia. China traditionally relied heavily on coal for heat and to produce electricity, but China's serious air pollution problems in its bigger cities has forced it to adopt an ambitious plan to build 150 nuclear power plants over the next two decades. This plan will help control air quality, but it makes China dependent upon international sources for uranium as well as for other natural resources. To sustain its growing manufacturing and consumer economies, China now uses 20 percent or more of almost every industrial hydrocarbon or mineral resource.

Asia and Africa

Chinese foreign policy places great importance on good relations with the oil-producing countries, many of which have an Islamic population. It is therefore important for China to be seen as friendly toward Islam in general and the Muslims of China in particular. For example, in 2010 the China Guangdong Nuclear Power Group signed a long-term contract for the supply of uranium by Kazatomprom, the uranium producer owned by Kazakhstan. China also entered into agreements with Bangladesh, another predominantly Muslim state, for cooperation and import to China of natural resources including oil, gas, minerals, and agricultural products.

China's drive to secure future resources has brought it into competition with India, the regional power to its southwest. China seems to be winning. In a major setback for India's pride and India-China bilateral relations, China outmaneuvered India to win a contract for extensive gas imports from Myanmar. Construction on the new Myanmar-China Gas Pipeline will involve China laying over 900 kilometres of pipeline inside Myanmar without cost to Myanmar, which will then receive royalties on the sale of its gas.

Africa has been one of the key zones of interest for China. Ruchita Beri notes that China has strengthened its political, military, and economic interest in several African states to combat influence from international actors, especially the United States, to out-compete regional competitors such as India and Taiwan, and especially to secure a future supply of natural resources.[61] In 2003 China cancelled debts to African countries worth US$ 1.27 billion. By doing so, China hoped to open up reliable new supplies of natural resources. During his 2014 visit to four African nations, Chinese Premier Li Keqiang signed over 50 new investment and trade agreements. At that time, it was estimated that Chinese direct investment in Africa was over $25 billion and growing rapidly, and that 85% of African exports to China were raw materials.[62]

---

[60]As reported by the U.S. Energy Information System. http://www.eia.gov/todayinenergy/detail.cfm?9d=15531.

[61]Ruchita Beri, "China's Rising Profile in Africa," in *China Report* (vol. 43, no. 3, July–Sept. 2007). 297–308.

[61]http://www.ingoldwetrust.ch/china-its-tentacles-reaching-all-over-the-globe.

China has economic motivations to be on perceived as friendly toward Islam, but the rich resources of Xinjiang Province means that China cannot tolerate a strong separatist movement among Xinjiang's Muslims. Taking advantage of the world-wide concern with Islamic terrorism, China has been able to crack down on Uyghur movements advocating either separatism or more autonomy.

We have seen that one reason for the strained bilateral relationship between China and India is that India not only harbored the Dalai Lama's government in exile, but that India has continued to support the Dalai Lama and has repeatedly allowed him to leave India to speak around the world. China's continuing policy of suppressing the Tibetan culture remains a concern for India. With a new airport, rail line, and station, Han migration and tourism into TAR has increased. Given its large Muslim minority, India also is concerned about the treatment of Muslims in China. But there are other causes, besides religious ones, for the tension between the two emerging Asian superpowers. China and India continue to compete for access to the natural resources of Southeast Asia, especially Burma (Myanmar).

The West

The United States granted Most Favored Nation status to China in 1980, thus allowing China's trade goods to enter the United States with the lowest tariff rate. Some members of the United States Congress called for the ending of most-favored-nation status after the 1989 Tiananmen Square massacre, but it was renewed annually before being made permanent in 2001. The name Most Favored Nation was changed to Permanent Normal Trade Relations in 1998 to reflect the fact that the status had become the norm. The fact that the United States has a very large trade imbalance with China year after year has been a cause of concern.

The Chinese treatment of Falun Dafa members has been an impediment to its relations with Western states in particular, and has threatened China's most-favored-nation status. Falun Dafa members in Europe and North America have been successful in keeping China's alleged human rights abuses under media attention. The attention given to China's human rights record during the lead up to the 2008 Olympics was due in part to Falun Dafa criticisms.

Hosting the Olympics was a long-term goal of China's foreign policy. Objections from human rights organizations hampered China's earlier bids, but hosting the 2008 Olympics was a major achievement for China, and putting a damper on protests before and during the event was a challenge. Foreign governments found themselves under pressure from human rights advocates to boycott the 2008 Olympics, especially after China reacted so strongly to protests among Tibetans. But the long history of the Olympics being apolitical prevailed.

The United States State Department's annual International Religious Freedom Report continues to anger China. Year after year, that report criticizes China for human rights abuses, including abuses against China's religious minorities. In response to the December 2010 Report, Hong Lei, speaking for China's Foreign Ministry, countered by insisting that

China maintains full freedom for its ethnic minorities and the practice of their religious beliefs. Lei chided the United States to stop such criticism and focus instead on matters that would strengthen rather than harm China/American bilateral relations.[63]

Although the West, as an important trade market for China, has some leverage for demanding that China improve its human rights stance toward its minorities and its religious organizations, China has leverage in that it has most of the world's commercially viable sources for "rare earths," the group of 17 rare minerals essential to the manufacturing of high tech electronics, including military technology. China controls as much as 97 percent of the world's supplies of some of the more essential of these rare earths. In 2010 China sent shockwaves through the high tech manufacturing sector when it dramatically raised the prices of rare earths and curtailed exports.

The rapid growth of Christianity raises an interesting theoretical question. Could such a large number of Christians influence Chinese foreign policy in ways more favorable to the predominantly Christian nations of the West? David Aikman argues strongly that it could. In his book *Jesus in Beijing: How Christianity is Transforming China and Changing the Global Balance of Power*, he calls attention to the growing numbers of Christians among Party leaders, military officers, judges, human rights lawyers, and other influential positions. They have, he suggests, a very positive view of Western style democracy and civilization, and they may someday promote a more Western-style democracy in China and lead to a more Western tilt in China's international relations.[64]

So, what can we conclude about the interface of religion and politics in China? On the politics side, we have seen a government intent upon controlling organized forms of all religions, but not suppressing religion *per se*, except during the decade of the Cultural Revolution. On the religion side, we do not see religious ideologues who are opposed to the Communist government. In most cases, we just have Protestants, Catholics, Buddhists (Tibetan and Han) and Muslims (Hui, Uyghur and other) wanting to practice their religion with as little interference from the government as possible. And we have a state that now wants to draw upon the energies of religions to advance social harmony and economic development.

The interface of religion and politics in modern China proves, or at least strongly suggests, two principles:

1. That an authoritarian central government can control religions by controlling the appointments of religious leaders and controlling the media;

2. That human spirituality is such that religious identity and practice will undergo resurgence whenever state suppression is relaxed.

---

[63]"China opposes USA report on its religious status," in *Foreign and Military Affairs*. (Nov. 26, 2010). www.chinadaily.com.cn/china/2010-11/26/cntent_11611845.htm.

[64]David Aikman, *Jesus in Beijing: How Christianity is Transforming China and changing the Global Balance of Power* (Washington D.C.: Regnery Press, 2006), 306.

> Our next destination is India, where we plan to see for ourselves how the world's largest democracy interfaces with growing religious fervor from both Hindus and Muslims.

STUDY QUESTIONS

1. What was Marx's view of religion and how does it compare with the government's approach to religion in contemporary China?

2. What motivates Uyghur separatism?

3. What influence does the Dalai Lama have on the governance of Tibetan Buddhists in China?

4. Are the restrictions put on Christianity in China a help or hindrance to the growth of Christianity in China?

5. Compare the government policies toward Falun Dafa in Hong Kong vs. the mainland.

6. How might China's internal treatment of Muslims be relevant to its international trade and relations?

7. Do you foresee any major changes concerning religion and politics in China?

FURTHER READING

Aikman, David. *Jesus in Beijing: How Christianity is Transforming China and Changing the Global Balance of Power.* Washington, D.C.: Regnery Press, 2006.

Ashiwa, Yoshiko, and Wank, David L. *Making Religion, Making the State.* Stanford: Stanford University Press, 2009. Essays on the politics of religion in modern China.

Back, Eugene, and Zhu, Brother. *Crimson Cross: Uncovering the Mysteries of the Chinese House Church.* Blountsvill, Alabama: Fifth Estate, 2012. Stories of several house church movements.

Chang, Jung. *Wild Swans: Three Daughters of China.* New York: Simon and Schuster, 1991 and 2003. A three generational autobiography that reads like a work of historical fiction. A wonderful source about Chinese politics as experience by ordinary people.

Chau, Adam Yuet, ed. *Religion in Contemporary China: Revitalization and Innovation.* Abingdon: Routeledge, 2011. Articles by various authors based on field research.

Dalai Lama. *Freedom in Exile: The Autobiography of the Dalai Lama.* New York: HarperPerennial edition, 2008. Writings by the world's most influential Buddhist.

Dreyer, June Teufel. *China's Political System: Modernization and Tradition.* New York: Pearson, 5th edition, 2006.

Israeli, Raphaeli. *Islam in China: Religion, Ethnicity, Culture, and Politics.* New York: Lexington Books, 2007. A good introduction to the diversity of Islam in China.

Kaltman, Blaine. *Under the Heel of the Dragon: Islam, Racism, Crime, and the Uyghur in China (Ohio RIS Global Series)* Athens: Center for International Studies, 2007.

Mitter, Rana. *A Bitter Revolution: China's Struggle with the Modern World.* Oxford: Oxford University Press, 2004. A good account of the way China attempts to deal with its problems.

Masden, Richard. *China's Catholics: Tragedy and Hope in an Emerging Civil Society.* Berkeley and Los Angeles: University of California Press, 1998. A good but dated account of Catholics in China.

Ownby, David. *Falun Gong and the Future of China.* New York: Oxford University Press, 2008. An overview of the movement based on interviews and published writings.

Shirk, Susan L. *China: Fragile Superpower: How China's Internal Politics Could Derail its Peaceful Rise.* Oxford: Oxford University Press, 2007. A comprehensive assessment.

Woo, Terry Tak-lin."Chinese and Korean Traditions," in Oxtoby, Willard G, Amore, Roy C. and Hussain, Amir, eds. World Religions: Eastern Traditions. 4th edition. Toronto: Oxford University Press, 2014. An introduction to the religions of China.

Xin, Yalin. *Inside China's House Church Networke Postmodern City: The Word of Life Movement and Its Renewing Dynamic.*Lexington: Emeth Press, 2009. An appreciative discussion of the Word of Life Movement.

WEBSITES

ww.buddhanet.net/e-learning/buddhistworld/china-txt.htm. Gives an overview of the history and varieties of Buddhism in China, but without any focus on current politics.

www.english.gov.cn Official web site for the Government of China. A good source for the point of view advanced in the Chinese media.

www.falundafa.org. Site of the Falun Gong or Falun Dafa organization, giving their side of the dispute with China.

www.freetibet.org. Site of the Free Tibet Campaign, a movement started by Tibetans in exile and their supporters.

www.islaminchinda.worpress.com This site carries interesting pictures news stories on the Hui Muslims of China. There are links of pro-Hui blog sites.

www.uyghuramerican.org Official site of the Uyghur American Association.

www.uyghurcongress.org Official site of the World Uyghur Congress, headquartered in Munich.

KEY PEOPLE

Bodhidharma The Buddhist monk who brought the Chan (Zen) school of Buddhism in China.

Li Hongzhi Founder and leader of Falun Dafa.

Chiang Kai-shek Leader of the Guomintang (Nationalist) Party during the Civil War period.

Konfuzi (Confucius) The ancient Chinese Sage whose teachings shaped Chinese cultural values.

Dalai Lama Title of the leader of one branch of Tibetan Buddhism and temporal leader of Tibet until the current era of Chinese control.

Laozi Ancient Sage who taught a minimalist theory of government.

Li Hongzhi The founder of Falun Dafa.

Sun Yat-sen Leader of the early Republic Period of China who was revered by both the Nationalists and Communists.

Mao Zedong Leader of the Chinese Communist Party and first Premier of the People's Republic of China.

Mengzi The second Confucian sage, after Confucius.

Zhuangzi (Chuang Tse) Second Daoist Sage who advocated a relaxed way of life and a minimalist government.

GLOSSARY

ahimsa Non-violence, as taught in Buddhism.

Amida Buddha A Buddha venerated in Pure Land Buddhism.

Buddhism An Indian religion that became established in China.

Chan (Zen) A sect of Mahayana Buddhism stressing simplicity and enlightenment.

Civil War The prolonged struggle between the Guomintang and Communists from 1927 to 1949.

Confucianism A school of social and political thought begun by Confucius.

Cult of Mao Refers to the way that Mao was treated almost like a deity during the Cultural Revolution.

Cultural Revolution A period (1966-76) of suppression of all religion and old culture.

Dalai Lama A title of the head of the Galugpa sect of Buddhists and before 1959 the head of government in Tibet.

Daodejing A Daoist text attributed to Laozi.

Daoism A traditional religion of China.

East Turkistan Islamic Movement (ETIM) A movement advocating more autonomy for Uyghurs in Xinjiang, which it calls East Turkistan.

Falun Dafa (Falun Gong) A Qigong movement with Buddhist roots, now outlawed in China.

feng shui A traditional set of practices meant to control spiritual energies.

Four Olds Old customs, culture, habits and ideas -- the slogan for what was to be destroyed during the Cultural Revolution.

Gang of Four The pejorative nickname for the four people to led the Cultural Revolution.

Guomintang Nationalist Party during the Civil War in China.

Han A dynasty in classical China and term for ethnic Chinese.

Hanification The process of increasing Han people and culture in traditionally ethnic areas such as Tibet.

Hinayana The oldest school (vehicle) of Buddhism, also known as Theravada.

house churches Unregistered Christian congregations in China.

Hui A Muslim minority of China.

koan A story, often paradoxical, used in Chan Buddhism as an aid to enlightenment.

Legalist An ancient Chinese political philosophy which sought to bring order by strictly enforced, written laws applying to all.

Little Red Book A collection of Mao's sayings, used during the Cultural Revolution.

Long March 1934-35 journey of the Red Army toward safety in the Northwest.

Mahayana The school (vehicle) of Buddhism most common in China.

mandarin A term for civil administrators in traditional China, and a term for the northern dialect of Chinese used by the government.

minority peoples The 55 ethnic groups of China, as distinct from the Han Chinese.

Nirvana A State of absolute bliss

Panthay Rebellion A nineteenth-century revolt of Hui Muslims in southern China.

parinirvana A Buddhist term for complete and final liberation upon death.

Popular Religion A term for the traditional Chinese religious practices centered on spirit rituals, fortune telling, and wish granting. Also called **Folk Religion.**

qi (chi), qigong Physical exercises and movements intended to maximize good energies in the body and mind.

Red Guards Bands of youths who enforced the dictates of the Gang of Four during the Cultural Revolution.

San Jiao The traditional system of "three religions" in China.

Shinto The "Way of the Spirits," meaning the traditional religion of Japan.

State Shinto A term for the cult of the Emperor before and during World War II in Japan.

Three-Self Church An organization of Protestant churches recognized by the Chinese government.

Tiananmen Square A large public square outside the "Heavenly Gate" entrance to the Imperial City.

Taiping Rebellion A mid-nineteenth century peasant revolt led by quasi-Christian reformers.

Tibetan Autonomous Region (TAR) The current name for three provinces of China that cover part of the former Tibet.

Theravada One of the Hinayana Schools of Buddhism now found in Sri Lanka and Southeast Asia.

Uyghur A Turkish ethnic group whose home region is now part of China.

Uyghur Autonomous Region The traditional Uyghur region now ruled by China.

Vajrayana The school of Buddhism popular among Tibetans.

wuwei A Daoist goal of effortless or spontaneous action.

Yihewani Chinese Muslim organization, from Arabic Ikhwan, "Brotherhood."

zazen "Sitting Meditation (zen), as practiced in Chan Buddhism.

Chapter Three

India

Secular Policy versus Religious Demands:
Dalit Rights, Hindu Nationalism, Muslim Demands

In this chapter you will learn about:

- religion and politics in Thailand, Myanmar, Sri Lanka, and Nepal
- the background of religion and politics in India
- secularist policy verses communal demands
- the struggle of Dalits for basic rights
- the goals of Hindu Nationalists
- Hindu-Muslim conflicts

STOPOVERS IN THAILAND, MYANMAR, SRI LANKA, AND NEPAL

Landing in Bangkok's impressive new Suvarnabhumi Airport, we head toward the backpacker area around Khaosan Road. The name refers to the "polished rice" which used to be sold here, but now the Khaosan Road area teems with young travelers from seemingly every other country. They mostly just hang out, shop, eat, drink, and exchange travel tips. We settle into our room and hop on the 'water taxi,' a fast moving boat that goes from pier to pier along the Chao Praya River like a public bus making stops along a street. The water taxi barely stops long enough for us to hop on. We pass barges that are home to Thai families, complete with a pet dog and a TV antenna. We spot some traditional Thai style homes, built on stilts near the river. We get off at the Royal Palace. The King lives elsewhere in a newer palace. This one was built to look like a European palace, except that it has three tall, Thai style cupolas along its roofline. The Thais joke that it is a Western building with three Thai hats.

On the palace grounds we enter the famous Temple of the Emerald Buddha. This building and its precious Buddha statue located high above the altar at the far end give us a glimpse of the close relationship between religion and politics, Thai style. Three times a year the King comes to change the clothing draped on the Buddha image. Thailand has three seasons: cool, rainy and hot, so the king puts appropriate seasonal clothing on the statue at the beginning of each season. It is a very important cultural and

HRH Crown Prince Maha Vagiralongkorn of Thailand changing the attire of the Emerald Buddha from rainy season to winter season.
Photo:http://www.nationmultimedia.com/specials/nationphoto/show.php?pid-14806

political ceremony watched by high officials in person and on television by Thais everywhere. It shows that, although all Thais serve the king, the king serves the Buddha. The traditional relation of religion and politics is alive and well in Thailand. The king must be a Buddhist but the elected parliamentarians do not. Buddhism enjoys a favored status as the majority religion. Does it also show the Muslims of Southern Thailand that they do not really fit into the Thai political culture?

Separatist Fighting in Southern Thailand

One of the biggest issues in Thai politics arises from the demands by the Muslims in the south of Thailand for more regional autonomy. The population of that part of Thailand is mostly Malay Muslims rather than Thai Buddhists. The region is relatively poor and, arguably, has not received its fair share of government assistance in the past. The region has long been a stronghold of local warlords, but now the situation has been complicated by demands for more autonomy or independence. The trouble was not started by outsiders, but once it started it got the attention of Islamic jihadists. Farther down the Malay Peninsula is Malaysia, a prospering Islamic country, and so some ethnic Malays of southern Thailand want to break away from Thailand and join their ethnic and religious counterparts in Malaysia. The Thai government does not want to lose this territory, so no easy solution is in sight.

Religion is not involved in the bitter conflict between the political factions known as "yellow shirts" and "red shirts." The one group wears yellow shirts to rallies because yellow is the color of the day of the week on which the king was born. Displaying yellow is a symbol of their loyalty to the monarchy and their opposition to the regime of exiled former Prime Minister Thaksin Shinawatra, and to his sister, Yingluck Shinawatra, the current Prime Minister. The "reds" faction, which strongly backs the Shinawatra regimes, is especially strong in the northern and rural areas. The "reds" have easily won recent elections.

Sulak's Buddhist Critique of Consumerism

Before leaving Bangkok we go to visit the Spirit in Education Movement, a non-governmental organization (NGO) run by **Sulak Sivaraksa**. *Sulak has twice been charged in a Thai military court with* lèse majesté, *literally "harming the king," meaning the offense of speaking ill of a king. He was not found guilty, but the charges succeeded as a form of harassment. However, one time he left the country and spent several months in exile. His lectures in various cities of Europe, Canada, and the United States during that exile helped make him an internationally known peace activist.*

Before we leave, Sulak talks to us about his favorite topic, the problems caused by globalization in general and consumerism in particular. He reminds us of Rene Descartes' famous saying, "I think, therefore I am." Sulak says the new attitude that sums up the consumerism attitude that has swept the world is "I shop, therefore I am." We laugh at this, because it hits home. Asians had been content when they had basic shelter, traditional clothing, and enough rice and other food to eat, but now they do not feel worthy unless they can buy the latest fashions and electronics, Sulak laments. And to make matters worse, he explains, many of the fields that grew crops for the local Thai families are now growing pineapples and other export crops for multinational corporations. Sulak draws upon the Buddhist ethic of moderation—Buddhists follow a Middle Path on many things—as his inspiration to help the people and the politicians resist the excesses of consumerism and greed. It is another example of a religious leader trying to influence public policy, for the better it seems. Too bad most of us, whatever our religious affiliation might be, do not follow a middle path on these matters. I recall a Thai monk once telling my class, "Enough is better than too much."

We thank Sulak and prepare to fly to Myanmar, where the self-serving military junta may be giving way to democracy—or not!

Military Junta versus Democracy in Myanmar

Flying into Yangon, we arrive at the first of the nations we will visit that were colonies of a European country until the mid-twentieth century. Myanmar was ruled by the British, who were never very careful in the English spelling of the cities and countries they ruled. After independence, many former colonies have corrected those spellings. "Burma" is now corrected to Myanmar, and Rangoon, the former capital, is now spelled Yangon.

After gaining independence under the leadership of Aung San in 1947, Myanmar, like Thailand, has gone through periods of military rule interspersed with democracy. A military junta assumed power in 1962 and has only recently begun to relinquish power. Known as the State Law and Order Restoration Council (SLORC), the ruling military council reluctantly agreed to democratic elections in 1990, thinking that it would easily win. But a coalition of pro-democracy Burmese, led by **Daw Aung San Suu Kyi**, won the election in a landslide. Yet the military council refused to resign, and she found herself under house arrest. Myanmar is one of the poorest and worst-ruled countries in the world. The generals who sat on SLORC profited from the trade in opium or by selling Myanmar's teak and other natural resources, mostly to the Chinese.

There has been some religion-based resistance to military rule from time to time. For example, in 2007 Buddhist monks led protests against the military, but were brutally suppressed. Seeing their rulers bring harm to monks was the last straw for many Burmese, but they were powerless to do much against a military dictatorship. The government's weak response in the aftermath of the devastating typhoon in 2008, and its reluctance to allow outside assistance, increased the world's attention to the problem. Some activists wanted the United Nations to move into Myanmar to protect its citizens. But outside powers have not been inclined to send in an army of liberation, and there was a fear that China, wanting to maintain its near-monopoly on Myanmar's resources, might resist the regime change. ASEAN (Association of Southeast Asian Nations) and its member nations have vacillated between maintaining an official boycott and trading with Myanmar. But SLORC finally gave in to external pressures and announced a "Roadway to Democracy" in 2011. Daw Aung San Suu Kyi was elected to parliament in 2012.

Although civilian government now rules, the real power remains with the military.

Ugly Separatist Fighting in Beautiful Sri Lanka

We fly to Colombo's Bandaranaike International Airport on the island country of Sri Lanka. This airport was built by Canadian aid money in the 1970s and was named after former Prime Minister Bandaranaike. After his assassination by a Buddhist monk, his wife Sirima Bandaranaike became the first woman leader of a modern democracy in 1960. To get a better feel for the Buddhist element here, we travel "up country" to the Central Highlands by train. The train winds slowly through the steep hills lined with coconut plantations. We arrive in Kandy, the seat of the last independent government before the British period. Kandy is a beautiful little city built around a lake. Overlooking the lake is the most sacred Buddhist temple on the island. It is named the Temple of the Tooth because Buddhists believe that it contains a very sacred relic, an eyetooth retrieved from the Buddha's cremation ashes. We stand on the street between the temple and the river, looking up at a balcony. We are standing where crowds of Sri Lankans have often stood to hear important announcements by political leaders from this balcony. Reflecting on this mix of politics and religion, we begin to understand why some Tamil Hindus feel excluded from Sri Lanka's political culture. The Sinhalese people, the ethnic majority, have a strong belief that their beloved island is the "Bulwark of Buddhism," the place where original Buddhism survived after it was driven from India. This motivates them to mix Buddhism and politics.

We arrive in time to see one of the world's most famous religious processions, the Kandy Perahera. Instead of parade floats, it features elephants parading in groups of three. Leading each group of elephants are dancers and musicians representing different villages. The place of honor goes to the last division of the parade, representing the Temple of the Tooth. Four other temples come first, including both Buddhist and Hindu ones. So the symbolism of Buddhist-Hindu cooperation is built into the ritual, but the symbolic superiority of Buddhism is there as well.

Among the countries of South Asia, Sri Lanka has been through the longest period of instability, starting from the late 1970's when some Hindu **Tamils** of the north started demanding more autonomy in a country they perceived to be overly dominated by the **Sinhalese** majority, most of whom are Buddhists. The most militant of the Tamil groups, the infamous **Tamil Tigers** (Liberation Tigers of Tamil Eelam, or **LTTE**) fought a guerrilla war against the government starting in 1983, despite the stronger resources of the Sri Lanka army.

From 1987–1990 an "Indian Peace Keeping Force," a detachment of the Indian army, was sent by Prime Minister Rajiv Gandhi to put down the Tamil separatist movement. India had long been threatened by its own separatist movements, especially by the Sikhs in the Punjab region, and so it had a motive to suppress separatist activities in neighboring Sri Lanka. The de facto invasion of the Tamil area of Sri Lanka was very unpopular among the Tamil population of south India. Tamil resentment led to the assassination in 1991 of Rajiv Gandhi by a female LTTE suicide bomber.[1] Rajiv Gandhi's military advisors had assured him that the more highly trained and disciplined Indian army would quickly overrun the LTTE resistance. That did not prove to be the case, and both the LTTE and Indian army took heavy casualties before the Indian army withdrew without achieving anything significant and with great loss of its prestige in the region.

The Tamil Tigers might have been satisfied just by gaining more regional autonomy when they began the civil war, but once they tasted some success both the Tigers and the

---

[1]The LTTE is sometimes "credited" with popularizing the suicide bomber tactic that has become so widely used by terrorists.

government hardened their attitudes. The Tigers then demanded total independence for the predominantly Tamil north as well as the Eastern Province, which has a mixed population of Tamil, Sinhalese, and Muslims. The non-Tamils of the Eastern Province did not want to be governed by the Tigers, but the Tigers insisted on having the Eastern Province as part of their nation because of its relatively large Tamil population and because the northeast region has more resources and better rainfall.

This civil war was not started as a religious conflict. Rather, it arose when the Tamils of the relatively poor north demanded better conditions and a bigger share of the national wealth. The fact that the government was dominated by those who spoke Sinhalese made access to government positions difficult for Tamil speakers. In this political context, it is understandable that once the conflict reared its ugly head, the fact that the Tamils are mostly Hindus and the Sinhalese mostly Buddhists complicated the matter. Some Buddhist leaders, both lay and monk, took a Sinhalese Buddhist nationalism position, which exacerbated the tensions between the two groups. In the late 1970s the overwhelming majority of both ethnic communities wanted to see a peaceful solution. By the 1990s both sides could hardly say anything good about the other. Religion did not start the war, but it played a role once the war had started.

Given the strong *ahimsa*, "non-violence" ethic in traditional Buddhism, how can Buddhist monks and their lay supporters justify violence and war against the LTTE? P. Schalk

Temple of the [Buddha's] Tooth Relic, Kandy Sri Lanka. In the past important political speeches have been made from the Temple's portico (seen in the foreground), which associates Buddhism with the state.
Photo: Ji-Elle, Wikipedia Commons.

lists several reasons given by the political Buddhists to justify their "war for peace" stance. One is the claim that the ends justify the means, or they turn to the stories of war against the Tamils in the island's past. Some hold that the *ahimsa* ideal does not apply in this time and place, or they deny that unnecessary violence is being used at all.[2]

One of the names for the Sinhalese nationalist position is *Sinhalatva*, meaning "Sinhala-ness." When we get to India, we will discuss the parallel Hindu Nationalist movement known as *Hindutva*, "Indian-ness" or "Hindu-ness." *Sinhalatva* is both a Buddhist nationalist and Sinhalese nationalist movement. Its proponents tended to favor a concept known as "war for peace," which means that they supported the war against Tamil separatists. The movement formed a new political party, the **National Heritage Party** (**JHU**, Jathika Hela Urumaya) and won nine seats in the 2004 parliamentary elections. Because the leadership and some of the elected members were Buddhist monks, it caused quite a controversy because, traditionally, it was thought to be inappropriate for a monk to hold a political office. In the past, a monk who wished to take up a secular position would first become a layman. Buddhist monks are not under a vow to remain monks their whole lives, so this is not seen as a problem. The JHU party is staunchly Nationalistic and pro-Buddhist. It would like to see restrictions placed on the sale of alcohol and on overly zealous Christian evangelism. It also led a request for the United Nations to investigate human rights abuses in the United States.

Two especially zealous monks who had been leaders in JHU broke away from that organization to found a new, more militant party known as **BBS**, for **Bodu Bala Sena** ("Buddhist Power Force"). It held its first convention in 2012, and adopted a platform that opposed concessions to minority religion, weakening of the unitary constitution, and special laws for non-Buddhists. It also wants an end to government funding for practices thought to be immoral, such as vasectomies or tubectomies. It has become increasingly aggressive in opposition to Muslims, and has sometimes stormed into hotels, colleges, and government offices in protest. More moderate Buddhists have spoken out against the BBS's extreme positions and tactics.

In sharp contrast with the BBS, some organizations in Sri Lanka, such as Sarvodaya, continue to work toward peace and harmony among members of all religious groups. The government also took a positive step in 2015 when it created four government Ministries for each of the four main religions: Buddhism, Hinduism, Islam and Christianity. This governmental structure should help assure the minority religions that their concerns will be heard.

We take the return train to Colombo, take time for a swim in the Indian Ocean, then catch our flight to Kathmandu, Nepal, another troubled South Asian country.

---

[2] Peter Schalk, "Operationalizing Buddhism for Political Ends in a Martial Context in Lanka: The Case of *Simhalatva*," in *Religion and Violence in South Asia: Theory and Practice.* ed. John R. Hinnells and Richard King (Abingdon and New York: Routledge, 2007), 149–150.

Maoist Revolt Against a Hindu Monarchy in Nepal

As we approach Tribhuvan International Airport, the amazing view of Kathmandu Valley with the Himalaya Mountains in the background makes us forget the bumpy flight up to this elevation. After clearing customs, we immediately head for Durbar Square, where the kings used to hold court in old Kathmandu. In the ancient practice, here and most places, justice was administered each morning by the king. We have the saying, "Justice delayed is justice denied," but our modern system with two or more years of waiting for a court case would have seemed absurd and immoral in old South Asia. We could learn a lot from ancient cultures like this.

We see the large old building said to have been built entirely from the wood of one huge tree. The modern name Kathmandu for the city and the valley derives from its name, Kasthamandap, "House of Wood." Walking further around Durbar Square we see several Hindu temples and historic buildings severely damaged by the 2015 earthquake. There is a lingam, the sacred, phallic symbol of the god Shiva, and the ring symbol of the corresponding female principle. The area near the temple is used as an open-air barber shop. Across the square, images of the god Shiva and his consort, the goddess Parvati, look out from an upstairs window of their temple, welcoming visitors like good hosts. All these Hindu temples surrounding the king's court area and the nearby palace reminds us that Nepal was officially a Hindu kingdom, with power devolved to an elected parliament. Or at least it was a kingdom until the royal family self-destructed and the Maoist rebels got stronger.

A tragic event in 2001 radically changed Nepali politics. After quarrelling with his parents about the choice of his bride, Crown Prince Dipendra left the family dinner party, went to his room and put on combat fatigues. He returned with an automatic gun and shot and killed eleven people, including his parents, the queen and king, as well as his sister and brother. He then shot and wounded himself. Ironically, given that he was the crown prince and the king was dead, he was made the king while he lay wounded in the hospital. He died from his wounds, however, so the king's younger brother Gyanendra was crowed the new king.

The problem was that King Gyanendra was not well respected by the Nepalese, and he soon was locked into a political showdown with the Parliament. The King suspended the Parliament and took power back to the monarchy. Meanwhile the Communist Party of Nepal-Maoist, which had long been active in the rural areas, was emboldened by the loss of confidence in the monarchy and the parliamentary mess. The Maoists started to attack inside Kathmandu and the two other cities in the Kathmandu Valley where most Nepalese live. By 2006 the Maoists were in a strong negotiating position, and India opened relations with them under a "12 Point Agreement" calling for the stablishment of an absolute democracy.[3]

---

[3]To view the 12 Point Agreement on line, see http://www.telegraphnepal.com/news_det.php?news_id=774.

Tourism and Elephant Preservation

Accompanied by two friends I had taken an elephant ride in the jungle to look for rhinos in the Chitwan National Park, an animal habitat preservation area and tourist attraction in southern Nepal. Along the way our mahout climbed down off the elephant and disappeared into the jungle to heed the call of nature. Our elephant began to stomp its feet, shake his head and wail! The three of us just looked at each other in disbelief! The beast could have taken off at any moment, to anywhere. The mahout beside us spoke to him in Nepali to calm him down but with no luck. Laughing, he proclaimed "bad elephant," which became his nickname. The rest of the three-hour ride was a blast, especially when the two mahouts began to race. Bad Elephant won! Back on terra firma I went over to thank Bad Elephant for a great ride, and he lightly ran his trunk over my head and down the side of my face.

The next day we crossed the river to visit a sanctuary the government runs to care for and breed domesticated elephants. After seeing the big males and breeding females, and after dodging the calves as they chased each other around the calving ground, we started biking back into town. A storm hit and we were soaked. The road had turned to mud and it was getting darker. I heard Jen, then Roy, and then Irene yell something as each turned the corner onto the main road. "What?" I yelled back. Starting my turn on to the road I heard "ELEPHANT!! LOOK OUT!" I skidded to a stop. My heart pounded. Trotting straight towards me was Bad Elephant. Bad Elephant snorted as he moved out of the way, and the mahout and I exchanged Namaste, and then they were gone.

—Michelle Morrison

Elections for a constitutional assembly were held in 2008, with the Maoist party being asked to lead a coalition government. The Maoist party rose to this strong position through armed guerrilla warfare and grass roots support from many of Nepal's rural poor who felt excluded in the old system under which an elite of high class and high **caste** Nepalese held control of parliament. The Maoist rise to power was in part a class struggle, but not in the classical Marxist sense of the urban workers against factory owners. Rather, it was the rural poor against the landowning class, and then the urban poor against the upper castes.

Nepal has the most active Maoist movement in the region, but India's militant communists, called **Naxalites**,[4] are quite active as well, so India finds itself fighting Naxalite terrorism at home while recognizing a Maoist-led government to its north.

---

[4] The name Naxalite refers to the location where this communist movement staged one of its first actions.

We take a bus south from Kathmandu toward India. We stop at Chitwan National Park long enough to ride through the park on an elephant and look for white rhinos. Then we take the bus further south to Lumbini Park, to see the place where Buddha was born. This is one of the four great pilgrimage sights connected with the Buddha. We cross the border into India, our main country of interest in South Asia.

INDIA

The South Asian Region

South Asia is an area of extremes. It has, as a region, the world's largest population and the world's highest mountains. India is the world's largest democracy and has the largest Hindu population. Pakistan has the world's second largest Muslim population. South Asia is also politically diverse. There are countries with functioning democracies, ones ruled by the military from time to time, one (Nepal) with a recently overthrow kingship, and one (Bhutan) in which the king is trying to get his subjects to move toward democracy! The region also has areas of extreme poverty and religious-based violence.

One issue in the region concerning politics is the tension between civilian democracies and military rule. Both Pakistan and Bangladesh have had their civilian democracies interrupted by periods of military rule. Another problem is the instability caused by assassinations of political leaders, including India's Mahatma Gandhi (1948), Indira Gandhi (1984), and her son Rajiv Gandhi (1991), Bangladesh's Prime Minister Mujibur Rahman (1975), Nepal's King Birendra (2001), and Pakistan's Benazir Bhutto (2007).

Although the interface of religions and politics is important and interesting in all of the South Asian countries, we will focus on India because it is so large, so much a land of extremes, so religiously diverse, and well, just because it is India.

RELIGIOUS BACKGROUND

India is home to four of the world's best known religions: **Hinduism**, **Jainism**, **Buddhism**, and **Sikhism**. As if that were not enough, it has become a home for the Zoroastrians who migrated from Persia (Iran) and are now known as Parsees. And there are perhaps twenty million Christians, and small numbers of Jews, Baha'i, and almost everything else under the hot, Indian sun.

Hinduism

Hinduism is an umbrella term given to the complex assortment of beliefs, gods and goddesses, festivals, and practices that are native to India. Unlike the more doctrinal religions originating in the Middle East, Hindus do not stress conformity to a certain creed. Nor is

Hindu Holy Men (*Sadhus*) pose,
for tips, at the Pashupati (Shiva)
Temple in Kathmandu, Nepal.
Photo: Roy Amore

there anyone quite like a pope. Some Hindus worship Shiva and his family of gods and goddesses, and some worship the god Vishnu and his family. It does not seem to matter to Hindus. Historically there have been relatively few wars or serious conflicts (compared to Europe for example) between the Shiva worshippers (Shaivas) and the Vishnu worshippers (Vaishnavas). Nor is there any forced consensus on the nature of god. Whereas most Hindus believe in lots of gods and goddesses as person-like powers, the Vedantin Hindus hold that the highest concept of god is as an impersonal power, something like the Dao of Daoism or the Absolute of some forms of Western mysticism.

What gives Hinduism its sense of oneness, then, if it is so diverse? Two things. First, all forms of Hinduism give some degree of respect to the Vedas and the Brahmin priesthood. The Vedas are the oldest of the Hindu sacred books, and the Brahmin priests officiate at the rituals. Brahmins in general—meaning the Brahmin class—are all those, male and female, born to Brahmin parents, whereas Brahmin priests are those male Brahmins who have taken the special training to become priests. Most persons in the Brahmin class are not priests. Traditionally, many were owners of land and cattle. Many still are. As for the Vedas, they are given great respect but are not much read or known by the ordinary Hindus, who greatly prefer the more popular Hindu stories with plots. The two most important of the latter are the Mahabharata and the Ramayana epics. The Mahabharata tells of the long exile of the five Pandava brothers and their victory in the great civil war for the throne among the Bharata royalty. The Ramayana tells the story of the god-king Ram and his wife, the goddess-queen Sita, and that story will be very relevant to our third issue involving the Hindu efforts to build a Ram temple in Ayodhya.

Buddhism and Jainism

Buddhism and **Jainism** started out as closely related religions growing out of Ganges spirituality, the ascetic beliefs and practices found along the Ganges basin 2,500 years ago. Both believe in karma, rebirth and the idea that occasionally a major leader arises and teaches a dharma that helps people move along a path to nirvana. Jainism and Buddhism differed from Hinduism in many ways. They downplayed the role of the gods and did not accept the authority of the Vedas or the Brahmin priests. Persons from any social class could become Buddhist or Jain monks. In this and other ways, The Buddha and Mahavira, the Jain leader, were ahead of the modern Hindu reformers by 2,400 years. They rejected caste discrimination, advocated intercaste dining and admitted women into training. If Indian society had followed their teaching against caste, the first of our three topics in this chapter, about caste discrimination, would no longer be an issue.

Although similar in teachings and practice at their beginnings, Jainism and Buddhism developed separately and followed their own destinies. Jainism spread throughout most areas of India and prospered for several centuries before assuming its current role as a minority religion that goes largely unnoticed in India.

Buddhism also spread throughout India, but unlike Jainism it spread beyond India into Sri Lanka, Southeast Asia, and, thanks to the famous Silk Road, north into Central Asia and then across to East Asia. Last of all, Buddhism spread northward into the Himalayan region, including Tibet. Despite its great success elsewhere, Buddhism gradually died out in India by the twelfth century, perhaps in part because Hinduism had assimilated many Buddhist and Jain teachings, thus blurring the distinction. But also, Buddhism was mainly centerd in monasteries, and the Muslim era in northern India brought the destruction of its monasteries. From around 1200 to the Chinese takeover of Tibet in 1959, there were few Buddhists in India except for Assam in the far northeast. As discussed in the China chapter, the Chinese takeover of Tibet led to many Tibetans migrating to India, so there is now a visible Tibetan Buddhist presence in India, especially in the hill areas of the northwest. Also, as discussed in this chapter, a statesman from a low class background, **Dr. Ambedkar**, converted to Buddhism along with thousands of other **Dalits** (a name meaning persons of the oppressed classes).

Sikhism

Sikhism is a much more recent religion. It arose in the Punjab area in 1499 when a spiritual man named Nanak received a call from God and became a Guru, a teacher of a new religion intended to unite all religions. Guru Nanak lived in a time and place in which there were great conflicts between Muslims and Hindus. He came to the position that "there is no Muslim and there is no Hindu," meaning that people should get beyond that old distinction and just worship God. He taught the oneness of God, as in Islamic theology, but he drew a lot of spiritual practices from the Hindu tradition, such as the practice of singing devotional hymns. He referred to God as Sat Nam, "True Name." Many people in the Punjab area embraced the Sikh tradition as developed under the leadership of the 10 Gurus, Guru Nanak and nine later men. By the death of the tenth, Guru Gobind Singh, in 1708, it was a religion distinct from both Hinduism and Islam, with its headquarters in the beautiful Golden Temple at Amritsar.

Sikhism has played an important role in Indian politics. During the Mughal period (1526–1857) the Sikhs took up arms to defend themselves against what they perceived to be harassment and forced conversion to Islam. Once armed, there were fierce battles with Mughal forces, and for a brief time in 1783, a Sikh army took Delhi, the Mughal capital.[5] In the British period, in an attempt to quell sedition, the British officer in charge of the city of Amritsar ordered his men to open fire on a large crowd of Sikhs trapped in a compound where they had gathered to celebrate a holy day. This shameful act by the British helped undermine their authority in ruling India. In the 1980s some Sikhs were agitating to form a separate country in the Punjab area, believing it was unfair that the Muslims had gotten their own state and Sikhs had not when India was partitioned into Pakistan and India. To put down this separatist movement, Prime Minister Indira Gandhi ordered Indian forces to move into the Golden Temple at Amritsar in an attempt to capture the separatist leader and seize what was expected to be a large cache of arms and munitions. The military action, under the now-infamous code name Operation Blue Star, was a disaster, leading to the death of many Sikhs and some physical damage, but not to the temple itself as rumors had it at the time. Sikhs were outraged, and four months later a Sikh bodyguard to Indira Gandhi assassinated her in revenge.

Zoroastrianism, Islam and Christianity

The name **Parsee**, or Parsi, just means Persians. The Parsees came to Gujarat on the west coast of India to escape Islamic persecution in Persia, now Iran, in the eighth century. Many now live in Mumbai. They follow the religion that goes back to the prophet Zoroaster, who lived in the sixth century B.C. (or earlier) in Persia. They are a small but thriving community, known for their success in business. They are important for the economic life of India, but keep a low profile on the political scene.

The other important religions in India are Islam and Christianity. Christianity was very important during the British period, but it now enters the political arena mainly when there is a backlash to what are perceived to be overly aggressive missionary tactics by evangelical Christians. Islam, on the other hand, has played a major role in India politics from before the Mughal period to the present.

We shall see how the granting of a Muslim state, Pakistan, and then later political concessions to the Muslims of India has touched off a backlash among right wing Hindus, helping create a Hindu Nationalism that will be the focus of our second and third issues.

---

[5]The lower level of the largest Sikh gurdwara (temple) in Delhi contains a museum of paintings and documents about the strife between Muslims and Sikhs during the Mughal period.

POLITICAL BACKGROUND

Historical India

Indians take great pride in the fact that their civilization traces back thousands of years, as do the Chinese and Egyptians, among others. Many of us find the Harappan, or Indus civilization, fascinating. Here was a state-of-the-art civilization covering the largest area of any ancient civilization known from this time period, around 5,000 years ago. It covered much of modern Pakistan and western India and extended as far east as Delhi. Archeological remains show careful town planning with some well laid out, broad streets, water and sewage systems, standardized weights and measures, and many other factors suggesting good governance.[6] But we know almost nothing about who ruled the city or how they did it.

Our ignorance of the ancient Harappan era is offset by a surprising amount of information on subsequent Indian political history. We have the two Epics, plus manuals on governance. We know that kingship was the norm, but with an interesting twist. A king was to retire and turn the throne over to his crown prince when he began to get gray hair. (There's a tale about a king who pays his barber handsomely to dye his graying beard.) There was also a strong republican tradition in old India in which the power was vested in a council of elders drawn from leading families.

There is a Buddhist story about how kingship started. The people got together and elected a "king,"called the "Great Elect," and kingship was established, but by the will of the people rather than through military might. The Hebrew Bible contains a similar story about how kingship got started in Israel, but it puts more emphasis on the role of god. The people ask the prophet Samuel to anoint a king. He warns them about the dangers of a centralized government, and then reluctantly casts lots to select Saul as the first king of Israel.[7]

In the early third century B.C. Alexander the Great conquered much of Western India, but the battles were so difficult and the diseases so alarming that his men convinced him to turn back. He died on the way home and two of his underlings took over the Indian portions of the former empire. Before long an Indian named Chandragupta restored Indian rule and put together a large kingdom, founding the Mauryan Dynasty. The Mauryans ruled sternly but with justice. Their approach was that of the philosopher king in the Greek tradition. In addition to the normal matters of governance, they sought out and sat at the feet of the great religious leaders of the day. They followed a policy of religious pluralism, giving support to Hinduism, Jainism, and Buddhism.

The next major era was that of the Gupta dynasty (320–550). After that, regional dynasties ruled until the Mughals consolidated power in northern India in 1526.

---

[6]For pictures and articles on the latest archaeological finds at Harappa, see www.harappan.com.

[7]I *Samuel* 8:1–11:15.

The Mughal Period

> *We arrive in Delhi and do a walking tour of Old Delhi, starting at the Red Fort, the palace built to accommodate Shah Jahan when he moved his residence from Agra to Delhi in 1639. We stare in awe at the size of the Red Fort—we would have to walk almost 2.5 kms (1.5 miles) to get around its outer walls. We also note that its sandstone really is quite red. Next we walk along Chandni Chowk, the "Moonlit Market" area that served old Delhi and still has interesting shops. We visit two old Jain temples, a Hindu Shiva temple, and then follow a narrow old roadway, elbowing our way through the crowd of people, bicycles, goats, and dogs until we reach our destination, the Jama Masjid, the grand Mughal mosque. We sit on its steps and enjoy some people-watching.*

The political history of the Mughal Empire is important to the third issue to be discussed, the Babri (Babar) Mosque. Babar came to India in 1526 and defeated the Delhi Sultanate, and then made himself the ruler. A huge controversy today centers on the question of whether or not Babar's general tore down a Hindu temple to build a mosque in the city of Ayodhya. Four years after becoming the ruler, Babar died and was soon succeeded by his son Humayun, who further developed the Mughal reign. The long reign (1556–1605) of Akbar, Babar's grandson, was the zenith of Mughal power and glory.

Akbar did some interesting things in terms of our subject of religion and politics. He evidently was quite concerned about the problem of ruling a people divided between Islam and Hinduism. His policy was to allow multiculturalism, and he supported both Hindu and Muslim institutions. But he took this spirit of cooperation a giant step further. He attempted to amalgamate Hinduism, Islam and Christianity into a new entity called "Religion of God" (Din-i-ilahi). It was a nice try for religious harmony, but it did not take.

Akbar's son Jahangir was a great patron of painting, gardens, and the arts. His successor, Shah Jahan was a great builder, giving us the great Mughal buildings in the old part of Delhi and the Taj Mahal. He had the Taj built of the finest white marble as a tomb for his wife.[8] The Taj Mahal was a magnificent structure, but it was built at huge cost of money and labor. The story is that when it was finished, Shah Jahan planned to build a matching tomb across the river for himself, made of black marble. The people resisted this idea, and his son took over the rule. Shah Jahan was kept under house arrest in a spacious palace apartment at Agra, with a view of his wife's tomb in the distance. This may rank as one of the world's great love stories.

Shah Jahan's successor was Aurangzeb, whose approach differed markedly from that of Akbar. Aurangzeb had what we might now call an Islamist approach. He reversed the policy of religious tolerance and introduced **Shariah** law. Many contemporary Indian Muslims admire him for introducing a truer from of Islam, whereas many Hindus look

---

[8]In India and elsewhere, it was common for a great ruler to have family or personal tombs built during their lifetimes.

back on his era as a time or repression and discrimination against Hinduism and Indian culture. Our second issue, Hindu Nationalism, reveals how some Hindus want to turn back the clock and restore the old Indian culture and the primacy of Hinduism.

After Aurangzeb's death in 1707 his empire came apart, partly because the British now controlled several regions for trade purposes. The British had come to India to profit from trade through the privately-held East India Company. The East India Company had started trading in the early 1600s, and eventually got the permission of Jahangir to establish some trading bases on the coast. By 1688 it had established itself so well that it went to war with Aurangzeb and, as a result, won control of several coastal regions. By 1757 British officer Robert Clive took the authority upon himself to conquer and take control of more regional kingdoms.

By the 1840s and 1850s the trading company had gotten so involved with matters of governance, such as collecting taxes, building forts, putting down rebellions, and replacing traditional rulers, that the British had little choice but to take over the entire country, or else downsize their trade. They justified their rule of India not on the basis of profiteering, but on the basis of their duty to bring proper civilization, justice, and the rule of law to the backward nations. This attitude is summed up in the phrase "white man's burden" that now seems politically incorrect on so many levels. One of the reforms the British tried to impose was to outlaw the practice of Sati (or Suttee), the practice among some social classes in some parts of India for widows to "voluntarily" throw themselves on their husband's funeral pyre to follow him into the afterlife. The British were understandably shocked by this practice and outlawed it, but that did not completely stop it. They also passed laws banning discrimination against the "untouchables," and the continuation of just such discrimination will be our first issue in this chapter.

There was resistance to British rule from the very beginning. The first serious rebellion was in 1857 when some Indian soldiers (*sepoys*) serving in the British army rebelled and sided with the Mughal emperor. The British put down this Sepoy Rebellion, and then changed the nature of their army. They also made the decision to rule directly, and not through the East Asia Company.[9]

In 1858 the governance of India was transferred to Great Britain, with Queen Victoria on the throne: the British Raj, or "reign," officially began. The British colonized Burma and Sri Lanka as well, which were also areas where the East Indian Company had established trading ports. Indian leaders of various backgrounds and religions joined the Indian National Congress, which began in 1885. Its main goal was to get the British to leave India and to introduce Self Rule (*Swaraj*) in its place. Its leaders included Jinnah, the founding Prime Minister of Pakistan, Nehru, the founding Prime Minister of modern India, and Mahatma Gandhi, who advised the Congress leaders behind the scenes without holding public office. Under Gandhi's advice, Congress pushed hard for independence but always in a non-violent way. However, other Swaraj factions resorted to terrorist measures.

---

[9]www.gatewayforindia.com has helpful articles on the days of the East India Company and Indian history. For example, see www.gatewayforindia.com/history/british_history1.htm.

The All-India Muslim League had been founded in 1906 and had taken the lead in demanding a separate Muslim state. Jinnah, its leader, was a sophisticated man who had been educated in the West. He was a leader in the Congress Party, but went against its policy when he demanded an independent Pakistan.

Independence and the Partitioning of British India

After the Second World War ended, the new Labor government in Britain decided to grant India its independence in 1947, but the powerful lobby by Jinnah and the Muslim League convinced the British that it was necessary to partition India into a Muslim Pakistan and a secular India. The partitioning set off a terrible period of death and forced migration, as millions of Hindus fled Pakistan into India, and many Muslims of nearby regions fled India.

Pakistan and Bangladesh
Pakistan consisted of East Pakistan and West Pakistan, one on either side of India, with Jinnah and the Muslim League in power. The two parts of Pakistan had different languages, cultures and economies, but they were regions heavily populated by Muslims and so they became one state. When East Pakistan pushed for independence from West Pakistan, the Indian army assisted it, and it gained independence under the name Bangladesh in 1971. So the India of the Raj days is now three countries: Pakistan, Bangladesh, and India.

Pakistan was set up as a Muslim country, originally under Jinnah's rather secular and Western approach. In more recent decades Pakistan has followed the trend among Muslims toward a more traditional Islamic society, and now has become the home of very Islamist **Madrasahs** (schools) that gave birth to the Taliban of Afghanistan and other Islamist movements. Bangladesh has been a more moderate Muslim country than Pakistan, but recently it has experienced violent terrorist attacks by radical Muslim groups.

Secularism and the Nehru Political Dynasty in India

Upon gaining independence, the Congress Party came to power under Jawaharlal Nehru's leadership. Nehru and Congress favored a secularist government, based upon Gandhi's principle that the state should treat all religions as equally valid (*sarva dharma samabhava*). This became the basis for the style of state secularism in India. Gandhi did not like proselytizing, whether on an individual or state level.

The Congress Party has been led by the Nehru family dynasty since independence. Nehru's daughter, Indira Gandhi, succeeded him as leader of the Congress Party and as Prime Minister. After her assassination, her son Rajiv Gandhi became Prime Minister, and now Sonia Gandhi, Rajiv's Italian-born wife, is the leader of the party. The next generation of this "Nehru Dynasty" is now active in politics as well. Sonia and Rajiv's son Rahul is in the Congress Party, but the children of Rajiv's younger brother are active in the rival **BJP** party (to be discussed below)!

Religion and politics interact on a daily basis in India. The biggest issue remains the longstanding communal strife between Muslims and Hindus, which figures strongly in Nepal and Sri Lanka as well. We will look at only three of the many possible issues arising from the interaction of religion and politics in India. The first concerns the ongoing struggle of the lower castes. The debate about how best to bring about the economic development of India's poor is a worthy one, but our interest here centers on the division within Hinduism between those who want to cling to an ancient social hierarchy system and those reform-minded Hindus who want to end the discrimination.

Our second issue focuses on the rise of what has been called **Hindu Nationalism**, or Hindu fundamentalism. This will require an introducion to a host of organizations and political parties.

The third issue involves the controversy over whether or not a Hindu temple should be built on the spot of an old mosque in the city of Ayodhya. This issue has already set off riots and mass killings, and it threatens to touch off even worse communal strife between Muslims and Hindus in the future.

ISSUE 1: DALIT RIGHTS VS. THE HINDU UPPER CLASSES

Along the ghats at Varanasi, with the burning ghat just ahead. The smoke from the tower is from the modern crematorium. The smoke nearer the water is from bodies burning on a traditional pyre, which is more expensive due to the cost of fuel.
Photo: Roy Amore

In our hotel in the old section of Varanasi, we have set our alarms to 4:30 a.m. We walk silently through a series of narrow streets, amazed at how many Indians are up at this hour. For us, this 5:00 a.m. walk is a rarity, but it is routine for them.

We squeeze with the throng through a narrow passage and suddenly we stand in awe before one of the world's great tourist sights, the ghats of Varanasi at sunrise. The ghats are a series of wide platforms or "steps" that lead down to the water level. They need several of these platform levels because the water level varies so much during the year. We contract for a boat ride and drift slowly down the Ganges as the timeless life of ancient India greets the new day. People are taking their morning baths here. Prayers are being said there. Vegetable sellers are setting up shop on some of the ghats. And so much else. Then we approach one of the famous burning ghats, the platforms where Hindu corpses are burned before their ashes are scattered in the sacred Ganges. We learn that the man who owns the cremation business is nicknamed "the king of the Dalits," for he is from the former "untouchable" class, now called Dalit, "oppressed ones." Handling corpses is a polluting thing in traditional belief, so he and his fellow Dalit workers are extremely low on the social pecking order. On the other hand, he is the owner of a thriving funeral business, and has therefore earned the "king" moniker. We tip the boatmen and head back through the crowded streets for breakfast, having seen more incredible things before 8:00 a.m. than most tourists do all day.

How the Hindu Class, Caste and Purity System Discriminates against the Dalits

The **Dalits** ("Oppressed Persons") of India have been called by many names. In the early British period they were often called "outcastes" or "untouchables" because the Brahmin and other upper-class Hindus considered it to be **ritually polluting** merely to contact them, or even to have their shadow cross one's body! To understand this ancient belief system that destines a person at birth to a privileged or oppressed social status, we need to review the Hindu concepts of class, caste, and ritual purity.

We will start with term *class* because it is the easiest to understand. Ancient Aryan civilization in India divided the ruling classes into three functional divisions. The term for class (*varna*) originally meant "color," indicating that each class had a symbolic clothing color. The ruling class (Kshatriya or Raja) included soldiers, administrative officials and the royal family. The priestly class (Brahmin) included those families whose male members could, if properly trained, function as priests (compare the tribe of Levi in traditional Israel). The middle class (Vaishya) included the businessmen and others who enjoyed a middle level social status. Persons in those three classes had the privilege of attending the sacred rituals and, for young males, undertaking a sacred initiation ritual in which one was said to be reborn as an adult member of the upper class, Vedic society. Similar to the symbolism of the Christian baptism, the initiate was said to have been reborn. He was now "Twice Born," once from the womb and once ritually from the Vedas. There is a fourth class, the Shudra, consisting of those who are not in the upper three classes. Shudras were considered Hindu, but were not allowed to attend some Hindu rituals or undertake the initiation ritual.

The term *caste* refers to the thousands of traditional occupational groups. The Sanskrit word for caste is *jati*, "birth," meaning your birth grouping. In Indian languages, one would not say "What is your caste?" but "How were you born?" Similar to the guilds of traditional Europe, Indian society was traditionally structured around occupational groups. Members of the same occupation lived in the same quarter of the town. They chose their own leaders, made their own rules for their group and settled internal disputes in their own caste courts. Their children were automatically members of the caste, for life. Importantly, those children could marry only members of that caste, or sometimes closely related castes. The names of the castes reflect the historic occupations, not the modern ones. For example, a family might have moved to the city and become factory workers, but would still be a member of the Toddy Tapper (tree climbers) caste. Even though caste membership is not so important for many contemporary Hindus, it still figures in traditional arranged marriages. Castes have a relatively high or low social ranking in relation to other castes, so traditional Hindus avoid arranging marriages to lower ranked caste members.[10]

Traditionally, each class and each of its many caste subdivisions is situated somewhere on a hierarchy determined by ritual **purity**, an archaic notion found traditionally in many societies. The concept is that humans are relatively pure/impure depending upon such things as their birth status, their contact with foulness or death, and other ritual factors. In this belief system, people may be temporarily impure from such things as contacting blood (including menstruation), touching a corpse, or giving birth (due to blood and fluids). Undergoing the proper ritual will restore one's purity. But in Indian thought, some social groups are always impure, so much so that their attendance at a ritual would render it invalid.

At the top of the purity hierarchy were the Brahmins. Toward the bottom were those groups who were, either by occupation or by social tradition, considered impure. The lowest social levels were considered so impure that to merely touch them brought impurity upon oneself; which explains the outmoded term "untouchable."

Some Dalits come from families that traditionally practiced occupations deemed to be polluting in this ritual purity system. For example, in India and elsewhere in Asia,[11] leather workers were very low on the impure scale, because they touched dead animals and worked with the foul smells involved in the tanning process.[12] Other occupations, such as

---

[10]Although most castes are named after their traditional occupation, other social groups (castes) that tend to intermarry exclusively may be determined by belonging in a particular religious group such as a form of Christianity.

[11]For an example of another country in which a severely low social status was forced upon leather workers, read about the Burakumin in Japan.

[12]In Vikram Seth's novel *A Suitable Boy*, a Hindu girl has to choose between two suitors, a Muslim and a

In the early 1990s I was invited to the Bangalore home of a high ranking official of Karnataka State in southern India. As a Dalit and an Ambedkar Buddhist, he is a zealous political advocate for Dalit and women's rights, as well as environmental laws. He is very proud of just having passed a law that he hopes will cut down on the pollution by diesel trucks and buses in Bangalore.

Our talk turns to the Dalits. He strongly believes that the Dalits must abandon the lowest of jobs they have held in the past to transition into occupations with better pay and higher social status. One of the lowest of the traditional Dalit jobs was to empty the chamber pots of higher class homes. Each morning the Dalit arrives at the home, puts the chamber pot on his head, walks to the dump and returns the empty pot. My host described the debate in parliament over his proposed legislation to prohibit hiring anyone to empty the chamber pot. He described how much resistance there was to the bill from high class parliamentarians, who demanded to know, "If this bill were to pass, how could we empty our chamber pots?" His reply: "Well, one way I know of is to put the pot on your head and walk to the dump." We both had a good laugh, and then he added, "But they were not amused!"

workers at cremations or burials, also were classified very low because they involved handling human corpses. Barbers and washermen are also classed very low. Note that it does not matter whether or not a worker is physically clean. Nor does it matter whether or not they actually work in that occupation. Someone from a leather working family, even generations back, who now works in a clean, modern office building might still be discriminated against in some rural areas today, especially when it comes to arranging a marriage.

The castes thought to be impure were sometimes called "the fifth class," or 'outcaste' because they weren't classified in one of the four social classes. Mahatma Gandhi coined a nicer name for them, *harijan*, "children of God," but that did not gain much acceptance by them. Now, most of them prefer the term *Dalit*, meaning "Oppressed Ones," for it implies the truth—they are regular people who have been oppressed by the Hindu establishment for centuries. Many Dalits have converted to Islam, Buddhism or Christianity to escape the stigma.

Economic Factors for Oppressing the Lower Castes

In the rural areas, there are strong economic reasons for upper class Hindus to stick to the old discrimination practices. Dalits form a pool of cheap laborers. In the 1990s I interviewed Dalit farm workers who were harvesting sugar cane for long hours under an incredibly hot sun. The men were cutting the cane and dropping it by the armfuls on the ground. The women were carrying these heavy armloads of the cane stocks to a finishing area, where other women were cutting the leaves off the cane and arranging it for sale. For their gruelling twelve hour day, the men were getting the equivalent of US $1.20

Hindu who works in the shoe business. In the process, she sees first-hand the foulness of the traditional tanning process.

and the women US $.90 per day, not per hour. I wondered what would happened if they banded together and demanded better wages or working conditions, so I asked the Dalits working in the cane fields if they had considered striking for better pay. "If we did that," they told me, "the landowner would truck in workers from other villages and we would have nothing." Besides, as I found out from other interviews, the landowning class just has too much influence with the police, the courts and other persons in power positions. Complaints by Dalits to the police tend to be ignored. Even worse, reprisals may occur. Lawyers who agree to represent Dalits find that many of their richer clients subsequently refuse to hire them. Some NGOs staffed by both Dalit and non-Dalit lawyers are trying to correct this by providing very inexpensive legal services to Dalits. Fortunately, there are many Hindus who are embarrassed by the traditional religious-based prejudice against the Dalits and some of them contribute money and time to help correct centuries of oppression.

In the traditional village system, the Dalits get no benefits and no pay except on those days when there is work to be done. They were traditionally not allowed to live inside the boundaries of the village, but they could come in during the day to do menial tasks such as empty the night soil from the homes of higher castes, remove dead animals, or routine manual work such as digging or construction. They could not bury their dead in the regular cemeteries, nor could they go into the regular Hindu temples or drink from the regular wells. They were not slaves, but they could not escape the social stigma of being a Dalit by moving to another village.

These are very serious restrictions. For example, India is very prone to dry periods, and during a drought the traditional prohibition against drinking from the regular water sources often has become life threatening. When the Dalits' usual source of water, such as a local stream, dried up, they were forced by extreme thirst to drink water from ruts, ditches or highly infested pools of standing water. This led to outbreaks of diseases, and they traditionally had very little access to medical care. They quite rightly complained that the cattle of the Brahmin landowners had better water to drink than they did.

Their only recourse was to move, but moving a family or group of families a long distance is very problematic for those with little money or other resources. And where can they move? It's not like India has a lot of unclaimed areas open to homesteading. I once interviewed a family living in a small shack near the side of a major road in Mumbai. The man had built it himself from scrap materials and dirt. From the outside it looked crude, but on the inside it looked like a real home. In the traditional style, the floor was packed earth and the cooking was done over an open fire pit. The furnishings consisted of a larger and smaller cooking pot, a pot for boiling water, enough cups and thali (thin metal plates) for the family, and some thin sleeping mats rolled up and stacked along a wall during the day. Everything in the home could have been carried in a single sack or two, and that is just what had happened. Driven from their traditional village over a hundred kilometres away by a chronic lack of drinking water, the family had migrated to the big city. Here they had access to city water by walking four blocks to a water pipe sticking up out of the ground, but they were illegal squatters. To keep the sides of the roads from

Dalits in India march to demand more government positions for their lower ranking Dalit caste. This reflects 'inner reservation' politics among Dalit groups advocating for a bigger slice of the reservation system jobs. Picture taken during a procession insisting on an inner reservation for Arunthathiyar by Aathi Thamilar Peravai at Dharmapuri on 24th August 2008.

Photo: Adhiyamaan, Wikimedia.

being crowded with squatter shacks, the city removed such homes occasionally. The family told me that in the two years they had lived there, the city had bulldozed their house four times. When that happens, the family just grabs their few possessions and stands outside while their house is destroyed. Then, they salvage what they can and rebuild.

Intercaste Dining

Traditionally it was thought by the upper classes that they dare not eat with the lower classes, lest they, too, become ritually polluted. The social norm was that an upper-class person could accept raw food, but not cooked food, from a low caste person. This was a convenient rule for the upper classes because it meant that Dalit workers could harvest the food and bring it to the house, leaving it just outside. The upper-class members of the house could then get the food and prepare the meals. Dalits were not allowed to eat in the same area as the upper-class persons, but leftovers could be given to the Dalits. This applied to drinking water as well. No upper-class person was to accept water from a Dalit. To protest this teaching, Buddhism told a story of the Buddha accepting water at a well from a Chamar women (Chamar, a leather work caste, is considered one of the lowest).

As I have pointed out elsewhere, this story is quite similar in both plot and meaning to the story of Jesus accepting water from a Samaritan women at a well.[13]

The traditional prohibition against intercaste dining continues in some schools in rural districts, along with other forms of discrimination. In 2008 three teachers in a rural village were arrested for alleged acts of discrimination against Dalits.[14] The teachers were accused of forcing the Dalit students to eat in a separate area and of throwing plates of food at them (perhaps to avoid close contact?). Also, when the teachers caned the Dalits, they used a separate cane and then immediately washed their hands, which they did not do after caning the other students. In this village, the old caste pollution rules are obviously dying a slow death. The police are enforcing the policies of the constitution, whereas the teachers are enforcing age-old caste rules.

Reservation System and Politics

How to reform this oppressive system? That was the question asked by reform minded Hindus such as Mahatma Gandhi and Nehru, by organizations such as Ramakrishna Movement, and of course by Dalit leaders themselves. During the Raj, the British response was to outlaw untouchability, to make it unlawful to discriminate against low caste persons. This established a nice legal principle, but did not change social customs. The British also tried a more positive, affirmative action approach. They introduced a "reservation system" involving reserved seats for Dalits in colleges and civil service positions. This meant the British had to define who was eligible for these school entrances, scholarships, and eventual government jobs. So the British drew up a schedule (list) of the low castes qualified for this program. Hence, during the British period, the lower caste people were often called "the scheduled castes" or just SC. There was also a schedule of the Scheduled Tribes or ST. Later, to make the list more complete, another list was added called the "Other Backward Classes" or OBC. So in law, these three groups qualified for school and employment reservations.

After Independence, India set out to write a new constitution. The principal author of that constitution was Dr. B. R. Ambedkar, a Dalit member of Parliament. As a schoolboy, he had experienced plenty of discrimination. Once, when he was asked by the teacher to go to the blackboard, the upper class students rushed there first to remove their lunch tins stacked next to the board. They dare not have an "untouchable" touching the blackboard that was itself touching their lunches![15] Another time, he and his brother were thrown out of a cart after their caste status became known. On that same trip, people refused to give them any water to drink.[16] Offsetting this discrimination, however, was encouragement from a Brahmin teacher, from whom he got the Brahmin name Ambedkar, and money

---

[13]Roy C. Amore, *Two Masters, One Message* (Nashville: Abingdon Press, 1978), 40–41.

[14]*India Together*. 11 January 2008. ⟨http://www.indiatogether.org/2007/aug/edu-caste.htm⟩.

[15]Dhananjay Kerr, *Dr. Ambedkar: Life and Mission*. 3rd Edition. (Bombay: Popular Prqakashan, 1971), 18.

[16]*Ibid.*, 12.

from the local Muslim ruler, so that Ambedkar was able to attend university. Then he earned a doctoral degree in economics in England. Returning to India, he represented Dalits in Parliament. Understandably, the constitution he authored enshrines very progressive principles of equality for all persons regardless of social status or gender.

The 1950 constitution, authored mainly by Dr. Ambedkar, set the reservation levels at 15 percent for scheduled castes and 7.5 percent for scheduled tribes. The reservation system continues to play a role in Indian politics. The 1980 Mandal Report, named after the parliamentarian who headed a government commission charged with reviewing and recommending policies on how to help the oppressed castes and tribes, supported the previous "reservation" system and called for the number of reserved places to be increased. This led to a backlash among upper class Hindus who felt that it took affirmative action too far, making it too difficult for their sons and daughters to gain admissions and civil servant positions.

Playing to the Dalit vote continues to be important in Indian party politics. Even before Independence, Mahatma Gandhi, Nehru and other Congress Party leaders were eager to include the Dalits under the umbrella of Hinduism, which was understandable in party politics but ironic in that traditional Hinduism had done so much to exclude them from temples, rituals and communal events. Congress wanted their support against the drive for a separate Pakistan. Since Independence, politicians of most parties have made promises to uplift the backward classes, but little has been done except for the reservation system.

To gain more direct access to the political process, Dalits have formed political parties. The most important of these is the Bahujan Samaj Party (BSP). The term Bahujan means "majority people." It is meant to suggest that the party represents the majority. The BSP has been strongest in Northern India, especially in Uttar Pradesh, where it held the majority of seats after the 2007 elections but failed to hold its majority in 2012. In the 2014 national elections, the BSP failed to win any seats in the Lok Sabha, the Lower House of Parliament.

In addition to becoming more active politically, there is a growing body of Dalit literature. This literature often describes the economic and social struggles of India's vast underclass, and it sometimes depicts upper class Hindus as the oppressors. Some works have thus become a target of protest from upper class Hindus, who have organized protests and book burnings. For example, the book *One Part Woman* by Perumal Murugan has been the subject of such intense protests that its writer has publicly stated "Perumal Murugan, the writer, is dead. As he is no God, he is not going to resurrect himself.... As an ordinary teacher, he will live as P Murugan."[17]

Not all Dalits wanted to identify with Hinduism, which many saw as the agent of their oppression. Many converted to Islam, and some to Christianity. Dr. Ambedkar also blamed Hinduism for the problem, and he used to say that he was born a Hindu, but would not die a Hindu. After studying Islam and Christianity, he chose to become Bud-

---

[17]www.bbc.com/news/world-asia-india-30808747.

dhist. His reading of Indian history suggested to him that most of the Dalits had been Buddhists before being absorbed in the Hindu-dominated social order. In October 1956 he and his wife were formally converted to Buddhism in Nagpur, right in the heart of Hindu India. Then, the thousands of other Dalits who attended the ceremony converted as well.[18] After 1200 years of absence, he said, Buddhism had returned to India. It was not just a religious conversion; it was a political protest against centuries of publicly sanctioned oppression.

The reservation system is not enough and India political parties are still trying to do more. In 2007 the Congress Party-led ruling coalition proposed a fifteen-point program to bring additional help to the backward classes. **Narendra Modi**, the controversial BJP Chief Minister of Gujarat State at the time, accused the central government of "communal budgeting," and said that his own proposal to help the socially disadvantaged was much better because it was "social budgeting" rather than communal or caste budgeting. He cited the case of the Mushars, a caste with a very low literacy rate. His point seems to be that affirmative action plans should target the poorest of the poor by measures based on poverty indicators such as low education instead of the more broad-sweeping caste identity. Another problem is that some low level castes and tribes that are not currently on the list are agitating to be included in the reservation system. The Gujjars, for example, have mounted large protests in Delhi to demand that they be included on the list of Scheduled Tribes. In June 2008 they brought traffic to a standstill on some major highways in New Delhi. This tells us that Indians of lower social status see value in the policy of setting aside reserved seats.

ISSUE 2: THE RISE OF HINDU NATIONALISM AND THE BJP PARTY

"Shiv Sena has mass, BJP has class—We need each other."

The BJP is a major India political party with roots in, and strong support from pro-Hindu, anti-Muslim factions. To help understand the rise of the BJP party, we need to understand its roots in previous right-wing Hindu organizations such as the RSS and Shiv Sena, as well as the Hindu Nationalist concept of Hindutva.

RSS

The **RSS,** or Rashtriya Svayamsevak Sangha (National Volunteer Association), was founded by Dr. Keshan Hedgewar before Independence. He had been fervently against the British rule even as a schoolboy. There is a story about his refusing to eat sweets handed out at school in honour of the King's birthday, saying that he's not our king! He also refused to attend a fireworks celebrating the king's birthday. With some friends he

---

[18]Kerr, *Dr. Ambedkar,* 500–501.

tried to tunnel into a British fort to replace the Union Jack with an Indian flag. He got expelled from school for yelling out *Vande Mataram*, "Hail to the Motherland," which came from an old patriotic song made up to counter "God Save the Queen." Later, while studying medicine, he was involved with several activities the British considered seditious. Hedgewar started the RSS in 1925 in Nagpur, the same city in which Dr. Ambedkar would later organize the mass conversion of Dalits to Buddhism.

Hedgewar's goal in starting the RSS grew out of his great zeal for Hinduism. One of his ancestors had been appointed "Defender of Dharma" by the famous Hindu thinker Shankara. So, he fell heir to this family tradition of studying the Vedas and defending the faith. His new organization was intended to instil pride and discipline among Hindu boys. It was also intended to be a Hindu counter to the **Muslim League**, an organization that had become quite influential and would later demand the partitioning of India to create a Muslim Pakistan. The RSS started as a school club. The boys met at 5:00 a.m. every Sunday for paramilitary-style drills, exercises, and instruction in Hindu principles, wearing the khaki shirts and shorts that later became their signature uniform. The movement spread to other high schools and then to universities. Like Gandhi and other reformers, Hedgewar was against caste discrimination. He instituted inter-caste dining among the RSS youth, which made it attractive to Dalits as well.

Shri Guruji (M. S. Golwalkar) took over the leadership of the RSS after Hedgewar's death in 1940. Guruji's RSS was adamantly opposed to the partitioning of India and criticized Nehru and the Congress for giving in, however reluctantly, to the demands of their old adversary, the Muslim League and Jinnah. When Independence Day came, RSS members were among the few in India who refused to celebrate, because Pakistan had been allowed to separate. For the same reason Gandhi did not celebrate the Independence he had fought for during the second half of his life.

The RSS never evolved into a political party, but it had great political influence behind the scenes. When Gandhi was assassinated shortly after Independence by the Hindu extremist N. Godse, it was blamed on the RSS by Nehru and some of the other Congress leaders. The RSS was probably not directly involved, but all right wing Hindu groups came under suspicion. The RSS was banned for a while and Guruji was put in jail. The next leader, M. D. Deoras had to take some other difficult policy decisions. When the Mandal Commission Report called for raising the percentage of reserved seats for Scheduled Castes and Tribes, he supported the increase, thereby going against the wishes of many upper-class Hindus. On the other hand, the RSS was very supportive of the drive to build a new Ram temple at Ayodhya, to be discussed as our third issue.

RSS-trained Hindus remain active in Indian intellectual life, promoting nationalist and Hindu causes. They have spearheaded a movement that critics have labelled **Revisionist History**. Through publications, speeches and websites, conservative Hindus have attempted to correct, from their point of view, the textbook version of India history. For example, they do not accept what they label the "**Aryan Invasion**" approach.

This issue itself has an interesting history. Western historians had written about an "Aryan invasion" into northwest India during the second millennium B.C., and this point of view made its way into both Western and Indian textbooks. The name "Aryan" came from the Indian and Iranian branch of this culture, but later Hitler appropriated the term, laying down a propaganda that wrongly turned "Aryan" from a civilization into a race and wrongly made Germany its homeland. The "revisionist" historians zealously refute what they call the "Aryan invasion theory," holding that the Aryans have been in India since long before the alleged invasion and that in fact India may have been the homeland of the Aryans, some of whom migrated westward into Europe.[19] The nationalist historians are fighting an out of date position, for Western scholars now usually describe a slow infusion of Aryan civilization into India rather than an "invasion." Some of the RSS-backed revisionist writings, for which they managed to get government funding, contained passages and interpretations quite inflammatory to Muslims.[20]

The RSS has given rise to several related organizations, all sharing the general goals of right wing Hinduism. This grouping is called the Sangh Parivar, or the Rashriya (Swayamsevak) Sangh Family, or often just The Parivar. The Parivar includes organizations for women, farmers and many others. There is an interesting youth division, spun off from the VHP to be discussed below, named the Bajrang Dal, or Army of Hanuman. Bajrang is one of the names for Hanuman, the famous monkey who helped Ram and Lakshman defeat Ravana and rescue Sita. For this reason, in English the Bajrang Dal is sometimes called the "Monkey Brigade." Individual members of the Monkey Brigade have been involved in killing Christian missionaries, making bombs for terrorism, and committing terrorist acts against Muslims, but the Bajrang Dal leadership denies that it supports such violent acts.

The Bajrang Dal was especially active in support of BJP candidate Narendra Modi, discussed below, during his successful 2014 national election campaign. Its members organized rallies and parades, proudly wearing their swords as they marching in parades.

Shiv Sena

The name **Shiv Sena**, meaning the army of the god Shiva, itself suggests a militant, pro-Hindu party. It was founded in 1966 by **Bal Thackeray**, who drew upon his fame as a cartoonist. At the time, the party's two main platforms reflected his two interrelated concerns. First, he was staunchly anti-communist. Second, he was anti-immigration. The immigrants he was against were coming into his home state of Maharastra from poorer regions to the south and causing poverty and restlessness among the local underemployed working people. The relation between these two issues was that the local unemployed youth were being actively recruited into a growing communist movement. Later, Shiv Sena

---

[19]Michael Witzel has been the leading Western scholar among those challenging the nationalistic Indian historians, pointing out serious flaws in their arguments. See Michael Witzel, "Autochthonous Aryans? The Evidence from Old Indian and Iranian Texts," *Electronic Journal of Vedic Studies*, Vol. 7, Issue 3 (May, 2001).

[20]Aligarh Historians Group, "The RSS Coup in the ICHR: Its First Fruits," *Social Scientist* (vol. 7, no. 11, June, 1979): 59.

broadened its appeal outside its home state by forming coalitions with other right-wing Hindu parties.

Thus, Shiv Sena started as a party supporting local Hindu unemployed youth and evolved into a component of the Hindu political right wing. It does skirt on the edge of militancy, however. "It has been accused of instigating many riots in the state, including the Mumbai riots of the late 1960s, the Bhiwandi riots in 1984 and the Mumbai riots of 1992–1993."[21] In June 2006 Thackery took a public stance against increased Muslim numbers in Parliament, the military, and public service. He called upon Hindus to work together to make sure that additional Muslim representatives did not get elected. He even went so far as to suggest that he and his followers should work together with the Naxalites (Indian Maoists) to defeat Muslim demands.[22] That is, a far-right religious Shiv Sena leader prefers to work with terrorists over Muslims. For a party that started with an anti-communist platform, this takes Islam bashing to a new low, it would seem.

Shiv Sena's success, however limited, is partly because it was able to ride the nationalistic Hindutva tide, to which we now turn.

Hindutva and "Saffronization"

The concept *Hindutva* has been the main policy of the Hindu-based parties. V. D. Sarvakar coined the term in the early 1920s. The grammar of the term is straightforward. It consists of the word *hindu* plus the ending *tva* (-ness). But depending upon what the speaker wants to emphasise, it can mean either "Hindu-ness" or "India-ness," because the root of the terms Hindu and India is the same. So, a Hindutva policy embraced by a government such as the BJP could stand for nationalism and Indian pride. Or it could imply a very pro-Hindu position, sometimes called Hindu fundamentalism by critics. The article "Hindutva—The Great Nationalist Ideology" on the BJP website exploits the ambiguity.[23] It claims that Hindutva just implies Indian nationalism and a secular state with equal treatment of all religions. Yet the article is full of pro-Hindu references and traditions, and it alleges Muslim mistreatment of Hindus from the time of Babar to the 1992 Ayodhya mosque issue (discussed below). Elsewhere on the BJP website, Muslims are blamed for agitating for their own family law, for causing the partitioning of India, and for making other political demands.[24]

One problem for the Hindu defenders of the Hindutva policy is that they write from the conviction that, if only real pride in India could be restored, then the Muslims, Christians, Buddhists, and others would return to Hinduism, as their original religion and the true religion for Indians. This approach naively assumes that because one's ancestors may

---

[21]Syed Firdaus Ashraf, "Know Your Parties," 2004, in rediff.com/election/2004/apr/23espc3.htm.

[22]www.rediff.com/news/2006/jun/20bal.htm

[23]www.bjp.org

[24]www.bjp.org

have converted to Islam in the distant past, whether by force or other reasons, their current descendants will return to the Hindu fold.

Actually, there have been "re-conversions" to Hinduism by groups of Muslims, Buddhists or Christians. The Indian term for this is ***ghar wapsi***, "home coming" or "returning home." Hindu Nationalist organizations have arranged for well publicized events in which a group "return home" to Hinduism. The motivation may be more economic that spiritual. For example, in some cases the "conversions" may just be a way for a disadvantaged group to gain ration cards or some other form of government assistance. During the British Raj, Indians who converted to Christianity in order to get steady work or regular food (rice) for their families were sometimes called "rice Christians," but now the economic rewards have shifted to the Hindu side.

To gain votes from Dalit communities, the BJP party has looked for communal stories or festivals that could be reinterpreted in such a way as to bring Dalits into the Hindutva identification camp.[25] This meant that it has become necessary to set aside the traditional practices of upper-class Hindus excluding Dalits from water supplies, temples, and many public places to make Dalits feel that Hinduness is now their true home, or at least feel that voting for a Hindu Nationalist party will gain them some immediate benefits in terms of local development projects, welfare monies, or more self-determination.

In India the color saffron is associated with Hinduism. The main reason is that Hindus who "renounce the world" to become holy men or women normally wear saffron colored robes. The term Saffronization is used, mainly by critics, to characterise the movement to further the Hindutva agenda in public policy. The Saffronization movement is especially relevant in education. In the public education system, Hindu Nationalists promote the use of materials presenting Indian history from their perspective. In the private sector, the RSS-backed organization Vidya Bharati operates over 20,000 formal and informal schools providing education which, according to its website, "has its roots in Hindutva. So it is crystal clear that revival of Hindu Philosophy is the be-all and end-all of our educational Renaissance."[26]

BJP

The **Bharatiya Janata Party** (Indian People's Party) arose in 1980, with leadership heavily drawn from the RSS. Whereas the Shiv Sena organization had strong grass-roots appeal across various social classes and castes, the leadership of the BJP was upper class. And class figures heavily in Indian politics. There was a slogan among their supporters that summed up the relationship between these two organizations: "Shiv Sena has mass, BJP has class—We need each other."[27]

---

[25]Badri Narayan, *Fasinating Hindutva: Saffron Politics and Dalit Mobilisation* (New Delhi: Sage Publications, 2009).

[26]Vidyabharti.net/organization.php

[27]Thomas Blom Hansen and Christophe Jaffrelot, ed.s, *The BJP and the Compulsions of Politics in* India (Oxford, Oxford University Press, 1998), 131.

1998 was a banner year for the coalition of pro-Hindu parties that governed the country. Under a BJP government, India successfully tested nuclear devices. This caused alarm in Pakistan and around the world, but was a source of great pride and patriotism among most Indians. In terms of popular approval, the BJP hit its zenith. With 87 percent approval of the nuclear tests and a surge of India pride, the BJP led government was in a strong position to advocate for its Hindu Nationalist agenda.[28]

Hansen and Jaffrelot state that the BJP has "always oscillated between a militant and a moderate approach to politics."[29] As examples of the militant approach, they call attention to the way the BJP has politically exploited issues arising around Hindu sensitivities such as cow protection and the Ayodhya temple. For the most part, the more militant approach has been left to the RSS and its various subgroups, leaving the BJP at both the federal and state levels to take the more moderate approach. The BJP at all levels has been reluctant to criticize the more militant approach or to take legal action against the acts of violence that have arisen within the arena supported by militant Hindu rhetoric.

The party leadership itself reflected the tension between the Hindu Nationalists and those wanting a moderate position to gain more widespread support. The former Prime Minister A. B. Vajpayee led the moderate camp, while the second-most influential party leader, L. K. Advani, was a strong advocate for a more Hindu Nationalist position.

During the 2007 election in the northwest state of Uttar Pradesh, the National Commission of Minorities issued a strongly-worded statement of concern about controversial media on a CD that the BJP distributed in the state. The Commission found the contents of the CD to present a biased and inflammatory image of Muslims. It felt that the content was offensive to the Muslim community and that the CD was calculated to arouse hatred toward Muslims and to disturb India's social harmony.[30] The national level of the BJP distanced itself from the CD, but did not seem to mind the way it generated interest in the party.

As a counter to the anti-Muslim CD issued by the Uttar Pradesh BJP, the group of social activists called Act Now for Harmony and Democracy issued its own CD titled "*Secular Voices*" on which twenty seven famous India personalities make their pitch for social harmony among India's various communities.

In Gujarat state, Narendra Modi led the BJP to a decisive re-election victory in the 2007 state elections. He received a strong mmandate for a new term as Chief Minister even though the federal-level Congress Party poured extensive resources into the campaign against him. Meanwhile, the national level of the BJP party did not fare well after losing the 2004 elections. As the most successful of the BJP state politicians, one would have expected Modi to be the darling of the national party, but he was not. The implication of his complicity with the pogrom against Muslims after the Godhra train fire, discussed below, was one of the reasons. However, by the 2014 national elections, Modi was the national leader of the

---

[28]Seshia, "Divide and Rule in Indian Party Politics, 1048.

[29]Hansen, and Jaffrelot, *The BJP*, 1.

[30]www.rediff.com/news/2007/apr/11uppoll5.htm

BJP party despite the way his controversial past left many Muslims fearful of their fate under a Modi-led national government.

Modi had received about 40 percent of the Muslim vote in the latest Gujarat elections, and in the 2014 national elections he led the BJP to an overwhelming victory, winning 282 seats while the Indian National Congress took only 44. Narendra Modi is now Prime Minister of India. Many Muslims voted for him, despite his controversial past, because they thought they would do better under his leadership, based on his economic record as leader of Gujarat state.

ISSUE 3: THE BABRI MOSQUE CONTROVERSY AND MUSLIM-HINDU VIOLENCE

Since Independence, serious outbreaks of violence have flared up periodically in India, especially in the North and in areas with large populations of both Hindus and Muslims. Gujarat State, Mumbai and Kolkata have been hot spots. In more recent years, most of the violence has been inflicted by Hindu mobs against Muslims, perhaps because their majority status gives them the upper hand. Yet there have been prolonged periods of peaceful coexistence.

The Babri Mosque was a hot political issue in the late 1980s, and it figured strongly in the 1989 elections. The issue helped the BJP stir up support among conservative Hindus, but some critics accuse the Congress Party of playing to the Hindu sentiments as well.[31] The most recent flare-up started in 1992. Surprisingly, it was touched off by a new Ramayana Epic TV series. The Ramayana (Ram Story) tells the epic saga of an ancient Prince named Ram (or Rama) from the city Ayodhya. He is forced into exile, accompanied by his faithful wife Sita and his insightful brother Lakshman. After Sita is abducted by Ravana, the demon king of Sri Lanka, Ram and Lakshman set out to rescue her with the help of a magical monkey named Hanuman. They succeed and Ram returns to Ayodhya and rules as a just king. Ram and Sita represent the ideal man and woman in Hinduism. Ram came to be revered as a god, as one of the ten major avatars (incarnations) of the god Vishnu. As his birthplace and home, Ayodhya became a holy city. A large percentage of Hindus watched the Ramayana TV series, and it sparked interest in Ayodhya and especially in the site of the Babri Mosque or **Masjid**—India uses the Arabic term *masjid*.

VHP

The conservative Hindu organization known as VHP is an important actor in the interface of religion and politics surrounding the Babri Mosque controversy. Its full name has several variations. It is usually given as **Vishva** (or Vishwa) **Hindu Parishad**, but in English **World Hindu Council** (or Conference) is also used. It was started in 1964 by conservative

---

[31]Asghar Al Engineer, *Babri-Masjid Ramjanambhoomi Controversy* (Delhi: Ajanta Publications, 1990), 1.

In the summer of 1992 I led a group of students on a study tour of small–scale development projects in India. All summer long, tensions were building over the Hindu plan to build a temple on the spot of the Babri Mosque. Almost every day, the front page stories in every newspaper involved coverage of the gathering of Hindu work parties in Ayodhya, a traditional regional capital in north central India. When we arrived in Mumbai the "communal strife" between Muslims and Hindus was running high. The Muslims were concerned about repeated calls by the right wing organizations for the destruction of the Babri Mosque in Ayodhya and the building of a Ram temple in its place. The police were concerned over the likelihood of riots, and the atmosphere was further charged because the Muslims were celebrating the Ashura festival, involving groups of Muslims moving through the streets to the main river. And Hindus returning from a pilgrimage to Ayodhya were stirring up right wing Hindu sentiment. The city went under a limited curfew. We took a day trip out of the city to the Ashram where Mahatma Gandhi had lived. There in a peaceful setting beside the river we listened to the guide talk about Gandhi's notion of Satyagraha, the power of truth, and how truth and justice will eventually win out over hatred and violence. We read what Gandhi had written about the need for people of all religions to practice tolerance and live in peace. Why oh why, I wondered, do people turn their backs on the wisdom of their religious sages and listen to religious demagogues?

Hindus who wanted to protect and defend Hinduism within India and to unite Hindus worldwide. The spiritual leader and President was a swami, a Hindu holy man, and the first General Secretary, S. S. Apte, had an RSS background. It invited the Dalai Lama as well as Sikh and Jain leaders to its first conference in 1966, and stressed the idea that all of the religions of Indian origin should work together. Through the 1970s the VHP remained low profile and was not extremist, although some of its members engaged in bashing Muslims, Christians and communists.[32] Apte in particular took a stance against Christianity, Islam and communism as three "religions," each with the goal of taking over the entire world. He was suspicious of the values of modernity and socialism he saw in Nehru's policies. The perceived threat by Christianity within India had two forms. There was the aggressiveness of evangelical missionaries and the movement among the tribal Naga people of Assam for more independence. Many of them had been converted to Christianity, and the VHP saw that as a treat to Indian cultural and political unity. The VHP goal was an "Undivided India."

To its credit the VHP had sided with reform Hindus and denounced the abuses of the caste system. It was socially active on this, setting up clinics and other services to help the Dalits. It even supported the policy of raising the reservation percentages for the Dalits and other backward groups. However, when increasing numbers of the Dalits were converting to Christianity, the VHP lobbied the government to exclude Dalits from the reservation system if they had converted to Christianity. This position made sense to them because they were trying to stop the weakening of India/Hindu cultural values through increased conversion to non-Indian religions, but as a public policy it seems wrong to say

---

[32]Manjari Katju, "The Early Vishva Hindu Parishad: 1964 to 1983", *Social Scientist*, vol. 26, No. 5/6 (May-Jun., 1998): 34.

that a person who was qualified for affirmative action last year is no longer eligible due to having changed religions. The reservation system was supposed to have been about uplifting the economically disadvantaged classes, not about religious identity. Underlying all this is the fact that many of the lower classes in India have turned to Islam, Christianity or Buddhism to escape the social stigma the Hindubacked caste system imposed upon them.

The VHP had other projects. One was that of **cow protection**, which had been important to them from their start. Cow protection includes more than just a ban on hurting or killing cattle. To Hindus the special status afforded to cows is a symbol of all that is good about Hinduism. However, allowing cows to wander about at will and to take naps on highways, causing traffic congestion, goes against the tide of modernization. Multinational food chains, most of them originally featuring a beef menu, are among the targets of conservative Hindu protests. The McDonald's chain in India has to inform the Indian public that it does not serve beef (for the Hindus) or pork (for the Muslims). McDonald's also has to avoid using beef flavoring in the french fries. In the United States, a Hindu sued McDonald's after learning that although McDonald's had announced a policy of switching to vegetable oil for cooking its fries, it allegedly seasoned the fries with beef flavoring before cooking.[33]

The building of a Ram temple in Ayodhya was another issue of longstanding importance to the VHP. They had tried to purchase the out-of-service Babri Masjid and had taken the matter to court. Building on the Ramayana TV series, conservative Hindu organizations such as the VHP demanded that the Babri Masjid give way for the building of a temple in honor of Ram's birth. An archaeological report suggesting evidence of an older, larger temple foundation was published in one of the conservative Hindu magazines in 1990, further stirring up Hindu militancy on the issue.[34]

Controversial History of the Ramkot Site

To better understand the Babri Masjid controversy, we travel north to Ayodhya, the city in the state of Uttar Pradesh associated with the birth and kingship of the god Ram. We watch episodes of the Ram Lila, the story of Ram, being enacted on a stage by actors and musicians engage in in Kathak-style traditional dance. The audience consists of both foreign tourists and Hindu pilgrims. The next day we tour the town and note the many active mosques as well as the many groups of Hindu karsevaks (pilgrim "workers"). We climb the 76 steps of the impressive Hanuman Garhi, the old fort with a temple dedicated to the monkey god Hanuman. This honors the monkey who helped Ram get Sita back from her captivity in Sri Lanka. Finally, we visit Ramkot, the hill on which Ram is said to have been born.

---

[33]www.all-creatures.org/aip/nl-23may2001-fries.html.

[34]For a book length statement of the VHP point of view see *History versus Casuistry: Evidence of The Framajanmabhoomi Mandir presented by the Vishva Hindu Parishad to the Government of India in December-January 1990-91* (New Delhi: Voice of India, 1991).

> *We see that the Hindus have not been allowed to build a new Ram temple here, nor have the Muslims been allowed to rebuild the Babri Mosque. However, Hindus are holding a puja (worship service) on the site.*

Hindus and Muslims are locked in a bitter controversy over whether Hindus will get to build a temple or Muslims will get to rebuild a mosque on a certain hill in the city of Ayodhya. To understand the reasons why this has become such a politically charged issue, we need to review its complex and disputed background.

Hindus, led by the VHP, use the name Ram's Birthplace (Ramjanamabhoomi) for the temple they want to build. Their claim is that the Babri Mosque, meaning the Mosque of Mughal Emperor Babar that stood on the site until its destruction in 1992, was built over a previous Ram temple on the same site. Hindus also hold that the builders of the mosque tore down the existing Ram temple to make room for the mosque, which was completed in 1527. The site itself is a hilltop called Ram Fort (*Ramkot*) by Hindus. Some critics have questioned the historical existence of Ram, but most Hindus do not. Some go even farther and think they know historical details about Ram, such as the fact that he was born on Ramkot. Indians take their astrology very seriously, and some have used a method they call archaeoastronomy to determine the dates associated with Ram, and at the same time confirm that he was a real person. It starts by reading the traditional epics looking for references to the position of the planets in relation to the constellations mentioned there. It then uses planetarium software to ascertain the year in which such an astral pattern occurred. This approach, according to one of its proponents, has determined that Ram was born in 5114 B.C. and that his defeat of Ravana occurred when he was 39 years old.[35] Many scholars do not accept such an old date, however.

The Muslim side of the controversy is led by the **All-India Babri Masjid Action Committee**. It argues that there is no proof that there was a Ram temple torn down to make room for the Babri Masjid, and therefore the mosque should be restored.[36]

The controversy therefore plays out this way. The Muslim faction objects to the idea of replacing the Babri Mosque on the grounds that religious sites are protected by law. The Hindu faction claims that the Ram temple was unjustly torn down under Babar and it is only fair that this injustice to rectified.

Here is what is known of the controversial history of the site. It is likely true that it was built under the reign of the first Mughal ruler, Babar, and was named in his honor. His general, Mir Baqi, was in charge. The mosque had three domes, which may have been added later. It was situated on Ramkot, with an adjoining well whose water was thought to have medicinal properties. There are historical fragments suggesting that Hindu temples were previously located there, but these are disputed by the Muslim faction.[37] The evi-

---

[35]www.rediff.com/news/2007/nov/20inter.htm

[36]http://sify.com/news/othernews/fullstory.php?id=13237310

[37]For an example of an argument for the Hindu position drawn in large part from Muslim sources, see

The three domes of the Babri Mosque, as seen before their destruction in 1992.
Photo: "Babri Mosque 7" by Original Uploader - w:ar:File:بابری Babri Mosque 7.jpg. Licensed under Public Domain via Wikimedia Commons - http://commons.wikimedia.org/wiki/File:Babri_Mosque_7.jpg#mediaviewer/File:Babri_Mosque_7.jpg

dence that there was a temple specifically dedicated to Ram is far less certain, although most Hindus now hold firmly to that belief.

There is some evidence that both Hindus and Muslims used to worship at the site in the 1800s or even earlier. In the late 1800s some Hindus tried unsuccessfully to get permission to build a small Hindu temple there. During the later days of the Raj there were repeated conflicts at the site between Muslims praying in the mosque and Hindus coming to pray at a small Ram shrine nearby. A British official tried to solve the problem by having a fence erected to separate the two groups, but stone throwing and other problems led him to a more radical solution. He closed down the mosque. Locked and out of service, the mosque slowly deteriorated from lack of maintenance.

Giving in to pressures from conservative Hindus, the government permitted the area to be unlocked in 1986, to allow Hindus to enter the area near the mosque to worship. The mosque itself remained out of service. Abdullah Bukhari, the Imam of the historic Jama Masjid in Delhi, led a protest against allowing Hindus to enter the area. By 1989 a ceremonial laying of a foundation stone for the new Ram temple took place with approval of the Congress government, under Rajiv Gandhi. Hindus were given to expect that the full temple would soon be built. Muslim protests became more intense. With the VHP agitating on one side and the Imam on the other, a long-abandoned mosque emerged as the line in the sand drawn between zealous Muslims and zealous Hindus. The BJP gov-

---

Harsh Narain, *The Ayodhya Temple-Mosque Dispute: Focus on Muslim Sources* (Delhi: Penman Publishers, 1993).

ernment of Uttar Pradesh and the Congress Party government in the capital, New Delhi, were unable to find a compromise solution. Hindus offered to raise the money privately to buy the mosque, but Muslims would not consider that. They might have before it became so symbolic, but not afterward.

In the summer of 1992, as thousands of Hindus made a pilgrimage to Ayodhya as *karsevaks*, persons offering work-service to god, another archaeological report appeared alleging to have found evidence of a medieval Hindu temple on the spot. Subsequent archaeological evidence has found occupation on the site reaching back at least 3000 years, with evidence of temple objects of various periods. One inscription appears to refer to Ram, but under the name of Vishnu. There was some possible evidence of Muslim presence at the site before the Babar period as well. During that summer Prime Minister Rao called upon the karsevaks to cease their preliminary construction plans, as per court order. The Hindu leaders vowed to ignore the court order and the pressure from the central government. Meanwhile, the local BJP-led state government of Uttar Pradesh, being sympathetic to the cause, refused to intervene by force. The state government expected the central government to declare a state of emergency in Uttar Pradesh and set up a system of governance run from the New Delhi—as allowed for in the Indian constitution. But Prime Minister Rao did not do so.

By the fall of 1992, whole trainloads of karsevaks had gone to Ayodhya, spending as much time there as they could afford, and had returned home to spread the word about the need to build the Ram temple and recruit even more volunteers. The crowd of karsevaks was getting larger and more impatient by the day. The government ordered the area closed, and police were stationed around the perimeter. The conservative Hindu organizations were getting frustrated. They had issued a series of ultimatums, giving dates by which they were going to start construction with or without official permission. The deadlines had come and gone with nothing happening.

Then on December 6, 1992, a few *karsevaks* broke through the police lines. Two climbed on the roof and began to tear off tiles. Most *karsevaks* gathered there cheered wildly, and many more soon stormed through the police lines. Before long the three domes were gone and the Babri Mosque was in ruins.

There was massive celebration across the nation by many Hindus and massive protest by many Muslims. More moderate spokespersons from both communities feared the worst and called for calm. It did not help. The worst outbreak of riots, violence, and reprisals since the Partition followed. Thousands were killed or seriously hurt. Houses and shops were burned. Stores were looted. Old communal wounds were opened. Muslims blamed both the state and national governments for complicity in the event, either by not doing enough to secure the mosque, or by secretly wanting it to be destroyed. The controversy was made worse by party politics. Ayodhya is in Uttar Pradesh state, whose government was formed by the BJP under the leadership of Chief Minister Kalyan Singh, whereas the central government in New Delhi was formed by a Congress Party-led coalition. Before long, even a former Prime Minister called for both Prime Minister P. V. Narasimha Rao and Kalyan Singh to be put on trial for criminal negligence, or a more severe charge. It was subsequently revealed at a public hearing and other forums that the same former Prime Minister and at least one state Chief Minister had warned Prime Minister Rao about the situation in the weeks before the December 6th incident. There were accusations that a deal had been brokered in which Rao agreed to not send in troops to protect the mosque. His critics said that Rao should have known that the right wing pro-Hindu BJP government of Uttar Pradesh was not adequately protecting the mosque. Therefore, he should have dismissed the state government and ruled the State from New Delhi, bringing in sufficient troops to protect the mosque.

Having not dismissed the Uttar Pradesh government in advance of its failure to protect the mosque, Prime Minister Rao went to the other extreme in the aftermath of the riots. He dismissed not only the Uttar Pradesh government but also the other three state governments under BJP control. He also banned the most radical of the Hindu and Muslim organizations held responsible for fanning the flames of communal hatred and violence. The banned groups include the RSS.

Later Rao wrote a book entitled *Ayodhya: 6 December 1992*, published after his death at his request, on the central government's role during the time of the destruction of the mosque.[38] One of his stated reasons for not acting was that the issue was before the courts, but critics have pointed that that the court order did not restrict federal intervention.

One karsevak who participated in the destruction of the mosque later wrote an article for a paper saying that the BJP and other leaders on the platform had instigated the destruction by stirring up the crowd. He explains that he supported it at the time, but later regretted it after seeing how much violence and religious hatred was unleashed. His concluding admonition is that people should be devout, but without falling under the sway of religious extremism. [39]

The VHP and RSS continue to press for the building of the Ram temple. For example, in 2006 the International President of the VHP fanned the flames of communal discontent when he said that it was one of the greatest insults possible to Hindus worldwide that the Ram temple was not being constructed.[40] And the BJP continues to give them political support. The temple has not been built, nor has the mosque been restored. The interplay of religion and politics has India between the proverbial rock and a hard place.

Various parties to the controversy have appealed to courts in an effort to gain the legal right to rebuild the mosque or the temple. The Allahabad High Court issued a surprising ruling in 2010 that angered all parties. The three judges accepted the archaeological evidence that a Hindu temple existed on the site previously, but avoided saying whether Babar's general had torn down a temple to build the mosque. The court ruled that the area near the former Babri Mosque should be divided among three parties. A Sunni Muslim group was given ownership of a plot of land near the former mosque site, and two other

[38]P. V. Narasimha Rao, *Ayodhya: 6 December 1992*. (New Delhi: Penquin/Viking, 2006).

[39]www.sacw.net/new/rajwade092003.html

[40]www.rediff.com/news/2006/sep/13ram.htm

sites were given to Hindu organizations. The judges foresaw a future in which the Ramkot hill would host both a mosque and a Ram temple. Many groups initiated appeals to the High Court's decision, and the Court itself stayed its own ruling indefinitely. In 2011 the Indian Supreme Court issued a ruling that stayed the Allahabad's ruling, but did not make any replacement ruling. The status quo remains.

The Godhra Train Incident, Indian Pogroms, and Narendra Modi

As we have seen, the destruction of the Babri Mosque in 1992 did not end the controversy. Hindu karsevaks organized mainly by the VHP continued to stream back and forth to the site by bus, train, and car. In 2003, almost ten years after the destruction of the mosque, a train carrying karsevaks and others caught fire in the town of **Godhra** in Gujarat state, leading to the death of 59 passengers. Many Hindus believed the initial rumors about Muslims at Godhra throwing lighted torches into the train cars while blocking the doors. This set off massive violence against Muslims in many Gujarat cities and towns. Thousands of Muslims were killed by gangs of Hindu thugs who burned Muslim shops and homes.

We see here an example of how people inclined to religious hatred will take vengeance on any member of a religious community, even if they know for sure that their victim had nothing to do with the offense. In this case, Hindu ruffians killed Muslims in Mumbai in reaction to the (false) belief that a few Muslims in the distant town of Godhra had killed Hindus. A subsequent investigation has concluded that the fire did not start from external sources or anything thrown into the train. It was not caused by Muslims.

The Gujarat police did little to stop the mob violence. There have been repeated accusations of police involvement, either as organizers or as participants in civilian clothes. Then there are accusations that the BJP government may have sanctioned the violence. In her book *War Talk* Indian author and essayist Arundhati Roy has denounced the violence as a government sponsored "pogrom," thus comparing the Hindu attacks on Muslims with Russian attacks (pogroms) on Jews in the early 1900s.[41] Elsewhere she writes, "Within hours of the Godhra outrage, the Vishwa Hindu Parishad (VHP) and the Bajrang Dal put into motion a meticulously planned pogrom against the Muslim community."[42]

Roy puts the blame on a Hindu culture of hatred. "Hundreds of RSS shakhas and Saraswati Shishu mandirs across the country have been indoctrinating thousands of children and young people, stunting their minds with religious hatred and falsified history. They're no different from, and no less dangerous than, the *madrassas* all over Pakistan and Afghanistan which spawned the Taliban."[43] Agnivesh and Thampu write, "It could o down in history as an instance of state-permitted terrorism, a great deal worse than

---

[41] Arundhati Roy, "Democracy," *War Talk* (Cambridge, MA: South End Press, 2003).

[42] Arundhati Roy, "Democracy: Who's She When She's at Home?," in *Harvest of Hate: Gujarat Under Siege* ed.s Swami Agnivesh and Valson Thampu (New Delhi: Rupa and Co., 2002), 114.

[43] *Ibid*, 120–121.

'cross-border terrorism' as it turns innocent citizens into enemies and refugees in their own homeland."[44]

One expert in Hindu Nationalism, C. Jaffrelot, notes that besides the usual explanations for Hindu-Muslim tensions, two political factors are at work. One is a militant ethno-religious ideology, the Hindutva movement. The other is the way that the Hindu Nationalist-based political parties have used the communal tensions for votes. But the 2002 pogrom in Gujarat was an extreme event. "This time, Hindu-Muslim violence was not so much a reflection of the routinized logic of communal riots in India, but rather the result of an organized pogrom with the approval of the state apparatus of Gujarat acting not only with the electoral agenda in mind, but also in view of a true ethnic cleansing."[45]

Prime Minister Narendra Modi
Photo: Wikipedia Commons

The Chief Minister of Gujarat state at the time was Narendra Modi, who later became Prime Minister after leading the BJP to victory in 2014 despite his controversial role following the Godhra train fire. His career reveals the way the various Hindu groups intertwine. Modi started out as a leader in the RSS, but was recruited to work in the BJP. He served as General Secretary in other states before taking over as Chief Minister of Gujarat. Like other BJP state leaders, and like the national policies during the years when the BJP led a majority coalition, his policies are pro-Hindu and pro-development. His economic successes are enviable. During 2006–2007 for example, the growth rate for India as a whole was an impressive 8 percent, but Gujarat State led the way with a 12 percent growth rate.

Modi's economic successes have made him somewhat immune from the charges that under his leadership, public officials and police may have played a significant role in encouraging or at least allowing Hindu mobs to harass or kill Gujarati Muslims. However, in mid-2007 the federal level Supreme Court of India became quite active in the case, demanding that the Gujarat Government give an accounting of a 2005 incident in which a Muslim couple was taken from a bus allegedly by police and killed.[46] As A. Roy points, so far no one has been held accountable in Gujarat for the killing of approximately 1000

---

[44]Swami Agnivesh and Valson Thampu, ed.s, *Harvest of Hate: Gujarat Under Siege* (New Delhi: Rupa and Co., 2002), 9.

[45]C. Jaffrelot. "The 2002 Pogrom in Gujarat: The Post 9/11 face of Hindu Nationalist anti-Muslim Violence." In John R. Hinnells and Richard King. Ed.s. 2007. *Religion and Violence in South Asia: Theory and Practice.* London: Routledge. 174.

[46]BBC News, http://news.bbc.co.uk/2/hi/southasia/7141662.stm.

Muslims in the aftermath of the Godhra train incident, but now the India Supreme Court may force a more active and in-depth investigation.

Overview and Theoretical Discussion

The first issue concerned the struggle of India's Dalits for the equality enshrined in the Indian constitution and legislative acts but not yet realized in Indian society, especially in the rural areas. Starting with the British Raj, efforts were made to uplift the backward classes, as they put it at the time. After Independence, progressive-minded Hindus, Buddhists and others have shaped the constitution and the laws in ways supportive of social equality and have instituted a strong affirmative action policies in government sectors. Yet real progress has been slow.

Because Dalits are over 50 percent of the population in many areas, they have great potential for asserting their interests in a democratic state, but first they need to find ways to make their votes count more effectively. The current emphasis on reserved places helps the relatively few Dalits who go on to university and who seek civil service appointments, but the majority of Dalits remain day laborers and are largely unaffected by this government initiative.

The Dalit issue shows the way in which religion can work on both sides on an issue. On the one side, traditionalist Hindus hold on to a system that ranks social groups in a hierarchy based upon religious tradition and an archaic notion of pollution that is hard for most modern people to understand. There are both social and economic motivations for sticking to the caste system. The social ones are that almost everyone is able to take pride in being ranked above some others. Even among the Dalit groups there are those who have traditionally felt they were better than other castes. The economic reasons are that it is advantageous to landowners and other employers to have a large pool of cheap laborers eager to work under almost any circumstances. Also, it means that the lowest caste workers were not able to complete for middle level positions. In the minds of its supporters, the caste system has the sanction of the Hindu dharma anchored in the revealed wisdom of the ancient Seers, the Indian parallel to the prophets of Middle Eastern religions.

On the other side, for over two thousand years the Buddha and other social reformers have denounced caste discrimination and the elite who benefited from it. In the modern era, Mahatma Gandhi, Ramakrishnan and many other Hindu leaders took up the cause of equality for the Dalits. The British outlawed caste discrimination, and after Independence the Dalit parliamentarian Dr. Ambedkar authored a constitution enshrining the values of social equality.

The most controversial issue in Indian politics concerning the Dalits is the reservation system. Is it really working? Should the quotas be increased? How can India help the Dalits without touching off an upper-class Hindu backlash? Some Hindus resent the way that Dalits have converted to Islam, Buddhism, or Christianity in large numbers, yet how can one blame people for leaving a religion that has traditionally excluded them from its temples and major rituals, from wells and meeting halls, and from advancing into better paying positions?

The second issue dealt with the political implications of the rise of Hindu Nationalism and its Hindutva policy. Hindu youth organizations such as the Shiv Sena and right wing Hindu organizations such as the RSS, VHP and other groups of The Parivar have lobbied and agitated for Hindu causes such as cow protection and a prohibition on serving beef. They have also been very critical of past Muslim suppression of Hinduism and more recent legislation giving concessions to Muslims. The most successful political party advocating the goals of the Hindu Nationalists is the BJP, which currently heads the national and several of the state governments.

As seen in our third issue, the conservative Hindus also want to go back to the pre-Mughal days when there was, in their view, a temple to Ram standing where the ruins of the Babri Masjid now lay. The VHP, having evolved from a movement hoping to promote Hindu values and unite diaspora Hindus into a militant movement, has led the drive to build the Ram temple in Ayodhya. Violence has broken out on a number of occasions. One was fuelled by Muslim anger at the destruction of the old mosque in 1992. Ten years later, the violence was led by Hindu mobs in Gujarat in retaliation for the perceived but wrong notion that Muslims had caused a train fire in Godhra. The BJP government of Gujarat was implicated in the mob violence, but it still won the 2007 elections and its leader rose to lead the BJP to victory nationally, and is now Prime Minister.

Theoretical Discussion

Nehru's Secular State vs. Communalism in Party Politics
Underlying most of these issues is a struggle between two models of statecraft. There is the secular model stemming from the Enlightenment and championed in India by Jawaharlal Nehru. It tries to keep politics and policy apart from religious convictions, laws and customs. The other model wants to base public policy and laws on religious tradition, and in the case of India this model is held by two bitter rivals: the Hindu Nationalists as represented by The Parivar and the Islamists as represented by the All-India Babri Masjid Action Committee.

Some critics have pointed out that by embracing Hindutva and its implied Hindu supremacy, the BJP is compromising the secularism built into the Indian constitution under the influence of Gandhi's principal of treating all religions the same. One such critic of Hindutva is happy that the constitutional review set up when the BJP first came to power nationally in 1998 did not compromise secularism (as he assumes the BJP wished) but rather "debated and settled the issue of equality of all citizens before the law irrespective of their faith, and affirmed the principle of equal, non-discriminatory treatment of all religions by the state (Sarva Dharma Samabhava) as a minimalistic definition of secularism."[47]

---

[47]Praful Bidwai, " 'Sarva Dharma Samabhava' forgotten" (The Free Press Journal, Dec. 24, 2014), http://freepressjournal.in/sarva-dharma-samabhava-forgotten/.

Ramesh Thakur has made an interesting case for the erosion of secularism in Indian politics since Independence. His line of reasoning starts with the observation that the secularism laid down by Nehru and spelled out in the constitution envisioned a state that protected religious freedoms but did not grant exceptions to the law based on religious identity. He believes the trouble started with the introduction of the Government of India Act of 1935, during the latter days of the Raj, because it led to the formation of parties and voter blocs along religious lines.

Nehru was able to maintain secularism, but it began to erode in the era after Nehru, as political parties found it expedient to pander to religious groups to gain votes. This included his own Congress party under the leadership of his daughter, Indira Gandhi, and his grandson, Rajiv Gandhi. Continuing this line of argumentation, Thakur suggests strongly that the concessions made to religious minorities, especially the Muslim minority, have led to problems in the long run for both Muslims and non-Muslims. It started with legislation giving exceptions to Muslims in the area of family law. Most importantly, allowing Muslim men (but not Hindu, Christian or other men) to marry up to four wives, in accordance with Islamic law. Then the Hindu Succession Law of 1956 liberalized the rights of property inheritance for women, but Muslim inheritance was to be governed by Islamic laws, giving women a lesser amount. Thakur feels that in granting these exemptions to Muslims, India severely compromised its secularism approach.[48]

The case of Shah Bano, Thakur continues, should have been dealt with as one of an individual's needs before a secular law, but instead became a cause for Islamist demands. Shah Bano was a destitute elderly Muslim woman who went to court in an effort to get some support from her former husband, who had divorced her. The secular courts tended to look favorably on her case, but an Islamic faction turned the case into an excuse to demand that Islamic law cover Muslim cases. Parliament gave in to the demands and passed the Muslim Women (Protection of Rights on Divorce) Act in 1986. Thakur laments that rights guaranteed to Shah Bano under the constitution were taken away by this Act. India had moved another step toward a two-law state. An Islamic law of sorts for Muslims and a secular law for all others.[49]

But how did this series of concessions by a Congress Party-led government adversely affect Muslims in India, as Thakur's claims? His answer is that the departure from India's secularism and the concessions to Muslims set off a backlash among conservative Hindus. The BJP party was able to exploit this backlash and rise to power, at first in several of the states of the **Hindi Belt**. The term *Hindi Belt* refers to the states of northern India where Hindi is the main language. They tend to be overpopulated and economically backward. They are also the region where the right wing Hindu parties do especially well. Besides holding power at the state level, the BJP has led coalitions that governed at the Center

[48]Ramesh Thakur, "Ayodhya and the Politics of India's Secularism: A Double-Standards Discourse", *Asian Survey* (1993: 33, 7): 649–650.

[49]*Ibid.*

(national level) based on its strength in the Hindi Belt combined with dissatisfaction with Congress over alleged corruption.

Some Muslims worried that the conservative Islamic effort had focused exclusively on demands for separate treatment in the area of family law, whereas little attention had been given to the pressing economic needs of the many poor Muslims. Some Muslims asked, had the Islamist faction just gained concessions that will keep the Muslim community economically backward?[50]

Is the interface of religion and politics in India an example of Huntington's *Clash of Civilizations* thesis? There certainly has been a clash of some sort. Thousands have been killed in Muslim-Hindu riots, protests and, to use Arundhati Roy's phrase, pogroms. But is this a clash between the Islamic civilization and the Hindu civilization, or is it just a good old fashioned struggle for land and

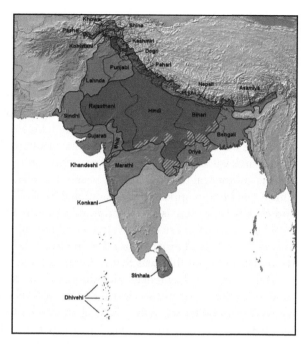

Map of the so-called Hindi Belt, the areas in north-central India where Hindi and closely related dialects are spoken. This is a region of strong support for the BJP party.

Photo: Based on Indoarische Sprachen Verbreitung.png by BishkekRocks [GFDL (http://www.gnu.org/copyleft/fdl.html) or CC-BY-SA-3.0 (http://creativecommons.org/licenses/by-sa/3.0/)], via Wikimedia Commons

property between two groups who happen to hold different religions that define two great civilizations? Maybe the answer lies in between these two options. Maybe in Indian religion and politics we have a clash between Muslim and Hindu extremists who would not have been able to garner mass support for their causes if it were not for the strong power of social identity that religion can generate. India would not have been partitioned without the power of playing the religion card. The Babri Masjid mess could have been solved with some compromise on the local level if religious extremists on both sides had not been able to rally religious sentiments throughout the country. Huntington's description of how religious identities harden the lines of a conflict is relevant here and in the case of Sri Lanka.

---

[50]Hasan Abdullah, "Muslim Personal Law: Case for an Optional Reform Act," *Statesmen Weekly* (25 January, 1992).

Is Herberg's pendulum effect in India? Is religious identity becoming notably more important here? The answer seems to be yes. The role of religion in Indian politics has increased lately, fanned by the flames of the Babri Masjid and Godhra train events.

Hindu Fundamentalism

All three of our issues involve Hindu conservatism or nationalism. The old social patterns of discrimination against Dalits are being kept alive by conservative Hindus. The traditionalists who maintain caste discrimination may qualify as fundamentalists under Lawrence's theory in that they follow an ideology that rejects modernity. In this case, modernity's values of social equality of opportunity, human dignity, and equality in law are seen as antithetical to thousands of years of Indian social custom as engrained in Hinduism. When Hindus appeal to the traditional book, *The Laws of Manu*, to support their caste and class beliefs, there is also a scriptural literalism at work.

Is it fair to say these conservative Hindu groups are fundamentalist? In his book *The Saffron Wave*, T. B. Hansen argues that the BJP is a Hindu Nationalist party but not a fundamentalist one, on the basis that it doesn't adhere rigidly to doctrine or textual beliefs.[51]

But if we use Lawrence's definition of fundamentalists as those reacting against modernity, the case is not so clear. The Hindu Nationalists embrace modern secularism as a government policy when they fight against concessions to Muslims, but they also exhibit nostalgia for the past that reminds us of religious fundamentalists everywhere.[52] They dream of the days of "greater India," before the loss of Pakistan and Bangladesh. Some even go so far as to wish for India to embrace all the Aryan lands mentioned in the Vedas, which would include parts of Afghanistan. They also want to revert to the days before many Indians turned to non-Hindu religions.

Those Hindus who fervently support the building of a Ram Temple in Ayodhya also have fundamentalist characteristics. They want to turn the clock back to a time before Babar when they believe there was a temple commemorating Ram's birth on a certain hill in Ayodhya. They will not compromise by agreeing to build a temple in a nearby spot. And conversely, neither will the leaders of the Muslim side agree to rebuilt the Babri Mosque on any nearby spot. It recalls Tariq Ali's term "Clash of Fundamentalisms" but in a different context.

The BJP has been hard-pressed to distance itself from the more militant and more fundamentalist VHP organization without alienating the VHP's conservative Hindu supporters. This attempt to embrace a far-right Hindu group has sometimes brought the BJP to the attention of critics who would prefer a national party to avoid association with extremist positions. Sanjay Ruparella writes about the way the party has been pulled in two directions. On the one hand, the BJP's role as a national party and leader of a national coalition has forced it away from its ideology and toward a more moderate set of policies.

---

[51]Thomas Blom Hansen, *The Saffron Wave* (Princeton: Princeton University Press, 1999).

[52]Bruce Lawrence, *Defenders of God: The Fundamentalist Revolt against the Modern Age* (San Francisco: Harper & Row, 1989).

On the other hand, he argues that the BJP, while giving lip service to the more moderate policies, at that same time circumvented those policies in favor of more right-wing actions.[53]

International Relations

To what extent is the interplay of religion and politics in India affecting its relations with other countries? India's most important relation is with Pakistan because of the ongoing dispute over control of the Kashmir region and the nuclear threat the two countries pose to each other. Pakistan has reason to feel threatened by increased political influence by The Parivar. Although Pakistan tested its own nuclear device in 1998, Pakistan is well aware that it was a BJP government that proudly tested a nuclear device and that Hindutva extremists dream of reuniting greater India.

India's relations with China have been adversely impacted by India's continuing to provide a supportive environment for the Dalai Lama and other Tibetan refugees. But China's hold on the Tibetan Autonomous Region is now so secure that it can put that issue behind it. There is an unresolved border dispute in the Himalayan region that has been on the back burner for decades. Prime Minister Singh visited China in 2007 to work on the border and trade issues, but no progress was made on the border. The Hindutva agenda does not pose as much of a threat to China as it does to Pakistan. China is more concerned with accessing resources in support of its growing economy, and as the two countries compete for oil and minerals, their relationship could become more strained.

Relations with the United States have been easier when religion is kept out of Indian politics. The efforts of George W. Bush's policy of giving India nuclear assistance would not have been possible in an atmosphere of nuclear tests. The United States wants to maintain good relations with both India and Pakistan, and so India needs to avoid policies leading to anger and protests among its Muslim population if it wishes to maintain good relations with the West.

Good or Bad?

All things considered, is the interface of religion and politics in India a bad thing or a good thing? Would reforms for the Dalits have come about quicker if the pattern of social discrimination did not have religious sanction? Probably so. Would reforms for the Dalits have come about more slowly without the efforts of Hindu reformers such as Gandhi? Probably so. Would the people of Pakistan and Bangladesh be better off today if religious-based demands had not led to the partitioning of India? A Muslim who finds it important to live under a Muslim government would likely answer differently than a secularist answering in terms of economic development or access to natural resources. Would there have been deaths and destruction surrounding the Babri Masjid without religions getting involved in the political process? Most likely, not.

---

[53]Sanjay Ruparella, "Rethinking Institutional Theories of Political Moderation: The Case of Hindu Nationalism in India, 1996–2004," *Comparative Politics* vol. 38, no. 3, (April 2006): 317–336.

Whether or not India would be better off if religion stayed out of politics and politics stayed out of religion, given India's history and its current ethos, neither of those things is about to happen.

> As we head for the Delhi airport we reflect on our experience that in India, the home of Hinduism, the main religion and politics interfaces have been between Hindus and Muslims. Our next stop is Saudi Arabia, historically the home of Islam and in modern times a kingdom which relies on a very conservative form of Islam for legitimizing support.

STUDY QUESTIONS

1. What was Nehru's view of the ideal relationship between religion and politics?

2. In what ways may party politics have compromised secular democracy in India?

3. How did Dalits become oppressed and what—if any—government policies would improve their social-economic role?

4. What are the political implications arising from Hindu-Muslim tensions in South Asia?

5. What are the goals and organizations associated with the movement known as Hindu Nationalism?

6. What role do religious minorities such as Sikhs, Christians, Buddhists, Jains, and Parsees play in Indian politics?

FURTHER READING

Agnivesh, Swami and Valson Thampu, ed.s, *Harvest of Hate: Gujarat Under Siege.* New Delhi: Rupa and Co., 2002. Social activists discuss the violence of Hindu extremists.

Amore, Roy C. *Two Masters, One Message.* Nashville: Abingdon Press, 1978. Discusses the parallels of the lives and teachings of Buddha and Christ.

Hansen, Thomas Blom and Christophe Jaffrelot, ed.s, *The BJP and the Compulsions of Politics in* India. Oxford, Oxford University Press, 1998. Essays on Hindu Nationalism.

Hansen, Thomas Blom. *The Saffron Wave: Democracy and Hindu Nationalism in Modern India.* Princeton: Princeton University Press, 1999. Scholarship on Hindu Nationalism.

Hasan, Zoya, ed. *Parties and Party Politics in India.* New York: Oxford University Press, 2004. Essays on Indian party politics.

Hasan, Zoya and Ritu Menon. *Unequal Citizens: A Study of Muslim women in India.* New Delhi: Oxford University Press, 2004. An India scholar's view of the role and status of Muslim women.

Kerr, Dhananjay. *Dr. Ambedkar: Life and Mission.* 3rd Edition. Bombay: Popular Prqakashan, 1971. Life of Buddhism most famous modern convert.

Marino, Andy. *Narendra Modi: A Political Biography.* New York: Noida: HarperCollins India, 2015. A balanced treatment of the Indian Prime Minister's political life.

Mitta, Manoj. *The Fiction of Fact Finding: Modi and Godhra.* Noida: HarperCollins India, 2014). Critique of the politics of public inquires.

Narayan, Badri. *Fascinating Hindutva: Saffron Politics and Dalit Mobilisation.* New Delhi: Sage Publications, 2009.

Narayanan, Vasudha. "Hindu Traditions." In *A Concise Introduction to World Religions,* 3rd edition, edited by Willard G. Oxtoby, Roy C. Amore, and Amir Hussain. Toronto: Oxford University Press, 2015.

Narian, Harsh. *The Ayodhya Temple-Mosque Dispute: Focus on Muslim Sources.* Delhi: Penman Publishers, 1993. Argues the Hindu point of view in the dispute, using Muslim sources.

Pai, Sudra. *Dalit Assertion and the Unfinished Democratic Revolution: The Bahujan Samaj Party in Uttar Pradesh.* Delhi: Sage Publications Pvt., 2002. A good account of Dalit political pressure in one Indian state.

Rao, P. V. Narasimha. *Ayodhya: 6 December 1992.* New Delhi: Penguin/Viking, 2006. Description of the Ayodhya events.

Roy, Arundhati. *War Talk.* Cambridge, MA: South End Press, 2003. Essays by an engaging, activist author.

Wilkinson, Steven I. *Votes and Violence: Electoral Competition and Ethnic Riots in India.* New Edition. Cambridge: Cambridge University Press, 2006. A good source on the issues surrounding communal strife.

WEBSITES

www.bjp.org The official site of the BJP Party.

www.dalitnetwork.org A site dedicated to information about Dalits and Dalit rights, with emotionally moving pictures and stories.

www.gatewayforindia.com An Indian news source with links to many topics, including politics and religion.

www.islamonline.net/servlet/Satellite?cc=Article_C&cid=1156077771094&pagename=Zone-English-Muslim_Affairs%2FMAELayout. An article reflecting the Muslim point of view on the destruction of the Babri Mosque.

www.rediff.com/news A good source for coverage of news stories originating in India.

KEY PEOPLE

Dr. B. R. Ambedkar A politician leader of the Dalits who led a mass conversion to Buddhism and authored the Indian constitution.

Mohandas Gandhi A leading advocate for Indian independence, social equality, sustainable development and buying local, and leader in the Congress party.

Indira Gandhi Daughter of Nehru and former Prime Minister of India.

Rajiv Gandhi Son of Indira Gandhi and former Prime Minister.

Dr. Keshan Hedgewar Founder of the RSS, an important Hindu Nationalist group.

Indira Gandhi Daughter of Nehru and former Prime Minister of India.

Daw Aung San Suu Kyi Leader of the main opposition party in Myanmar and recipient of a Nobel Peace prize.

Narendra Modi Leader of the BJP party and the Prime Minister starting in 2014.

Jawaharlal Nehru Congress party leader and first Prime Minister of independent India.

Bal Thackery Founder of the Hindu Nationalist organization, Shiv Sena, 'Shiva's Army'.

Thaksin Shinawatra A popular former Prime Minister of Thailand who now lives in exile due to charges against him in Thailand.

Yingluck Shinawatra The younger sister of Thaksin who is currently Prime Minister of Thailand.

Sulak Sivaraksa Thai social critic and leader of several Buddhist organizations dedicated to sustainable development and social justice.

GLOSSARY

All India Babri Masjid Action Committee The Muslim organization coordinating the effort to rebuild the Babri Mosque and resist the building of a Ram Temple at Ayodhya.

Aryan Invasion The now outmoded theory that Aryan people forcefully overran India over 3000 years ago.

Babri Masjid The mosque, named after Babar, that used to stand on Ramkot.

Bajrang Dal The Hindu Nationalist youth movement named after the monkey god Hanuman, often called the Monkey Brigade in English.

Bharatiya Janata Party or **BJP** A leading conservative party in India, with Hindu Nationalist backing.

Bodu Bala Sena or **BBS** Meaning "Buddhist Power Force" is militant Sinhalese Buddhist organization led by monks who oppose concessions to Muslims and Christian missionizing

Buddhism A religion tracing back to ancient India that values meditation, moderation and enlightenment.

caste A term for the traditional social divisions based mainly on one's birth group in India and Sri Lanka

Dalits The 'oppressed people', the lower social castes in India

Ghar Wapsi "Home coming," a term by Hindus to describe a conversion of Muslims, Christians or Buddhists "back to Hinduism."

Indus Civilization or **Harappan Civilization** The civilization that flourished in parts of Pakistan and India over 4000 years ago. It is referred to by a main river, the Indus, or by a main city now called Harappa.

intercaste dining An occasion where higher and lower caste persons eat together and/or receive food from each other.

Hindu Nationalism A term outsiders use to describe conservative Hindus who wish to restore Hinduism to its traditional role in Indian culture.

Hinduism The traditional and majority religion of India.

Hindutva A term used by Hindu Nationalists meaning both "Indian-ness" or "Hindu-ness."

Jainism A religion tracing back to ancient India that practices ahimsa and values asceticism and enlightenment.

karsevaks Hindus who go on pilgrimages to serve their god.

Madrasah Schools for Islamic studies.

Muslim League The organization of Muslims that advocated for a separate state called Pakistan for Muslims.

National Heritage Party or **JHU** A Buddhist based political party in Sri Lanka.

Naxalites A Maoist Communist movement active in parts of India, named after its town of origin, Naxalbari.

The Parivar or **Sangh Parivar** The "family" of Hindu Nationalist organizations and political parties.

Ramkot The hill in Ayodhya were Ram is said to have been born and where a temple to him may have once stood.

Revisionist History A term for the way some Hindu Nationalists want to revise textbook and other presentations of early India history.

ritual pollution or impurity An archaic notion that humans can be relatively pure/impure depending upon their birth status, contact with death, and other factors.

RSS or **Rashtriya Svayamsevak Sangha** A right wing Hindu organization known for its militancy.

Shariah Islamic law, based upon the Quran and other early Islamic sources.

Sikhism A religion, originating in the Punjab area of India, and stressing the oneness of God and the guidance of the Gurus.

Tamils An ethnic group, and language, found in Southeast India and throughout Sri Lanka, especially in the north and northeast.

Tamil Tigers or **LTTE** The short forms of the name Liberation Tigers of Tamil Eelam, a militant organization that led a long civil war in Sri Lanka.

Saffronization A term describing the movement to make Indian educational and other public institutions reflect conservative Hindu ideas and values.

Shiv Sena Meaning the god "Shiva's Army," it is an Hindu revivalist organization founded in 1966.

Sinhalatva A term meaning Sinhala-ness, used to those who take a strong pro-Sinhalese stance in Sri Lankan religion and politics.

VHP or **Vishva Hindu Parishad** Also called the World Hindu Council, an organization dedicated to promoting Hindu cooperation and conservative interests, especially the building of a Ram temple at Ayodhya.

Chapter Four

Saudi Arabia

The Rise and Spread of Salafi Wahhabism:
Wahhabis, House of Saud, Islamic Terrorism, Arab Spring

In this chapter you will learn about:

- the political and religious background of Saudi Arabia
- the concerns and role of Salafi Muslims
- the House of Saud and the Kingdom
- the rise of terrorism among Muslims
- the Arab Spring and its implications for Saudi Arabia
- the case for labeling Wahhabism as fundamentalist

> *The Mutawwaeen [religious police] were... tapping on windows of tardy shop closers.... 'Prayer! Come to prayer! Remember god!' they boomed, ordering merchants to close for the required thirty-minute break. ... In a... shop... a merchant had lingered to chat with a woman customer.... Thwack! Down came the switch on the flustered Yemeni merchant's wrist. 'Stop that!.... Are you flirting with her? Close your shop now! And you,' he said, his eyes narrowing as he inspected the woman's translucent veil, a middle-class hallmark. 'Go home to your husband.' I caught a glimpse of her face as she readjusted her veil before leaving the shop: humiliation, fury, and indignation. Glancing at my uncovered face, she shrugged under her veil. The Mutawwa was young enough to be her son. What had happened to the kingdom's traditional deference to one's elders?*
>
> Judith Miller[1]

---

[1]Judith Miller, *God has Ninety-nine Names* (New York: Simon and Schuster, 1996), 103.

130

Our flight from Delhi arrives at King Khaled Airport, just north of Riyadh, the capital of Saudi Arabia. This is the heartland of the Wahhabi version of Islam we came here to understand. Saudi Arabia is the largest, richest and most important of the Arab Gulf States of the Arabian Peninsula. The region has two features of huge importance to the interface of religion and politics: it holds the world's largest oil reserves and it is the homeland of Islam.

As we travel toward the downtown we note that this is not a beautiful city with great tourist attractions. It is the capital because it is near the home town of the ruling Saud royal family. It used to be only a small city, and of course it is not one of the two major holy cities of the Kingdom. Today, this is a sprawling city with two large towers dominating the landscape, plus many neighborhood mosques gleaming in the desert heat.

RELIGIOUS BACKGROUND: PROPHET MUHAMMAD, HOLY SITES

The Arabian Peninsula is the homeland of Islam. The Prophet Muhammad was born in Mecca and later moved to Medina, and within those two cities are the two most holy sites for Muslims. The government of Saudi Arabia takes great pride at being the protector of these cities and their holy sites.

Prophet Muhammad

Early Life of Muhammad

Muhammad was born into the dominant trading tribe called the Quraysh in Mecca, Saudi Arabia in A.D. 570. Mecca was an important religious city because it was the home of the **Ka'bah**, the temple said to have been built by Abraham on the site where the angels had built a temple at the time of creation. Allah, the Arabic word for God, corresponds to the Hebrew term *Eloh*, which appears in the Hebrew Bible as *Elohim*—the plural of majesty of *Eloh*. Muslims understand *Allah* to be the same God as worshipped by Jews and Christians.

Abraham was a strict monotheist who thought it naïve and wrong to believe that idols were anything more than just shapes of materials such as wood or stone. So there were no idols in the original temple in Mecca. However, the Arabian Peninsula was home to tribal religious traditions that were polytheistic and used idols in their worship. Through the centuries between Abraham and the time of Muhammad, over 300 idols had found their way into the Meccan temple. There were images of many gods, including a Rain God, and three goddesses who were considered to be daughters of Allah. The images included a Christian one of Madonna and child. An annual festival attracted pilgrims, including Christians, from surrounding areas. Trading was the economic base of Mecca, but the income from the annual pilgrimage was quite important as well. In the ancient world,

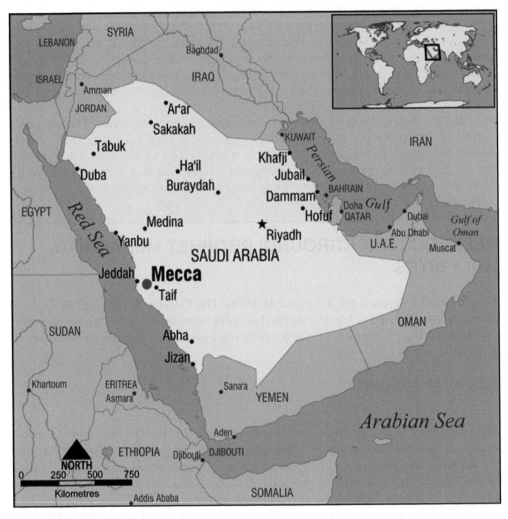

Map showing the location of Mecca, Medina, Saudi Arabia and surrounding states.

Map: Norman Einstein: Wikimedia Commons

being a pilgrimage destination brought both economic gain and political prestige to a city. Muslims call this period of polytheism and idol worship before Muhammad's reforms the "Age of Ignorance."

Muhammad became an orphan at an early age and was raised by relatives who got him work in the caravan trade rather than sending him for a formal education. Learning to read and write was not expected of most people at the time. He was therefore illiterate, but bright, industrious, and had a reputation for being trustworthy. As a young man he was put in charge of caravans. In his mid-twenties he married Khadijah, a widow who owned the caravan business for which he worked. Besides running the caravan business, he found time to spend long hours at prayer, either at the **Ka'bah** or, especially in the month of **Ramadan**, in a cave on Mount Hira a few kilometres outside Mecca.

Call to Prophecy

During one of his stays in the cave, he received a call to prophecy via an angel. When there was no subsequent follow up, he was uncertain of the authenticity of the call, but his wife Khadijah had confidence in his divine mission. Soon he began to receive revelations from God, in the form of Arabic poetic verses called **surahs**. The earliest surahs reaffirmed the monotheism of Abraham, denounced the worship of idols and false gods, and warned of a coming Day of Doom, similar to the Judgement Day expected by John the Baptist and Jesus. Muhammad recited these surahs at prayer gatherings he held near the Ka'bah. A small but loyal group of followers accepted him as a new prophet, but the merchant elite of the town feared his message, not so much because of their love of polytheism but because they feared the loss of revenue from the annual pilgrimage to Mecca. The surahs condemned the pollution of the ka'bah with these idols, and Muhammad called for their removal.

After the death of his uncle and wife in the same year, 619, his enemies in Mecca made life difficult for Muhammad and his followers. In that same year he experienced his **night journey,** *mi-raj,* during which an angel took him to Jerusalem. From there he was taken into heaven to talk with God and some of the earlier prophets. In a later chapter we will discuss the Dome of the Rock in Jerusalem commemorating this event.

Hijrah, Migration to Medina

In 622 an invitation came for him to move to Yathrib, a city to the north of Mecca, where he would become the political leader. Yathrib needed a strong, outside leader because it had a divided population. Approximately one third of the city was Jewish, while the majority Arabs were divided along tribal lines. He and most of his Meccan followers moved to Yathrib. This migration, **Hijrah**, is a really important event in Islam. It marks the coming together of Islam as a religion and Islam as a political system. From this point forward, Islam and politics are conceptually one. The Muslim calendar dates from the *Hijrah*.

Once in Yathrib, Muhammad established an Islamic Commonwealth by formatting an agreement, now known as the Constitution of Medina, calling for fair treatment to all citizens, including the Jews and Christians. It treated all tribes and religious adherents as members of a larger *Ummah*, or "community." Yathrib was renamed **Medina** "The City" (of the Prophet) in his honor. At first Muhammad sought to accommodate the Jews. He saw himself as a prophet in the long line of Jewish and Arabic prophets. He made the Jewish Day of Atonement a recognized holiday and he had Muslims pray facing Jerusalem, in the Jewish manner. But after two years it became clear that the Jews accepted him as a political leader but not as new prophet with a new revelation. This is a fateful period in the history of religions, for if the Jews of Medina had embraced the new prophet, religious history might have taken a very different turn. As it happened, Muhammad later turned against the Jews because they sided with the Meccans during the Battle of the Trench.

Based on an interpretation of Jewish law, he had the Jewish men beheaded and enslaved the women and children. Sadly, a chance for peaceful cooperation between the two traditions was lost. The Day of Atonement did not become a Muslim holiday and prayers were said facing Mecca.

War with Mecca and Consolidation of Leadership
After assuming leadership of Medina, a war broke out with Mecca, started in part by Medinan raids on Meccan caravans. Muhammad and the Muslims successfully defeated a larger Meccan army in the Battle of Badr in 624. But the Meccans won a return engagement the following year. It was following this critical battle that Muhammad decided to expel the Jews from Medina. The Meccans attacked Medina in 627, but a trench dug around parts of the city held off the Meccan cavalry and the Medinans won this Battle of the Trench. By 630 Muhammad had put together such a large coalition of tribal groups around Arabia that the Meccans surrendered their city without a fight. The Muslims entered Mecca and destroyed the idols in the temple, which was then rededicated as a temple in the monotheistic tradition of Abraham. Muhammad preached a farewell sermon on a hill outside Mecca. Today, standing on that hill and contemplating the words of that sermon is a central ritual of the pilgrimage to Mecca.

Muhammad had put together a commonwealth based upon religious authority and backed by military might. By the time of his death, only ten years after his move to Medina, he was the religious and political leader of most of Arabia. After his death, the surahs revealed to him during his years as a prophet were collected as the Quran. It is considered to be the word of God as revealed through Muhammad, the "Messenger of God."

The Four Rightly Guided Caliphs and Shariah

After Muhammad's death in 632 there was no tradition in place for choosing a successor. The Quran did not address the issue directly, nor had Muhammad given specific guidance on the matter. There was a group of senior advisors, called the Companions of the Prophet, and they met to decide a course of action. One obvious approach was to have the most senior of the advisors, **Abu Bakr**, become the Successor (*kalifah*, or Caliph in the usual English spelling) of the Prophet, and that is what was determined. Note that this is similar to the way a new pope is chosen, by a meeting of the senior leaders rather than a vote by the full community. Although the older Abu Bakr was chosen as leader, there was considerable support for the youngest of the Companions, Ali.

As the new leader, Abu Bakr was faced with a crucial decision. Some of the tribal leaders in the Muslim federation wanted to leave the fold. They held that their commitment of loyalty was to Muhammad, who was now dead, and so they were no longer bound to stay within Islam as a political entity. Abu Bakr refused to allow them to leave, which led to a war. After winning this civil war with the dissident tribes, he established the principle that the commitment carried over to the Successors of Muhammad.

Umar became the second Caliph, soon to be replaced by Uthman. When the party of Ali finally got its way, with Ali's selection as the fourth Caliph, things turned badly for the party of Ali. After Ali's death, his adversary, **Muawiyah** became the fifth Caliph and relocated the Caliphate from Medina to Damascus. The first four caliphs are known as the "Rightly Guided Ones." We will see how the era of the **Salaf**, the first three generations of Muslims became the golden age for the **Salafi** interpretation of Islam that came to dominate in modern Saudi Arabia.

The Messenger of God, Shariah, and the Four Schools of Law

Islam holds that God has inspired numerous Hebrew and Arabic prophets (nabi). Five of these prophets hold a special status called Messenger (rasul). They are Noah, Abraham, Moses, Jesus, and finally Muhammad, the "seal" or final Messenger. The five Messengers made God's law known to humans. The term for the "law" here is Shariah, which literally means a path to a source of water. The implication is that God has, through Messengers, shown humans the proper Way. The Shariah as revealed to Muhammad is understood to be complete, so there is no expectation of a future Messenger.

The Shariah needs interpreters to spell out in detail how it applies to everyday life. That task fell to Islamic legal scholars. They based their legal opinions on four sources. The most authoritative source is the Quran. The second source is the Sunnah, which encompasses the words and deeds of Muhammad, mainly as contained in the Hadith—the 'traditions' containing sayings or actions attributed to Muhammad. The third source is the Reasoning of the jurists, and the fourth is the Consensus of the community.

As Islam developed and spread throughout the Middle East, among Sunni Muslims four different Schools of Shariah interpretation coalesced around four outstanding jurists. The Hanafi School is the most widespread and was favored by the Abbasid Caliphate and the Ottoman Empire. The Maliki School spread from Medina to parts of the Africa and the Gulf states. The Shafi'i School spread from Egypt to southern Arabia and on to Southeast Asia, where it remains the main legal tradition. The conservative Hanbali School was followed mainly in central Arabia, from where its influence has spread along with the Wahhabi form of Islam discussed below. Most Shi'i Muslims follow another school of interpretation called Ja'fari.

The Sunni-Shi'i Split

The division between Sunni and Shi'i arose in part because not everyone agreed with the selection of the first three Caliphs. There were some who felt that Muhammad had made it clear that Ali was to be his successor. They based this claim on *hadith* ("traditions" about the sayings of Muhammad), especially one *hadith* relating that Muhammad once held up Ali's hand before a crowd and announced that anyone to whom he (Muhammad) was a master, Ali was also their master. Ali was Muhammad's younger cousin and so he was a blood relative, unlike Abu Bakr. Ali was also Muhammad's son-in-law. The supporters of Ali did not get their way at first, but he did become the fourth caliph. As of that time, the issue was more a matter of succession policy than a hard division within the Islamic community.

Ali became the caliph after a very unfortunate event in 656. Under the short period of the first three caliphs (632–656), Islam had spread rapidly throughout the Middle East. Uthman was from the Umayyad family and had appointed relatives as governors over important areas such as Damascus and Cairo. The Umayyad relative in Cairo was extremely unpopular and a group of Arabs and Egyptians journeyed to Mecca to appeal to Uthman to replace him. They protested outside Uthman's house without success. Then in an outbreak of anger and mob violence they stormed inside and killed Uthman. So, Ali took over in a very difficult situation. Part of his problem was that the mob that killed Uthmar had included his supporters. He was a gentle man by nature it seems and did not have the crowd punished or executed. Muawiyah, the Umayyad governor of Damascus was furious at this and, holding up the bloodied shirt of his relative Uthman, demanded vengeance. Muawiyah, originally from Mecca, had served in the Islamic army. Drawing upon this and his role as governor of Syria, he commanded a large and loyal military force in Syria.

An Islamic civil war broke out as Aisha, the young widow of Muhammad, and other important people from Mecca formed a rebel army with the intent to avenge Uthman's murder. They marched to Basra, Iraq, and it was near there that Ali and his army engaged them in battle. Aisha led her rebel group from the large camel given to her by supporters. Much of the battle took place around her camel, so it is known as the Battle of the Camel. Ali's side won. Ali had the male rebel leaders killed but pardoned Aisha and gave her a pension for life.

Muawiyah had not joined in the Battle of the Camel but he had led Syria in revolt against Ali's leadership, so Ali turned his attention to asserting his caliphate there. First, he established his headquarters in Kufa, in 656. This move from Medina in Arabia to Kufa in Iraq continues to be very important in Iraq's political and religious history. As we shall see, most of the important events of early Shi'i history happened in Iraq. After settling in Kufa and attempting to broker a deal with Muawiyah, Ali marched his army against Muawiyah. The armies met in the Battle of Siffin along the Euphrates River in Syria. After two days of indecisive fighting, during which Ali's army may have had the advantage, Muawiyah's side suggested the dispute be submitted to Muslim arbitrators. This was agreed, and Ali withdrew his army back to Kufa. Months later, the arbitration meeting was held, but resulted in a stalemate between the two claimants to the caliphate.

After the Battle of Siffin, Ali's leadership suffered several setbacks. A large contingent of his army rebelled. They became known as the Kharijites, dissenters, and they rejected both caliph claimants and held that any pious Muslim could be selected as the leader. They called themselves Shurat, and a small number of Shurat still exist.

Ali engaged in a battle against the dissident Kharijites and defeated them. Yet some of the surviving Kharijites became quite hostile to all those who were claiming leadership of the Muslim world. They planned to assassinate Muawiyah and Ali on the same day. The plan partially succeeded. Muawiyah escapted the assassins, but Ali was struck by a poisoned sword while praying in Kufa, and he later died. The story is that he was buried in secret

Early Sunni Caliphs and Shi'i Imams	
Sunni Caliphate Tradition	*Shi'i Imamat Tradition (Twelver list)*
4 Rightly Guided Caliphs (Medina)	1. Ali ibn Abu Talib (632-61)
Abu Bakr (632-634)	2. Hasan ibn Ali (661-70)
Umar (634-44)	3. Husayn ibn Ali (670-80)
Uthman (644-56)	4. Ali ibn Husayn (680-712)
Ali (656-61)	5. Muhammad ibn Ali (712-32)
Umayyad Caliphate (Damascus)	6. Ja'far ibn Muhammad (732-65)
Muawiyah (661-80)	7. Musa ibn Ja'far (735-99)
others (680-750)	8. Ali ibn Musa (799-817)
Abbasid Caliphate (Baghdad)	9. Muhammad ibn Ali (817-835)
As-Saffah (750-4)	10. Ali ibn Muhammad (835-868)
Al-Mansur (754-75)	11. Hasan ibn Ali (868-74)
others (775-1258)	12. Muhammad ibn Hasan (874- ?)

well outside Kufa, to avoid evildoers from harming his corpse, Later it was thought that the burial place was Najaf, and so that city became holy in Shi'i Islam as the burial place of Imam Ali. The shrine of Ali remains a very important pilgrimage site.[2]

Hasan did not have a strong army. In the meantime, Muawiyah had strengthened his army and consolidated his power. To avoid further bloodshed, Hasan reluctantly agreed to allow Muawiyah's claim to the caliphate to go uncontested. Shi'i Muslims believe the terms of the agreement called for the leadership to pass to Hasan's younger brother Husayn after Muawiyah's death. But that did not happen. Muawiyah's son Yazid became the next caliph, as recognized by Sunnis.

Muawiyah was recognized as the fifth caliph by most Muslims of Arabia, Syria and Egypt, which he now had under his control. Those Muslims accepting the Muawiyah caliphate and its successors are called Sunni, meaning those who follow the tradition, *sunnah*. Those Muslims who remained convinced that Hasan, his younger brother Husayn and that line of subsequent Imams were the true leaders are known as the **Shi'a Ali**, the Party of Ali. The term is often shortened to just Shi'a, or Shi'i. A person who follows Shi'a is a Shi'i, which is sometimes given an English ending as Shi'ite.[3]

Martyrdom of Husayn and the Growing Tension between Shi'i Imams and Sunni Caliphs
Sunni Muslims use the term Imam, leader, for whoever leads prayers at a mosque. But Shi'i Muslims use the term to refer to those they consider to be the true religious and

---

[2] Visiting the shrines of past Imams is an important part of Shi'i spirituality. Also, it used to be a common practice for the corpses of Iranian Shi'is to be transported to Iraq for burial in the cemeteries associated with the holy cities of Najaf and Karbala. Note that it is not unusual for adherents of a religion to seek burial near its holiest sites.

[3] Spellings vary in English. In this book Shi'a refers to the sect (Party), and the spelling Shi'i is used for the adherents and as the adjectival form.

political leaders after Muhammad. So to Shi'i Muslims, Ali abu Talif was the first Imam, his elder son Hasan was the second, and his younger son Husayn the third, and so on.

The martyrdom of **Imam Husayn** is the next major event in Shi'i history. Husayn, also spelled Hussain or Hussein, refused to accept the legitimacy of the Umayyad line of caliphs. In a battle at Karbala, Iraq in 680, Husayn and a very small army fought against a much larger force loyal to the Umayyad Caliphate. Rather than merely being defeated, the Shi'is fighers were all killed and their bodies mutilated. Husayn was beheaded and his head was taken to the Umayyad caliph. The Shi'i women and children wept when they saw Imam Husayn's riderless horse returning to camp.

Ashura, the Remembrance of Imam Husayn's Martyrdom

Husayn's martyrdom is remembered each year in a ritual known as **Ashura** because the martyrdom occurred on the tenth day, known as Ashura, of Muharrum, the first lunar month of the Islamic year. When political conditions permit, thousands of Shi'i pilgrims come to Karbala each year to commemorate Ashura. Other Shi'i Muslims hold the ritual in their home areas. It is a time of sadness for them. It reinforces the division between Sunni and Shi'i.

The ritual re-enacting this martyrdom was important in shaping the Shi'i consciousness of being very different than Sunni. Before 680, Y. Nakash argues, Islam was divided along two lines, depending on whether one supported Ali or Muawiyah, but this division did not involve separate rituals or distinct interpretations of Islam.[4] This reminds us of the way Eastern and Western Christians in the early Christian centuries were one worldwide church, but with different languages, theologians, and customs. Later disputes led to a lasting separation between the Eastern Orthodox and Roman Catholic Churches.

The martyrdom of Husayn and its ritual re-enactment during Ashura provides a way for Shi'i Muslims to identify with what they believe to the side of right and truth. The death of Husayn becomes for them a great sacrifice in the struggle of right against wrong. The all-important suffering and death of Husayn functions for Shi'is a bit like the role that the death of Jesus on the cross plays for Christians, although the two theologies are not the same because Husayn is not seen as god on earth as Jesus is by Christians. (Following its understanding of the monotheism of Abraham, Islam strongly denounces the sin of "association," meaning that Muslims refuse to equate (associate) any human, image, or anything else with god.)

As the remembrance of Ashura evolved over the years, it came to include five rituals. One ritual involves memorial services, sometimes spread over the first ten days of the month. The services are intended to invoke a strong sense of mourning, and audible weeping over the suffering of the Imams is encouraged. Another ritual is a visit to the tomb of Husayn in Karbala either on the day of his death or the fortieth day after the death (Arba'een), in accordance with the Shi'i tradition of commemorating a martyrdom on the fortieth day.

---

[4]Yitzhak Nakash, "An Attempt to Trace the Origin of the Rituals of 'Ashura'," Die Welt des Islams (1993, 33, 2), 161–181.

Experiencing Ashura in India

My students and I are staying in a hotel on the river in Ahmedabad, India. The monsoon rains are late and the river is nearly dried up. It's as wide as the Mississippi, but mostly it is rocks. Only a small, shallow trickle flows just outside my hotel window. We hear parade noises and look outside for a parade. But how can there be a parade in a dry riverbed? Yet there it is. A group of maybe twenty men are parading over the rocks toward us. Scores of children follow along.

Four of the men are carrying something heavy on their shoulders. It looks like a small version of a Hindu temple. No wait, it's more like a small mosque. They carry the miniature structure to the water and release it so that it can flow down the river. But the water is so shallow that it gets stuck on the bottom after going a little ways. No problem. Three boys wade into the water to give it a push. Soon there are twenty boys and girls in there helping it along.

More groups come. This goes on all day, well into the night and continues the next day. There must have been a hundred groups, and each one carried one of the structures. Some were small, but two or three were taller than a person and required several bearers to carry. Some of the big heavy ones just would not float away, but stayed stuck on the rocks, awaiting the imminent monsoon rains.

The students come by to ask me what this is. It's Ashura, I say. It commemorates Imam Husayn's martyrdom, the most solemn time of the year for Shi'i Muslims. One student says she thought Ashura was earlier in the year. It's on a lunar calendar I say. It moves around, like the Christian Easter.

But what are the things they are putting in the water? Those are miniature replicas of the Shrine of Imam Husayn in Karbala. These Muslims cannot make the trip to Iraq, so they make models of the shrine here. When the ritual is over, they release them on the water. They will make new ones next year. Some year, some of them may be able to go as pilgrims to the real shrine.

areas. It was started in the mid-tenth century by a Shi'i ruler in Bagdad. A fourth ritual takes the form of a play representing the battle. This is thought to have begun with the support of a Shi'i regime in Iran. The fifth is ritual flagellation. The use of steel knives and other instruments to cut the skin and draw blood may have begun in the 1600s in the region that is now Azerbaijan. At the point in the play in which Imam Husayn is beheaded, the flagellants would draw their own blood as a way of identifying with the original martyrs of the story.[5]

---

[5]Flagellation of one's skin is a very ancient practice found in many old religions, including forms of Hinduism and Christianity in the Philippines. Besides the pious discipline it takes to continually hurt oneself, there may be a physiological explanation. The abrasions on the skin cause the body to release adrenalin and other substances which play a role in heightening the spiritual experience. Sunnis do not practice flagellation, and during the rule of Saddam Hussein the practice was banned. After his fall, the practice resurfaced during Ashura.

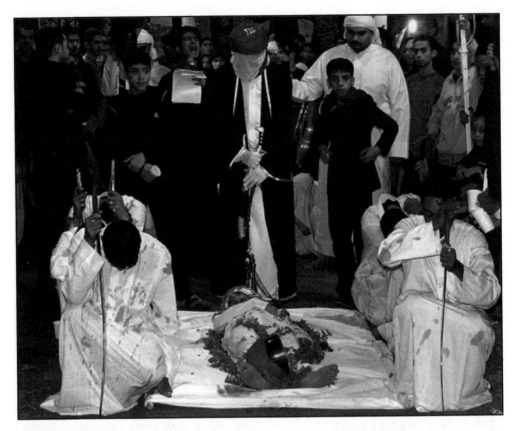

A scene from an Ashura re-enactment in Bahrain. In this scene Imam Hussayn is standing over his son who has been martyred.

Photo: "Ashoora" by Ahmed Rabea–Flickr. Licensed under CC BY-SA 2.0 via Wikimedia Commons—http://commons.wikimedia.org/wiki/File:Ashoora.jpg#/media/File:Ashoora.jpg Ashura

We learn from this review that the Karbala massacre and its remembrance through the Ashura rituals are very important for Shi'i identity. We can also see that the rituals have developed over time and in several places. There is no set pattern that all Shi'i follow. There is also the possibility that some of the Ashura traditions developed under outside influence. Y. Nakash suggests that the last rituals of public procession may have been influenced by Christian processions and that the flagellation practice may owe something to Italian Christian fraternities that practiced drawing blood in sympathy with the death of Jesus.[6]

There are also economic and political reasons at work with regard to pilgrimages. In some periods the Shi'i pilgrimage to the shrines of Imam Husayn at Karbala and Imam Ali at Najaf rivalled the pilgrimage to Mecca. It served the interests of the rulers of Iraq to have the pilgrimage destination be in their territory rather than in Arabia.

---

[6]*Ibid.*

Varieties of Shi'a Islam

Shi'a is an umbrella term for a variety of related types of Islam. They all share a belief in the line of Imams through Husayn, but they differ on when that line stopped and on the names in the lineage. We need a brief review of these groups to better understand the interplay of Shi'a and politics.

The Twelvers, or Imami

The majority of the Shi'i in Iraq, Iran and Afghanistan belong to the branch of Shi'a called the **Twelvers** or **Imami** because they believe that there were twelve true Imams following Muhammad. The Twelver list of Imams starts from Ali and omits all of the other caliphs recognized by Sunni Islam. Following Ali's two sons Hasan and Husayn, it continues with Husayn's son and so on until the twelfth one, Imam Muhammad ibn Hasan, whose title is al-Mahdi.

According to one story, at the funeral of the eleventh Imam in 874, his five-year-old son insisted on leading the prayers on the grounds that only an Imam should lead the funeral prayers of an Imam. This precocious act is taken as a confirmation that he was the true twelfth Imam. Then the story gets really interesting. According to the Twelvers, Imam Muhammad al-Mahdi, while still a young boy, went into hiding, a very special kind of hiding called **occultation**. The term occultation refers to the belief that a highly spiritual person may temporarily disappear from the world and then later reappear. Although Christians do not use the term, one might consider Jesus to be in occultation between his Resurrection and this Second Coming. According to Twelvers, there was a smaller occultation (874-939) during which Imam Mahdi is said to have communicated through an inner circle of leaders, and a larger occultation period from 939 to the present in which he is out of communication with the world. Except that we will see that Ayatollah Khomeini's followers thought Imam Madhi communicated with Khomeini during his spiritual retreat in the 1960s.

Twelvers await the return of Imam Muhammad al-Mahdi before the Day of Judgment. Islam believes that Jesus was a true prophet and that he will play a major role in the final days. The Mahdi's role is similar, and most Twelvers think he and Jesus will both play a role on the Day of Doom, or Judgement Day. Later we will discuss Muqtada Sadr and his militia named the Mahdi Army after Imam al-Mahdi.

The Ismailis

The next most numerous division of Shi'a is the **Ismaili** one. Its name comes from the seventh Imam, a boy named Ismail who was the eldest son of the sixth Imam. According to the Twelvers the seventh Imam died quite young and so they turned to his younger brother as the next Imam. But Ismailis say his father faked the boy's death to protect him. There are subdivisions of the Ismailis. Most Ismailis believe the line of Imams ended with Ismail, who went into occultation. However, the Nizari division of the Ismailis believe the line of Imams, known by the title Aga Khan, is still intact. The current Aga Khan is considered the 49th Imam. He is a modernist leader who has been active in improving the role of women and helping fight poverty.

The Ghulat Sects

Sometimes a variety of Shi'a sects are grouped together as the **Ghulat** Sects, a term that refers to those divisions of Shi'a who partially deify Ali. This view is sometimes associated with Abdullah Ibn Saba, a historically vague contemporary of Ali. The name *Ghulat*, here meaning "exceeders," refers to the fact that more orthodox Muslims look upon them as exceeding the boundaries of proper Muslim monotheism. Some Shi'i believe that Ali can intercede on behalf of his followers, along the theological lines of Christ or saints in Christianity. In his book *The Extremist Shiites*, M. Moosa suggests that there may have been some Christian influence on the Ghulat movement.[7]

Zaidi Sect

The Zaydi (or Zaydi, or Zaidiyyah)) is a Shi'i sect found mainly in Yemen. The sect is named after Imam Zayd ibn Ali, the fourth Imam. He led a rebellion against the Umayyad Caliphate. Zaydi beliefs and legal traditions are closer to Sunni Islam than that of the other Shi'i sects. The militant political movement in Yemen known as the **Houthis**, named after a former commander Hussein Badreddin al-Houthi, is a Zaidi group that is very active in Yemini politics. As a Shi'i activist movement, it is more aligned with Iran, in contrast to the Sunni led Gulf States.

Political Power

The height of Shi'i political power was the Fatima Caliphate (909–1171) that ruled from Cairo. It was known for its tolerance of other forms of Islam as well as of Christians and Jews. Since those days Shi'is have been out of political power in most countries, living as a minority population under either Sunni or western control.

Otherwise, political power has usually been held by the Sunni. The Umayyad Caliphate in Damascus and the Abassid Caliphate in Bagdad were headed by Sunni caliphs. Sunnis controlled the Seljuk and Ottoman Empires centered in Turkey.

POLITICAL BACKGROUND: OIL, OPEC AND POLITICAL POWER

The discovery of oil on the Arab Peninsula in the 1930s combined with the high price of crude oil from the 1970s to the present has brought enormous wealth to the business and political elite of the region. This is especially the case in Saudi Arabia and the United Arab Emirates (UAE). The formation of OPEC, the Organization of Petroleum Exporting Countries, in 1960 created a way for the largest oil-exporting countries to cooperate

---

[7]Matti Moosa, *The Extremist Shiites: The Ghulat Sects* (Syracuse: Syracuse University Press, 1987).

to limit supply and thereby move the price upward. But OPEC struggled for years to get crude prices to go up. At its founding in 1960, crude prices were around $16 per barrel and falling. The price continued to fall for the next 13 years.

Regional politics brought tensions within OPEC. When the Arab-Israeli War (also known as the Six Day War, or to many Arabs, The Setback) occurred in June 1967, many of the Arab states involved were also OPEC members. They wanted more control over the flow of oil for political reasons. They formed a related group, the Organization of Arab Petroleum Exporting Countries. In response to the 1973 Yom Kippur War between Israel and a coalition of Arab states led by Egypt and Syria, the Arab oil-exporting states undertook an oil embargo to punish the Western powers for shipping vast supplies of oil to Israel in support of the war. This interface of religion and politics caused crude oil prices to spike to over $40. The Iran-Iraq war of early 1980s took the price of crude to over $60 per barrel, an unheard of amount at the time. By the late 1980s the price had crashed to under $20. The price recovered during the first Gulf War, but after that a series of OPEC production cuts was needed to get it back over $20 a barrel. The price was around $25 when the World Trade Center was destroyed, which caused an immediate price spike and a long term trend upward to over $100 per barrel. A look at a chart of oil prices overlaid with Middle East wars and international terrorist events shows how the history of oil prices directly correlates with religio-political events.[8]

In this chapter we will discuss the role the oil revenues have played in the spread of Wahhabi Islam throughout the Gulf region and beyond.

ISSUE 1. SALAFI ISLAM AND WAHHABI EXTREMISM: SALAF, AL-WAHHAB, TAWHID, INFIDELS

Outsiders often use the term **Wahhabi** or Wahhabism for the very conservative form of Islam that dominates in Saudi Arabia. Followers of the tradition itself use other terms, such as Salafi, meaning "Followers of the Salaf." Or they use Arabic terms referring to themselves as those who defend the doctrine of the oneness of god by stressing god's Unity. We will start by defining the Salaf and the Unity doctrine before turning to the life and teachings of the most important of the Salafi, Ibn Abd al-Wahhab, the namesake of the Wahhabis. The Arabic spelling for Wahhabi is *wahhabiyyah*.

Salafi Islam

The term *Salaf* means "Predecessors" or "Ancestors" and refers to the early Muslims of Saudi Arabia. Salafis are those who pride themselves in following the forms of Islam developed in the first three generations of Islam. The first three generations in Islam are that of the Companions of Muhammad, their Successors, and the Successors of the Successors.

---

[8]See for example, http://www.wtrg.com/prices.htm.

The confidence in the first three generations is based upon a hadith in which Muhammad is reported to have called the first three generations the best. "The best of people is my generation, then those who come after them, then those who come after them."[9]

The belief is that Islam was pure and uncorrupted in the early period. The Salafi are reactionaries in that they wish to restore original Islam. The name *Salafi* has a similar meaning to Muslims as the term Theravada, "Way of the Elders" to some Buddhists. The leaders of the Protestant Reformation were also motivated in part to get back to an earlier version of Christianity. When reactionaries dream of restoring things the way there were at some time in the past, they usually focus on what they idealized in the past period and ignore the problems of the period. Judith Miller calls attention to the problems of this early period to make this point. There were, she writes, three caliphs murdered, a split between Shi'i and Sunni, arguments over succession, wars and massacres, enslavements, and loss of some of the gains for women made in the time of the Prophet.[10]

The Stress on Tawhid, God's Unity

Salafi Muslims denounce practices that have arisen since the time of the Salaf. They have two main concerns, which are interrelated in their minds. One concern is that foreign, meaning non-Arabic or at least non-Saudi influences, have been incorporated into Islamic practice over the years. These foreign influences include several practices surrounding the graves of famous Muslims. (In the chapter on Iran and Iraq we will see how important this practice is to Shi'is.) Visiting grave sites is practiced to a lesser degree by Sunnis as well, so the dispute is more over the nature of the visit and the size of the grave marker. We will return to this issue after introducing the concept of the sin of association.

Another example of outside influence, according to Salafis is the style of Islamic philosophy that grew under the influence of Greek philosophy. The wedding of Greek philosophy and Quranic thought is usually considered one of the great achievements of the Abbasid Caliphate of Baghdad. One of Islam's great contributions to the West was to preserve Greek manuscripts and philosophical debates during Europe's Dark Ages. Most of Aristotle's works had been lost in Europe but not in Islamic universities, for example. To the Salafis, Islamic philosophy is a suspicious later development. They wish to stick to the style of Islamic thinking that prevailed during the period of the Salaf.

The Salafi rejection of foreign influences includes western notions of political parties, parliaments and democracy. They reject the idea that it is acceptable for a majority of Muslims to vote to change Shariah. Therefore, the whole concept of a legislature is thought to be based on a wrong practice.

The second Salafi concern is to defend the Unity of god, known as *tawhid* in Arabic. Muhammad saw himself as a defender of the monotheism of Abraham over against the polytheism that had become common in Arabia before Muhammad, during the time that Islam calls the "age of ignorance." The opposite of Tawhid is to commit *shirk*, the

---

[9]See, for example, http://alqamardesigns.wordpress.com/2007/05/20/salafi.

[10]Judith Miller, *God Has Ninety-Nine Names*, 96–97.

sin of "association." The underlying concept is that it is forbidden for monotheists to associate anything with god that is not god. For example, Abraham, according to Islam, denounced the idea that the sun and moon were gods. Therefore, to suggest otherwise is *shirk*. Before Muhammad's army rededicated the **Kaaba** to the one god of Abraham, there were over three hundred idols of gods in the Kaaba, enough to have one for each day of the year.

For Salafis, the practice of venerating the tombs or shrines of famous Muslims of the past borders on *shirk*. It does not seem to Shi'is that they are compromising their monotheism when they visit the shrine of Imam Ali or Imam Husayn, as discussed in the next chapter, but to the Salafis it is both a foreign practice and *shirk*. The key question might be put this way. Is there in any sense a chance that the dead is being revered like a god? "Not really," the Shi'i might answer. "Yes there is," the Salafi might counter.

We turn now to two important thinkers who gave shape to modern Wahhabi Islam in Saudi Arabia. The first was a conservative Kurdish Muslim who lived long ago, in the time of the Crusades. The second is al-Wahhab himself, who lived in Arabia in the eighteen century, in the very time and place of the formation of the first Saudi regime.

Ibn Taymiyyah

Taqi ad-Din Ahmad ibn Taymiyyah (1263–1328) was a Kurd whose family had migrated from Turkey to Damascus because the Mongols were causing great trouble for eastern Islam. He was a respected scholar who held that Islam should rely primarily on its early sources, the Quran and the Sunnah. Ibn Taymiyyah held firmly to the idea that the period of the Salaf was the pure and true time of Islamic thought. He denounced the Mongols, who had recently converted to Sunni Islam, as non-Muslim rulers because they did not rule by Shariah, but by their Mongol traditions. He called for a jihad against them. He was imprisoned several times for his criticism of proposed laws or his sharp rebuke of other Muslim thinkers. He died in a prison in Cairo, but his legacy lived on as one of the many thinkers followed by the Salafis.

Admiration for the Kharijites
As one modern scholar points out, ibn Taymiyyah was unusual among Islamic scholars in that he looked favorably upon the **Kharijites** (or Khariji in Arabic). That was the party that turned against both rivals to leadership of Islam in the days of Imam Ali. It was the Kharijites who attempted to kill the fifth Caliph, Muawiyah, and did assassinate Imam Ali. The Kharijites have the dubious reputation of being the first Muslims to use terrorist actions against other Muslims. Not only did they carry out assassinations, they argued that true Islam required such action. They were the first to put forward Islamic justifications for killing other Muslims.[11] Ibn Taymiyyah did not approve of all of Kharijite thought, but he seems to have admired their zeal and their strictness, and especially their truthfulness.

---

[11]A. Abukhalil, *The Battle for Saudi Arabia: Royalty, Fundamentalism, and Global Power* (New York: Seven Stories Press, 2004), 54.

Ibn Taymiyyah Mosque, Umm al-Fahm

Photo: By Moataz1997 (Own work) [CC BY-SA 4.0 (http://creativecommons.org/licenses/
by-sa/4.0)], via Wikimedia Commons.

Besides his qualified admiration for the Kharijites, ibn Tamiyyah took a theological position that differed from mainstream Islamic theology. He taught that those suffering in the fires of hell will eventually be released from hell and will join god in heaven. This understanding of hell is more like that of ancient Zoroastrian belief or New Testament concept that bad persons in hell will be redeemed upon the second coming of Christ.

Ibn Taymiyyah was a strict literalist in his interpretation of the Quran and Sunnah. This literalness applied to all aspects of his Quranic interpretation, but one aspect brought criticism from his Islamic peers. If the Quran talked about the hand of god, he took that to mean that god literally had a hand. This view got him in trouble. It even got him put in jail. His fellow Islamic thinkers accused him of making the mistake of talking of god as if god were a human. This is called anthropomorphizing god, ascribing human (*anthro-*) form (*morph-*) to god. There are many passages in the scriptures of Judaism, Christianity and Islam which describe god in human terms, but the more mainstream approach in Jewish, Christian and Muslim thought is to take the anthropomorphic passages of the scripture in a metaphoric way and hold to the doctrine that the actual nature of god is beyond human knowledge.

Sufism, the mystical strain of Islamic practice, was condemned by ibn Taymiyyah. He was especially critical of some of their forms of prayer. He took the position that some

Sufis were in fact infidels rather than true Muslims. He also denounced Shi'i Islam, but he stopped short of calling for the death of all Shi'is. His strict adherence to what he considered to be the original and only permissible forms of prayer led him to criticize the Muslim practice of calling upon Prophet Muhammad to intercede in prayer. Using Muhammad for such intercession was allowable while the Prophet was alive, but not so afterward, he taught. Stressing the unity of god, he denounces any practice by Sufis, Shi'is or Sunnis that might imply that some other agency is the object of prayer. The age-old practice of praying at the tomb of dead "saints," to use a Christian word, was especially wrong from his point of view.

Somewhat out of step with mainstream Islam, ibn Taymiyyah practiced a simple, ascetic lifestyle. He never married nor allowed himself to partake in the beauty of nature. This is quite against some interpretations of Islamic theology, which, like Judaism, saw the natural world as god's handiwork to be celebrated and enjoyed. Living a simple and ascetic lifestyle was actually more akin to Sufi practice.

Ibn Taymiyyah was persecuted for his radical thought, and he died in prison. Yet his notion that heretical Muslims deserved to die as well as his literalist approach to the Quran and the early Islamic traditions remained alive in the Muslim world. It was a precursor to the ultra-conservative forms of Islam found in the more recent Islamic resurgence. Some have gone so far as to see the thought and practice of ibh Tamiyyah as the forerunner of modern fundamentalist Islam. Through the centuries ibn Tamiyyah's radical interpretation was not necessarily the normative form of Islam, even in Saudi Arabia. At least, not until al-Wahhab so successfully championed its cause in the eighteenth century in partnership with political power.

Ibn Abd al-Wahhab

Ibn Abd al-Wahhab (or Wahab) was born in Arabia into a family of Sunni scholars in 1703. He lived in the Najd region of Arabia, in a time when there was no central ruler. His family followed the Hanbali school, the most strict of the four schools of Shariah law. There are no detailed, reliable accounts of his life. His modern Saudi admirers stress that he travelled extensively in his youth, studying in various centers of Islamic learning. The modern accounts also relate that he was quite a precocious student who memorized the Quran at an early age. Whatever foreign study he may have undertaken, we do know that he studied in Medina. That is where he became exposed to the strict literalist thought of ibn Taymiyyah. He is said to have admired ibn Taymiyyah's knowledge of the Hadith as well as his role in resisting the Christian Crusades. Ibn Abal-Wahhab's admiration for ibn Taymiyyah as both a fighter and a pious scholar may have played a role in the all-important partnership with Saudi power that he later embraced. It has been said that he looked upon the Quran and the sword as the foundation of Islam.[12]

---

[12]*Ibid*, 54.

Offering prayers for the dead, at Rumi's center in Konya, Turkey. This type of prayer was rejected by a-Wahhab.
Photo: Roy Amore

After his training, he returned to his home town and got the ear of the local ruler. From an early age he was almost obsessive in his indignation about veneration of grave sites. There was an important grave of one of the Companions of Muhammad in his area which was frequented by pious local Muslims. Upon al-Wahhab's insistence, the local ruler had the grave levelled and the trees associated with the grave site were cut down. The ruler forbade any grave rituals to be performed there.

Al-Wahhab's Stress on Tawhid, God's Unity

Al-Wahhab did not leave many writings. He compiled a small book of hadith, but very little else. The title of his collection of hadith, *Book of Tawhid*, reflects his central theological concern, the Oneness of God. Or, as his critics might say, his lifelong obsession. Tawhid, for al-Wahhab, covers lots of ground. He starts with its main and original meaning, referring to the oneness of God as the sole divinity of the world. This is of course consistent with the monotheism of Abraham, the Shema of Judaism ("Hear O Israel, the Lord thy God is One"), and the first pillar of Islam ("There is no god except The God").

Al-Wahhab also understands the Tawhid concept to embrace the ninety-nine names of God. This idea of the ninety-nine names of God is part of the main Islamic tradition. The concept of a "name" of God is equivalent to an "attribute" of God in traditional Christian and Jewish theology. In theological affirmations such as "God is Truth," "God is Love," or "God is Merciful," the terms Truth, Love, and Merciful are God's names or attributes. Al-Wahhab's fear seems to have been that someone might mistakenly take the name as a separate divine entity, a lesser god.

Another aspect of al-Wahhab's broad application of the Tawhid doctrine was that the Unity of God demands that worship be purified from any elements that might, in Wahhab's mind at least, compromise the oneness of God. This is the point at which he parts company with mainstream Islamic thought. He expands the scope of Tawhid to such an extent that many forms of Muslim prayers became suspect for him. This was especially the case with the practices surrounding the prayers for the dead.

Opposition from the Ulama

The **ulama**, religious scholars, of the Najd area objected strongly to al-Wahhab's extreme positions. They preached against his views in the mosques. They wrote letters to al-Wahhab and his disciples. And they wrote epistles, longer letters meant to be widely circulated, in which they systematically refuted al-Wahhab's interpretations. One such epistle was written in 1743, when Al-Wahhab would have been around forty years old. Unlike later biographies written by his admirers long after his death, this epistle reflects a time when he was just a controversial scholar and not yet the namesake of the Islamic interpretation favored by the al-Saud rulers. He had stirred up so much controversy that some regional leaders were calling for his arrest or death. One local leader wrote to a regional leader with the threat to withhold paying the land tax unless al-Wahhab was put to death.[13]

The author of the epistle criticizes al-Wahhab for downplaying the role of the four schools of Shariah, suggesting that it is inappropriate to strike out on one's own to reinterpret Quranic based thought. The implication is that it is very presumptuous to depart from the norms of Shariah tradition. Al-Wahhab thought of himself as following the Hanbali school of Shariah, however. The epistle also criticizes al-Wahhab for agitating for reversing the long standing policy of exempting the local residents from paying the land tax out of respect for the fact that the graves of some of the companions of the Prophet were located there. Al-Wahhab's motivation for this was presumably to further weaken what he took to be the wrongful prayers of intercession done at the grave sites. Anything he could do to weaken the grave practices was justifiable to him. The epistle's author also criticizes al-Wahhab for condemning prayers of intercession. In the process he calls attention to the extremist way that al-Wahhab denounced al-Busiri as an infidel, even though mainstream Sunnis admired al-Busiri as the author of a eulogy for the Prophet.

This epistle has added comments from other Islamic scholars from Mecca and Basra, showing that there was serious and widespread opposition to al-Wahhab during his lifetime.[14]

---

[13]S. Traboulsi, "An Early Refutation of Muhammad ibn 'Abd al-Wahhab's Reformist Views," *Die Welt des Islams*, New Ser., Vol 42, Issue 3 (2002): 376.

[14]*Ibid.*, 387.

Labels His Opponents as Kafir, Infidels

> We leave Riyadh for the Eastern Province (Ash Sharqiyah), the home area of most Shi'is of Saudi Arabia. We want to get a firsthand look at the economic and social life of the Kingdom's Islamic minority. From the air as we fly to Dammam, the Eastern Province's capital, we can easily see that this region is home to huge oil fields and refineries. With its great natural resources, it seems obvious that there is no way the Kingdom would ever tolerate a Shi'i separatist movement. From the air we can also see that we are flying into a desert area. We look down upon Bedouin camps, with their colorful tents, camels and motorbikes. We land at King Fahd International Airport, an enormous expanse of airport facilities in the middle of a desert. We take the public bus downtown, then switch to dababs, four wheeled vehicles that are a cross between a motorcycle and a four wheeled off road vehicle. We ask our drivers to take us to King Fahd Park, where we see an interesting mosque reflected in a large pond. We temporarily forget that we are in the middle of a desert.
>
> The Dammam area has grown greatly in population in recent decades, largely because Saudi policy has been to encourage Sunni citizens to move here. We learn that the Sunnis tend to do business and interact mainly among themselves, leaving the Shi'i out of the economic prosperity. The Shi'is mainly are confined to the manual labor jobs in the oil industry. We learn that the areas of high density Shi'i population lie in and around the oasis towns of Qatif and al-Hasa, so we travel by bus to Qatif.
>
> Arriving in Qatif, we can see the effects of Wabbabi-based rule on a Shi'i area. We learn that Shi'i towns here used to have a religious center called a husseiniyya. The name reflects its origin as a place for remembering the martyrdom of Imam Husayn at Ashura, as discussed in next chapter. The husseiniyyas became centers of Shi'i learning and practice. They remained in operation while the region was under foreign rule, including the Portuguese and Ottomans, but were closed down after Eastern Arabia was captured by the Al-Saud in 1913. We also learn that Qatif was traditionally a center of Shi'i learning and piety, with such close ties to the holy city of Najaf in Iraq that it was called "little Najaf."[15]

Throughout his life al-Wahhab took a "my way or the highway" approach to his Islamic opponents. His strong tendency was to denounce anyone who disagreed with him as a *kafir*, an infidel who was not a true Muslim. This extremist position made him unpopular with many mainstream Sunni Muslims during his lifetime. His own father worried about his excesses. One of his most important critics was his own brother, Sulayman. Actually it is likely that one reason why the family relocated was due to the trouble caused to his father by the young al-Wahhab. After his father's death, he moved back home, perhaps in part because there was an attempt on his life.

Sulayman wrote a book criticizing his brother. He questioned the basis of authority for his brother's extreme teachings. That book is now banned in Saudi Arabia, but is appreciated by Shi'is who have come under attack by Wahhabis.

One of al-Wahhab's most controversial acts involved a woman accused of adultery. She is said to have confessed, and he got four male witnesses to witness to her alleged adultery, and then he sentenced her to death by stoning. He ordered her to be tied down and then the people stoned her to death. Many local Muslims were aghast at this and it became very controversial.

Fateful Move to Diriyah and Last Years

At the age of forty-two al-Wahhab was in serious trouble in his home town. The local ruler was demanding that he be killed, and there was an attempt on his life. Not surprisingly, he decided to move. He chose to relocate to a market town called Diriyah. Its local ruler was Muhammad ibn Saud. This meeting of al-Wahhab and the founder of the House of Saud changed Arabian history. In our next Issue, focusing on the House of Saud, we will pick up the story of the rocky start to their relationship and the role that ibn Saud's wife played in encouraging the partnership that would shape the future of Saudi Arabia and modern Islam, and to a growing extent, the whole world.

Modern Diriya, Saudi Arabia
Photo: Swisshippo. Dreamstime. http://www.dreamstime.com/royalty-free-stock-image-diriyah-old-city-near-riyadh-image5641466

Having been very active in public affairs by issuing controversial rulings and aligning himself with rulers, al-Wahhab withdrew into a life of prayer during his final years. He died in 1791, but by that time his interpretation of Islam had taken hold. His partnership with the House of Saud would prove to be crucial to his brand of Islam. Through that partnership, the Wahhabi version of Salafi Islam became normative for Saudi Arabia and then spread around the world.

Wahhabi-Shi'i Attacks and Tensions

The Sacking of Karbala and Name Calling
From the time of ibh Taymiyyah to the present, the Sunni Salafi-Wahhabi clerics and their political partners have been very critical of the Shi'is (also known as Shiites). Thy have attacked Shi'is and their shrines from time to time. A Wahhabi army sacked the Shi'i holy city of Karbala, Iraq in 1801. Destroying the city of the shrine of Imam Husayn was the ultimate insult to Shi'is. It is an event that still brings tension to the Sunni-Shi'i relationship, especially to the Wahhabi-Shi'i one. The shrine had been previously destroyed by one of the Abbasid Caliphs, and later in 1843 it was robbed of its gold and other valuables by the Ottomans. All of these attacks fuel Shi'i resentment toward Sunnis.

Shi'i militants have sometimes countered with their own demonstrations or attacks. Starting in 1913, the Ottoman Empire's policy of tolerance for various sects of Islam and other religions was abruptly replaced with the Salafi-Wahhabi view that Shi'a was an unorthodox form of Islam to be suppressed.

The Shi'is sometimes refer to the Wahhabi as *Nasibi*, a pejorative term that refers to those who dislike Imam Ali. Conversely the Wahhabis call the Shi'is *Fafide*, "Dissenters," a term that refers to the way that Shi'is do not accept the validity of the Umayyad and Abbasid Caliphates or even the first three of the Medinan Caliphs. Such name calling reflects the continuing disagreement about whether or not Muhammad appointed Ali as his successor. The fact that the Shi'is are a significant minority within Saudi Arabia has caused a governance policy for the House of Saud, to which we now turn.

ISSUE 2. THE HOUSE OF SAUD: ORIGINS, RELIGION, OIL, RELATIONS WITH THE UNITED STATES

The Saud family gives its name to and is firmly in control of the Kingdom of Saudi Arabia. But this has not always been the case by any means. We begin with a brief history of the House of Saud's rise to power, and then consider its partnership with Wahhabi Islam, the role of oil, and its relations with the United States and other countries.

---

[15]"The Shiite Question in Saudi Arabia." International Crisis Group, Middle East Report no. 45 (September 19, 2005): 1. http://merln.ndu.edu/archive/icg/shiitequestion.pdf.

Rise to Power, Three Times

The Al Saud, the House of Saud, has taken political control of Arabia three times. It began in the late 1700s when a local village chief, Muhammad ibh Saud gained political power in Diriyah, in central Arabia.

Partnership with al-Wahhab
Diriyah is the same market town to which the controversial Salafi cleric al-Wahhab relocated in 1744. The story is that at first ibn Saud was very reluctant to have anything to do with the extremist cleric, but his wife encouraged him to meet with al-Wahhab, saying that this was a great opportunity that God had presented.

The meeting went well. Soon a partnership was formed between ibn Saud as the political authority and al-Wahhab as the religious authority. The marriage of ibn Saud's son to al-Wahhab's daughter sealed the bond between religion and politics, Saudi style. This somewhat unlikely partnership has lasted over two hundred years, continuing with their descendents. Al-Wahhab is respectfully referred to by his title, Shaykh, and so this is known as a partnership between the Al Saud (House of Saud) and the Al al-Shaykh (House of the Shaykh). Normally the House of Saud appoints a Grand Mufti, the highest religious authority, who is from the Al al-Shaykh.

From the 1770s to 1819, the first Al Saud kingdom was put together through conquest of most of Arabia. Yet they did not have the military capacity to hold such a large territory in the face of external attack. In 1818 the Ottoman Empire encouraged Egypt to attack the Saudi Kingdom. The capital, Diriyah, fell and soon the first Saudi Kingdom ended.

The second Al Saud kingdom (1824–91) was based upon the same partnership between the House of Saud and the Wahhabis. It ended through a civil war. Intrigue within the Saudi ruling family itself was a significant cause of the fall, and many surviving members of the Saud family fled to Kuwait.

The Third and Current Kingdom
The third Kingdom of Saudi Arabia began on a small scale in 1902. The Saud family had been living in Kuwait for over a decade in an impoverished state under the protection of Sheikh Mubarak. Then twenty-year-old Abdul Aziz ibn Saud talked the Kuwaiti Sheikh into equipping him for a return home. The Saudis had made a few unsuccessful raids into Arabia earlier. Equipped with forty camels and a few men, the tall, charismatic ibn Saud set out to gain a foothold in Arabia. He had only limited success in his strategy in picking up tribal fighters and equipment along the way. Realizing that with his small force of only two hundred men he had no chance in a conventional battle, he devised a daring plan to sneak into the capital, Riyadh. The story is that the raid seemed so foolhardy that only six of his two hundred men came with him. The others waited at a camp, to see if they should come to assist or flee for their lives.

Ibn Saud scaled the city wall and hid in the house of an old friend. His plan was to then attack Ajlan, the Amir of the city who was from the Rashid, an old rival of the Saud family. Ibn Saud sprang from hiding, and the Amir fled but was killed by one of ibn Saud's men. In the turmoil the Amir's guards thought the city was under a major attack. Ibn Saud boldly stepped into the open and proclaimed himself the new ruler. The guards accepted this, and Riyadh had fallen to a "force" of seven men. The Rashid regime had been repressive and unpopular, which made the transition to Saudi rule much easier. Ibn Saud made his father the Sheikh, but his father then turned it over to him. This deference to age was seen as a good thing.[16]

From his base in Riyadh, ibn Saud conducted raids into the surrounding areas and then into Western Arabia, which was under the control of the Hashemite Sherifs, whom he eventually expelled in 1924. He was then the ruler of much of Arabia, but he had little revenue to support his regime. Fortunately for him, perhaps, several western countries were willing to provide him aid because each wanted to gain influence over the others.

The Creation of the Ikhwan

To bring stability to the kingdom and conquer most of Arabia, King Abdulaziz, or ibn Saud, undertook a complex social reform that turned out to work brilliantly. The first step was to convince many of the Bedouin to abandon their nomadic, herding way of life and participate in a new *Hijrah*. Similar to Muhammad's original migration (*Hijrah*) from Mecca to Medina, the Bedouin were asked to migrate from a nomadic to a settled life and to adopt a more strict set of Islamic practices under the guidance of the Wahhabis. The plan called for the development of agricultural settlements around wells traditionally owned by tribes. The settlements had clerics ready to instruct the settlers in proper Islamic behavior as taught by Wahhabis. Each settler was called a brother, *akh*, and collectively they were called **Ikhwan**, the Brotherhood.

In its early years, the Ikhwan system worked well for both the Al Saud and the Wahhabis. For the Wahhabis it was a chance to convert nominal Muslims to strict Salafi adherents. For the Al Saud, it was a militia. The Ikhwan became the Al Saud army of conquest. They were willing to fight and plunder for God and the kingdom. Their attack on other cities of Arabia was for them a *jihad*, a holy struggle. Ibn Saud gradually expanded his territory, controlling Najd and its surrounding area by 1921. His rival, the Sharif of the Hashimite king of Hijaz, remained his last main obstacle to the control of the holy cities Mecca and Medina, and most of Arabia. Great Britain had been propping up both ibn Saud and the Sharif with funds, but in 1923 Britain withdrew support from both regimes. This move favored ibn Saud, who was left with better funding sources. Perhaps in an act of desperation, Sharif had himself proclaimed a Caliph in 1924, but later that year ibn Saud conquered the holy city of Mecca. He took Medina the following year. He took control of the emirate of Asir in the South in 1926.

By 1932 the Ikhwan had helped bring most of Arabia under the Al Saud regime and under Wahhabi Islam. In September 1932 the various conquered territories were officially unified as the independent Kingdom of Saudi Arabia. The Kingdom established Salafi, based on the teachings of ibn Wahhab, as its official form of Islam.

---

[16]James W. Flanagan, *David's Social Drama: A Hologram of Israel's Early Iron Age* (Sheffield: Almond Press, 1988), 229–300.

The Ikhwan army advancing.
Licenced under Public Domain via Wikimedia Commons - http://commons.wikimedia.org/wiki/File:Ikhwan.jpg#/media/File:Ikhwan.jpg

The Destruction of the Ikhwan

Even before 1932, a rift was growing between the Ikhwan and the Al Saud. Having become Wahhabi zealots, the Ikhwan was critical of many of the practices and norms evolving in the Kingdom. To the Ikhwan, the Saudi family seemed too modern, too Western, and too prone to introduce new things like automobiles, radios, telephones, and taxes. They found it particularly un-Islamic for the Al Saud to impose a tax on tobacco because it was illegal. According to Wahhabi norms, one should not smoke in the first place.

Shi'i Minority Rights

Ibn Saud's wars of expansion led to his taking control over eastern Arabia in 1914. The region around the al-Hasa oasis is populated by Shi'i rather than Sunni Muslims. Ibn Saud's approach to governing a Shi'i population was determined more by political realism than by Wahhabi ideals. Contrary to the wishes of his Wahhabi spiritual advisors, he allowed some latitude to the Shi'is in return for their acceptance of his authority. However, through the years the Saudi regime's partnership with the Wahhabi clerics has led to a policy of discrimination against the Shi'is in the Kingdom. Although Shi'is form at least 13 percent of the population and are a majority in the Eastern Province, they have been assigned a second-class status because they are not considered true Muslims by Wahhabi-influenced state policy. For example, they are not allowed to serve in the army. To improve their minority conditions, some Shi'is turned to socialism or pan-Arab nationalism in the 1950s and 1960s. After the founding of the Shi'i militant group Hezbollah in 1982, many Shi'is turned to it as a means toward increased Shi'i power. The Saudi refusal to let Shi'is join the army became particularly aggravating to Shi'is when the government brought in foreigners during the 1990–91 Gulf War.[17]

So that they may move toward equality in citizenship, Shi'i leaders have asked the Saudi government to lessen their dependence on the Wahhabi clerics. They want a mandatory military service for males, thus gaining for themselves the status of defending the country. They also want economic improvements and a move toward more democracy. So far it has not made much difference. More recently Shi'i leaders called for a move toward democracy, beginning at the local level and with suffrage for women as well as men. But when a limited version of local democracy was introduced in 2005, women were excluded.[18]

Oil Riches and the Difference It Makes

In the late 1920s King ibn Saud was short on money. He had befriended English businessman Jack Philby. While riding across the desert in 1930 Philby suggested to the king that he and his government were like people unknowingly sleeping on a buried treasure. This excited Ibn Saud, but not about prospecting for oil, as intended, but for water to irrigate cash crops. A water engineer was brought in who saw little hope of finding large artesian water resources. He did, however, suggest that the geology was favorable for oil.

Socal (Standard Oil of California) struck oil in nearby Bahrain in 1932 and therefore they were quite interested in exploring in eastern Arabia. They obtained the exploration rights, but the early results were quite discouraging. Socal hit dry well after dry well for almost three years, and was about to cease explorations. Then, oil was struck in nearby Kuwait in 1938, which would later bring riches to ibn Saud's close ally Sheikh Ahmad. And just a few weeks after the Kuwait strike, serious amounts of oil were struck in exploration well 7 in Arabia. The kingdom had been overly dependent upon the income from the annual Mecca pilgrimage, which was subject to fluctuation during years of political turmoil. In this era of the Great Depression, the number of pilgrims making the Hajj was way down. In great need of the oil revenue, King ibn Saud pressed ahead with the plan to

---

[17]Yitshak Nakash, *Reaching for Power: The Shi'a in the Modern Arab World* (Princeton: Princeton University Press, 2006), 129–130.

[18]*Ibid.*, 130–133.

build a pipeline to the coast and a terminal for shipping. In just over a year after discovery, oil exports began. The boom years for the Saudi princes were beginning.[19]

The discovery of Saudi Arabian oil came on the eve of World War II, and both the Axis and Allies sides were scrambling to contract for reserves. The Axis countries, Germany, Japan, and Italy, each bid for Saudi oil and courted the Al Saud royals. But Casoc (California-Arabian Standard Oil Company, the Saudi Arabian subsidiary of Socal) had locked up the rights. This was a great boon for both the company and the Allies.[20]

Thanks to oil revenue, the government went from being nearly bankrupt in the 1930s to having enormous reserves currently. Meanwhile, the income of the numerous members of the royal family has gone from modest levels to off-the-chart levels. To keep the thousands of members of the royal family content, a huge portion of the oil revenues is divided among the family members, who in turn have often parlayed that money into successful investments abroad, particularly in the United States and in major European cities. The enormous wealth of the large royal family has led to excesses in lifestyle, which has left them open to criticism by conservative Muslims. The oil money has allowed the government to pay for extensive medical and other services for the people, but the non-royals do not directly participate in the oil riches. During periods when international oil prices have dropped sharply, it has been difficult to maintain the "allowances" paid to the various members of the royal family.

Relations with the United States

Prior to 1931 the United States did not have diplomatic relations with Saudi Arabia. The two countries signed a friendship agreement in 1931 and a trade treaty in 1933. Prior to that time Great Britain had been the main Western power involved with Saudi Arabia. The fact that an American oil company was developing an interest in Saudi Arabia was influential in the rise United States interest. The oil industry quickly became a key lobbying factor in United States-Saudi relations, and remains so today.

To help Saudi Arabia's economy and to gain influence, the United States began foreign aid to the Kingdom in 1943. In the discussion of oil above, it was noted that the Allies were keenly aware of their need to keep Saudi oil resources on their side during the second World War

Whereas oil and foreign assistance drew the two countries together, the rising Zionist immigration to Palestine caused tensions. In a famous meeting between ibn Saud and Franklin D. Roosevelt, they got along very well, but ibn Saud took the occasion to point out to FDR that it seemed unfair to punish the Palestinians for the crimes against the Jews

---

[19]Daniel Yergin, *The Prize: The Epic Quest for Oil, Money, and Power* (New York: Simon and Schuster, 1991), 300–301.

[20]Later, the Philby part of the story had a negative side for the West during the Cold War. It happened that Jack Philby used some of the money he made from helping with the oil contract to send his son to Cambridge University, and H.A. R. "Kim" Philby went on to a career as a British spy. It was later revealed that he was a double agent, with his real loyalties lying with communism and the Soviet Union. *Ibid.,* 290.

committed by Hitler's Germany. He was making the point that the Palestinians were suffering loss of their land and control of the region for no reason of their own doing. FDR later commented that he learned a great deal about the Islamic position on Palestine from this meeting. But FDR died shortly after the meeting and was not able to change United States policy toward a more pro-Palestinian approach. Under Harry Truman's presidency, the United States pursued a pro-Israel policy while maintaining friendly relations with the Saudis.

During the Eisenhower years in the 1950s, Saudi Arabia became a key ally to the Eisenhower Doctrine, which gave generous military and foreign aid to countries helping in the fight against communism. The United States had built an air base in Saudi Arabia. In a meeting between Eisenhower and King Saud in 1957, the King went home with a huge increase in his aid package, while Eisenhower got a five-year renewal on the air base and a solid anti-communist leader in the Middle East. By the time of John Kennedy's presidency, King Faysal had led a palace coup to come to power in Saudi Arabia. Faysal and Kennedy got along well, despite the ongoing tensions caused by the suffering of the Palestinians. But all was not well for King Faysal. The popularity of Egypt's Prsident Gamal Abdel Nasser was spilling over into other Middle Eastern countries. Nasser and his admirers were critical of the excesses in lifestyle enjoyed by the Saudi royal family and others in the gulf region. King Faysal needed the support of the United States to control the wave of criticism sweeping into the Kingdom. This worked well for the United States, which was becoming more and more dependent on Saudi oil as its own reserves were depleting.

Meanwhile, as the United States continued to back Israel, Nasser's Egypt turned more toward the Soviet Union for assistance. When Egypt was defeated in the 1967 Arab-Israeli War, leaving Muslims without a strong army with which to mount a resistance against Israel, there was a tendency in the Arab world to look to Islam as the sole answer to their problems. Whereas Wahhabi Islam had previously been perceived as too extreme by other Arab countries, various forms of Islamic extremism began to gain popular appeal in the Middle East. Nasser was assassinated in 1970, and the Saudis again became the dominant power in the Middle East.

Observers have noted that throughout the post-World War II era, the Saudis seem more comfortable with Republican than Democratic presidents. Several reasons have been suggested. One is that in the Saudi view the Democratic Party has been more pro-Israel than the Republican Party. That may not be true in reality, but it seems so to the Saudis. Another reason is that the Saudis feel that the Republican Party is more influenced by the oil lobby, and therefore more likely to align itself with Saudi interests. The Reagan years reinforced this Saudi view. The Soviet invasion of Afghanistan alarmed both the Saudis and the United States, and their relationship became closer and more involved. The United States agreed to supply the Saudis with high-level military equipment, including F–15 fighter jets and early warning radar systems. Also, the American air base was kept in place and put into more use.

The need for resistance fighters against the Soviets in Afghanistan led to the American financing of Islamic militants such as Bin Laden. This leads to our third issue, the rise of Islamic terrorism and Al-Qaeda.

ISSUE 3. THE RISE OF ISLAMIC TERRORISM AND AL-QAEDA

I was travelling with students in China on the day the World Trade Center was targeted by terrorist-controlled planes. For the next few days everywhere we went in China people were coming up to us and saying they were sorry about what had happened. A month later we were in Varanasi, India, in the heavily Muslim old part of the city. Given all the trouble in the world, we were a little apprehensive. As we walked through the narrow streets, a cow takes exception to one of our students and comes after him. He escapes serious harm, and turns to me to ask, "How did it know I was Jewish?" Soon afterwards I am bothered by a tout who won't take "no" for an answer. He keeps offering me one thing after another: Boat ride? Watch? Jewelery? What? I assure him I don't want ANYTHING. "Oh yes you do," he says with a knowing smile, "You want bin Laden!"

The Soviet Union lost influence in Egypt with the 1979 signing of a United States-brokered peace agreement between Egypt and Israel. In the same year, the Islamic Revolution in Iran caused the United States to deploy a large American naval fleet into the Persian Gulf. The Soviet Union perceived these events as a blow to its influence in the Middle East, and it decided to invade Afghanistan as a way of gaining influence and power in the region. In the aftermath of the Soviet invasion of Afghanistan in 1980, the Reagan White House, following long-standing Cold War policy, moved to build resistance against this expansion of communism through almost any means possible. In cooperation with the Saudis, the CIA recruited, equipped, and financed Islamic fighters who were moved into the mountains of Afghanistan to fight with the Mujahideen, the Afghan "Jihadis" who were resisting Soviet occupation. There, they successfully made life so difficult for the Soviets that they withdrew by 1989.

Under the diplomacy of Saudi Prince Bandar, the Saudis played an important role not only in giving rise to the Islamic fighters in Afghanistan but also in assisting the Reagan White House in its funding of the Contras in Nicaragua and CIA operations in Lebanon. Funds to support the Mujahideen in Afghanistan were also channelled through Pakistan in a covert action codenamed Operation Cyclone.

The Rise of Al-Qaeda and Osama bin Laden

Al-Qaeda, "The Base," was founded in 1988 by Abdhullah Azzam to assist veterans of the Islamic resistance in Afghanistan. Azzam was soon replaced by his former student, Osama bin Laden. There are at least two theories about the origin of the name al-Qaeda. One is that it comes from a training base that was used in the Afghanistan war. The other takes the Arabic term in its figurative meaning of "method" or "precept." Azzam, as early as 1987, called for an "al-qaeda al-sullah," meaning a "vanguard of the strong."[21] Perhaps both meanings played a role. The name took on its current meaning of a worldwide network of Islamic extremists during the publicity surrounded the trial of those accused of bombing United States embassies in Africa in 1988. In presenting its case, the FBI described al-Qaeda as a worldwide organization, headed by Osama bin Laden. It has been argued that the FBI needed a specific adversary to conform to the way the United States antiterrorism laws were written. It would be an overstatement to say that the FBI created al-Qaeda, but the publicity from the trial helped al-Qaeda become what it is today.

Life of Osama bin Laden

Osama bin Laden was born in 1957 as the seventeenth of what would eventually be the 52 children of Muhammad Awad bin Laden. His father was a wealthy business man who had immigrated to Saudi Arabia from nearby Yemen. The father started as an unskilled laborer. He was a porter at the docks. In a story that recalls the American dream, his father had started a company and watched it grow into the largest construction firm in Saudi Arabia. His mother, one of his father's four wives, had Syrian ancestry.

Osama married at age 17. While studying in Jeddah, he came under the influence of one of his teachers named Abddullah Azzam, the man who later founded al-Qaeda. Azzam was an adherent to a strict Wahhabi interpretation of Islam. In his book on the Bin Laden family, Steve Coll calls attention to young Osama's fascination with technology and airplanes, foreshadowing his later choice of terrorist means.[22]

In 1979, at age 22, he went to Afghanistan to fight with the Mujahideen resistance to the Soviets. Before leaving he had conversations with members of the royal family, for in those days he and other Saudis like him were being supported by Saudi and CIA funds. After the Soviet-Afghan war, he returned to Saudi Arabia to work for the family construction business. When his old teacher, Azzam, founded his organization to help fund the Mujahideen veterans, bin Laden became its financial officer and the main Saudi donor to the cause. He had inherited quite a fortune when his father died, which gave him the means to do this.

In 1990 bin Laden became outraged at the way the Al Saud allowed American troops to use Saudi Arabia as a base for the first Gulf War. He wrote to the Grand Mufti urging him to denounce the royals for their decision to allow the United States troops on the soil of Arabia, the homeland of the Prophet and Islam. The Grand Mufti did not, however, renounce the House of Saud. Bin Laden wrote more widely circulating treatises denouncing the USA military presence. By 1991 his criticisms were so bothersome to the government that it forced him into exile. He went to Sudan. Later, the government renounced his Saudi citizenship and the bin Laden family disowned him as well.

The failed attempt to bomb the World Trade Center in New York in 1993 led to the conviction of six Muslims whom the American government believed to be connected to

---

[21]J. Burke, "Al Aqeda," *Foreign Policy*, No. 142 (May–Jun., 2004), 18.

[22]Steve Coll. 2008. *The Bin Ladens: An Arabian Family in the American Century.* New York: Penguin Group.

bin Laden. He was suspected of being connected to the ambush of humanitarian workers in Somalia, but that connection was never proven. He did chide the United States later for being a "paper tiger" because it left Somalia after the deaths. By 1996 his suspected role in various terrorist plots led the United States to get him expelled from Sudan. He moved with his three wives and ten children to Afghanistan, where he befriended the Taliban leader Mullah Omar. The bond between the two was fixed when bin Laden married one of Mullah Omar's daughters. By 1998 bin Laden was openly calling for a jihad against all Americans, military or civilian. Four persons later convicted of bombing American embassies in Africa were said to be followers of bin Laden. In 2000 a terrorist who attempted to explode a bomb in the Los Angeles airport later said he was trained in a bin Laden-sponsored camp.

Following the September 11, 2001 destruction of both World Trade Center towers and partial destruction of the Pentagon, the United States implicated bin Laden as the mastermind of the attacks, naming al-Qaeda as the organization headed by bin Laden. The following year the United States invaded Afghanistan to oust the Taliban and capture bin Laden. The United States instituted a reward for the capture or death of bin Laden, initially at twenty-five million dollars, with a later raise to fifty million.

In 2011, ten years after the World Trade Center destruction, an American Special Forces team of Navy Seals undertook Operation Neptune Spear, authorized by President Obama after intelligence suggested bin Laden was living near a military academy in Pakistan. The Navy Seals team killed bin Laden and his body was buried at sea. Presumably the USA did not want his grave site to become a pilgrimage destination. The USA claimed it had intelligence sources proving that at least one Pakistani general was complicit in allowing bin Laden to live near the military in a complex that may have been built for that purpose. The Pakistan government denied that it was complicit in sheltering bin Laden. Whether or not the Pakistani government was directly involved, the affair put a severe strain on the USA-Pakistan bilateral relations.

Bin Laden, Wahhabi Islam, 9–11, and Ideology
Religiously, bin Laden comes from the fold of Wahhabi Islam. He was critical of the Al Saud royal family, but not directly critical of the Wahhabi clerics. One of his goals was to overthrow the Saudi monarchy, replacing it with a government based on Shariah.

It is thought that al-Qaeda joined forces with the international division of an Egyptian terrorist organization, al-Jihad, in 2002, although some scholars argue the two groups are more rivals than partners. The fame of bin Ladin attracted copycat Islamic organizations, leading to an informal network of organizations and cells around the world.

J. Burke argues that al-Qaeda has become an ideology, one that he calls "al Qaedasim."[23] One of its goals is to rid the Islamic countries of regimes which do not rule by Shariah and Islamic principles as understood by conservative interpretations. Another is to rid the Islamic world of Western influence. It is felt that Western powers, from the crusades

---

[23]J. Burke, "Al Qaeda," *Foreign Policy*, No. 142 (May–Jun., 2004), 18.

through the colonial era to the present, desire to control the politics and natural resources, especially oil, of the Islamic region. This theme plays well in the Arab world. During the second gulf war, Arab TV coverage tended to call it the "War for Oil."

This ideology does not reject all things modern. On the contrary, Islamic terrorists make great use of the modern technologies, including videos, internet sites and blogs, and television. They are quite dependent upon these technologies to globalize their appeal and impact. Their version of Islam is not exactly mainstream, however, for they tend to go outside the traditional *ulama*, feeling free to interpret the Quran and Islamic traditions for themselves. They have not followed traditional Islamic guidelines for war, especially in regard to killing civilians. The norms of terrorism do not conform to traditional Islamic norms.

The Islamic State as the Culmination of Militant Salafi Ideology

The founding of the **Islamic State** can be seen as the culmination of the aspirations of militant Salafi ideology. However, although Al-Qaeda was the best known organization of militant Salafis, the **ISIS** (Islamic State of Iraq and Syria) broke its affiliation with Al-Qaeda in Iraq before declaring an Islamic State. Whether or not the Islamic State sees itself as part of the Al-Qaeda network, it shares the Salafi ideology. It wants an Islamic state governed by Salafi-style Muslims, with a version of Hanafi Shariah as the legal basis of the state. We will discuss the Islamic State more in the next chapter.

ISSUE 4. THE ARAB SPRING AND ITS IMPACT ON THE SAUDIS

The Arab Spring

The term **Arab Spring** refers to the protest movements that spread across much of the Arab world beginning in 2010. We will look at how it started in Tunisia and then spread rapidly with the help of social media.

Origins of the Arab Spring in Tunisia's Jasmine Revolution

Revolutions and reformations have a way of spilling over from town to town, rural to urban, or occasionally even country to country. For example, there had been sporadic attempts to reform the Catholic Church before, but when a young priest and professor named Martin Luther posted 95 theses about controversial church practices for debate on a church door in a small German city in 1517, the demands to reform and modernized the Church spread to other German cities. With the help of the newly invented printing press, Luther's demands for reform spread throughout Europe. When the Pope ordered him to cease his protests, he refused, and his followers soon separated to become the Lutheran Church. Other protesting groups also broke away from Rome, and Protestant Churches became the majority religion in most countries of northern Europe. Three hundred years later, the French Revolution of 1848 similarly touched off rebellions across Europe and

Arab Spring protest demonstration in Tahrir Square, Cairo, Egypt
Photo: Goldman fund [CC0], via Wikimedia Commons

beyond. But unlike the Protestant Reformation, the European Revolutions, although given the promising label "Springtime of the Peoples," did not lead to lasting change.

Among the Arab regions there had been repeated efforts, known as the Pan-Arab movements or Pan-Arabism, to unite all Arabs politically. So far these have met resistance from nationalists and those who fear domination by a more powerful Arab neighbor, such as Egypt. But in December 2010 a different kind of political unity, one calling for more democracy and less corruption, swept across the Arab states. It started in Tunisia when a 26-year-old vender named Mohamad Bouazizi burned himself to death after police had beat him and confiscated his cart because he didn't have a permit. Thousands of Tunisians took up the cause of his protest against police corruption and tactics. A widespread series of protest demonstrations quickly followed, in what came to be called the Jasmine Revolution. After 29 days the protest succeeded in getting Tunisian President Ben Ali to resign, ending his 23 years of police-state style leadership. The role of cell phones and social media in spreading the protest and coordinating the demonstrations was a modern version of the role of the printing press during the Protestant Reformation.

The Spread of the Arab Spring in the Region
Popular Arab television networks, such as Al Jazeera and Al Arabiya, also played a major role because watching their coverage of the protests in Tunisia sparked protests against

corrupt regimes throughout the region. Egypt and Libya soon erupted with protests. Word of where and when to meet was spread on social media so effectively that the protesters grew more bold and numerous each day. The daily protests at Tahrir Square in downtown Cairo emerged as the focal point of the attention of Arabs and the rest of the world. With international news crews filming events, the regime of Egyptian President Hosni Mubarak didn't dare fire at the protestors. Yet it became so desperate that it got the camel drivers who normally give rides to tourists at the nearby pyramids to bring their camels to try to disperse the crowd at Tahrir Square. The regime was forced to give up power to a caretaker military government.

The scene was similar in Libya. Protests began in mid-February 2011, and within three days a revolutionary military force was in control of Benghazi, the second largest city. Using its superior air power, Muammar Gaddafi's long-standing regime fought back, leaving thousands dead. By August a coalition authorized by the United Nations intervened by enforcing a no-fly zone, which neutralized Gaddafi's air superiority. That, plus some bombing by the United States and France, gave the edge to the revolutionary forces and they were able to take the capital, Tripoli. Gaddafi clung to power, holding out in Sirti, his home city, but he was killed in October 2011 when it was overrun.

The Arab Spring events in Yemen started with similar protests in early 2011, but when the protestors failed at first to overthrow the regime of President Ali Abdullah Saleh, an assassination attempt left him badly wounded. He continued to rule indirectly from his hospital room in Saudi Arabia. The states of the Gulf Cooperation Council (GCC) brokered a peace deal which called for Saleh to resign in exchange for guaranteed immunity. After repeated delays, he accepted the GCC terms and resigned.

In contrast, the protests of the Assad regime in Syria have not led to a relatively swift outcome. At first it seemed that the various protest groups were gaining territory and momentum sufficient to overthrow Assad. Instead the situation has evolved into a prolonged civil war, with several outside nations supporting either the Assad regime or one of the various protest factions. The tensions between Sunni interests, led by Saudi Arabia, and Shi'i interests, led by Iran, exacerbate the civil war. Sunni-Shi'i conflicts are especially relevant in Bahrain's version of the Arab Spring, where the most of the protestors are Shi'i whereas the monarchy is Sunni. Despite large protests and brutal police tactics against protestors (supported by money and troops from Saudi Arabia), the regime of King Hamad remains in control.

Fearing that the Jasmine Revolution would spread as far as China, Chinese officials quickly took measures after a few Chinese Internet postings called for a Jasmine Revolution in China. Despite China's traditional love of jasmine flowers for their beauty and as a flavoring for tea, officials blocked Internet postings using the term jasmine, cancelled an annual Jasmine festival, and even deleted a video of the President singing a traditional song about jasmine.[24]

---

[24]"Catching Scent of Revolution, China Moves to Snip Jasmine," *The New York Times* (10 May, 2011). http://www.nytimes.com/2011/05/11/world/asia/11jasmine.html?_r=0

The Muslim Brotherhood's Short-Lived Regime in Egypt

The **Muslim Brotherhood** arose in Egypt in 1928, when Egypt was under British control. Hassan al-Banna, the Brotherhood's founder, had been influenced by the Salafist movement, which had made its way from Saudi Arabia to Egypt.[25] Al-Banna called for changes across a broad religious and political spectrum. Politically, he wanted an end to British control of Egypt. Religiously, he wanted more Islamic values to be realized in public and family life. He understood Shariah to be God's unchanging laws governing human behavior at all levels from the family up to the state. Socially, he called for better, and more Islamic, social, educational, and medical services. Toward that goal, the Muslim Brotherhood founded schools, hospitals, and other service organizations.

The Muslim Brotherhood in Egypt has often been described as fundamentalist, radical, or revolutionary, but it had become more mainstream through the decades. It did not play a leading role in the Arab Spring movement in Egypt, but it eagerly entered candidates for the post-Arab Spring elections in 2012. It easily won, taking advantage of being the only established and well known party contesting the elections, and Brotherhood leader Mohamad Morsi began a new regime. The Brotherhood had gone from being denounced and periodically outlawed to being the governing majority. Writing during this time when the Brotherhood formed the government in Egypt, Roy Olivier argued that the Muslim Brotherhood in Egypt was no longer a revolutionary movement. It had conservative views on gender roles and favored censorship of un-Islamic matters, but it tried to work with the existing regimes in Egypt and Tunisia rather than take up arms.[26]

Having become Egypt's first ever democratically elected head of state in June 2012, Morsi seemed to overreach his authority by taking such matters as declaring his legislation was not subject to court review. He also proposed to institute a new constitution that critics saw as a way to enshrine Islamist laws not wanted by many Egyptians. New protests emerged over these perceived abuses of power, and by June 2013 the military took power. The Brotherhood protested loudly that the coup d'état made a mockery of the new democracy and the will of the people, but the Western powers and many Egyptians welcomed the change. Having pushed toward Islamist values too far and too fast, without the backing of the military, the Brotherhood had held onto power for just over one year.

The Possibility of an Arab Spring in The Kingdom

The Backstory of "Petro-Islam": Islamic Terrorism and Saudi Politics

In the late 1970s two things happened that scared the Saudi family into a change of course. There was an occupation of the Grand Mosque in Mecca by Saudis outraged in part at their government's excesses. And there was the Islamic Revolution in Iran, which threatened to undermine the authority of the Saudi regime. After all, if conservative Muslims in Iran could rise up and overthrow their monarchy, it could happen in Saudi Arabia

---

[25] J. Burke, "Al Qaeda," *Foreign Policy*, No. 142 (May–Jun., 2004), 36.

[26] Roy Olivier, "There Will Be No Islamist Revolution," *Journal of Democracy 24*.1 (Jan. 2013): 14.

as well. The Al Saud reacted by stepping up internal security and by giving more influence and money to the Wahhabi clerics. As part of the package intended to maintain the loyalty of the Wahhabis, the clerics were given the green light and necessary funding to expand their brand of Islam abroad. Saudi-funded mosques were built in numerous countries, including Pakistan, Iraq, Afghanistan, Germany, Great Britain, Canada and the United States. Some observers estimate the number of mosques built by Saudi oil money to be over 1500 worldwide. Madrasahs (Islamic schools), were also built throughout the world. This phenomenon has been dubbed "petro-Islam" by some observers.

Along with the funding to build these mosques and madrasahs came the money to staff them with imams and teachers who had been trained in Wahhabi Islam, usually within Saudi Arabia. More moderate Muslims were often marginalized from local leadership positions, and some mosques became the centers of fiery sermons denouncing the west and its values. For example, Muslims in India have become divided through the introduction of a Wahhabi version claiming to be the only true Islam.[27] Although the original intent of the Saudi government was to gain the support of its Wahhabi clerics, and the intent of the clerics was to spread their brand of Islam, critics contend that the net effect of this worldwide expansion of Wahhabi Islam was to provide a breeding ground for radicals. This is not to say that the majority of the members of these mosques support radical Islam or terrorism. But just as Wahhabi Islam has been a breeding ground for Saudi militants such as Osama bin Laden, the Wahhabi-sponsored mosques have been suspected of creating terrorists, however unintentionally.

An Arab Spring in The Kingdom?

To combat the Arab Spring protests that were popping up in nations around it—Egypt to its west, Yemen to its south, Syria to its north and Bahrain to its east—as well as starting within its borders, the Saudi Arabian kingdom moved quickly to stop the protests before they could bring about the fall of the regime as in Tunisia, Libya, and Egypt. In the article "Saudi Arabia's Forgotten Shi'ite Spring," Ahman Khalid Majidyar writes that the House of Saud quickly employed several strategies. One strategy aimed at the Sunni majority involved job creation and income improvements for workers, along with housing subsidies. Another strategy, aimed at Shi'i protesters mainly, involved tightening controls, banning public gatherings, and detaining protest leaders. A very effective strategy was to blame the unrest on the Shi'i minority, thus lessening the support for change among the Sunni majority. Finally, the House of Saud used its considerable influence in the region, partly through the Gulf Cooperation Council (GCC), to keep other authoritarian regimes in the region in power.[28]

The House of Saud had good reason to fear a Shi'i uprising. Although not more than 15 percent of the Saudi population is Shi'i, they form a majority in the oil-rich Eastern

---

[27] Y. Sikkand. "Stoking the Flames: Intra-Muslim Rivalries in India and the Saudi Connection," *Comparative Studies of South Asia, Africa and the Middle East* Vol. 27, No. 1 (2007): 95–108.

[28] Ahmad Khalid Majidyar, "Saudi Arabia's Forgotten Shi'ite Spring," AEI Outlook Seriest (August, 2013), 4.

Province and many oil field laborers are Shi'i. The Eastern Province has the world's largest oil reserves and is home to the largest oil company, Saudi Aramco. Any serious protests in that regime could have caused a major disruption in Saudi oil production and export capabilities. Given the history of Wahabi attacks on Shi'is and their shrines, as well as the ways that Shi'is are treated as second-class citizens in the kingdom, there were certainly grounds for protests. Adding to the threat was the fear of Iranian influence, for there had been some revolutionary zeal among Saudi Shi'is, led by the Organization of Islamic Revolution in the Arabian Peninsula (IRO), following the 1979 Islamic Revolution in Iran. Majidyar notes that to encourage Shi'i resistance, Iran maintains Arab language radio and television (Al Aram) stations that broadcast accusations of corruption and other charges against the Saudi royalty, while encouraging revolutionary activities.[29]

These strategies succeeded in avoiding a regime change in The Kingdom as well as in GCC neighbor Bahrain.

From Arab Spring to Islamic Revival

With the possible exception of Tunisia, the Arab Spring did not fulfil its promise. There were regime changes, but critics may argue that the aftermath was often a replacement of one authoritative regime with another. Both within and beyond the Arab region of the Middle East, there is an Islamic Revival movement which appears to be a more lasting game-changer. We will revisit this topic in the concluding chapter when we step back from our country by country approach to survey "the big picture."

OVERVIEW AND THEORETICAL DISCUSSION

After a brief review of the rise of Islam and its holy sites in Arabia, we considered four issues important to the interface of religion and politics in the kingdom. The first issue concerns the House of the Shaykh. A very conservative interpretation of Islam, tracing back through ibn Tamiyyah, was fervently advocated by al-Wahhab, known as the Shaykh. This form of Islam is known as Salafism to Muslims, but others often refer to it as Wahhabism due to the pivotal role of al-Wahhab.

The second issue dealt with the al Saud, the royal family that forms the political side of the twin powers of religion and politics in Saudi Arabia. The Saudi kings have relied on the support of the House of the Shaykh for the authority to rule during each of the three phases the kingdom. There is an ongoing arrangement in which the two Houses mutually support each other and ward off challenges to each other in their respective arenas of authority—political or religious.

The third issue, Islamic terrorism, focused on Osama bin Laden and his real or symbolic leadership of an Islamic resistance to the Saudi monarchy, to Israel, and to Western influence in Islamic countries. Agreeing with one or all of those goals does not make

---

[29]*Ibid.,* 1.

one a terrorist, but using indiscriminate violence to cause terror among your perceived enemies does. The success of Sunni ISIS in taking control of Sunni territory, combined with ISIS's expansionistic goals, has brought the West and Iran closer together in the sense that they now have a new enemy that they fear more than they fear each other!

The fourth issue discussed the rise of the Arab Spring. Having started in Tunisia, the Arab Spring touched off democratic or at least anti-oppression demonstrations and demands throughout much of the Arab world. However, the Arab Spring did not get much traction in Saudi Arabia or the nearby Gulf States.

Theoretical Discussion

"Fencing in" the Fundamental Laws in Comparative Religions

The Salafi stress on the doctrine of Tawhid amounts to an extreme form of monotheism that zealously denounces any practices that might even approach idolatry. In comparative religions we can see a tendency for legalistic religions to go to great lengths to avoid even coming close to breaking the religious laws that are considered fundamental to the faith. In the chapter on India we discussed the way some Brahmins imposed great restrictions on the Dalits to guard their own purity. Brahmins refused to take food or water from "untouchables," avoided letting a Dalit's shadow fall on themselves, and did not allow Dalits to spend the night inside the village. In the Talmudic era, Jewish rabbis added layer upon layer of laws as buffers against breaking the Torah commandments. For example, the Torah commandment to not cook baby goat in its own mother's milk was expanded by interpretation so many times that keeping strict kosher came to mean never allowing any meat to mix with any milk product at a meal. Then the rabbinic court ruled that one could not even use the same cooking pots, plates or serving dishes for a meat meal on one occasion and a milk meal on another. This total avoidance of mixing meat and milk was all created as buffer laws around the central concern. The Rabbis called this process "fencing in the Torah." Although the Salafi would not use the concept "fencing in," in comparative religion terms they have also built buffer rules around the central concern, the unity of god.

Women, Wahhabi Salafism, and Theories about Fundamentalism

Salafi Islam, especially in its modern Wahhabi manifestation, is a textbook case of religious fundamentalism. First, there are several similarities between Wahhabi Islam and the Christians for whom the term *fundamentalism* was coined a century ago. One strong similarity is that both are literalists. Christian fundamentalists affirm the inerrancy (without error) of scriptures, and thanks to the legacy of ibn Taymiyyah, Wahhabi Muslims also stand firmly for a literalist interpretation of the Quran and the hadith. There are some differences, however. For Christian fundamentalists, the thrust of their affirmation of Biblical literalism was to reject liberal academic criticism of the Bible and to reject Darwinian and other scientific positions that do not conform to a literal reading of the Bible. Wahhabi Muslims are not that concerned about questions raised by science or by academic criticism of the Quran. Rather, their literalism is a rejection of what they perceive to be innovations in Islamic practice since the days of the Salaf.

In conformity with Bruce Lawrence's definition, Wahhabi Islam reacts against the secular values of modernity. It idealises an early, pure Islamic era of the first three Islamic generations (Salaf). It rejects the relativism of secularism in favor of the certainty that arises from affirming that the Quran is the literal word of God. Lawrence's observation that Christian fundamentalists do not reject modern technology, just modernist values, does not fit the Wahhabis, however. They have a history of being suspicious of new technologies, such as recorded music or television as foreign and unIslamic. Some Wahhabis have even condemned sports such as soccer as foreign.

Other characteristics of religious fundamentalism found in Wahhabi Islam include a downplaying of the role of women, a mistrust of pluralism, and a condemnation of religious opponents as not being true believers—as reflected in the Salafi rejection of Shi'i Muslims and even the denunciation of Sunni Muslims who follow different practices.

The restrictions placed upon women, however, is the most striking of all the fundamentalist traits observed in Wahhabi Saudi Arabia. One restriction that has gained the world's attention recently is the regulation against women drivers. Although women are allowed to drive cars elsewhere in Islamic societies, Wahhabi requests have led the Saudi Kings to ban female drivers. There is no specific law against females driving, but females are not allowed to get a driver's licence. This amounts to the same thing for Saudi women, but ironically women with a foreign driver's licence can legally drive. And in rural areas some women drive cars without being challenged. Some brave Saudi women activists, such as journalist **Wajeha Al-Huwaider**, have protested the ban from time to time, so far without success. Posting videos of Saudi women driving on YouTube has brought world attention to the Wahhabi-inspired policy. One woman filmed herself driving, and families in passing cars can be seen giving the thumbs up gesture in support. In December 2014, the cases of two women—Loujain al-Hathloul and Maysa al-Amoudi—who had been detained for over a month for driving, were transferred for trial in a terrorist court. The reason for the transfer is thought to be due to comments they made on social media.[30]

The king seems to be supportive of women being allowed to drive, but the religious conservatism of the Wahhabis keeps the change from happening. But why are the Wahhabis so concerned about women driving? They take pride in living by the values of the Salaf, but there was no ban in that period on women driving camels or whatever the equivalent of driving cars might be. And there is no Quranic or Hadith passage directly relevant to the question. One reason is that, from a Wahhabi point of view, the idea that women should always have a male protector, or guardian, when they appear in public implies that women should not be allowed to drive cars. The Quran specifies who has too close a relationship to be eligible for marriage to a woman (or inversely, to a man). The lists include close relatives and close in-laws as one might expect, but it also includes a person with

---

[30]"Saudi terrorism court to 'to try women drivers,'" *BBC News*, December 25, 2014. http://www.bbc.com/news/world-middle-east-30602155

Saudi Activist Wajeha al-Huwaider protesting for women's right to drive.
Photo:

a wet-nursing relationship.[31] The Arabic term **mahram** refers to a person ineligible for sexual relations and therefore marriage. A woman appearing in public is supposed to have a mahram, a male guardian, although the term mahram is now used to include a broader range of men who can serve as a guardian. The underlying concept is that a woman needs a male to protect her against other males who might make sexual advances. This doesn't directly relate to driving, because in practice a woman might drive the car while her guardian rides with her, but the Wahhabi fear seems to be that letting women drive will lead to more independence from males. Other reasons are also given, such as that women will have to come into contact with non-mahram males if, for example, they are stopped by the police or there is a traffic accident. One sheikh, based on a so-called medical study, stated that driving was bad for a woman's pelvis and ovaries.[32]

There have been severe restrictions on the political rights of women as well, but that is changing. In 2013 women were appointed for the first time to the Consultative Assembly, the kingdom's advisory parliament. Women were not eligible to vote in or be candidates for municipal elections, but that was to change in the 2015 elections.

Traditional Kingship vs. Democratic and Theocratic Alternatives

---

[31] It was common practice in old Arabia for more affluent families to hire another woman to nurse a baby.

[32] The Young Turks news report, "Ovaries Get Damaged When Women Drive, Says Saudi Sheik." https://www.youtube.com/watch?v=fPLBdwbFuvw

In Huntington's terms, Wahhabi Islam clashes with western civilization on many levels. One of the cornerstones of western civilization is the ideal of democracy, but Wahhabi Islam rejects democracy on the grounds that laws are not to be made by democratic vote, but by interpreting the Quran and the hadith. This is a "contradiction between a force that sees itself as a custodian of the divine message, hence as having a monopoly on truth, and a system built on relative truths and opinions."[33] Secularism, another characteristic of western civilization, is rejected as well because it refuses to grant authority to any one religious tradition.

The House of Saud and its historic partnership with the House of the Shaykh, the descendants of al-Wahhab have combined to provide the religious and political governance of the kingdom for much of the past three hundred years. Oil revenues have made the difference in Saudi Arabia. From the discovery of oil in the late 1930s, oil has provided the money the large royal family needs to live an extravagant lifestyle while at the same time provided both funding for Salafi causes and enough money for services to keep the people relatively satisfied under the monarchy's regime.

International Relations: Saudi Arabia and the United States
The fact that an American company won the first oil exploration rights in Saudi Arabia has had a major impact on international relations. Oil has brought the Saudis and the United States into a longstanding partnership that now embraces not only the oil industry in both countries but also banking, investments and even covert operations.

The book with the intriguing title *House of Bush, House of Saud: The Secret Relationship Between the World's Two Most Powerful Dynasties,* by C. Unger makes the case for the unusually close relationship between the two Bush presidents and the Saudi royal family. It argues that Prince Bandar became a close friend of the first President Bush and then later was close to his son also. Through Prince Bandar and large investments in the United States, the argument goes, the bin Laden family also came to be exceptionally close to the Bush White Houses. Not Osama bin Laden himself, but the bin Laden (or bin Ladin) family who remain in Saudi Arabia and whose business, the Saudi Binladin Group, wins most of the major construction contracts issued in the kingdom through its close contacts and intermarriage with the Saudi royal family.

Unger documents the way members of the bin Laden and Saudi families were flown out of the United States in the aftermath of the 2001 attacks, even though private flights were still officially grounded. He assumes that this was arranged during a White House meeting shortly after September 11 between President Bush and Prince Bandar. The Bush White House has denied involvement.

The Bush, Saudi, and bin Laden family connections extend deep into the oil, investment, and banking industries, Unger argues. He goes into detail about several of these connections, including those with the Carlyle Group, a global investment firm. He criti-

---

[33]Abdel Salam Sidahmed and Anoushiravan Ehteshami, ed.s, *Islamic Fundamentalism* (Boulder: Westview Press, 1996), 13.

cizes the Bush White House for going soft on Saudi Arabia in the United States' global war on terrorism. Unger does concede that if the Saudi regime were to be replaced, the new regime would likely be much less friendly toward United States and Western interest.

STUDY QUESTIONS

1. What is Salafi Islam and why is it sometimes called Wahhabism?
2. Why has the bond between the House of Saud and the House of the Shaykh held together for so long?
3. What are the origins and tactics of Islamic-style terrorist organizations?
4. How did the Arab Spring start, spread, and end without regime change in Saudi Arabia?
5. What forms of women's rights protests are found in Saudi Arabia?

FURTHER READING

Abukhalil, As'ad. *The Battle for Saudi Arabia: Royalty, Fundamentalism, and Global Power.* New York: Seven Stories Press, 2004. Good on most of the topics in this chapter.

Bradley, John L. *Saudi Arabia Exposed: Inside a Kingdom in Crisis.* New York: Palgrave MacMillan, 2005. Good on everyday life in the Kingdom.

Coll, Steve. *The Bin Ladens: An Arabian Family in the American Century.* New York: Penguin Group, 2008. A Yemini family becomes construction millionaires in Arabia.

Cooke, Miriam. *Women Claim Islam.* New York and London: Routledge, 2001. Islamic Feminism revealed through literary works in the Arab world.

Davidson, Lawrence. *Islamic Fundamentalism.* Westport: Greenwood Press, 1998. Includes a chapter on Saudi Arabia.

Hussain, Amir. "Islamic Traditions." In *A Concise Introduction to World Religions*, edited by Willard G. Oxtoby, Roy C. Amore and Amir Hussain. Toronto: Oxford University Press, 2015. A introduction to Islam.

Lippman, Thomas W. *Inside the Mirage: America's Fragile Partnership with Saudi Arabia.* Boulder: Westview Press, 2004. A journalist's account of the United States-Saudi relationship.

Miller, Judith. *God Has Ninety-Nine Names.* New York: Simon and Schuster, 1996. A journalist's eyewitness account of several Islamic countries, including Saudi Arabia.

Milton-Edwards, Beverley. *Islamic Fundamentalism since 1945.* London and New York: Routledge, 2005. Deals with causes for and diverse forms of Islamic fundamentalism as an ideology.

Roy, Oliver. *Globalized Islam:The Search for a New Ummah.* New York: Columbia University Press, 2004. Includes a chapter on bin Laden.

Unger, Craig. *House of Bush, House of Saud: The Secret Relationship Between the World's Two Most Powerful Dynasties.* New York: Scribner, 2004. An investigative journalist's fascinating report.

Yergin, Daniel. *The Prize: The Epic Quest for Oil, Money and Power.* New York: Simon and Schuster, 1991. A very well researched history of oil that opens up much of modern political, military and industrial history.

WEBSITES

atheism.about.com/library/FAQs/islam/countries/bl_SaudiIndex.htm About.com's site on Saudi Arabia, with links to articles on religion and politics.

www.carnegieendowment.org/events/index.cfm?fa-eventDetail&id=876 A 2006 article on efforts at political reform in Saudi Arabia.

countrystudies.us/saudi-arabia/54.htm An article on the role of Ulama in Saudi Arabia.

www.hermes-press.com/BushSaud.htm An article by M. Mairesse on "The Bush-Saudi Connection."

www.islambasics.com/view.php?bkID=151&chapter=0 A site on ibn Wahhab's life and work, written from a Muslim point of view.

KEY PEOPLE

Wajeha Al-Huwaider A female activist in Saudi Arabia

Imam Ali The fourth Caliph according to Sunni history and the first Imam according to Shi'i history.

Wajeha Al-Huwaider Author and journalist who is an activist against restrictions on women in Saudi Arabia.

Ibn Abd al-Wahhab An eighteenth century Islamic thinker who greatly influenced later Salafi thought, especially on the strict interpretation of *tawhid*.

Abu Bakr The first Caliph

Osama Bin Laden The best known leader of the Al-Qaeda network.

Imam Husayn The son of Imam Ali who was killed in the massacre at Karballah.

Muhammad The "Seal of the Prophets" through whom the Qu'ran was revealed.

Muawiyah The fifth caliph and founder of a new Umayyad Caliphate in Damascus.

Taqi ad-Din Ahmad Ibn Taymiyyah A conservative Islamic scholar (1263–1328) whose writings laid the foundation for Salafi theology.

GLOSSARY

Al-Qaeda The "Base," the most commonly used name for the organization formerly headed by Osama bin Laden, combining Wahhabi thought with terrorist tactics.

Al Saud The House of Saud, the extended royal family of Arabia.

Al-Shaykh the House of the Shaykh, meaning the extended family tracing ancestry back to al-Wahhab.

Hadith the "traditions," sayings attributed to Muhammad or other respected early Muslims.

Hanbali The most strict of the four schools of Islamic law, followed by Salafi Muslims among others.

Hijrah The "migration" of Muhammad from Mecca to the city afterward known as Medina.

Houthis A militant movement of Zaidi Shi'is active in war-torn Yemen.

Ikhwan The "Brotherhood" of Bedouins who adopted a settled lifestyle and Wahhabi theology.

Islamic State (ISIS) A state established in parts of Syria and Iraq by a militant Islamist organization.

Ka'bah The cube shaped temple to Allah in Mecca.

kafir An infidel, in Islamic thought.

Kharijites An early Islamic group who carried out assassinations on other Muslims.

mahram The Shariah term for a person so closely related that it is forbidden to have sexual relations with them. The term is used in a more generic sense of protector or guardian.

Mecca or Mekkah The holy city in Saudi Arabi, the focus of Islamic prayers and pilgrimage.

Medina The "City" of the Prophet, a holy city in Saudi Arabia.

Night Journey The trip Muhammad is said to have taken to Jerusalem and then up into heaven.

Ramadan The month in the Islamic calendar during which Muslims fast from dawn until dusk.

Rasul A 'Messenger' of God, used especially to describe the role of Muhammad.

Salaf The first three generations of Muslim leaders after Muhammad. Thought to be especially pure in their practice of Islam.

Salafi A Muslim who admires and seeks to emulate the purity of the Salaf period.

Shariah Islamic Law, as revealed throught Prophet Muhammad as the Messenger of God.

Shi'i or Shi'a A Muslim who follows any one of several Islamic traditions tracing back through a line of Imams to Imam Ali and the Prophet Muhammad.

Shirk In Islam, the sin of "associating" anything with God, thereby compromising God's Unity or Oneness (tawhid)

Sunni Muslim who follows the majority Islamic position tracing back through the Caliphs to the Sunnah and Muhammad.

Sunnah The words and deeds of Muhammad, and the namesake of a Sunni Muslim.

Surah A section of the Quran.

Tawhid The Unity or Oneness of God, in Islamic thought, in contrast to polytheism or idolatry.

Ulama Religious scholars in Islam.

Ummah The "Community" of all Muslims.

Zaidi A Shi'i sect found mainly in Yemen.

Chapter Five

Iran and Iraq

The Rise of Shi'i Activism:
Sunni-Shi'i Tensions, Political Activism, New Caliphate, and The Islamic State

In this chapter you will learn about:

- the religious and political background of Iran and Iraq
- the ongoing tensions between Sunni and Shi'i Muslims
- political and social activism among Shi'i clerics
- the rise and goals of ISIS and the Islamic State

> *In the Fall of 1995, I was met at the airport by… my new translator…. The revolution was changing, but too slowly to permit Western-educated Iranians to fulfill their professional aspirations….*
>
> *Tehran looked much better to me than it had during my earlier visits…. Tehran's streets were now well maintained and clean…. The once-omnipresent soldiers on the streets were gone. The revolutionary graffiti that used to cover public buildings had been erased: Billboards advertising "Nokios," the latest cellular phones, Kodak, Ray-Ban, Winston, and Xerox were now as ubiquitous as Koranic verses had been only a few years ago. Women still covered their heads, but they tied their scarves more loosely. The "uniforms" had also changed. Some women, particularly the young, wore pastel manteaus and even more brightly colored head scarves, along with obvious makeup. The other day, Nahzi told me, a woman broadcaster had worn a bright pink head scarf on state television!… What happened to the ban on "Bad Hijab?"*
>
> Judith Miller[1]

[1]Judith Miller. 1996. *God Has Ninety-Nine Names.* 447–448.

*Our next stop brings us to the most eastern region of the Middle East. As we arrive in Tehran's new **Imam Khomeini** airport its name reminds us of why we came here. We want to visit the home of the Islamic Revolution that started the modern rise of political Islam, especially among the Shi'i Muslims who will be the main subject of this chapter. Our trip downtown gives us a view of a huge metropolis crowed with drab buildings, traffic, and air pollution. Once downtown, however, we see large mosques, majestic palaces, and more museums than we can count. We stroll through the huge bazaar, where there are clusters of gold shops, spice shops, cloth shops, and practically everything else from traditional handicrafts to the latest electronic gear.*

RELIGIOUS BACKGROUND: POLITICAL ISLAM

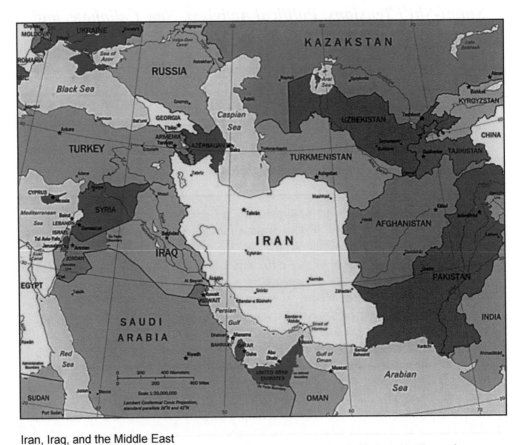

Iran, Iraq, and the Middle East

Source: United States. Central Intelligence Agency. *Southwest Asia*. [Washington, D.C.]: Central Intelligence Agency, 1996. http://www.veteranstoday.com/2014/07/19/neo-russian-iranian-cooperation-on-regional-security/

This chapter focuses on Shi'i Islam in Iran and Iraq. When Muhammad moved from Mecca in 622 to accept the political and spiritual leadership of the city now known as Medina, religion and politics combined in Islam. The combining of prophethood and political leadership is rare in history. One could argue that something similar happened when Moses became leader of the Israelites during the period of wondering in the wilderness. Buddhism and Christianity, however, developed for two or three hundred years before gaining any access to political power.

The combination of political power and Islamic spirituality has been a great strength to Islam, but as discussed in the previous chapter it also led to a leadership crisis during the era of Ali, when two claimants to leadership each gained partisans, complete with armies. We will continue the discussion of Shi'is and the history of tensions between Sunni and Shi'i Islam as our first issue.

Iran and Iraq have sometimes been under one empire, but in the modern period they have distinct political histories. As a political background to our three issues, for Iraq we will focus on the rule of the **Ba'ath Party** and its most important leader, **Saddam Hussein**. For Iran our focus will be the period of the rule by **Shahs**. Although the two regimes were so different politically, they did share a trait relevant to our topic of the interface of religion and politics: both the Shahs and the Ba'athists were secularist regimes. This frustrated the religious conservatives, and pent-up anger would later fuel a Shi'i revival in both countries.

> *We take an early morning plane from Tehran to Shiraz, the capital in the 1700s. We visit the shrine to Iran's national poet, Hafez, who lived here in the 1300s. His beautiful lyric poetry is revered by Iranians today, but the underlying ideas in his poems would not meet with the approval of the conservative clerics who hold authority here today. Next we ride the bus for almost an hour before arriving at Persepolis, the ancient capital. After we climb the hill to the top of the ruined city, we are in a perfect place to reflect on Persia's long and important political history.*

Iran

The name *Persia* used traditionally in the West comes from the Greek name for the region, Persis, derived from the Pars area in southern Iran. The Shah requested that the country be called Iran in 1935. The word *Iran* is the Persian way of spelling *Aryan*, the name used for the "noble" people in India and Iran. In the India chapter we discussed how the so-called "Aryan Invasion" theory was a favorite target of the Hindu Nationalists. The language and culture of ancient Iran and northwest India were closely related. The main language in Iran is Persian (or Farsi), a modern Persian language of the Indo-Iranian family of languages. There are many dialects of Persian spoken there, and Kurdish and Armenia are used as well. Arabic is used for Islamic prayers and Quranic studies of course, but in general the divide between the Arabic and non-Arabic Middle East falls at the Iraq-Iran border.

Although the Iranian region is quite mountainous and subject to droughts, it was the home of some major empires in the past. Starting in the sixth century B.C., the Median Empire ruled a large territory from what is now northern Iran. The Mede people may be ancient ancestors of the Kurdish people, some of whom now want an independent Kurdistan. The Achaemenian Empire (648–330 B.C.) started by Cyrus the Great combined the old Median territories and Babylon into a powerful political entity ranging from Egypt to modern Pakistan. Cyrus was very important for Jewish history as well, because after he conquered Babylon he freed the Jews from their Babylonian Captivity. Some Jews remained in Babylon, some moved to the Persian capital, and some returned to Jerusalem, where they rebuilt the temple.

After Alexander the Great's conquest of Persia in 334 B.C., the Iranians re-established control under the Parthian Empire (249 B.C.–A.D. 224), which put an Eastern limit on Roman expansion. This was followed by the Sassanian Empire (224–651), which was the high point for the Zoroastrian religion.

Islam came to Iran during the time of the second caliph, Umar. His army conquered Iran in 642–644 and began the centuries-long process of replacing Zoroastrianism with Islam. Those few who refused to convert are the ancestors of the Parsees discussed in the India chapter. During the rule of the Damascus-based **Ummayad Caliphate**, the Iranian Muslims were marginalized, but the subsequent **Abbasid Caliphate** (750–1517) based in Baghdad integrated them into Islam, as we will discuss below.

The Seljuk Turks took control of Iraq in the eleventh century. They were Sunni Muslims but there were intervals of rule by Shi'i Muslims. The Mongol invasion started in the early 1200s and brought great destruction to both the population and the culture of Iran.

The Safavid Dynasty beginning in the early 1500s brought Shi'i Muslim rule and culture. It gave shape to the predominantly Shi'i Iran of today. The Ghajar Dynasty brought the rule of a Turkic elite beginning in 1781. Its founder, Agha Muhammad Khan took the title Shah, king. The term *shah* is related to the Indian term *kshatriya* for the ruling class.

A military officer overthrew the Ghajar Dynasty and established the new **Pahlavi Dynasty** in 1925. His ruling name was Reza Shah Pahlavi. Like Ataturk in Turkey, he set out to modernize and westernize Iran. As we will see, those two policies, combined with his dictatorial style, created a significant resistance and led to a backlash and eventual revolution led by the clerics.

The influence of European powers had begun in the 1700s and intensified in the twentieth century, heightened by the discovery of oil in Iran in the early 1900s. During Worldd War II the Allies needed Iranian oil. They helped force Reza Shah to step down because he favored the Nazi side. He was replaced by his more pro-Allies son, Mohammad Reza Shah Pahlavi, who was the Shah on the Peacock Throne[2] in the period leading up to the Islamic Revolution. W. Forbis suggests that the establishment of the Islamic Republic in 1979 marked the fall of the world's oldest monarchy.[3] Characterizing the past

---

[2]Named after the peacock image on the ornate throne, for the peacock was seen as a king's guardian

[3]William Forbis, *Fall of the Peacock Throne: The Story of Iran* (New York: McGraw-Hill, 1981).

2500 years of Iranian history as a continuous monarchy may be an overstatement, but 1979 marked a major turning point in modern Iranian history. We will need to ask it if also marks a major turning point in world history as well.

Iraq

Iraqis are proud of their history tracing back to ancient Mesopotamia and its many achievements. For example, King Hammurabi of Babylon wrote what may have been the world's first written law code in the 1700s B.C. Ancient Babylon had advanced math, sailing, city planning, writing, and its famous hanging gardens in Baghdad.

The height of Islamic power in Iraq came when it was the home of the **Abbasid Caliphate**. The name Abbasid derives from the ruling family being descendants of Muhammad's uncle Abbas, one of the Companions of Muhammad. Whereas the Umayyad family had led the resistance to Muhammad in the early days in Mecca, here was a family, the Abbasid, with a family connection to Muhammad. An Abbasid had defeated the Umayyads and been proclaimed caliph, founding the Abbasid Califphate in 750. The Umayyad Caliphate had been in Damascus, but the second Abbasid caliph, al-Mansur, moved the Caliphate to Baghdad in 762, located in a newly built, round city. The Al-Mansur district of Baghdad is named after him.

The Abbasid Caliphate was very good at including the culture and learning of its Persian subjects. The first Abbasid had defeated the Umayyads with the help of the recently-converted Persian Muslims, and one reason to move the court to Baghdad was to be closer to Persia. For the first time non-Arabs; that is, Persians, were included at court. Islamic culture had expanded beyond its Arabic base. The ancient rivals, Persia and Mesopotamia, were working in harmony.

Rise of a Shi'i Regime

The Abbasids had difficulties with the various divisions of Shi'i Islam. Even though they had come to power with the support of some Shi'i factions, the Abbasid efforts to win the lasting cooperation and support of various Shi'i factions did not succeed. By 945 a Shi'i faction known as the Buyid Dynasty had taken virtual control of the area, reducing the Abbasid Caliphate to the status of a powerless figurehead. The Buyid period was the height of Shi'i power in Iraq. It was not until after the fall of Saddam that Shi'is again had a real chance to rule the country.

Ottoman Period and British Periods

The **Ottoman Empire** (1300–1922) ruled Iraq from its headquarters in Turkey. The Empire expanded to include all or most of Turkey, Arabia and Palestine. It defeated Iran in 1517, thus extending its influence there. By the mid-nineteenth century the empire was badly in debt to European banks and was in decline. It made the mistake of allying with Germany in World War I and so lost its territories, mostly to the French and British.

After the collapse of the Ottoman Empire during World War I, the modern state of Iraq was created. The boundaries were drawn at the Paris Peace Conference of 1919–20 by the winning Allies. M. McMillan in her book *Paris 1919: Six Months that Changed the World* gives a careful history of the conference and the geographic messes it created. It set up the British Mandate in Palestine, but that is a topic for the Israel–Palestine chapter. It created the modern state of Iraq, despite the fact that the new entity threw together Kurdish, Shi'i and Sunni populations with a history of not getting along well.[4]

The British Mandate in Iraq began in 1920, but it soon met with resistance when there was an uprising in the same year. The British delegation, under the direction of then cabinet minister Winston Churchill, ordered the use of high-tech military to suppress the "Iraq Revolt." In an early example of what would later become the norm in later wars, airplanes were used to drop artillery, firebombs and mustard gas. Note that later Saddam would be highly criticized in the West for using gas against his people.

Rise of the Ba'ath Party
The Arabic word *ba'ath* means resurrection or revival. Beginning in the 1930s three teachers in Damascus, Syria, advocated a revival of Arab nationalism and espoused a non-Marxist socialist economy. They founded the Ba'ath Arab Socialist Party in 1947. This was just one year before the establishment of modern Israel and the defeat of the Arab countries who went to war in protest. After that war the Ba'ath party's approach to a modern and united Arab nationalism began to catch on in other Arab countries. In Iraq the party was established under the name Arab Ba'ath Socialist Party in 1954.

Ba'athists tend to be secular Sunni Muslims who believe in nationalism and pan-Arab (all Arab) cooperation. The Party's motto is Unity (pan-Arabism), Freedom (anti-colonialism), and Socialism. In 1963 the Ba'ath party came to power in Syria, where it remains in power, and ruled briefly in Iraq. The Iraq and Syrian parties split in 1966, partly over the Syrian party's more pro-Soviet stance.

The Iraqi Ba'ath party returned to power in a 1968 coup led by General Ahmad Hassan al-Bakr. He ruled the government of Iraq with an iron fist but there were dissidents and purges within the party. Saddam Hussein took control in 1979 and ruled strictly until his defeat by the United States–led coalition in 2003. Great controversy has surrounded the Bush White House's policy of dismissing Ba'athists from the post-Saddam regime. At first the goal was to keep them completely out of leadership roles, but with the rise of Sunni-based terrorist resistance, by 2008 the United States relaxed that policy.

ISSUE 1: SUNNI-SHI'I TENSIONS

The two main divisions of Islam are intermixed in this region, so our first issue will review the history of this division between Sunni and Shi'i and then consider its impact on recent politics.

---

[4]Margaret McMillan, *Paris 1919: Six Months that Changed the World* (New York: Random House, 2002), (Back matter).

Political Power

Political power has usually been held by the Sunnis. The Umayyad Caliphate in Damascus and the Abassid Caliphate in Bagdad were headed by Sunni caliphs. Sunnis controlled the Seljuk and Ottoman Empires centered in Turkey.

There have been some periods in which Shi'i Muslims held political power, however. The height of Shi'i political power was the Fatima Caliphate (909–1171) that ruled from Cairo. It was known for its tolerance of other forms of Islam as well as of Christians and Jews. Since those days Shi'is have been out of political power in most countries, living as a minority population under either Sunni or western control.

Political Strength of Shi'is in Iraq and the Region
Whereas the Shi'i-Sunni population ratio is fairly close in Iraq, the other two countries of the region go to the two extremes. Estimates put the Shi'i population at only 15 percent in Afghanistan. At the other extreme, around 93 percent of the Iranian population is Shi'i.[5]

Southern Iraq is a Shi'i stronghold. Much of central Iraq is Sunni, and the Kurds in the Northwest are mostly Sunni. There are more Shi'i than Sunni Muslims in Iraq, but historically the wealth and power were in Sunni hands. Even though the Shi'is are over 60 percent of the population, they were not well represented in the Ba'ath Party government of Saddam Hussein. After his overthrow, Shi'is were able to win a majority of the seats in the new parliament on the basis of their numbers and the fact that some Sunnis boycotted the elections.

Having won the election, Shi'i political leader Nouri al-Maliki of the Islamic Dawa Party was chosen as the new Prime Minister of post-Saddam Iraq in 2006. Under Shi'i control, the government began to replace Sunni civil servants and military personnel with Shi'is.

The attempt to restore order and bring economic prosperity to Iraq has been marred by many problems, including serious violence and killings between the Shi'i and Sunni Muslims, sometimes referred to as a "civil war." Through harassment and killings, neighborhoods have been "cleansed" of either their Shi'i or Sunni minorities.

Faced with a loss of political and economic power, many Sunnis withdrew support for the Maliki government. Civil strife between three main factions—Kurds, Sunni Iraqis and Shi'i Iraqis—led to a breakdown in government services and security. The conditions were such that a breakup of Iraq into Kurdish, Sunni, and Shi'i states seemed not only likely but even desirable. Under the triple threat of becoming a failed state, of being overrun by the Islamic State, and of losing the military and economic support of the United States, Maliki stepped down in 2014 in favor of a different Shi'i politician, Haider al-Abadi. Al-Abadi pledged to form a more inclusive government. A major goal was to win back the support of Sunni tribal leaders who had pledged their support to the Islamic State faction.

---

[5]See www.islamicweb.com

ISSUE 2: POLITICAL ROLE OF THE CLERICS IN IRAN

From the time of the Hijrah in 622 when Muhammad accepted the leadership of the city that came to be known as Medina, Islam and politics have gone hand in hand. Whereas Christianity did not gain any political control in the Roman Empire until three hundred years after the death of Jesus, Muhammad was the political leader of Arabia for a decade before his death in 632.

In the traditional Sunni system the Caliph was the political leader. He had the responsibility of overseeing and protecting Islam. The actual interpretation of Quranic-based law was put in the hands of Quranic scholars. Thus, unlike kings, in theory the Caliph did not make laws, but enforced the laws as interpreted by the Quranic scholars.

In the Shi'i traditions, on the other hand, there was not such a strong division between the political leader and spiritual authority. This provides a clue into the strong political role of the clerics, especially the Shi'i clerics in modern Iraq and Iran. From Iran's Ayatollah Khomeini to Iraq's al-Sadr, the political role of Shi'i clerics stands out.

Ayatollah Khomeini

We turn to the story of an Iranian cleric whose radical criticism of the corruption, westernization and secularism of the Shah led to his exile and eventual return to lead what most likely was the most important interface of religion and politics in the twentieth century.

Khomeini before the Islamic Revolution
Ruhollah Khomeini was born in the town of Khomein south of Tehran, into a family claiming descent from Imam Ali and his wife Fatima. As such he was entitled to the honorific title Seyed (or Sayyid), meaning "Master" or "Leader." His family was known for its devotion to Shi'i Islam . His father was murdered when he was still an infant. The event was taken to imply that the baby was bad luck. His mother remarried and, perhaps at the insistence of her new husband, gave the baby to the care of her sister. As F. Hoveyda points out, when Ruhollah started Quranic studies, he would have learned that the Prophet Muhammad was also raised by his uncle.[6] This may have helped give him the sense of a special purpose that he exhibited later in life.

His studies at school included both the Quran and traditional subjects. His seminary training was mostly done in the holy city of Qom, a major shrine city and the center of Shi'i learning in Iran. Khomeini became a university instructor and wrote on Islamic history and philosophy. During that period of his life he was a respected Islamic academic who was not active in politics. He was, however, very critical of the Westernizing tendencies of the Shah, and his writings already reflected the belief that clerics should be politically involved.

---

[6]Fereydoun Hoveyda, *The Broken Crescent: The "Threat" of Militant Islamic Fundamentalism*. (Westport: Praeger, 1998).

Khomeini was upwardly mobile, and toward that end he became an assistant to an important Grand Ayatollah named Boroujerdi, who had found favor with the Shah. As the assistant to Boroujerdi, he had occasion to meet with the Shah, and the reports are that they instantly disliked each other. One wonders, however, if either one of them imagined that the young cleric would one day lead an Islamic Revolution overthrowing the Peacock Throne of the Shahs.

Khomeini also developed a relationship with a more conservative Grand Ayatollah named Kashani, with whom he had more in common in that they were both advocates of a strong political role for clerics. When Ayatollah Boroujerdi, who followed a more traditional approach that avoided political activism, learned of his assistant's friendliness with his rival Ayatollah Kashani, he dismissed Khomeini. This brought Khomeini even more into the conservative camp of activist clerics, as he turned against the more moderate Boroujerdi.

Besides his work as a teacher, writer, and rising clerical administrator, he found time to run a business in Qom with his brother. They were quite successful in business.

Khomeini's Spiritual Retreat

Khomeini withdrew for a month on a spiritual retreat. When he returned he seemed different to his friends. He seemed more detached, but strangely focused. It is interesting how many times the biographies of religious leaders speak of a noticeable physical change after a profound spiritual experience. Some examples are the transfiguration of Jesus, the golden hue of Buddha's skin, and the sudden matting of the hair of a Sri Lankan ascetic.

He was now convinced that God wanted him for a special task, that of cleansing the world of corruption. He belonged to the Twelver Shi'a sect. Before long the belief developed that during his retreat he had spoken to the hidden twelfth Imam, the one who has been in occultation for centuries. He already had built up a significant following of former students, but after the retreat he enjoyed more respect than ever. The feeling grew that God had given him a special mission.

The Clerics React Against the White Revolution

By the 1960s it was United States policy, under the Kennedy administration, to press Iran to modernize faster. Under this influence, the Shah instituted a series of reforms known as the **White Revolution**. It was not really a political revolution at all. Rather it was a far-reaching program to modernize the economy, reform the schools, and institute other matters inspired by western values. The original stage had six components.

1. *Land Reform*: Large land holdings were to be broken up and given to the peasants who had been farming it for landholders.
2. *Nationalization of Forests and Pasturelands*: The creation of plans for reforestation.
3. *Privatization of government industries*: This was to modernize the industrial economy.
4. *Profit Sharing*: Workers were to share in profits to help stimulate efficient production and raise the income of working families.

5. *Suffrage for Women*: For the first time women would be able to vote.

6. *Literacy Corps*: To correct the low literacy rates in rural areas, rural schools would be better funded and it would now be possible to serve as literacy teachers as an alternative to military service.

The clerics were divided on the White Revolution program. Much of it held promise for economically uplifting the country. Yet parts of the modernization program were threatening to the clerics, either by loss of income or loss of authority. The loss of income threat derived from the land reform provision. Many of the highest ranking clerics came from the landowning class, and so their family holdings were threatened. A more direct threat was that some of the income from land rental had traditionally gone to the clerical institutions. It is interesting how many countries of the world historically had a system in which temples and other religious institutions got their support from farm land rentals, thus making landlords out of religious institutions. Also, the educational reforms threatened to make the public schools better, thereby undermining the traditional Islamic schools.

Khomeini was very influential among those who opposed the White Revolution. He led a group of senior clerics who issued a decree demanding people to boycott the upcoming referendum on the White Revolution. The Shah reacted by denouncing the clerics. The war of words escalated, with Khomeini comparing the Shah to the Ummayad Caliph to whom the head of Imam Husayn was delivered. He also accused the Shah of promoting the interests of the United States and Israel over those of Iran.

Khomeini's slogan was that "Islam is in danger." He mixed this with anti-western and anti-Jewish themes. In June of 1963, on the 15th day of the Iranian month Khordad, the Shah had Khomeini arrested. This touched off three days of violence and protest known as the Movement of 15 Khordad.

By 1964 Khomeini was denouncing the Shah for allowing United States military personnel who committed crimes in Iran to be tried in American military courts. This is a modern version of the "extraterritoriality" provision in colonial treaties that so angered China. Why should, the argument goes, a foreigner not be subject to our laws? Of course the underlying suspicion was that the American courts would go easy on the alleged offenders. The Prime Minister, Mansur, summoned Khomeini to a meeting during which it is alleged that Khomeini insulted and slapped the Prime Minister. The Shah, it is said, was advised to have Khomeini killed, but instead he chose to exile him, perhaps because of a prohibition against executing a Grand Ayatollah.

Khomeini's leadership role in the protests and fateful encounter with the Prime Minister Mansur led to his exile, first to Turkey for a year, and then to Iraq. In exile he wrote extensively about how government should be based on Shariah law and principles, and should be administered only by those to know Shariah well. This amounted to saying that clerics such as himself should run Islamic countries, which is, of course, exactly what was going to happen. While in Iraq, his writings got the attention of the Iraqi Vice President, Saddam Hussein, who had Khomeini sent out of Iraq in 1978. This example of the interface of religion and politics was fateful, for by the 1980s each man would be leading his country in a war against the other. Khomeini found his way to France, where he met with many students.

Meanwhile, back in Iran former students of Khomeini kept the protest alive in his absence. His writings and speeches were smuggled into Iran and widely circulated. They issued a death sentence against the new prime minister and soon he was, in fact, assassinated. Khomeini's movement was becoming a serious rebellion, one that had proven itself willing to invoke violence. Most other Iranian clerics were against the use of violence.

The Islamic Revolution

By early 1979, Khomeini's strength had grown even though he was in exile. Iranians were fairly united in their opposition to the Shah's regime. To combat inflation, the Shah had imposed strict regulations that had the net effect of making the workers poorer and more frustrated over the gap between their wages and the wealth of the elite. Many groups within the labor sector held demonstrations to protest their wages. The influx of rural population into the cities caused further problems.

Although there was widespread dislike of the Shah's regime, both clerics and non-clerics were divided about what system of governance should replace the Shah's. There was a Marxist faction, a secular democracy faction, and the theocracy faction. A brief review of these three factions is needed before we describe the events of the regime change.

The Marxist Tudeh Party
The Tudeh Party had been founded in the 1940s as a Marxist approach to improving worker conditions. It gained many followers and organized labor protests in many parts of Iran. By the time of the Islamic Revolution in 1979, its followers were one of the factions fighting in the streets.

The Secular Democratic Movement
The democratic faction was favored by the more secular urban middle class. They were doing well enough under the current economic and political order that they feared a radical change, either to the Marxist left or the religious right. They favored a democracy without undue influence from either the west or the more conservative clerics.

The Nationalist Front was a democratic party started by western-educated moderates who wanted an independent but democratic Iran. Its founder, M. Mossadegh, became Prime Minister in 1951 and enforced the recently enacted Oil Nationalization Act which threatened the western control over (and profits from) Iranian oil. This lead to a CIA-sponsored coup which restored more power to the Shah, who was more passive about foreign oil profits.

The Liberation Movement of Iran under the leadership of Mahdi Bazargan was another of the secular democratic groups. Bazargan, its leader, was a Paris-educated professor of engineering whose revolutionary credentials included being jailed by the

Shah. The Liberation Movement played an important role in overthrowing the Shah, and Bazargan became the Prime Minister for a short time.

The Khomeini Theocratic Movement

Khomeini's speeches in exile, as circulated on cassettes, called not just for the overthrow of the Shah but for the establishment of a government under the control or guidance of the mullahs. He had said he would return to Iran only after the Shah departed, which happened in January 1979. Khomeini's arrival the following month was welcomed by thousands and covered by the international media. Now I understood why my friend in Paris had warned me of this Ayatollah's importance (see box).

The Shah had left "on vacation" but had not resigned. His government was still in place even though it was extremely unpopular. It was mainly being propped up by United States support. Khomeini set up a replacement government and threw Iran into chaos. When the army announced a neutral stance toward the two competing governments, the scale was tipped toward Khomeini's pick for Prime Minister, M. Bazargan, the engineering professor who led the Liberation Movement. During its formative period of rule, a power struggle took place between advocates of a secular government and advocates of a **theocracy**. As Prime Minister, Bazargan tried unsuccessfully to shape Iran as a theocratic Islamic Democratic Republic rather than an Islamic Republic, a theocracy. He lost that battle and resigned his position. The die was cast. Iran became a theocratic republic when the referendum on the change was approved by a 98 percent majority.

Taking Power and Taking Revenge

Ayatollah Khomeini had successfully rallied public support to his leadership, and an Islamic Republic was proclaimed with him as its Guardian, or Supreme Leader. This was a change from the traditional Shi'i approach in which the clerics were thought to have "guardianship in the social and legal sphere, not in the political sphere. The Islamic Republic set this tradition aside and institutionalized the rule of politically-committed clergy. However,

Ayatollah Khomeini, in 1979, the year of the Iranian Revolution
Photo: "بهپ و خمینی" by Unknown - پایگاه اطلاع رسانی امام خمینی. Licensed under Public Domain via Wikimedia Commons -

clerics and religious intellectuals who were uncomfortable with the Islamic Republic challenged this departure from tradition."[7]

After taking power, Khomeini's new regime launched an extensive campaign of revenge against the officials of the Shah's regime. Many were killed or imprisoned. The voices of moderation and secularism were lost in the excitement of Khomeini's victory. Only later did more moderate Iranians begin to find a voice.

The Hostage Crisis and Jimmy Carter

The aging and ailing Shah was allowed to come to the United States for medical care the following fall (1979). President Jimmy Carter had already angered Khomeini supporters by being too friendly with the Shah in his last days in power. In particular, a widely circulated picture of Jimmy Carter with his arm around the Shah symbolized to all Iranians what they disliked about western imperialism and secularism. Also, the new regime in Iran wanted the Shah returned to stand trial. The United States refused this request, which was unacceptable to many Iranians who saw the Shah as a corrupt ruler who exploited the people for personal gain. When the United States admitted the Shah as a medical patient,

---

[7]Gunes Murat Tezcur, *Muslim Reformers in Iran and Turkey: The Paradox of Modernization* (Austin: University of Texas Press, 2010). Kindle Edition, Chapter 5.

rather than returning him to Iran, it was the last straw for many Iranians, including some students who were about to take matters into their own hands.

A group of Khomeini student supporters marched to the American embassy to protest. To their surprise it seems, they were able to enter the embassy and take the staff hostage. It does not appear that this was Khomeini's idea, but once it had occurred he was able to leverage the situation to great benefit. The **Iran Hostage Crisis**, as it came to be called, was a major problem for the national pride of the United States. On the other hand it was welcomed throughout the Islamic world as a prideful act of defiance against western imperialism. Khomeini proclaimed that Iran would hold the hostages until the Shah was returned to Iran to stand trial. The hostage crisis was at a stalemate. Altogether it lasted over a year.

President Carter ordered a military rescue operation, code named **Operation Eagle Claw**, to rescue the hostages in April 1980. The plan was to bring in helicopters and planes to two staging areas the first night, and then storm the embassy the next night, escaping via the helicopters. There were two big weaknesses with the plan. One was that for the long distance to Tehran it had to rely on helicopters, which are slow and cannot fly long distances without refuelling. This meant that the operation would require two days, with a refueling stage in a remote, desert region. The other was that the operation required coordination among several branches of the United States armed forces, and there was no central command system in place for that kind of operation.

The Operation went very wrong. The coordination among the various American services did not go well. An unanticipated sand storm grounded several of the helicopters, which had not been designed for desert conditions. Several helicopters became dysfunctional, and when the rest of the helicopters arrived at the first refuelling stop, the shortage of helicopters and other problems caused the mission to be aborted, far from Tehran. The United States military had lost face. As a result of this failure, three years later in 1983 the American military created the central command system known as USCENTCOM. A religious uprising in Iran had led to a major restructuring of the United States military.

In response to the failed rescue operation, the Iranians moved the 57 hostages to scattered locations. The hostages were released voluntarily on January 20, 1981, the day of Ronald Reagan's inauguration as President, replacing Jimmy Carter. The voluntary release and the choice of the date reflected Khomeini's dislike of Carter's support for the Shah and failed rescue attempt.

Iran–Iraq War

The rise of Shi'i power in Iran combined with cross-border influence and border disputes led Saddam's Iraq to launch a war against Iran in 1980. Saddam likely thought Iran was weak militarily. It was a fight for oil, a fight against Shi'i influence in Iraq, and a fight between a rather secular Ba'ath government and a zealously Shi'i Iranian government. Taking advantage of its military offensive, Iraqi forces moved deep into Iran, but over the next two years they were driven back. The remaining six years saw Iran take the offensive. Meanwhile, the rest of the world stayed relatively neutral, although the Soviet Union functioned as Iraq's main ally and weapons supplier. To limit Soviet influence, the United

American hostages disembark from a plane in Germany after being freed on the day Ronald Reagan was inaugurated.
Photo: DOD via pingnews (public domain)

States reopened diplomatic relations with Iraq and supplied them with some military assistance. During the war, Khomeini had to suppress a leftist faction waging a civil war within Iran. The war ground to a halt in 1988. During the war and its aftermath, Khomeini had, by necessity, to compromise his stance against adopting Western technology. As J. Miller writes, "The longer he ruled, the more Khomeini equated the survival of his own government with that of Islam itself—a belief that fostered ever greater pragmatism, if not moderation, on his part."[8]

The Iranian Two Tier System of Government

The constitution of the Islamic Republic of Iran makes Twelver Shi'a the official religion of Iran. The constitution also calls for an unusual two-tier system of governance. There is a President and an elected legislature, but the real power lies with the cleric who is the Supreme Leader. Khomeini was the first Supreme Leader, and after his death in 1989, a like-minded leader, Grand Ayatollah Ali Khamenei, was appointed. The Supreme Leader is commander-in-chief and has veto power over every important decision made by the

---

[8]Miller. *God Has Ninety-nine Names,* 453.

government. He appoints the heads of the military branches, state controlled media and all other key posts.

The Guardian Council of the Constitution is a twelve-member upper chamber, consisting of six members chosen by the Supreme Leader and six by the Majlis, the Parliament. There is an Assembly of Experts, which is a body of more than 80 clerics, elected by the people from a list of approved candidates. The Guardian Council has disallowed female candidates on the grounds that they were not properly trained in religious law. This Assembly selects the Supreme Leader. The Majlis is a unicameral (one house) parliament with limited powers because it cannot go against the wishes of the Supreme Leader and the clerics. There are 14 seats reserved for Zoroastrian, Jewish, and Christian minorities, but not for the Baha'is, who are considered apostate.

The Iranian two tier system of government with supreme authority given to religion makes for an interesting contrast with the two tier system with secularism as supreme in China and in Turkey.

Reformist Islam and Women

Iran has a long history of modernist voices calling for more equality for women. Afsaneh Najmabadi's book *Women with Mustaches and Men without Beards* reveals the roots of Iranian gender equality reaching back into the twentieth century.[9] For example, one woman wrote that a male and female should be seen as the two wheels of a cart, working equally for a common purpose.[10] Many Iranians do not support the very conservative version of Islam advocated by the Guardian Council. They prefer a "Reformist Islam" which gives a more equal role to women and more freedom to the media, and which holds values more compatible with secularist, democratic ideals. As Hamideh Sedghi celebrates, women's voices in politics were instrumental in backing Reformist cleric Mohammad Khatami's 1997 Presidential victory.[11] Her book's subtitle, 'Veiling, Unveiling, and Reveiling," calls attention of the way in which the prescribed dress and associated roles of women have vacillated through the years. She describes how her grandmother was educated, while veiled, by a tutor at her home. Yet her mother, with an escort, was allowed to go to school outside the home, wearing a *chador*. The author herself attended a school without wearing a *chador*, except at a mosque. Upon returning from America after the Iranian Revolution, she was scolded by an Islamic revolutionary guard for not having her head and hair fully covered.[12]

Judith Miller describes the struggle by women publishers to maintain a feminist voice in the public media. Based on interviews with the woman who publishes the magazine

---

[9]Afsaneh Najmabadi, *Women with Mustaches and Men without Beards: Gender and Sexual Anxieties of Iranian Modernity* (Berkeley and Los Angeles: University of California Press, 2005).

[10]*Ibid.* 230.

[11]Hamideh Sedhhi. 2007. *Women and Politics in Iran: Veiling, Unveiling, and Reveiling.* Cambridge: Cambridge University Press.

[12]*Ibid.* 1.

Zaman, "Women," and others, Miller learned that a woman publisher has to be very careful not to cross the line or she will be closed down. A female publisher has an economic disadvantage because, unlike the magazines officially sponsored by the government, she does not receive free paper stock. Despite the risks, the editor of *Zaman* published articles pointing out that there is nothing in the Quran saying that women must wear black or not follow professions. In the magazine's issue on wife beating, she pointed out that Islam does not sanction such behavior by males.[13]

Azadeh Kian-Thiébaut calls attention to how the increasing role that women are playing in the education of their children, and especially the way Iranian women now interact with and pay more respect to their children's opinions, has led to a new generation of youth who expect and demand a more democratic society.[14] More democratic parenting has led to more democracy.

As with women's movements elsewhere, women activists in Iran range across a broad spectrum when it comes to their perception of the ideal role of religion in politics. Shabnam J. Holliday sees three loosely defined groupings or discourses. Two of these groupings are secularist. One secularist grouping tends to focus on issues, and is represented by the organization "Stop Stoning Forever." The other grouping is more associated with the Islamic Reformists, such as the group "Religious New Thinkers." This grouping, she suggests, has been more successful because it is aligned with the grassroots Reformist Movement. The third grouping is made up of those women who more Islamist and tend to support the Islamic Republic regime while seeking improvements in the lives of women.[15]

Shirin Ebadi had been a judge in Iran prior to 1979, but the conservative clerics administrating Iran after the 1979 Revolution decreed that women could not hold the office of judge. She was demoted to clerk and eventually retired from public service. Then she became a human rights author and activist. After later regaining permission to practice law, she continued to advocate for human rights and especially the rights of women and children. In recognition of her outstanding human rights activism, she was awarded the 2003 Nobel Peace Prize.

We have seen that in 1979 the Iranians were mostly united in opposing the Shah's regime, but were fairly evenly split over whether to replace the Shah with a democratic or a theocratic republic. But how do Iranians feel now after decades of theocratic rule? A 2013 survey by the Pew Research Center showed that 40 percent favor a large political role for clerics, whereas 30 percent favor little or no such role for clerics and 26 percent favored only a limited role for the clerics.[16] It seems that Iranians are still pretty evenly

---

[13]Miller, *God Has Ninety-nine Names*, 454.

[14]Azadeh Kian-Thiébaut. 2008. "From Motherhood to equal rights advocates", in Katourzian, Homa, and Shahidi, Hossein, *Iran in the 21ˢᵗ Century: Politics, Economics and Conflict.* London and New York: Routledge, 104–105.

[15]Shabnam J. Holliday. 2011. *Defining Iran: Politics of Resistance.* Surrey: Ashgate Publishing, 140-141.

[16]As reported by Reuters. http://blogs.reuters.com/faithworld/2013/06/12/iranians-mixed-on-having-religious-figures-in-politics-pew-poll/.

split on the subject, but other polls suggest that younger Iranians favor a move to a more democratic stance.

ISSUE 3: POLITICAL ROLE OF CLERICS IN IRAQ

> *Our flight from Tehran to Bagdad International Airport is a short one, yet we have crossed over some invisible but important boundaries. We have crossed into the Eastern limit of the vast Arabic language region, and we have crossed from a predominantly Shi'i zone into a region that has been dominated politically by Sunni Muslims for most of its history. We visit the al-Shaheed Monument, which consists of two large, blue oval shaped structures looking like a futuristic egg split in two. It honors Iraqis who died in the long and deadly Iran-Iraq war. Its beauty and simplicity make a sharp contrast to the brutality of the war which was started by Iraq's Saddam Hussein in 1980 and ended in a stalemate eight years later, after around a half million deaths. Later, by viewing the displays about the area's very ancient culture in the Iraq Museum, we develop an understanding of the great pride that Iraqis take in their long heritage. At the Bagdad Museum we see great displays showing what life was like in Bagdad for the past few centuries. Then we head south to the predominantly Shi'i area that proudly hosts so many important shrines and centers of Shi'i learning.*

The region of Najaf and Karbala in southern Iraq took on its present status as the center of Shi'i learning from the mid-eighteenth century. When that happened, many of the top Shi'i scholarly families moved from Iran to southern Iraq and became important religious scholars there. They, in turn, attracted many students from Iran and the region that is now India and Pakistan. Persian scholars came to dominate in southern Iraq. The two towns together attracted Shi'i pilgrims, along with the money and prestige that flows from being a pilgrimage destination and the area where relatives bring corpses for burial in an especially sacred area.

The Ottoman Empire undertook the policy of encouraging nomadic tribes to settle and take up agriculture during the nineteenth century. Southern Iraq had both the water and land needed for farming, so many of the tribes settled there. Once there, they came under the influence of Shi'i rather than Sunni Islam. According to Y. Nakash, this combination of being a scholar-pilgrimage center and having the capacity to accommodate settling tribes led to the conversion of many nomadic tribes to Shi'a and to the dominance of Shi'i Islam in southern Iraq. The conversion also meant that Shi'i Muslims came to outnumber Sunni Muslims in Iraq from the late 1800s to the present.[17]

In the process of affiliating with the Shi'i centers of learning, the tribes of southern Iraq adopted Shi'i rituals and customs as well as the Shi'i version of Shariah. Tribal leaders

---

[17]Yikshak Nakash, *The Shi'is of Iraq* (Princeton: Princeton University Press, 1994), 269.

intermarried with religious families, creating a new social order among the tribes that was complete with institutionalized religious and political authority.

Shi'is and Sunnis Cooperate in the 1920 Revolt

Under the newly formed League of Nations, the British rule of Palestine started in the summer of 1920, as the British Mandate of Mesopotamia. The boundaries of Mesopotamia (Iraq) had been determined by the 1919 Paris Peace Conference and the *Treaty of Sèvres*.[18] Seeing the Mandate as just another form of colonialism, a revolt against the British soon erupted. The Kurds of the north were in serious revolt, having never quite been subdued in the first place, and the Sunnis of the central region joined in the revolt.

The Shi'is of the south were the last to get involved. Given that many Shi'i tribes had only been converted to Shi'i culture within the past hundred and fifty years, the Sunni and Shi'i Iraqis shared many cultural traits. So it is not surprising that some Shi'i clerics joined the revolt as well. Besides the common Iraqi cause of wanting to expel the British, the Shi'i clerics wanted to establish a political system along Shi'i principles, which caused problems with the Kurdish and Sunni Iraquis of the center and north. In other words, they wanted a parliamentary system in which the clerics would have a strong voice behind the scenes. Although the Shi'i south did not fully cooperate in the Revolt, the level of cooperation among Kurd, Sunni and Shi'i Iraqis did go a long way toward the process of building a sense of unity and among the three communities thrown together at the Paris conference.

The British suppressed the Revolt at great cost in terms of money, equipment, and military personnel. They therefore wanted to find a less expensive way to rule Iraq, and in so doing they made two changes that would turn out to be very important for our story. First, they set up an Iraqi monarchy, but made sure that it was financially dependent upon the British. Second, they set up an Iraqi army that would take over for the British forces. To find experienced officers for the new army, they turned to those who had served under the Ottomans, which meant, in effect,, that they established a Sunni officer corps. There were Shi'i in the army, but mostly at the lower ranks. It would be from this Sunni officer corps that the later rulers of Iraq would emerge. Though they were a majority of the population, the Shi'i came out of this transition from British to Iraqi rule with little political power. The Sunni rulers, backed by Iraq's Sunni elite and Sunni-led army, did not want to share power with Shi'i and their conservative religious leaders. Shi'i Sheiks were allowed into the political process, but not the clerics. This was a situation that would last until the fall of Saddam.

The pan-Arab movement was sweeping the Arab Muslim world, and that made it easier for the Sunni leaders of Iraq to look down upon the non-Arab Iranian heritage of much of Iraq's southern clerics. The Shi'i clerical families with their Iranian roots were

---

[18]For the history of the events of 1919 that shaped the Middle East, see Margaret MacMillan, *Paris 1919: Six Months that Changed the World* (New York: Random House Trade Paperbacks, 2003).

either driven back to Iran or marginalized. By 1946 the headquarters of Shi'i Islam had been shifted back to Iran, and the Iranian Shahs played up the role of Iran's holy cities at the expense of pilgrimages to Najaf and Karbala in Iraq.

The Quietist Position of Grand Ayatollah Ali al-Sistani

Ali Al-Sistani is Iranian, having been born into a family of Shi'i scholars there in 1930. After studying in the center of Iranian learning, Qom, he went to Najaf, Iraq for further study. He rose in clerical rank very quickly and had a high rank by his early thirties. With the death of his teacher, the Grand Ayatollah of Najaf in 1992, he was recognised as the replacement and received the rank of a Grand Ayatollah. Now that he has more seniority, he is unofficially recognized as the leading Shi'i scholar of Iraq. He is the head of several theological training institutions, called Hawza, with thousands of students.

Al-Sistani was suppressed during Saddam's rule and his mosque was closed. Since the fall of Saddam he has been rather reclusive, but exercises great influence nonetheless, through his many former students and through issuing *fatwa*, rulings. He has been an important counsellor of moderation during the post-Saddam period. He called for women to vote in the elections. He helped calm the tension that arose when the Imam Ali Mosque was damaged by a Sunni attack in 2004. And he has tried to end the cycle of violence by those Shi'is who want to kill Sunnis in revenge for Sunni attacks.

Al-Sistani follows a **Quietist school** of Shi'i thought. Unlike Iran's Ayatollah Khomeini, Grand Ayatollah Ali al-Sistani, does not see theocracy as the proper polity in Shi'i thought. He sees a need for separate roles to be played by clerical and political leaders. It is the job of the clerics to make sure that the government rules in a way consistent with Shi'i culture and that it protects Islam. But he does not advocate the Iranian system of clerics ruling indirectly behind the scenes.[19]

The Activist Position of the Al-Sadr Clerics

In stark contrast to the Quietist school of Ayatollahs such as al-Sistani, an **Activist** style was developed by **Muhammad Baqir al-Sadr**, and then continued by his cousin known as **Sadr II** and his son **Muqtada Sadr**. It is a style that has combined social activism among the poor with militant defiance of political authorities, whether Ba'athist or post-Saddam.

Muhammad Baqir al-Sadr
According to Muhammad Baqir al-Sadr, there are two types of clerics. One type is represented by al-Sistani and the other Ayatollahs of Najaf. They rise to leadership roles through their scholarship and the consensus of their peers that they are pious and scholarly. The other type is more into social activism. This type endeavors to meet the needs

---

[19]Yitzhak Nakash, *Reaching for Power: The Shi'a in the Modern Arab World* (Princeton: Princeton University Press, 2006.

of their communities. Al-Sadr was proud of the second type. He did not see himself as a great scholar, but he endeavored to help his people.

His social activism embraced all whom he considered oppressed, including Kurds and Sunnis as well as Shi'is. Al-Sadr's activism and ability to organize the poor in pushing for better conditions during the 1970s became a threat to the Ba'ath Party elite, who had him killed in 1980.

Sadr II

After his release from prison following a Shi'i uprising in 1991, Muhammad Sadiq al-Sadr, a cousin of Muhammad Baquir al-Sadr, assumed the mantle of Shi'i activist leader within Iraq. He worked to bridge the gap between lofty Quranic scholarship and the lives of everyday working Shi'is. Toward that end, he developed a style of sermons at the Friday noon prayers at his mosque in Kufa that motivated the people to both apply Shi'i principles to the everyday lives and agitate to improve their socio-economic conditions. Known as Sadr II, he embodied his cousin's understanding that a cleric should be a political and social activist.

Sadr II would often preach against the United States, denouncing it as an imperialist nation seeking to dominate the Islamic world in pursuit of its self-interests. He amassed a large following, mostly of poorer Shi'i families. He was murdered in 1999 along with two of his sons. It was suspected that the killers were acting on behalf of the Saddam government, but nothing was proven. The government banned the holding of a public funeral for him, but over the next several days his supporters defied the ban and held memorial gatherings. The government used excessive force to crack down on those gatherings. It forced as many as four thousand families who supported the dead cleric to move from Baghdad to southern or western Iraq.

The Saddam government acted on the other theory of Sadr II's murder, holding that it had been arranged within the Shi'i community of Najaf. Four Shi'is were tried for the murder in a non-public trial and executed. Many of Sadr II's followers were arrested, including his fourth son Muqtada. Subsequently, in anticipation of the anniversary of his murder, police surrounded the mosques and banned the traditional pilgrimage walk from Najaf to Karbala on the fortieth day after Imam Husayn's martyrdom.

Muqtada al-Sadr Leads the Anti-United States Camp

After the death of Sadr II, his son Muqtada assumed the leadership of his father's movement, but kept a low profile due to the oppression by the Saddam regime. However, after the fall of Saddam and ensuing social chaos, Muqtada al-Sadr emerged as a serious critic of the United States and its new Iraqi regime.

Muqtada was suspected and later charged with the murder of another cleric. His followers rallied behind him and not much came from the charges. By 2003 the number of his followers swelled and he formed an alternate government to the Provisional Council imposed by the United States and its allies. His followers in the Sadr City part of Baghdad followed his guidance and elected their own city council. He also formed the

Mahdi Army, formally called the Imam Al-Mahdi Militia, being named after the twelfth Imam according to the Twelver Shi'a. He called for a street protest in the Sadr City area of Baghdad in 2004, causing a serious crisis for the Iraqi government. The interface of religion and politics was getting very intense!

In the 2010 parliamentary elections, Muqtada was quite active in politics as the leader of the **Sadrist Movemen**t, a political party named after his family of activists. Being supported by the poor and being critical of elites, his Movement is populist; that is, it represents ordinary people rather than the elite. The Movement was staunchly against what it saw as the United States occupation of Iraq. It won several seats in 2010 and was part of the National Iraqi Alliance coalition. In the months leading up to the 2014 Parliamentary Elections, Muqtada surprised everyone by announcing that he was stepping away from all politics and should no longer be considered the leader of any party.

ISSUE 4: THE NEW CALIPHATE AND THE ISLAMIC STATE

In 2006 a group of Al-Qaeda affiliates and other militant Wahhabi movements united to work toward an Islamic State of Iraq (ISI), meaning that they wished to establish Wahhabi style, Sunni control of Iraq. Later the territorial aspirations were expanded to include "greater Syria" and the name was changed to **ISIL**, for the **Islamic State of Iraq and the Levant**. The alternate name **ISIS**, for **Islamic State of Iraq and al-Sham** ("Levant" or greater Syria) is also used. The goal was to unite Sunni Muslims and resist both Shi'i and Western influence, with the ultimate hope of establishing a new Caliphate ruling most or all Sunni Muslims. ISIS withdrew from its association with al-Qaeda , preferring to focus on founding a state. ISIS has proven willing to use extreme forms of violence, including beheading civilians, to scare its enemies and spread its influence. In early 2014 ISIS surprized the world by easily taking control of most of the Sunni majority areas of Iraq except Baghdad, meeting with little resistance and taking advantage of the Sunni resentment of Shi'i rule in post-Saddam Iraq.

Having taken control of extensive areas of northern Iraq and Syria, ISIL declared a new caliphate in June 2014, with its leader, Abu Bakr al-Baghdadi, as the new caliph. The Kurdish population of Northwest Iraq resisted ISIL control, but Shi'i, Yazidi or Christian Iraqis living in ISIL-controlled areas were in grave danger. Those who did not manage to flee the rapid ISIL expansion were forced to convert or die. Some may have been given a third option of paying a tax. Shariah law permits non-Muslims to live within Islamic territory, but they are required to pay a special tax not levied on Muslims. The underlying principle was that this was to equalize taxes. Because Muslims had to pay the annual amount to charity and non-Muslims did not, the special tax leveled the taxation playing field. Without such a tax, it was feared, citizens would have an incentive to be non-Muslims. The leaders of the Islamic State sometimes claimed to be giving captured non-Muslims this third option—that of paying the special tax. However, reports from the conflict zones seem to suggest that the only choices may have been to convert or to die. The new regime confiscated the stored grain and farmland of those who had fled. As an example, one farmer who had fled received a phone call offering him the choice of either abandoning his grain and farm or returning to his farm on a condition of converting to Islam and paying a $500 fine.[20]

The Islamic State funds itself in several ways. The most important is by selling crude oil from the regions of Iraq it controls. Because the international community boycotts the purchase of Islamic State oil, it is forced to sell at deeply discounted prices on the black market. The collapse in crude oil prices in 2014 has greatly reduced this source of revenue. Indeed, some observers speculate the Saudis, perhaps with the approval of the United States, have deliberately flooded the oil market to undermine the ISIS economic position. Besides oil revenue, the Islamic State is thought to have confiscated gold, jewelry, and art objects worth millions of dollars for sale on the black market. Capturing and holding foreigners for ransom is thought to be a third source of important revenue.

The Islamic State dreams of controlling not only most of the Middle East but also large regions of Europe, Africa, and South Asia. It wants to control all of Northern Africa, organized as three regions named Maghreb, Habasha and Alkinana. It would set up all of South and Central Asia as an area named Khurasan. The Arabian Peninsula and numerous current nations north and northwest of Arabia, including southeast Europe, would be ruled as newly named regions. The formerly Muslim nation of Andalus would be restored, replacing Spain and Portugal in the Iberian Peninsula. These goals at first seemed totally unattainable, but as the Islamic State rapidly gained territory and military strength, the rest of the world became alarmed. Former enemies, such as the United States and Iran, found a common cause in reversing the spread of the Islamic State. For example, the tensions between Russia and the United States over whether Russia or NATO would dominate in the Ukraine were lessened because both nations now had reason to fear the Islamic State. Russia was concerned about the Islamic State's plans to expand into the predominantly Islamic regions of Southern Russia. The United States was concerned about the Islamic State's expansion in Iraq and Syria.

OVERVIEW AND THEORETICAL DISCUSSION

Our first issue called attention to the historical split between Sunni and Shi'i Islam as well as the ongoing political struggles between them. Like Protestants and Catholics in Europe, the two main divisions of Islam have sometimes coexisted peacefully, but sometimes not. From the time of the split, the Shi'is have usually been politically dominated by Sunnis, or by Europeans in the Colonial period.

---

[20]Maggie Fick, "Special Report: Islamic State uses grain to tighten grip on Iraq." *Reuters* (September 30 2014). http://www.reuters.com/article/2014/09/30/us-mideast-crisis-wheat-idUSKCN0HP12J20140930.

The second and third issues dealt with the political roles of the clerics in Iran and Iraq. We saw that those classified in the Quietist school tend to stay out of the political arena, preferring to focus on practicing and promoting Shi'i Muslim spirituality. Those classified in the Activist School, especially the Sadr family clerics, tend to get involved with providing social programs to needy persons. The activists sometimes become quite involved politically, as in the case of Muqtada al-Sadr and his Mahdi army. The more moderate position represented by the clerics of Najaf has given way to the activist style of the al-Sadr family in Iraq, Khomeini in Iran and **Hezbollah** in Lebanon. The activists have developed their own militia and set up their own network of charities and services to assist the poorest among the Shi'i communities. The Shi'i clerics of the right continue to hold power in Iran; while a broader range of Shi'i positions are represented in the government of Iraq.

The dramatic rise of the Islamic State was our last issue. The leaders broke ties with the Al-Qaeda network partly because they found it too moderate. Or perhaps they found it too focused on a few major terrorists actions rather than being focused on founding a state based on Shariah as understood in Wahhabi Islam. The Islamic State's rapid expansion took the world by surprise. Its acts of extreme violence shocked the world.

Theoretical Discussion

Struggles within Islam and with the West
The religious and political histories of Iran and Iraq show two kinds of struggles. The basic one is the struggle since the era of Imam Ali between the Shi'i and Sunni versions of Islam. When Imam Ali pursued the dissident army led by Aisha into Mesopotamia, modern Iraq, and then later decided to set up his headquarters there, followed by his death and that of Husayn, he made southern Iraq a holy area rivalling even Mecca for Shi'i Muslims. We can say that there is a Shi'i culture that extends from Iran over to Lebanon. With Iraq as its spiritual center, we have seen how Shi'i clerics have moved easily among Iran, Iraq, Syria, and Lebanon. Shi'i family and spiritual ties transcend national borders.

In hindsight we can see that the period of 1920 to 2003, from the 1920 Revolt to the fall of Saddam, marked a low period in the Shi'i influence on politics in Iraq. An important effect of the American defeat of the Ba'athists in Iraq was the restoration of Shi'i political power. Of course this was not the goal of United States policy under the Bush White House, but was foreseeable by some observers.

On a wider scale the struggle has been with western powers; first the British in the colonial era and then the Americans in the contemporary one. This wider struggle fits Huntington's Clash of Civilizations theory.

Tariq Ali's focus on United States' imperialism aptly describes the anti-American feelings that fuelled the Islamic Revolution in Iran. And Herberg's Pendulum theory seems helpful when we consider Shi'a in this region. Shi'is were rather dormant in the early part of the twentieth century, but toward the end of the century they began to get very active politically.

Do the clerics of Shi'i Islam and their followers fit the Fundamentalist label? They do have several of the family resemblances. They hold that spiritual authority is higher than secular or democratic principles. They want to apply Shariah rather than some more modern law code. And they seem to minimize the role of women in society, while at the same time saying that they hold women in great respect. Like Christian fundamentalists, they are against the secular values of modernity but not at all against modern technology. Quite the contrary, Muslims in this region have used technology, from Khomeini's cassettes to contemporary television and Internet sites, to their great advantage.

Differences between Iraqi and Iranian Clerics

There are significant differences between the Iraqi and Iranian Shi'i clerics. The Iranian clerics were less shaped by Arab culture, enjoyed better support from the government and merchant class, and ran better-endowed madrasahs. Also, there was a difference in the underlying meaning emphasized in the Ashura ritual. Whereas the Iranians stressed the martyrdom theme of Imam Husayn's death, the Iraqis stressed the Arab ideal of manhood, with themes such as masculinity, bravery and honor.[21]

Kurdish Separatism in Iraq

After the defeat of the Ottoman Empire in World War I, the Kurds had the chance to unite and form a state of Kurdistan as a British Protectorate. However, they were too divided along tribal and other lines to accept the kingship of a British-appointed Kurd leader. As the Turks strengthened under Ataturk, the possibility of carving out a Kurdistan from parts of Iraq and Turkey faded. The unwillingness of the Kurds to unite around a ruler, combined with the British, and then Iraqi, interests in the oil of the Kirkuk region, led to the inclusion of some Kurdish regions in Iraq, while regions farther to the North were included in Turkey. In this process the map as we now know it was drawn. Even though the Kurds of Iraq missed their chance in the 1920s to gain independence, more recently the Kurds of both Turkey and Iraq have pressed for independence, or at least more autonomy. The Kurds of Iraq live in an area with huge oil reserves, so their claim is seen as an economic as well as territorial threat to the Iraqi government.

Is Shi'i Regional Power at a Turning Point?

The rise of a Shi'i regime in Iran, enriched with oil money, has led to a marked increase in Shi'i influence in the region; not only in Iraq, Jordan, and Lebanon, but also in the Gulf States. Was the 1979 Islamic Revolution in Iran a major turning point in world history? In 1979, while those in the West were focused on the International Year of the Child, Pope John Paul's visit to Poland, the signing of the second Strategic Arms Limitation Treaty, the thaw in United States–China relations, the Three Mile Island nuclear plant accident, and the Unabomber, did we overlook the most important event of 1979? Will Shi'i political power be a force in Middle East politics for years to come? Will Iranian Shi'is, rather than Arab Sunnis, lead the struggle against western influence? Whatever the answer, there is no

---

[21]Yitzhak Nakash, *The Shi'is of Iraq* (Princeton: Princeton University Press, 1994), 271.

denying that Shi'i confidence and political power have increased throughout the Middle East as a result of the events in Iran.

Some of the clerics of Iraq have received encouragement, funds and other support from Iran. This is understandable because they share a Shi'i culture, and it is in the interest of Iranian Shi'i to be able to freely make pilgrimages to their holy sites in Karbala, Najaf, and elsewhere in Iraq.

Iranian and Iraqi Shi'i Influence on Hezbollah in Lebanon
There are deep connections between Lebanese and Iraqi Shi'i families. The Al-Sadr family has strong Lebanese ties. Muqtada Al-Sadr, the young cleric who has such a following among the poor, has Lebanese ancestry. One of his cousins, Musa Sadr, was a well-known philosopher and Shi'i activist in Lebanon who founded the **Amal Movement**, a Shi'i political party.

The Shi'is in Lebanon, unlike many Sunnis, had supported the idea of Lebanon as a state separate from Syria. They helped the French put down the Druze Revolt (1925–27), and they supported the constitution of 1936. However, after the Sunnis came into government roles, the Shi'is did not get much respect or a fair share of the government revenue. They were mostly poor and lived either in the rural south or in the working class areas of Beirut. Musa Sadr helped them organize and demand their rights. In 1969 he called for and got a government council for the Shi'i, whereas previously the Sunni-dominated council had, in theory, represented all Muslims of Lebanon. Before the war of 1975, Sadr spoke of the Shi'is of Lebanon as an oppressed people who needed to rise up, and he formed a militia named Amal, "Hope."

During a trip to Libya in 1978, Musa Sadr mysteriously disappeared, and never reappeared. This left a leadership vacuum for Shi'is right in the middle of the Civil War period (1975–80).

After the Islamic Revolution, members of the Iranian Revolutionary Guards went to Syria and on to southern Lebanon to spread the Islamic Revolution among the Shi'i population, who reside primarily in southern Lebanon. The movement has gained strength and has wide support among the Shi'i population in Lebanon. In retaliation for border incidents, in 2006 Israel launched an attack on **Hezbollah,** the "Party of God," in Lebanon. Israel attacked first by air and then with ground troops. When Israeli troops withdrew without a decisive victory, Hezbollah celebrated it as a victory in an **asymmetric war**, a conflict in which the two sides have unequal military forces. A stalemate in such a war is a nominal victory for the smaller force. Hezbollah suffered casualties during the action, but came out stronger and bolder. Hezbollah gained the admiration of many Muslims in the region, and the Israeli government of Prime Minister Ehud Olmert lost support among Israeli Jews.

By the mid-1980s the Amal movement was losing out to the newly formed Hezbollah, which had both the financial backing of Iran and the success story of the Khomeini's revolution as drivers. By 1990 the two competing Shi'i factions accepted a plan of cooperation brokered by Syria and Iran. Hezbollah's political wing has been active in politics and has gained stature after the 2006 war with Israel. Since 2006 Hezbollah has risen to the role of opposition in Lebanon, and some Christians have aligned with Hezbollah. In a break with its Iranian sponsors, the Hezbollah Party of Lebanon has not pressed for an Islamic state in Lebanon because it realizes that the Sunnis and Shi'is could not agree on Shariah and other Islamic principles. Nor would the Islamic State be acceptable to the Christians of northern Lebanon, who belong to the very old branch of Catholicism known as the **Maronite Church**.

The Oil Factor

The political drive to control and profit from oil reserves in the region continues to be a very important undercurrent for countries in the region, both in terms of internal politics and international relations, not to mention wars. Immediately after defeating the Ottoman Empire the British moved into the oil-rich area of Mosul, Iraq. By 1925 the British had control of the Iraq Petroleum Company with a seventy-five year oil concession. Since then the large oil companies have competed for control of the oil fields. Saddam's invasion of Kuwait was motivated to a large measure by Kuwait's sizable oil fields. The United States' willingness to go to war to restore Kuwait's independence was also motivated by the oil factor. Most western countries have become so dependent upon Middle Eastern oil that their foreign policy is driven by the goal of maintaining access to oil and securing the shipping lanes needed to transport it.

When the United States decided to invade Iraq and overthrow Saddam, the Bush White House and most of the American media labelled the war a fight "for freedom" and a "war against weapons of mass destruction" in the hands of enemies. However, Muslims in the Middle East watching Islamic websites such as Al Jazeera saw the invasion as "The War for Oil." Within Iraq, the oil reserves underlie all party politics.

> *We now fly to the place that may hold the dubious distinction of being the hottest of the world's hot spots in the interface of religion and politics. That place would, of course, be Israel and Palestine.*

STUDY QUESTIONS

1. How did the division between Sunni and Shi'i Muslims originate?
2. Which areas of the Middle East have large Shi'i populations and what political difference does that make?
3. What is the difference between the Quietist and Activist Schools of Shi'i Islam?
4. What nations or factions are supportive of or opposed to the Islamic State?
5. What factors will influence the expansion or contraction of the Islamic State?

FURTHER READING

Arjomand, Said Amir, ed. *Authority and Political Culture in Shi'ism*. Albany: State University of New York Press, 1988. A good but dated collection of scholarly essays.

Bayat, Asef. *Making Islam Democratic: Social Movements and the Post-Islamist Turn*. Stanford: Stanford University Press, 2007. Based on observation of Islamic trends in Iran and Egypt.

Cockburn, Patrick. *Muqtada Al-Sadr and the Battle for the Future of Iraq*. New York: Scribner, 2008. Gives the history of this important cleric's interaction with Iraqi society and politics.

Hoveyda, Fereydoun. *The Broken Crescent: The "Threat" of Militant Islamic Fundamentalism*. Westport: Praeger, 1998. Makes a strong distinction between mainstream religious Islam and fundamentalist political Islam.

Keddie, Nikki R., ed. *Religion and Politics in Iran: Shi'ism from Quietism to Revolution*. Yale: Yale University Press, 1983. A good but dated collection of scholarly essays.

Keddie, Nikki R. *Modern Iran: Roots and Results of Revolution*. New Haven: Yale University Press, 2006. A clearly written account ranging from historic Iran to the present.

Holliday, Shabnam J. *Defining Iran: Politics of Resistance*. Surrey: Ashgate Publishing, 2011. On the interaction of women and politics in Iran.

Moaveni, Azadeh. *Lipstick Jihad: A Memoir of Growing up Iranian in America and American in Iran*. New York, N.Y.: Public Affairs, 2006. An Iranian American woman's account of life as a student in California and as a journalist in Iran.

Moosa, Matti. *Extremist Shiites: The Ghulat Sects*. Syracuse: Syracuse University Press, 1988. An old but good source on the extremists sects of Shi'a.

Nakash, Yitzhak. Second Edition. *The Shi'is of Iraq*, 2nd edition. Princeton: Princeton University Press, 2003. Follows the story from their origins through to the first Gulf War.

Nakash, Yitzhak. *Reaching for Power: The Shi'a in the Modern Arab World*. Princeton: Princeton University Press, 2006. Great description of Shi'a throughout the Middle East.

Nasr, Vali. *The Shia Revival: How Conflicts Within Islam Will Shape the Future*. New York: W. W. Norton and Company, 2007. Good source on the diversity of Shi'a and its varieties in Iran, Iraq and Lebanon.

Parsi, Trita. *Treacherous Alliance: The Secret Dealings of Israel, Iran, and the United States*. New Haven: Yale University Press, 2007. A recent attempt to uncover the controversial intrigues of international relations.

Pratt, Nicola, and Enloe, Cynthia. *What Kind of Liberation: Women and the Occupation of Iraq*. Berkley and Los Angeles, 2010. A critical analysis of the status and role of Iraqi women from Sadaam's era to the United States occupation period, challenging the mainstream view in the United States.

Sekulow, Jay, et. al. *Rise of ISIS: A Threat We Can't Ignore*. New York: Howard Books, 2014. An introduction to Hamas and ISIS by a well-known lawyer and Evangelical.

Vakil, Sanam. *Women and Politics in the Islamic Republic of Iran: Action and Reaction*. London: Bloomsbury Academic, 2012. A good account of the issues and struggles through the past century, based on interviews.

Wiley, Joyce N. *The Islamaic Movement of Iraqi Shi'as*. Boulder: Lynne Rienner Publishers, 1992. Good source on Iraq before 1998.

WEBSITES

www.imamalinet.net/en/indexe/htm A site with pictures and information on Imam Ali and the Shi'i holy shrines.

www.al-shia.com A good site on Shi'a, written from a Shi'i viewpoint.

www.shia.org/ Another Shi'i site.

www.slate.com/id/2082980/ On the role of Clerics in Iraq and their influence on politics after Saddam.
www.islamicdawaparty.com/ The Dawa Islamic party official site.
www.sciri.btinterneet.co.uk/ Site of the Supreme Council for Islamic Resistance in Iraq.
www.leader.ir/langs/en/index.php Site of the Office of the Supreme Leader of Iran.

KEY PEOPLE

Ali al-Sistani A very well respected Grand Ayatollah.
Shirin Ebadi Iranian Lawyer and Human Rights activist who was awarded the 2003 Nobel Peace Prize.
Imam Hasan Elder son of and successor to Imam Ali.
Imam Husayn Younger son of Imam Ali. He died at the massacre at Karbala, Iraq.
Khamenei, Grand Ayatollah Ali Supreme leader of Iran
Khomeini, Grand Ayatollah Shi'i cleric who led the Iranian Revolution
Sadr A family of famous social activist clerics in Iraq.
Muqtada al-Sadr Influential Shi'i cleric in Baghdad region.

GLOSSARY

Abbasids Descendants of Abbas, one of Muhammad's Companions, who ruled as caliphs from Bagdad.
Activist School An attitude held by those Shi'i clerics who engage the world with a political agenda and/or social programs for the poor.
Amal Movement A major Shi'i political party in Lebanon.
Ashura A Shi'i ritual recalling the martyrdom of Imam Husayn and his supporters.
Asymmetric war A war in which one side has more military might than the other.
Ba'ath Party and **Ba'athists** Refers to a secular political movement that came to power in several Middle Eastern regions, including Saddam Hussein's regime in Iraq.
Ghulat A grouping of Shi'i sects who partially deify Imam Ali.
Hezbollah A Shi'i based, armed political party in Lebanon.
Imam For Sunni Muslims, the term for the leader of prayers at a mosque. For Shi'i Muslims, the term for the leaders in the lineage starting from Imam Ali.
Iran Hostage Crisis A period (1979–81) when Iran held United States Embassy staff members hostage for over a year.
ISIL and ISIS Alternate names for an organization whose goal it is to establish an Islamic State in the greater Syria area.
Islamic State A provisional government set up in territory controlled by ISIS.
Islamic Revolution or **Iranian Revolution** The movement that overthrew the Shah and brought Islamic Theocracy to Iran.
Ismailis or Seveners A Shi'i sect tracing back to Ismail.
Maronite Church A Lebanese division of the Catholic Church named after Saint Maron.
Occultation The disappearance of a spiritual person from the earth during an extended period.
Ottoman Empire A large empire based in what is now Turkey, under the rule of the Ottoman Turks.
Pahlavi A term for an old Persian language and the surname of a line of Shahs.
Quietist School An attitude held by those Shi'i clerics who prefer the life of scholarship and piety to social or political activism.
Shah An title of a king in traditional Iran.
Shi'i or **Shi'a** Those Muslims who identify with the Shi'a Ali (Party of Ali), thus recognizing a lineage of

leaders called Imams tracing back to Imam Ali. (Spellings vary in English. In this book *Shi'a* refers to the sect (Party), and the spelling *shi'i* is used for the adherents and as the adjectival form.)

Sunni Meaning those who follow the Sunna, the traditions of Islamic law as accepted by the majority of Muslims.

theocracy, theocratic Referring to a system of government where real political power is entrusted in the will of God, as interpreted by religious leaders.

Twelvers A widespread sect of Shi'i Islam

Umayyads A clan that ruled as caliphs from Damascus, Syria.

White Revolution An attempt by the Shah to modernize Iran.

Yazidi A minority religious sect whose main homeland is in Iraq.

Chapter Six

Israel and Palestine

Religion as a Basis for Land Claims:
Religious Nationalism, Religionization of Palestinian Nationalism, Jerusalem's Old City

In this chapter you will learn about:

- the Consociational Democracy of Lebanon
- the religious and political background of Israel and Palestine
- the conflicting claims for land
- the nature of Religious Nationalism among Jews
- the evolution of Palestinian resistance to Israel
- the complexities of governing Jerusalem's Old City

We land in Beirut's Rafic Hariri International Airport and our first question is, who was Rafic Hariri? Rafik (the airport uses the French spelling Rafic, but English spelling uses a k) Hariri was a rich businessman who was twice Prime Minister of Lebanon. He was assassinated by a massive roadside bomb in 2005. Many suspected Syria played a role in the killing, to eliminate a leader who favored increasing Lebanese independence from Syria. Some people think that Hezbollah played a role in the assassination. Our trip around the city shows the contrasts between the impoverished Palestinian refugee camps on the outskirts and the posh restaurants and buildings downtown.

We learn that there are over one million Syrian refugees in other camps, overwhelming Lebanon"s capacity to provide basic necessities.

STOPOVERS IN LEBANON AND JORDAN

Religion and Politics: Lebanese Style Consociational Democracy

The Lebanese system is designed to keep any one religious community from dominating. According to the Taif Agreement of 1989, worked out toward the end of the 15-year civil war, Muslims and Christians each get half of the 128 Parliamentary seats. This power-sharing arrangement ended the Christian dominance of Lebanese politics since at least the time of Lebanon's independence from France in 1943. Each of the Muslim and Christian blocs of 64 seats is then subdivided by religious subgroups. The largest Christian group, the **Maronite** Christians, get 34 seats, Greek Orthodox 14, Greek Catholic 8, and so on down according to population sizes.[1] Among the Muslim groups, Sunnis and Shi'is each get 27 seats, the Druze get 8 and the Alawite get 2. The latter two groups are not usually considered Muslim, but they come under the Muslim umbrella in this case. (We will introduce the Druze tradition in the Religious Background section.)

This model of power-sharing, under which various ethnic or religious communities (societies) are assigned a specified number of seats in parliament and specific leadership positions, is known as **Consociational Democracy**. Religious identity is constitutionally engrained in the Lebanese politics. The President has to be a **Maronite** Christian, the Prime Minister a Sunni Muslim, and the Speaker of Parliament a Shi'i Muslim. And this system of power-sharing applies to lesser positions as well. Everyone is expected to be a member of one of the recognized religions. Even positions in the civil service are allocated on the basis of religion. The Consociational way of mixing politics and ethnicity or religion is a model also used in Belgium, The Netherlands, and a few other nations.

It is hard enough to have a population split between Christians and Muslims, but Lebanese politics has to also take into account the role of other nations. Each of the three main religious groups has one or more external patrons. The Sunnis have Saudi Arabia, with its Salafi interests. The Shi'is have Iran and Syria as patron states. And the Christians have the backing of the West. In recent decades the increasing international influence of Salafi Islam has impacted Lebanese Sunnis. Also, the increasing influence of the more radical Hezbollah element among the Shi'is, as discussed in the chapter on Iran and Iraq, has encouraged the rise of Salafi influence among the Sunnis here.

When Israeli forces moved into southern Lebanon in July 2006, they did not crush the Hezbollah military strength as they expected. As a result of managing a stalemate in this **asymmetric war** the stature of Hezbollah increased so much in the region that by the summer of 2008 Hezbollah had been rearmed with the help of Iran. It was able to take control over parts of Beirut, signalling a possible restart to the civil war. Order was restored. Hezbollah had made its point that it was now a very strong force in Lebanese politics.

---

[1] The last official census, taken in 1933, showed the Christians were in a majority in Lebanon. The subject of the population sizes of the various religious groups is so politically sensitive that no new census has been taken. The political consensus is that no matter what the actual population proportions might be, Christians and Muslims will share power on a 50–50 basis.

We go to Martyrs' Square in the heart of old Beirut. It became the dividing zone during the long civil war. Looking eastward we see East Beirut, the Christian area. Looking westward, we see the Muslim area, West Beirut.

Leaving Beirut, we fly over troubled Syria to Amman, Jordan. Downtown, we climb to a museum atop a hill in the old section. We find ourselves at first in an open air museum from the Hellenistic era. Down below we see the ruins of the public theatre, a requirement of all ancient Greek cities. It is a reminder that Jordan was not always a center of Arabic culture. When we go inside the museum building, we see that this area has been a thriving cultural center since Neolithic times. We see statues of gods and goddesses from the days before Abraham's monotheism became normative around the Middle East. There are goddess statues that look like those from ancient Turkey, Iran and as far away as India.

We head south to visit Petra, the ancient caravan city in which the Nabataeans lived for centuries. Being expert rock carvers, they carved out homes, temples and tombs from the huge cliff surfaces. We learn that the famous narrow entrance between two cliff faces, as seen in an Indiana Jones *and many other movies, was actually the sacred ceremonial entrance to the city. It is lined with shrines and burials. Despite the heat, we climb the 500 or so steps to the top of the cliffs to see the stone altar where the Nabataeans sacrificed to their gods. The view from up here is spectacular. The Bible aptly refers to this kind of worship site as a "high place."'*

We go up Mt. Nebu to see where Moses stood to look over at the Promised Land. We wanted to come here before we go to Israel, to get an understanding of the Hebrew narrative in which they see themselves as having been given the land across from Mt. Nebu by God. We can see Jericho across the way, and now it makes sense why they started by conquering Jericho. It was the nearest town. From Mt. Nebu we can also see the place where many Christians think that John the Baptist baptised Jesus and other Jews. Moses is said to be buried in an unknown place near here.

Entering Israel through the Jordan Valley

We get a taxi to what Jordanians call the King Hussein Bridge and Israelis call the Allenby Bridge. We have our visas already, so we can cross there. We must leave our taxi in Jordan, and get an Israeli one after clearing immigration. The bridge's fame leads us to expect something grand, so we are a little let down when we see a very modest sized bridge. Having a similar first impression, former American Secretary of State Henry Kissinger is said to have remarked that this shows the power of public relations! As we approach Jericho the land looks a bit more impressive than it did from Mt. Nebu. The Bible describes how Joshua marched his men around the walls of Jericho, blew his trumpet, and the walls fell down. Could conquest of the largest town in the region have been that easy? Later the Crusaders tried the same approach. It worked, but with the help of artillery blasting a hole in walls.

> *We stop in Jericho long enough to ride the cable car to the top of the Mount of Temptation, where Jesus is thought to have been tempted by Satan. While we are up here, we check out the old Greek Monastery as well. If we had more time, we could take the camel ride through Wadi Qelt, visit Christian St. George's Monastery, and see Caliph Hisham's winter hunting palace, the site where Muslims hold that Moses is buried.*
>
> *We are driving now through the West Bank. Dusty Palestinian towns are here and there, around the precious few sources of water in this arid region. Surprisingly, it only takes 40 minutes to reach Jerusalem. Along the way we see the new Security Fence. It brings back unpleasant memories of the Berlin Wall that separated Germans along lines of political ideology during the cold war era. Here the barrier divides two peoples and at the same time, two religions.*

RELIGIOUS BACKGROUND: ISLAM, JUDAISM, CHRISTIANITY, BAHA'I, DRUZE

This region is the home of Judaism and Christianity and has sacred sites of Islam, **Baha'i** and the Druze. We reviewed the history of Sunni Islam in the Saudi Arabia chapter and Shi'i Islam in the Iran/Iraq chapter, so here we will give some background on Judaism, and briefly mention how these religions came to the region.

Judaism

The long history of Judaism here starts with Abraham's migration from Chaldea, (Southern Iraq) to the Canaan hills around 1800 B.C. It continues with his son Isaac and the settlement of the Jews, with their flocks of sheep and goats, in Canaan, now the West Bank. The twelve sons of Abraham's grandson Jacob, also known as Israel, fathered the twelve tribes of Israel. Centuries later they, or at least some of the Israelites, moved to Egypt to avoid famine conditions in Canaan. After several hundred years in Egypt, and a nasty turn of events in which they had become enslaved and put to work building pyramids, Moses led them out of Egypt, perhaps around 1280 B.C., into the "wilderness," meaning the sparsely inhabited desert region of the Sinai Peninsula, where Moses received the Ten Commandments on Mount Sinai. After forty years, the Israelites came to the East side of the Jordan River, crossed it, and under the leadership of Moses' successor Joshua, took control of nearby Jericho. As their population grew, they spread into surrounding areas. They formed a twelve tribe ritual and defence alliance, with each tribe having a territory. God was said to be their king. For practical leadership in times of war, disputes, or other crisis, they chose a "Judge." It was a man's world, but one of the best of the judges was a woman named Debra.

By 1000 B.C. they had adopted human kingship as their form of governance, but not without protest from the theological conservatives. The story is that the people asked the prophet Samuel to appoint a king of Israel.[2] He did so reluctantly, after warning them about kings. Kings will, he explains, take much of your crops as taxes, take your sons for their army and take your daughters to be servers in the palace. It is one of history's first warnings of the downside of having a powerful central governance structure. The people wanted kingship because they felt it necessary to compete against the surrounding nations, which had kings who maintained standing armies. So, Samuel appointed Saul as the first king and instructed Saul about how to conduct his war with the Amalekites. It would seem that Samuel favored a theocratic governance in which a prophet such as himself would make the major decisions after consulting with God through various forms of divination. The theocratic form of governance Samuel wanted reminds us of the system in contemporary Iran, where ultimate authority rests with religious leaders.

View of Holy Land as seen by Moses from Mt. Nebu. The map in the foreground shows the direction of major landmarks.
Photo: Roy Amore.

David became the second King of Israel. The young King David, an aggressive expansionist, conquered Jerusalem and made it his capital. He ruled both Judea, the southern group of two tribes including Jerusalem, and Israel, the group of northern tribes. David and then his son Solomon ruled over this "United Kingdom." David brought the Ark of the Covenant, representing God's dwelling place, into Jerusalem along with the special tent that housed the Ark. The plan was to replace the tent with a permanent structure. David's son Solomon did build a temple, in the style common in the region, to house the Ark. This was the golden age for the Jews and the only period in which one Jewish regime ruled over much of what is now Israel and the West Bank. Note that the historic northern area called Israel roughly corresponds with the today's West Bank region.

After being forcibly moved to Babylon during the Babylonian Captivity beginning in 586 B.C., the Jews were allowed to return after 538 B.C, when Cyrus the Persian conquered Babylon. Some did return and they rebuilt the temple in Jerusalem. They re-established kingship, but without the title king because of their subservience to the King of Per-

---

[2]There are several versions of the Biblical story of Saul becoming king. They are found in the I Samuel.

A model of the Second Jewish Temple.
Photo: Ariely [CC BY 3.0 http://creativecommons.org/licenses/by/3.0), via Wikimedia Commons

sia. Jews lost control of the region during the Hellenistic and Roman periods, but there were brief periods in which they re-established their independence. The final blow came after the Zealots, a radical independence party, made a bid for Jewish independence from Rome. The Romans took revenge in 70 by looting and destroying the second temple and by the forced dispersion (**Diaspora**) of the Jews. It is called a Diaspora rather than an Exile because to find places to live Jews moved to various regions. They became a scattered people who dreamed of one day returning to their homeland.

During the long Diaspora period, the Jews lost control of the region, but the Jewish claim to the territory is a theological rather than a political one. It is based on revelation to Abraham and to Moses that the Jews are meant by God to dwell in the region, as their Promised Land. Like claims based on revelation by Christians, Muslims or others, there is always going to be a disconnect between what is recognized in law or politics and what is claimed in revelation.

Islam in Israel and Palestine

After the death of Muhammad, Islamic rule spread quickly beyond Arabia. Just six years after Muhammad's death, the Byzantine Christians surrendered Jerusalem to the Muslims and the second Caliph Omar. Seeing Jesus as a true prophet and Christians as also "people of the Book." Omar ordered that Christian holy sites were not to be destroyed as if they were pagan. He issued a famous degree guaranteeing their safety. That guarantee lasted until 1009 when Caliph Kakim had them destroyed.

Islamic Holy Sites
The Quran describes Muhammad's Night Journey, an ascent to heaven on his white horse from the "farthest mosque" which Muslim tradition takes to mean the Al-Aqsa mosque built by the second caliph, Umar, on the Temple Mount in Jerusalem. The ascent is thought to have begun from the large rock outcrop on the Temple Mount near the Al-Aqsa Mosque. So, Caliph Abd al-Malik ordered the construction of the **Dome of the Rock** over the sacred rock. It was complete in 691. **The Al-Aqsa Mosque** has been rebuilt and expanded after damage by earthquakes. The current building dates from the mid-1000s. When the army of the First Crusade captured Jerusalem in 1099, the army converted Al-Aqsa into their headquarters and Church. It was returned to being a mosque after Saladin restored Islamic rule in 1187, after nearly a century of Christian Crusades came to an end.

Christianity in Israel and Palestine

The Jesus movement started in Galilee, now part of the **West Bank**, with Jesus preaching, healing, and warning people of the coming Kingdom of God. After his crucifixion by Roman officials in Jerusalem around A.D. 30, on what came to be called Good Friday, Christians came to believe that Jesus had risen from death on the third day, Easter Sunday. They were Christian Jews, who believed that the expected "Son of Man" had come. They also came to believe that he was more than a prophet and more than a human messiah (anointed agent of God). They believed he was in some mystical way also a divine Messiah (Christ, or *christos* in Greek), God on earth.

This later belief strayed too far from Jewish beliefs, and the Christian Jews gradually evolved into a new religion, Christianity. Under the leadership of Paul in particular, the decision was made that Christians did not have to follow the Jewish law. Circumcision was no longer required for males. Jewish dietary laws were optional. Christianity took on a life of its own. It now ignored the authority of the rabbis and rabbinic law. It developed its own worship service modelled on the Torah service of the synagogue, and with the addition of the Eucharist or Mass.

The Romans did not distinguish Jewish Christians from Jews when they ordered all Jews to leave Jerusalem in 70, so Christians were also dispersed. By the fourth century

The Temple Mount area with the Western wall below and the Dome of the Rock above. The plans for a permanent ramp up to the Temple Mount, to replace the temporary one seen in this picture, led to the Temple Mount Ramp Controversy.
Photo: Derek Barker.

Christianity started to become the main religion of the Roman Empire, both in its Eastern (Orthodox) and its Western (Catholic) halves. In this way, Christian control was established in Jerusalem, only to be lost to the Muslims in 638, as just mentioned.

Varieties of Christian Churches
There are numerous branches of Christianity now found in the region. Most Christians here are Roman Catholic or some variety of Eastern Orthodox. In the past few decades, various Protestant denominations have established a presence as well.

Christian Holy Sites
The region is dotted with sites of historical significance or sacredness to Christians. In Galillee there is Nazareth, the tiny hillside village were Jesus was raised. There is Capernaum where he lived during his adult years. Near Jerusalem is Bethlehem, his birth place. There is the garden of Gethsemane in which he was captured, and so many other places mentioned in the New Testament. Then there are the places associated with his crucifixion, burial and resurrection in the Old City area.

Minority Religions: Druze, Baha'i

Druze

A sectarian offshoot from Shi'i Islam occurred in Egypt during the eleventh century. It is known as **Druze**, after the name of one of its early leaders, al-Darazi. It combined Islamic monotheistic beliefs with some older ideas such as the transmigration of souls and the need to keep their sacred books secret from outsiders. They believe that the one of their leaders, named Ali, went into occultation in 1021, but will return with God to take part in the expected great era to come on earth. They were persecuted as heretics in Egypt. So they migrated north into parts of Syria, Lebanon and Jordan. Some Druze migrated to what is now the West Bank starting in the sixteenth century. They tended to settle in mountain villages, where they felt more secure. Today there are perhaps one hundred thousand Druze in Israel. The Druze have been more accepted by Jews than by Muslims. Many Druze men are career officers in the Israeli army.

Some Druze have immigrated to North America and elsewhere. The highest concentration of Druze in North America is in the greater Detroit area.

Baha'i

Baha'u'llah, "Glory of God" was a holy man who lived in Persia in the nineteenth century. He was from the Twelver sect of Shi'i Islam, and he became of follower of a man called the Bab, or "Gateway" to the returning Imam. In 1862 he announced that he had received a revelation and that he now understood himself to be the long expected leader. This claim was rejected by the Muslim rulers and he was imprisoned. While he was in prison his fame grew, so they moved him first to Baghdad. His followers made their way there as well. He was then imprisoned in Palestine, the most distant part of the Ottoman Empire from Persia. He spent his last years in Acre, Palestine. The Baha'i ('Followers of Baha) World Headquarters is now located in nearby Haifa. His burial shrine and those of other early Baha'i leaders are there as well. Baha'is do not play a major role in the politics of the region.

The Baha'i religion has spread around the world. It is sometimes called the world's newest religion. It holds more modern views than many religions on gender and racial equality and the need for harmony among all religions.

POLITICAL BACKGROUND: TENSIONS, CRUSADES, ZIONISM, MODERN ISRAEL

Tensions between Israelis and Palestinians

In 1998 when Israel celebrated the fiftieth anniversary of the founding of modern Israel, BBC News carried two stories. One was about the Israeli festivities, highlighted by an impressive flyover by military jets. The companion story was titled "The people with nothing to celebrate." It told of the Palestinian people who view the founding of modern Israel as *al naqba*, "the Catastrophe," the time when they lost their land. Most Palestinians were barred from attending the celebration, but they did not want to go anyway.

By the time of the sixtieth anniversary in 2008, nothing much had changed. Tensions between Israeli Jews and Palestinians were as high as ever. The second Intifada, 'Uprising,' was still in effect, settlements in the West Bank were still expanding, suicide bombers were still lurking, and each side blamed the other. Many Israelis think, if only the Palestinians would stop the violence, there could be peace. Many Palestinians think, if only the Jews would stop encroaching on our territory and pull back significantly, maybe we could co-exist.

The role of religious identity among the two peoples has increased since 1948, as we will discuss later. We will review the ugly history of the various wars fought between Israel and its Islamic neighbors. The conflict has spilled over into international politics. The threat of a renewed war between the Islamic countries and Israel remains, with the added danger that it could escalate into a world war.

Some background on the **Crusades**, **Zionism** and the founding of modern Israel may be helpful.

The Crusades

Pope Urban II, "God Wills It"
After spending the summer of 1095 in France, where it was cooler than Rome, Pope Urban II requested a large audience for a talk he was to give after his last Sunday service, during the Council of Clermont. Christian leaders from the Clermont region attended the outdoor talk, during which the Pope surprised his French flock with a moving call for the Franks, a term used for the rulers of vaious parts of Western Europe, to unite and fight the Turks. He told his audience that the Turks were defiling the holy places in the Holy Land and that their Eastern Orthodox brethren were under attack by the Turks. All Christians, both rich and poor, should march on this holy cause, he said. He appealed in particular to the French knights and noblemen to raise an army and march against the Turks the very next summer. "God wills it," he assured them, or perhaps that phrase first emerged from the crowd's enthusiastic cries. In either case, it became the slogan of the crusades. Urban II added, "God will lead you."

Actually, the Frank knights were not very eager to make war on the Turks, who were a long ways away. The truth was that the Turks had, for the most part, neither abused the Christian holy sites in the Holy Land nor barred Christians from making pilgrimages to them. After all, it was good business. The pilgrimage industry was in those days what the tourist industry is today.

Some Anti-Semitic German Christians reacted to the Pope's call to march on the infidels as an excuse to attack Jews in Germany. In hindsight, this is now sometimes called the first Holocaust.

The First Crusade

After continued demands by Urban II, the Franks organized the first war on the Turks in 1096. Later, this would be called the First Crusade, "War for the Cross." While the knights were taking their time, an eccentric, smelly barefoot man known as Peter the Hermit organized a rag-tag army of ill-trained and ill-equipped peasants known later as the People's Crusade. They walked toward the Holy Land, causing some trouble among local villages as they moved through. After some initial success against locals, they encountered and were hopelessly defeated by an army of Turkish regulars. The Turks celebrated, prematurely as it turned out.

The army of real knights, later known as the Princes' Crusade, eventually made it to Jerusalem in 1099 and wreaked havoc of the worst sort imaginable. After finally breaking through the walls, they went on a rampage and killed almost every inhabitant in Jerusalem, whether Muslim, Jew, or Orthodox Christian. It is reported that the narrow streets of the Old City flowed red with blood. Critics have wondered if this was Christendom's worst hour.

Some Christian knights stayed on and established various areas of Christian rule in various areas. These areas were collectively known as the Kingdom of Jerusalem.

The Fourth Crusade

The second and third crusades did not go well from the Christian point of view. The fourth was the most bizarre of all. The army marched to Venice, then the autonomous Republic of Venice, and not part of Italy. The Republic had the West's largest merchant fleet. The crusaders expected that, being a fellow Catholic, the Doge (leader) of Venice would supply them with ships to cross to the Holy Land. He agreed but explained that it would take time for that many ships to return and to be provisioned. In the meanwhile, he arranged for them to board in various houses in Venice. When he finally called the leaders to report that the ships, crews and provisions were ready, he presented them with a huge bill for the ships, supplies, crews and even their board and room while waiting. When they protested that they could not pay, he suggested that they could earn the amount by first doing a task for him. That task amounted to attacking and looting his main rival in the sea trade, Constantinople. Ironically, although helping their Eastern Orthodox fellow Christians was one of the two original goals announced by Pope Urban II, the fourth crusade wound up sacking the center of Eastern Orthodoxy, Constantinople. The valuable statues depicting the Biblical Four Horses of the Apocalypse were part of the loot brought back to Venice. Today, the original statues are kept in the Doge's Palace out of the weather, and replicas are displayed on a balcony overlooking San Marcus Square.

Salah al-Din's Restoration of Islamic Rule

Whereas the crusades began with a resounding Christian victory, however bloody, they ended with a resounding Islamic victory. The Islamic side was led by a Turk who had risen to be the Sultan of Egypt. He is known to Muslims by his Arabic name **Salah al-Din** and to the West as Saladin. He had spread his rule into Syria and had won small battles against

Four Horses overlooking San Marcus Square in Venice. They are replicas of the ones looted from Constantinople by the Fourth Crusade.
Photo: Roy Amore

the Christian forces, but suffered a major defeat in 1177. He withdrew with the remnants of his army to Egypt, where he regrouped, retrained, and prepared for a return engagement. He returned to Palestine and won some battles in 1187. He took most of the cities held by their Crusader rulers, the Knights Templar and Knights Hospitaller. Then he took Jerusalem. He then agreed to release the Christians for a ransom. Jerusalem and environments would remain under Muslim control until the founding of modern Israel in 1948.

The memory of the Crusades is still active among Muslims, creating a distrust of the West.

Zionism

The concept of **Zionism** refers to a return of Jews to Zion, the Biblical name for the sacred hill of Jerusalem, and by extension all of Jerusalem or all of Israel.

Restrictions, Persecutions and Pogroms
The underlying cause of Zionism was the discrimination against and persecution of Jews in Christian Europe. There were many contributing factors to this problem. One was that

the Jews tenaciously maintained their separate identity, refusing to assimilate into the local cultures. Another was that Christian tradition blamed the Jews for not accepting Christ and, worse, for playing a role in his death. Some parts of the Christian gospel accounts of the trial and death of Jesus describe the crowd; that is, the Jewish crowd, as calling out for Jesus' death. This may have been what actually happened, but some liberal scholars suspect the blame was put on the Jewish crowd for political reasons. In a time of Roman persecution of Christians, the Christian writers did not want to, or did not dare, play up the role of the Roman ruler in the death of Jesus.

Most European Christian countries treated the Jews as temporary refugees in the country. Restrictive laws varied from country to country and time to time, but as a generalization we can say the Jews typically were not allowed to own land or employ Christian workers. Jewish doctors enjoyed a good reputation, and one pope reacted to their popularity by forbidding good Christians to go to a Jewish doctor. The Jews in Venice were not allowed to employ Christians or compete with them for jobs. Jews could only be tailors or

Part of the Jewish ghetto in Venice. The wooden structure in the middle is a synagogue made by extending an existing room outwards. The Jews were not allowed to build higher. The cupola is over the Torah area, and does not stick up above the sight line to avoid criticism from Christians for competing with the church spires on the skyline.
Photo: Roy Amore

merchants of gold or used cloth. The restrictions were not as bad as the actual persecutions, killings and pogroms. The word *pogrom* refers to raids on Jewish villages or neighborhoods by Christian vigilante gangs. The pogroms involved killing, raping and looting.

Jews also typically had to reside within a certain area. As their population increased, these areas became over crowed and impoverished. The area set aside for Jewish use in Venice was a former island used as a foundry. The Italian name for foundry stuck, and in English we use the term **Ghetto** for these overcrowded Jewish neighborhoods wherever they were found. The term has come into modern English usage to refer to any poor, overcrowded, inner city neighborhood.

Dreyfus Trial

Alfred Dreyfus was a French soldier who was put on trial in 1894 on a charge of spying. A young Jewish reporter named Theodore Herzl covered the trial and became convinced Dreyfus was innocent and was just being blamed because he was Jewish. After the trial, Herzl decided that the only way Jews were going to be safe from pogroms, persecution and false accusations was if they could create their own Jewish state someplace. He convened a council of those interested in finding a Jewish homeland, and Zionism was born. After some failed efforts to find land for such a state elsewhere in the world, it was decided that the only recourse was to move to Palestine, their original homeland. The motivations were those of safety and economic improvement, and not theological ones. Jews did not really expect to gain control over the area. They were trying to escape persecution by Anti-Semitic Christians.

The Calls

The "Calls" to move back to Zion issued by some European Jews in the late 1800s meant that by 1900 Jews had begun to form a significant minority in Palestine. The Ottoman Empire allowed them to settle there. The movement to Israel by Jews intensified until World War I made the move difficult. After the war, the return to Zion movement resumed. As things worsened in Germany under the Third Reich, some Jews wisely fled. The number of Jews coming to Palestine began to alarm the Palestinians.

Modern Israel

British Mandate and the Balfour Declaration

The Ottoman Empire, already weakened economically, made the fateful decision to side with the Germans during World War I. After the defeat of the Germans, the Ottoman Empire crumbled. The victorious forces met in France to divide up the spoils of the war. Palestine became a British Mandate. Lord Balfour, the British foreign Secretary, had the difficult task of both making policy for Palestine and seeking a solution to the Jewish survivors of German rule who desperately wanted to move somewhere safer before another holocaust occurred. In his famous **Balfour Declaration** of 1917, Lord Balfour spelled out a British policy on Palestine. It basically opened the doors for Jews to immigrate to Palestine. With memory of pogroms and then the rise of the overtly anti-Semitic Nazi party,

---

Timeline: Modern Israel

1917	Balfour Declaration opens up Palestine for more Jewish immigration
1948	Modern Palestine founded, with 600,000 Jewish citizens plus Arab citizens War of Independence begins long period of intermittent wars with neighbors
1956	War with Egypt (Suez War)
1967	Israel captures Gaza, the West Bank, and East Jerusalem in Six Day War
1973	Syria and Egypt attack during Yom Kippur holy days
1979	Peace made with Egypt
1982	War with Lebanon
1987	Palestinian *Intifada* begins
1993	Oslo Peace Accords
1994	Peace with Jordan
2000	Second *Intifada* begins, Israel withdraws from Lebanon
2005	Israel withdraws from Gaza Strip
2006	War with Hezbollah in Lebanon

---

many Jews did move to Palestine. The Balfour Declaration stated that the communities currently residing in Palestine were not to be adversely affected by the Jewish immigration. In hindsight, that certainly was not what happened.

The Holocaust

Hitler's hatred for Jews was extreme. He referred to his plan to "solve" the problem of there being Jews mixed among the "Aryans" by killing them all as the "Final Solution." The plan called for all Jews under his rule to be rounded up and transported to various prison camps built for the purpose. Death came by means of the infamous gas chambers and cremation ovens the Nazi planners thought to be the most efficient way to kill and dispose of their victims. The most famous of those was Auschwitz in Poland.

In ancient Judaism most animal sacrifices involved offering only a small portion of the meat, fat and blood to God, with the rest of the meat being eaten by the priests and the family. Once a year, however, an entire goat was placed on the sacrificial fire. This sacrifice of the whole animal was called a **Holocaust**. Therefore, Hitler's plan to kill the whole Jewish population came to be called the Holocaust. The Nazis managed to kill at least five million Jews, plus millions of homosexuals, gypsies and political prisoners, before Hitler was defeated in 1945.

Founding of Modern Israel in 1948

When the World War II ended and the horror of the death camps became widely known, there was great pressure on the European community to find a lasting solution to the problem of periodic persecution of Jews. Jews in Israel were determined to have a state of their own. In 1948, they declared the modern state of Israel. Palestinians were in shock, rightly fearing that they were danger of losing control in their homeland.

The Jews in modern Israel came from throughout the Diaspora, not just from former Nazi territories. They did not all speak Yiddish, so a modernized Hebrew language was made the language of Israel. They also brought diverse cultural traditions with them. Most of the early Zionists who moved to Israel were **Ashkenazim**, Jews who shared cultural traits from northern and eastern Europe. **Sephardim**, Jews from Mediterranean regions, also arrived but tended to have less political power and a lower social ranking. The division between Ashkenazi and Sephardi Jews remains a factor in Israeli party politics.

Although the Zionists who founded Israel were mostly secular Jews, Orthodox Judaism was established as the official version of Judaism for the state. Since 1948 the political drive to make Orthodox Judaism the exclusive religion of the state has gradually softened, being replaced by a more pluralistic and individualistic conception of the relation between religion and politics. This change has been called the "Americanization" of religion and politics in Israel by one scholar.[3]

A Series of Israeli–Arab Wars

The surrounded Arab states reacted to the founding of modern Israel with a series of wars of protest. The 1948 Arab-Israeli War saw Egypt, Lebanon, Syria, Jordan and Iraq attacking Israel the day after its declaration of statehood. The Israeli Defense Force defeated the Arab coalition and in the process expanded Israeli control. Many Palestinians had fled their homes, becoming refugees in Jordan or Syria. Most have never returned. One of the sticky problems for a peaceful solution in the region is that Palestinian negotiators tend to be adamant about the **"Right of Return"** for the refugees, whereas Israeli negotiators are worried about such a big influx of Palestinians.

In 1956 Egypt nationalized the Suez Canal and closed it to Israeli ships. Israel responded by invading the Sinai Peninsula. After negotiations, Egypt agreed to open the canal to Israeli ships, and Israel withdrew from the Sinai.

1967 War
Egypt again blockaded Israeli shipping in 1967. Jordan and Syria signed a mutual defence pact with Egypt. War seemed likely. Israeli launched a pre-emptive air strike that took out most of the Egyptian military airplanes. Israel then severely damaged the airplanes of Jordan, Syria and Iraq. This decisive air dominance was followed by a rapid expansion of Israeli ground forces into Jordan, Syria and the Sinai. By the end of this "Six Day War," Israel had taken control of the West Bank, Gaza Strip, East Jerusalem and the Golan Heights. Balfour had expected that Jews and Palestinians could co-exist peacefully, but fifty years later, a new state of Israel had been formed and expanded.

Drawing upon an image from Jewish history, before the Six Day War, some commentators looked upon Israel as a David surrounded by an Arab Goliath. After the Six Day

---

[3]Martin Edelman, "A Portion of Animosity: the Politics of the Disestablishment of Religion in Israel. *Israeli Studies* Vol. 5, No. 1, (Spring 2000): 204.

War proved its military superiority and vastly expanded its territory, Israel seemed more like the Goliath than the David.[4]

The *Clash of Fundamentalisms* book has an appendix which reprints an interview made soon after the quick and total victory by Israel over the coalition of Arab states. In the interview, Polish-born journalist Isaac Deutsher said, "The war and the 'miracle' of Israel's victory have, in my view, solved none [of] the problems that confront Israel and the Arab states. They have, on the contrary, aggravated all the old issues and created new, more dangerous ones.... I am convinced that the latest, all-too-easy triumph of Israel arms will be seen one day, in a not very remote future, to have been a disaster in the first instance for Israel itself."[5]

1973 War and 1981 Attack on Iraq

In 1973 Egypt and Syria launched a surprise attack against Israel on Yom Kippur, the Day of Atonement. The surprise worked and Israel suffered several setbacks before regaining the upper hand. There was a risk that this 'Yom Kippur War' might have escalated into a Soviet-American war, but fortunately the cold war remained just that.

In 1981 Israel was becoming increasingly fearful that Iraq was developing nuclear missiles capable of reaching it. Israel made a successful pre-emptive strike on Iraqi nuclear facilities in 1981, setting back whatever nuclear development program the Iraqis had at the time.

2006 War with Hezbollah

Hezbollah fighters from Lebanon were making small raids into Israeli territory in 2006. In response, Israel launched a war on Hezbollah. Israeli air power easily destroyed airports and infrastructure, but the invading Israeli army met much more resistance from Hezbollah fighters than it expected. Israel pulled out of Lebanon. It was a stalemate, but the Arab world and the international press saw Hezbollah as the winner of the asymmetric war.

ISSUE 1: HAREDIM AND THE RELIGIOUS NATIONALISTS (ULTRA-ORTHODOXY, SETTLERS, ZIONISTS)

Our first issue concerns the influential role that the Religious Right plays in Israeli politics. It is seen as a good thing by the members of the Religious Right, of course, but it is seen as a problem by more secular Jews in Israel and by Palestinians trying to resist the encroachment of the settlements into their traditional territory.

---

[4]See, for example, Oakland Ross, "Still far from peace at 60." *Toronto Star.* (May 3, 2008): AA4. See http://www.thestar.com/news/2008/05/03/israel_still_far_from_peace_at_60.html.

[5]Isaac Deutsher. "On the Israeli-Arab War," New Left Review, 20 (June 1967). Reprinted as an appendix in Tariq Ali, *The Clash of Fundamentalisms*. New York: Verso. 394.

Most Israeli Jews are not especially religious in their personal lives or when it comes to politics. They have a strong identity with Judaism, but not a strong desire to see politics and public policy adhere to traditional Jewish norms. So, there is not that much interface between politics and Jews who are secular or moderately secular. They adhere to Judaism as a social identity and are not very active in organized expressions of Jewish religion. Several of the varieties of the most conservative Jews, however, have been quite active in trying to shape public policy or to expand the territory controlled by Israel and by Israeli Jews. We will begin with the Haredic Jews, the general term for the various groups of ultra-orthodox Jews. Then we will consider the nature and political role of a very different kind of Jews, the religious nationalists. We will see that the Haredic Jews and the religious nationalists are very different.

Haredi Jews and Ultra-Orthodoxy

A **Haredi**, or Charedi, is a Jew who adheres very strictly to the oral and written Torah traditions extending back to Moses. The term means one who Fears (the Lord). The plural form is **Haredim**, and the adjective used in English is Haredic. Heredic Jews are often referred to as **Ultra-Orthodox**, but many Haredim do not like that term.

The Haredim endeavor to follow the **Halakha**, Jewish traditional law, which they see as based upon revelations from God through Moses. The Talmud is the most authoritative source of Halakha, after the Torah itself. Haredi Jews understand Halakha to apply to every aspect of life. They are the Jewish equivalent to those Muslims who seek to live totally by Shariah. Most Haredi men wear old fashioned black clothes and a broad rimmed black hat while praying or walking out of doors, so it is easy to spot them on the streets of Israeli cities.

Some Haredi *poskim*, the "Deciders," or clerics who interpret Halakha, forbid secular diversions like television, films, and the Internet, but not every Haredi Jew goes to those lengths to avoid modernity. This refusal to accept modern things goes back to a ninteenth century German rabbi named Moshe Sofer, who is also called Chasam Sofer after the name of one of his books. He rejected the planting of a new form of wheat, and in the process laid down what became the broad principle that new things are forbidden by the Torah. This was a more extreme position than had been typical of Jews in the past and of Orthodox, as opposed to Ultra-Orthodox, Jews of

> **Reflections on Wearing Outdated Clothing:**
>
> *I'm walking in Jerusalem, enjoying the fascinating mix of buildings, peoples, sounds and smells. I happen to pass by a Yeshiva, a Jewish school. Coming towards me I see bearded young men all dressed in black, wearing old fashioned broad rimmed, black hats. Even though I know better, my first thought is that I am in Ohio among the Amish or in Ontario among the most conservative of the Mennonites? Later, in the Jewish museum in Prague, I see paintings from the eighteenth century of men who look and dress just like the twenty-first century Hasidic Jews. What motivates someone to refuse to change like that? What special meaning does it give them?*

the present. Orthodox Jews had been culturally conservative but did not reject new things so totally.

The anti-modernity position of Haredi Jews was in part a total rejection of the reform minded Jews of Germany of the early nineteenth century in Europe. At the time, reformers in the tradition of Jewish intellectual Moses Mendelsohn favored cultural assimilation for the Jews. Whereas other Jews resisted the German government's request for all citizens to take surnames to facilitate record keeping, he voluntarily changed his name from Moses ben Mendels, "Moses, Son of Mendels," to Moses Mendelsohn. The reformers wanted traditional Jewish life in the home, but in public they favored blending into the German scene. That meant dressing like Germans, and not wearing one's prayer shawl or *kippah*, cap, in public. It meant speaking German rather than Yiddish in public. It meant downplaying the traditional Jewish dream of one day returning to Israel. The reformers argued that by treating their stay in Germany as only temporary until their return to Israel, the Jews were setting themselves up for discrimination.

Most Jews of Germany and Poland found the ideas of the reformers unacceptable, and they continued to practice as they always had. They came to be called "Orthodox," in contrast to the Reform Jews. But the Haredim dug in their heels and rejected practically everything that was new, modern or secular. Like the Amish or Old Order Mennonites, their dress, lifestyle and whole culture did not change in the following centuries.

Baal Shem and the Hasidim

Israel ben Eliezer (1698–1759) was an orphan who was raised by the Jewish community in what is now Romania. He did not take to traditional Talmudic studies but rather turned to other means of support. He worked in a lime quarry for a while, ran a small inn, and in other ways earned a humble living. His fame came when he began to travel around Romania and the Ukraine. He developed a reputation for telling stories to children, for speaking to animals, and above all, for healing people in the name of God. Through this form of healing, he came to be called **Baal Shem Tov**, "Master of the Good Name," which is often shortened to **Baal Shem**. Like so many other Jewish figures, he is usually referred to by an acronym, through which Baal Shem Tov became **The Besht**.

The Besht represented a return to the simple piety of a pure worship of God. It appealed to those Jews who did not have the time or education to spend their days studying Torah. He offered an alternative spirituality which had Jewish roots but had been lost over the centuries. He was also inspired by his study of Kabbalah, the Jewish form of mysticism that has taken Hollywood by storm recently. He led spiritual retreats which became very popular. He preached about values such as mutual help, patience, and an ethic applicable to everyday life. Baal Shem was the model of the *tsaddik*, the "righteous leader" of Jewish piety. The Yiddish term *Rebbe* is often used as well. The Besht became the father of the Hasidic movement. After his death the movement was led by his disciple, who came to be known as the Maggid, "Preacher." The Maggid formulated the principle that leadership would pass to the eldest son of the former leader.

Reflections by a Jewish researcher on visiting an Hasidic celebration of the Purim festival:

I entered the Bobover Hasidim... [at] midnight on Purim.... [The] men's and women's sections were completely packed.... "We are waiting for the Rebbe [the Hasidi leader]. The play can't start without the Rebbe." I was... especially fascinated by the men's uniform black clothing, the smell of food and wine, and the sound of Yiddish.... [When] the Grand Bobover Rebbe, Shlomo Halberstam, arrived..., the women around me were whispering... "Look at the Rebbe; doesn't he look like an angel?"

Standing in the midst of the Bobover women, I wrote in my fieldwork notes, "What do I have in common with the Bobover, are we really members of the same tribe? We speak different languages, we live in different worlds set apart by our dress and life styles as well as our beliefs and world views." And I answered, "It is possible for people to share history, tradition, and even the Holocaust, but to live differently in the present and perhaps not to have a common future." However, the scenes, noises, and smells resulted in a nostalgic experience for me. They brought me close to my two pairs of grandparents who died before I was born, among them my maternal grandmother who died in Auschwitz. I remember also thinking about my maternal grandfather, who continued to be a Razvadover Hasid many years after he left... Galicia, for Germany after World War I.... At that moment, in the course of recognizing my differences with the Bobover, I felt closer to my grandparents than I ever did before.

Shifra Epstein, "Going Far Away in Order to Better Understand the Familiar: Odyssey of a Jewish Forklorist into the Bobover Hasidic Community," *The Journal of American Folklore* Vol. 112, No. 444 (Spring, 1999): 202.

The love of storytelling by Baal Shem inspired a wonderful tradition of Hasidic tales. Most are about a disciple observing and interacting with his master. From this encounter, the disciple learns a moral lesson to apply to his own life. More than one scholar has noted the parallels between this and the Zen Buddhist use of *koans*, stories of encounters between disciples and their masters that lead the disciple to enlightenment.

The Hasidic movement that The Besht founded became popular especially in Poland and Germany, and spread from there by immigration to Israel, the United States, and elsewhere. The greatest population of Hasidim in the United States is in Brooklyn, New York. The many Hasidic subdivisions usually trace their origin to a particularly pious or charismatic rabbi of Eastern Europe in the nineteenth century. For example, the Hasidic group known as Bobov or Bobover are named after Bobowa, their place of origin in southern Poland during the late nineteenth century. Today, Hasidic Jews, the Hasidim, constitute a large part of the Haredim.

Hasidic Worship

Hasidic Jews avoid worldly pleasures, but they are quite joyous in their worship. The Besht introduced ecstatic movement into Jewish worship. Music and psalms had been a part of the worship at the Jerusalem temple, but after its destruction in A.D. 70, only the synagogues were left as places for Jewish prayers. As an act of mourning for the loss of the temple, musical instruments were not allowed. Without changing the lament over the loss of the temple, The Besht and later his grandson introduced bodily movement into the prayer service in a way that brought a moving spiritual experience to Jews. The movements of the Hasidim have been compared to ecstatic dancing. They begin with quick movements of the hand and forearm and progress to movements of the arms, with jumping up and down, and with turning around. In comparative religions there are lots of examples of using such bodily movements to enhance one's spiritual experience. One author has compared the Hasidic dancing to the ecstatic dances of the Greek Bacchae.[6] One could add many other parallels to this list of comparisons, such as the Hare Krishna devotees who use some of the same movements in their ecstatic worship of Krishna. Also, in the European Union chapter, we will mention the somewhat similar Sufi practice of turning round and round to music, leading the practitioners of this approach to be called "Whirling Dervishes."

Lubavitcher Hasidim

The Baal Shem Hasidic movement spread into Lithuanian and Latvia, which were centers of Talmudic learning. A convert to Hasidim named Shneur Zalman wrote a philosophical work called *Tania* to combine Talmudic learning and the more emotional Hasidic approach. His followers were known by the acronym Habad or Chabad, but they are often referred to as **Lubavitchers**, after the name of a town in Belarus. The last Lubavitcher Rebbe, Menachem M. Schneerson, died in Brooklyn, New York in 1994 without a son to take over the leadership. Some Lubavitchers look upon Rebbe Schneerson as the long-awaited Messiah of Judaism, but of course other Jews reject this controversial claim. For one thing, it does not make sense, in traditional Jewish thought, to have a Messiah appear on earth without bringing about a new order and without bringing all Jews back to Israel.

Haredi Role in Israeli Politics

Although they like to remain apart from secular life in Israel, Haredi Jews do interface with political matters extensively by advocating for several public policies important to them. One is that they had sought and won an exemption from military service, which is otherwise required of all Israeli Jews. The basis for this is in part their piety and chosen life as a student of Torah. A few of them volunteered for service, however. But in 2014, after 65 years of exemptions, the **Knesset**, Israeli Parliament, passed a law requiring a gradually increasing number of young Haredi men to either join the army or a civil defense alternative. The goal was that a reasonable portion of Haredi would eventually serve in defense of their nation. Haredi Rabbis protested the change vehemently, both in Israel and abroad, but the law stands.

Another issue important to Ultra-Orthodox Jews is the continuation of the government payments to the **Yeshiva** system. Yeshivas are religious schools, and they are heavily subsidized. Most Haredi males go to a yeshiva, benefiting from the subsidies. After they get married many continue to study in special, subsidized schools for older, married men.

The Haredim also lobby to keep control over Rabbinical rituals exclusively in the hands of Orthodox rabbis, including the Haredi rabbis. Under Israeli law, marriages,

---

[6]Louis. H. Feldman, "Another Parallel to the Maenadism of the Bacchae: Hasidism in Modern Jewry," *The Harvard Theological Review* Vol. 42, No. 1. (Jan., 1949): 65–67.

divorces, funerals, and other rituals are not considered officially Jewish unless performed by an Orthodox rabbi. This excludes Conservative and Reform rabbis. Many Israeli Jews, especially those who have immigrated from North America, would like to have the laws changed to recognize Conservative and Reform rabbis, but the Orthodox and Haredi lobbies are too strong.

A strict public enforcement of Sabbath laws is another public policy interest of the Haredi. Orthodox regulations prohibit travel on the Sabbath. This is based upon the Torah idea that the Sabbath is a day of rest, as God rested on the seventh day of creation. Haredic influence has meant that buses may not run through certain Haredi neighborhoods on the Sabbath. Buses violating this prohibition have sometimes been stoned by Haredi.

Haredic Political Parties. There are several Haredi political parties in Israel. One might think they would have an even stronger voice if they united into one party representing all the various Haredi subgroups, but that has not happened. The main reason for having so many, small Haredi parties is that they are split along Ashkenazim versus Sephardim lines. Also, the many and various Haredi groups do not necessarily want to be in the same party. None of the Haredi parties has been very effective in parliament recently, and by 2008, journalists were asking the question: Is there any need for Haredic parties?[7]

Shas is an example of a Haredic party with a base of support among Sephardic Jews, as reflected in its original name, "The Worldwide Sephardic Association of Torah Keepers." Although it has been plagued by scandals involving charges of corruption, fraud, and forgery by high ranking members, Shas also enjoys the support of some non-Haredi Sepharic Jews and some Druze voters. The party won twelve seats in the 2006 elections.

The United Torah Judaism Party is a merger of convenience between two other Haredi parties. The Degel HaTorah, "Banner of Torah," party draws its main support from non-Hasidic Haredi Jews coming from Lithuania. It is therefore an Ashkenazi based party. The other component of United Torah Judaism is Agudat Israel, "Union Israel," a party whose leadership is mainly Hasidic Jews but which enjoys support from other conservative, Ashkenazi Jews. The two parties do not agree on many issues and tend to see each other as rivals, but it is in the interests of each to present a united party slate to qualify for more seats under Israel's proportionate representation system. Under that system, a party must get at least two percent of the vote to qualify for a portion of the seats. The danger for these two parties is that they might not qualify if they entered the race as separate parties. By uniting, they met the minimum in the 2006 elections and won six seats in the seventeenth Knesset.

Haredi Rejection of Zionism

It seems counter-intuitive that Ultra-Orthodox Jews who have chosen to move to modern Israel would not be Zionists, even avid Zionists. But no, they are not Zionists. The

---

[7]Aryeh Dayan, "Is the (Haredi) party over?" (2008) http://www.haaretz.com/hasen/pages/ShArt.jhtml?itemNo=%20420148&contrassID=2&subContrassID=1&sbSubContrassID=0&listSrc=Y.

reason has to do with the Jewish expectations of the coming Messiah. Hasidim and Jews traditionally understand that when the Messiah does come, Jews will then be called back to Israel. Zionism has it backwards, from their point of view, because Zionism called upon Jews to the return to Israel even though the Messiah has not yet come. To Moshe Sofer and later Hasidim, Zionism is an affront to God because the Zionists have done what only God was supposed to do through God's Messiah.

Another reason that the Hasidim rejected Zionism is that the early Zionists were not particularly religious Jews. Their call to return to Zion was because they were looking for a safe Jewish homeland, and not looking for a place to practice their religion more fervently.

In the early period of the founding of modern Israel there was a united Haredi party called Agudat Israel, or Agudath Israel. It served as an umbrella party for most Haredim. A dispute emerged within the party over the issue of whether or not a Haredi should partici-pate in elections. The more anti-Zionist faction, Edah haChareidis ('Haredi Community') went its own way. Popularly known as the Badatz, after the name of a Rabbinic Court, the Edah is noted for its anti-Zionist stance on many issues. Many of its members are Jews who lived in Palestine before the founding of modern Israel, which they basically oppose on theological grounds. The Edah holds that a good Jew, in this case an anti-Zionist one, should not vote in elections for the Knesset. Nor should the good Jew accept any govern-ment funding in any form. This means that they refuse subsidies for Yeshivas, refuse to apply for unemployment insurance, or even refuse to accept citizenship. They do have to deal with the government on a few matters such as registering births, marriages and deaths. The Edah community is itself divided between the Sephardic and Ashkenazic identities.

Having introduced the main ideas, groups and ideas of Haredic Judaism, we turn now to the Religious Nationalists, the other main type of Jewish political activism.

The Religious Nationalists (Zionism, Settlements)

Political Parties of the Religious Right
A survey on political behaviour showed that for Jews in the United States and in Israel the higher they ranked on the religiosity scale, the more their political views were similar on questions concerning Palestinians, the political role of Jews, and other religio-political issues.[8] In Israel, religion and fervent nationalism have often gone together. The term Reli-gious Nationalists is used for the various groups and parties that exhibit these two traits.

The main party of the Religious Nationalists has been the **National Religious Party (NRP)**. It was formed in 1956 by religious Zionists, who contrast sharply with the reli-gious anti-Zionists parties and groups. The inspiration for the party's ideology was pro-vided by Rabbi Abraham Isaac Kook. Kook had immigrated to Palestine from Lithuania in 1904, when Palestine was still part of the Ottoman Empire. He wound up in England

---

[8]Kenneth D. Wald and Michael D. Martinez, "Jewish Religiosity and Political Attitudes in the United States and Israel" *Political Behavior* Vol. 23, No. 4, (December 2001): 377–397.

during World War I. He is said to have had some influence on Lord Balfour and his important Balfour Declaration. Returning to Palestine after the Second World War, he became the first Ashkenazi Chief Rabbi in 1921. He was both a Zionist and a very orthodox Jew. In contrast to the anti-Zionists who saw the establishment of a Jewish state in Israel as an affront to God's plan, Rabbi Kook argued that God's plan was being carried out precisely through the return to the Holy Land. In contrast to the secular Zionists, he called for more adherence to dietary and Sabbath regulations.

The National Religious Party has won enough Knesset seats to be a part of most coalition governments. It has been a strong advocate for security concerns for the state of Israel and has become an advocate for the settlers' cause. When Prime Minister Ariel Sharon proposed to dismantle some of the settlements in Gaza in 2004, the National Religious Party quit his ruling coalition in protest.

Though not its original emphasis, the National Religious Party has made the continuation of the settlements in the West Bank its main agenda. It is committed to a **One State Policy**, meaning that its goal is the establishment of an Israel that embraces all the territory from the Jordan River to the Mediterranean Sea. The presence of the settlers obviously advances the cause of a One State policy.

Religious Nationalism and the Military

If the Israeli government ever commits to dismantling some of the settlements in the West Bank as part of a peace process, it will need to call upon the military to enforce the policy. The problem is that many members of the Israel Defense Forces are Religious Nationalists who support the settlements. Although Haredic Jews mostly do not serve in the military, Religious Nationalists serve in disproportionate numbers. They tend to volunteer for the elite units and many become career officers who subsequently form an important portion of the command chain. Based upon the past experience of dismantling settlements in Gaza, the military will most likely will have to forcibly remove settlers and bulldoze homes. The question is, will the Religious Nationalists follow orders on a dismantlement policy that goes so against their religious convictions?

Despite its support for the settlers and the fact that many Israelis also support the settlement policy, the National Religious Party's voter appeal had waned by 2006, when it won only three seats in the seventeenth Knesset. The struggling NRP merged with others to form the Jewish Home, a religious Zionist party.

Gush Emunim, Eretz Yisrael, and the Settlements

The name **Gush Emunim** means "Block of the Faithful." It grew out of the youth faction of the pro-Zionist National Religious Party in 1974, in the aftermath of the 1973 war. It later broke official ties with the NRP. Starting in 1977 under the right-wing Likud-led government, Gush Emunim spearheaded the settlement movements. With the blessing and cooperation of the Israeli government departments, numerous settlements were built mainly in the West Bank, but also in the Gaza Strip. Gush Emunim's settlement movement is called Amana. Gush Emunim's Council of Settlements, known as Yesha, lobbied for issues relevant to settlers, such as access to water, military protection and other practical matters.

Among all the parties, religious and secular, that support settlements, Gush Emunim stood out for several reasons. One is that it has made the expansion of the settlements its main party platform. Another is that, more than the other parties, it advocated expansion into former Palestinian territory. Its members brought both an expansionist ideology and youthful drive and enthusiasm to accomplish their goals. Gush Emunim no longer exists, but the cause is continued by others committed to their understanding of the Biblical Eretz Yisrael, "Land of Israel."

Water Rights and Environment Issues

We have rented taxis for the day. The drivers pick us up at our hotel in Amman, Jordan, at 6:30 for an early start on a busy day of sightseeing in the Jordan Valley. After seeing the area of natural pools where John the Baptist may have lived and baptized many Jews, including Jesus, we head further south. We are driving in the Jordan Valley over 300 metres, or 1000 feet, below sea level, the lowest point on earth. Even though it is still early in the morning, the heat is stifling here in mid-summer. What a place to live!

We reach our main goal, the Dead Sea. We pay ten Jordanian Dollars to enter a nice resort spa complex. We can't wait to try swimming here. We hurry right past the mud pits where other tourists are getting their whole bodies smeared with Dead Sea mud. "Make you young again," the masseuse calls to us. We enter the water, only to find that it is surprisingly difficult to swim in such salty, buoyant water. So we float on our backs, paddling with our hands as if we were in inner tubes.

From the water marks on the shoreline it is obvious that the water has dropped an unbelievable amount from its traditional levels, due to the overuse of the water of the Jordan River which feeds the Dead Sea. We see that some of the older resort spas, originally built near the shore, are now so far from the water that they have to give patrons a ride to the water's edge! Our spa is brand new, but if nothing changes, it will need to relocate in just a few years!

Access to water is a crucial matter because water is such a scarce resource in the region. Israel has been criticized by the international community for diverting most of the water resources to Jewish rather than Palestinian communities. Critics claim that new irrigation projects are begun in Jewish settlements while traditional Palestinian farm areas remain parched. In addition to the issue of who gets the water, there is the environmental issue arising from the fact that the Jordon River and Dead Sea are drying up due to the increasing diversion of water from the Jordon River for Israeli settlements and farms. In this case the interface of religion and politics has serious environment implications. The religious drive to expand Jewish presence in the West Bank has led the government to a pro-settlements policy, which in turn is causing serious long-term environment degradation on both sides of the Jordon River. The Jordon River has almost dried up in some spots. The water level in the Dead Sea has dropped eighty feet in the past fifty years, and has been dropping three feet per year on average since 1970. The Dead Sea has lost over a third of its water volume. Besides the upstream diversion for irrigation, both Israel and Jordon have projects to evaporate Jordon water to extract its minerals. The shrinking of the shore and loss of water has devastated the traditional tree and plant life along the shore. Unfortunately, this is an environmental disaster for waterfowl, because the area is a resting and feeding stop for an estimated 500 million birds that migrate between Europe and Africa.[9]

In 2013 the Israeli and Jordanian governments agreed to a plan calling for the construction of a pipeline to bring water from the Red Sea to the Dead Sea, to at least slow down its rapid rate of water loss. To address the underlying problem, Israel recycles water and has built a robust system of desalination plants intended to reverse the water crisis in Israel and the West Bank as of 2015.

Rabbi Kahane and the Kach

Rabbi Meir Kahane (1932–1990) was an Orthodox rabbi who was born in the United States. He founded the Jewish Defense League in 1968 to defend Jews against anti-semitism in general and to protect Hasidic Jews in Brooklyn in particular, where he recruited most of his members. Its tactics were extreme enough to get the JDL labelled a terrorist organization by some critics, and many mainstream American Jews disapproved of its tactics, but of course not with its goals.

After immigrating to Israel, he founded a party with the curious full name meaning "Kahane to the Knesset," popularly known by the acronym **Kach**. From its beginnings in the early 1970s, it did not win any seats in the Knesset until 1984. Its radical rhetoric caused the government to ban Kach from contesting future elections on the grounds that it was racist and inflammatory. Kahane was assassinated in 1990 in New York. After his death his son formed a breakaway party known as Kahane Chai, "Kahane Lives," based in a West Bank settlement. It was banned as well.

The Disproportionate Influence of the Religious Parties

As one scholar of Israeli politics points out, "If there was ever an example of a political group whose power is greater than its strength in the country, the religious parties provide it."[10] His basis for saying this is that the various religious parties combined never win over 18 percent of the Knesset seats, and yet they are often invited into the governing coalition. The reason is that Israel's two main parties, Likud and Labor, never win a majority, so they turn to the religious parties for support.

---

[9]John Ward Anderson, "For Dead Sea, a Slow and Seemingly Inexorable Death," *The Washington Post* (May 19, 2005). www.washingtonpost.com/wp-dyn/content/article/2005/05/18/AR2005051802400.html.

[10]Asher Arian. *Politics in Israel: The Second Republic*, 2nd Edition (Washington, D.C. CQ Press, 2005).

ISSUE 2: THE RELIGIONIZATION OF PALESTINIAN NATIONALISM (PLO, FATAH, HAMAS)

Our second issue concerns the way the various Palestinian nationalist movements have evolved from a relatively secular to a much more Islamic stance. This means that the fate of Palestine has become a rallying cry for Islamists worldwide. This is a seen as a good thing by those who want to see a movement toward more unity within Islam. It is seen as a bad thing by those who are trying to find a peaceful compromise settlement to the Israel/Palestine mess.

Arafat, the PLO and FATAH

Under the initiative of Nasser's Egypt, the **Palestinian Liberation Organization**, or **PLO**, was founded by the Arab League in 1964. Its goal was to liberate Palestine from Jewish occupation. The means to that goal included militant struggle. The militancy was thought to be justified by the Arab League's opinion that Israel was an illegal state. The PLO's first leader was Ahmad Shuqeiri, whose background was in diplomacy, not military action. During his first three years of leadership, in the period leading up to the 1967 Arab-Israeli War, he was quite confident in and boastful about a total Arab victory over Israel.

The devastating defeat suffered by the Arab side in the 1967 war brought about profound changes in the PLO. Many Palestinians had long hoped and expected that the Arab states would come to their assistance, defeating Israel and allowing Palestinians to return to their homes. After 1967, a new realism set in. The Palestinians became increasingly convinced that they had to rely on their own resources. As a result, they became more militant and the PLO became more important. As part of the transition, Shuqeiri resigned.

Fatah, Arafat, and the War of Attrition
Two years later, in 1969, **Fatah (the Palestinian National Liberation Movement)** factions had taken control of the PLO executive and soon chose their leader, **Yasser Arafat,** as the chairman of the PLO. He held that office until his death in 2004. Arafat was a fighter, not a diplomat. He had founded Fatah in the late 1950s. Operating out of surrounding Arab countries, it led attacks on Israel. His appointment to the chairmanship signalled the completion of the transformation of the PLO into a militant organization. He was bitterly denounced by Israeli leaders as a terrorist with whom they would never negotiate. Ironically he came to be seen as more of a moderate after the rise of even more aggressively militant groups such as **Hamas.**

Under Arafat's leadership, Palestinian men and women living inside Israel became more active in the resistance movement. His strategy was to engage in a protracted war of attrition. That is, a war in which the Israeli side would be the first to tire of losing its combatants. Israel reacted by putting many men and women into jail and by denouncing the PLO's tactics.

Ten-Point Program and the Rejectionist Front

By 1974 the PLO spelled out its goal further, stating that it sought an independent Palestinian state stretching from the Jordan River to the sea. That would mean the elimination of Israel. However the wording of the PLO's ten-point program was thought by some radical Fatah factions to suggest a possible abandoning of the goal of totally eliminating Israel as a state. Those more radical factions broke away to form the Rejectionist Front. The Rejectionists turned to surrounding Arab states for support. Their lack of internal cohesion and foreign support meant that most Palestinians continued to look to Arafat as their resistance leader.

As it turned out, the Rejectionists may have been right to suspect a change in Arafat's thinking. Beginning in 1993, the PLO expressed a readiness to accept a **Two-State Solution**, allowing for an independent Palestine and an independent but much smaller Israel. Israel in turn has accepted the PLO as the representative of the Palestinians.

Camp David Accords and Israeli-Egypt Peace Treaty

There was a serious drive toward peace undertaken in 1977. President Anwar Sadat of Egypt was making plans to meet with Israeli Prime Minister Menachem Begin in Tel-Aviv. The PLO and other Arab states were alarmed at the prospect of a peace agreement between Israel and Egypt, so they formed the Steadfastness and Confrontation Front. The Front was adamant that Arab states should not negotiate with Israel because that implied acceptance of Israel as a state. The Front's own position was that an interim Palestinian state should be established on as much territory as possible.

The Sadat/Begin peace initiative continued, despite the opposition of the Steadfastness and Confrontation Front. Sadat did break the Arab boycott against travelling to Israel. He not only went to Tel-Aviv to meet with Begin, he spoke before the Knesset. The first step had been taken toward a rapprochement between a major Arab neighbor and Israel. Jimmy Carter had made peace in the Middle East a major goal when he took office in 1977. He invited Sadat and Begin to Camp David, the Presidential retreat in the mountains of Maryland, for a two week period of intense negotiations. Began and Sadat were not on good terms, so Carter met them individually in their cabins to broker a hard won deal. This culminated in the Camp David Accords signed in the White House in 1978.

The Camp David Accords called for continuing negotiations between Israel and Egypt, which led to the signing of the Israeli-Egypt Peace Treaty in 1979. Israel agreed to withdraw from the Sinai Peninsula, where it had held territory since the 1967 War. Egypt agreed to recognize Israel, to allow Israeli shipping through the Suez Canal and elsewhere. In the process the two countries put a formal end to the war that had started with the creation of modern Israel in 1948.

Sadat and Begin shared the 1978 Nobel Peace Prize for their role in negotiating the treaty. Some critics grumbled that it was premature to think that peace had come to Israel and Palestine. A similar treaty was signed with Jordan in 1994. It put an end to the 1948 war, normalized relations between Israel and Jordan, and settled some boundary disputes. Anwas Sadat was assasinated by fundamentlaist Army soldiers in 1981.

The First Intifada (1987–1993)

Pent-up frustration over perceived mistreatment by Israeli policies, officials, and the army brought protesters out into the streets starting in 1987. The **Intifada**, "Uprising," began after an Israeli tank ran over and killed some Palestinians. Palestinians believed it had been done on purpose. The causes of the Intifada were much more deeply seated and long lasting than this single incident. The Intifada had started spontaneously among the Palestinian masses, but the PLO, Fatah, and other organizations soon got involved. There were rioting youth, suicide bombers, and some armed attacks. Perhaps most importantly for the future, Hamas was founded (to be discussed below).

Israeli Jews and international audiences watched TV news footage of Palestinian youths throwing stones at Israeli tanks and soldiers, who sometimes responded with bullets. By watching this footage, many Israeli Jews came to learn just how frustrated Palestinians in the West Bank and Gaza really were. There was little support in Israel for authorizing the soldiers to open fire on the youthful rioters. Despite an Israeli effort at restraint, the death toll among Palestinian youth mounted. An attempt at restraint by using clubs rather than guns led to several incidences of excessive beatings. The book *Rubber Bullets* describes the way in which the Israeli army switched to using rubber bullets in an attempt to control the rioters without killing them.[11] This eased the conscience of the Israeli public, the author reports, but still many Palestinian youths were killed or maimed.

Oslo Accords

The Declaration of Principles, more commonly known as the Oslo Accords, were negotiated in Oslo, Norway in 1993 and signed later that year in Washington, D.C. The Accords created the Palestinian Authority as the governing body over Palestinian-controlled territory and it called for the withdrawal of Israeli forces from parts of the West Bank and Gaza Strip. The plan was to move one baby step at a time toward a Two-State Solution, with the Palestinian Authority evolving into the full government of Palestine. The Accords were designed to extend for a period of five years during which more progress could be made on the road to security for Israel and self-governance for Palestine.

After the Oslo Accords, a Jewish extremist who opposed any compromise with the Palestinians assassinated Israeli Prime Minister Yitzhak Rabin. Israelis remained divided over how to move toward a peaceful coexistence with the Palestinians.

The Second Intifada

The Second Intifada was touched off by a visit by Ariel Sharon, then opposition leader and head of the Likud party, to the Temple Mount area in late September 2000. The Temple Mount is the most sacred site in Judaism because it is the site of the first and second temples. It is also the third most sacred site of Islam. It was routine for Jews to go to and pray at the Wailing Wall that runs along the western side of the temple mount area. But Jews did not normally go up the ramp to the main platform of the area because it leads to

---

[11]Yaron Ezrahi. *Rubber Bullets: Power and Conscience in Modern Israel* (Toronto: HarperCollins Canada, 1997), 207–216.

Jews praying at the Western wall.
Photo: Derek Barker

Haram-esh-Sharif, the "Sacred Area" of the Arabs, where Muhammad is believed to have ascended into Heaven and where the Al-Aqusa Mosque was built. But Sharon wanted to assert the right of Jews to go up on the mount. With full media coverage, an entourage, and many army guards, he toured the Temple Mount. The Palestinians were outraged, in part because their control over access to the Mount had been challenged, but also because the Palestinians tended to hate Sharon more than any other Jewish leader because of his past actions as an Israeli army commander.

The next day Palestinians rioted to protest Sharon's visit. Some threw rocks from the mount down upon the Jews praying at the Western Wall. Rioting soon spread around the city, and Israeli police killed some Palestinians while suppressing the rioters. The protests spread into Gaza and the West Bank, and the Second Intifada was born. October 2000 was marked by strikes, riots by Palestinians and, overreactions by Israeli police and military, as judged by an Israeli commission set up later by the government.

As it was sparked by the Sharon visit to the Temple Mount where the al-Aqsa Mosque is located, Palestinians sometimes call this the al-Aqsa Intifada.

The Al-Aqsa Ramp Controversy
In 2007 a controversy erupted when the Israeli government began to reconstruct one of the ramps leading up to the Temple Mount. This disputed ramp was used by tourists to get a view of the temple mount area. The old ramp had fallen into disrepair and had been out

of service. There would not have been a problem if the government had rebuilt the ramp in the same style and at the same location, but instead it started to build a bigger, stronger ramp which would start in a different place but still end up at the same place at the top. There was some consultation with Palestinian officials before beginning construction, but once the Palestinians saw what was being built, they protested strongly. Again, they threw stones from the Mount down upon Jews at the Western Wall.

What was not well-reported by the international press at the time, and not mentioned by Israeli defenders of the plan, was that the shifting of the ramp had the effect of opening up a lot more territory for Jews praying at the Western Wall. This was contentious because in the past the government had already torn down structures to make more room for Jews to pray. It was not the repair of a ramp that was at issue. It was perceived to be another instance of Jewish encroachment on traditional Palestinian space. It was a small matter, but it touched a nerve.

Hamas

We turn now to the other major party of Palestinian politics. Hamas is an acronym for an Arabic name meaning the "Islamic Resistance Movement." It grew out of the Gaza branch of the Muslim Brotherhood in 1987, during the first Intifada. Its first leader was Sheik Ahmed Yassin. The Palestinians were tired of waiting for either Israel to change its policies or the Arab countries to defeat Israel militarily. Conditions were especially bad in Gaza, where most Palestinians had lived in refugee camps for generations, with little hope of establishing a normal life. So the atmosphere was right for the rise of a group pledged to the total elimination of Israel and the establishment of Palestine as an independent state stretching from the Jordan River to the Sea. Gaza has remained the stronghold of Hamas support.

Hamas members believed that terrorist tactics against Israel were their best, and only viable, way to achieve their goals. They sponsored suicide bombings and other attacks against Israeli civilian and military targets. Hamas was particularly upset about the Oslo peace process. It gained a lot of support among Palestinian hardliners for its strong stance against any move toward recognizing Israel's right to exist.

After being postponed many times, Palestinian elections were held in January 2006. To the surprise of many, Hamas won a clear majority. For the first time the PLO found itself out of power, holding 76 of the 132 seats in the Palestinian Legislative Council, PLC. The PLO's Fatah Party won only 43 seats. Several reasons have been given for the defeat of the Fatah. One was that the PLO had a reputation for corruption among many Palestinians. Another was that Hamas had been active in arranging basic social services among the areas it controlled, mainly in Gaza. Although, Matthew Levitt calls attention to the way that Hamas charities often flowed money to their own activists rather than to the larger community.[12] Another was that Fatah infighting, or maybe just a failure to follow

---

[12]Matthew Levitt, *Hamas: Politics, Charity, and Terrorism in the Service of Jihad* (New Haven, Yale University Press, 2006). 92 ff.

sound election strategy, meant that in many election districts there were two or even three PLO candidates running for office. With the PLO vote split, it made it easy for the Hamas candidate to win the most votes.

After the Hamas victory, many countries refused to deal with Hamas and refused to transfer foreign assistance to the elected Hamas regime, leading to a severe financial crisis. With payments from donor countries cut off and having only an impoverished people as a tax base, Palestinian government workers, teachers, and many others found themselves going for months without pay. An already impoverished economy grew worse. Israeli travel restrictions made it impossible for the PLC to actually meet.

One unfortunate result of Hamas's election victory is that Fatah and Hamas factions have intensified their bitter fighting, leading to several deaths. Both parties maintain military wings. Izz ad-Din al-Qassam Brigades is the military wing of Hamas.

Hamas, or at least its al-Qassam Brigades division, has been declared a terrorist group by many, including the United States, Canada and the European Union. The United Nations recognizes the PLO, which has observer status at the United Nations. A branch of Hamas used to be permitted in Jordan by King Hussein, but his successor, King Abdullah II, closed down the Hamas headquarters, which subsequently moved to Qatar.

Former President Jimmy Carter undertook a dialogue mission to Hamas in 2008. He was criticized by the Bush White House for making unauthorized contact with a terrorist group. After the trip Carter announced that Hamas was ready to accept Israel as a neighbor if it agreed to pull back to its 1967 border (not likely) and if a majority of Palestinians approved of the acceptance of the peace deal in a referendum.[13] This would have meant a major shift in Hamas policy, but a Hamas leader Khaled Meshaal denied that Hamas would recognize Israel, saying that Hamas had offered a ten-year truce if Israel would pull back to its 1967 borders and allow sovereignty to Palestine with its capital in Jerusalem.[14]

Mahmoud Abbas
Mahmoud Abbas, popularly known by Arabs as abu Masen, took over the leadership of the PLO after the death of Arafat in 2004. He is a moderate leader who prefers negotiations over violence, but he has not been able to put a stop to Hamas-led attacks. The international community prefers to work with him rather than with Hamas, and tends to channel donor money through the PLO rather than Hamas.

After coming into power in Gaza, Islamist elements within the Hamas party tried to institute the enforcement of conservative Islamic dress for women and polygamy for men, but Hamas officials avoided enacting Islamist practices into law.

After Hamas formed the government in Gaza, Israeli stepped up the enforcement of its blockade of goods coming into Gaza. The blockade was intended to keep military supplies from entering Gaza, but it led to a shortage of basic supplies and brought

---

[13]"Carter: Hamas is willing accept Israel as its neighbor" *AP News* (April 21, 2008). apnews.excite.com/article/20080421/D9066D6O1.html and

[14]"Hamas rejects Israeli recognition." *BBC News*. (April 21, 2008). news.bbc.co.uk/1/hi/world/middle_east/7359661.stm.

hardship to Gaza residents. Various international organizations undertook efforts to bring humanitarian relief to Gaza. The "Gaza Freedom Flotilla," consisting of ships carrying supplies from several such organizations, was intercepted in international waters in May 2010 by Israeli security forces. The Israelis boarded the ships and made them divert to Israeli ports for inspection. Resistance to the boarding occurred on Turkish ship, and Israeli forces killed 10 people, most of whom were Turkish citizens. Israel had enjoyed good diplomatic relations with Turkey, but Turkey was outraged at what it and many other countries saw as the use of unnecessary lethal source in international waters. It took months for diplomatic relations between the two nations to normalize.

In response to missiles being fired from Gaza into Israeli towns near the border, there have been periodic military actions by Israel into the Hamas governed Gaza Strip. The 2014 Israeli military action in Gaza, known by Israelis as Operation Protective Edge, resulted in over 2000 deaths and widespread

A memorial in Gaza to those on the Turkish ship who lost their lives while attempting to deliver humanitarian relief to Gaza. Their names are inscribed on the base.

Photo: M. al-Haddad.

destruction of shops and homes. In the aftermath, Palestinians claimed that Israeli troops committed numerous war crimes during Operation Protective Edge. Palestine was in a position to pursue these claims formally when it became a member of the International Criminal Court in April 2015.

The terms of the ceasefire agreement after the 2014 Operation called for the Palestinian Authority to govern Gaza. The Hamas government had lost popular support in Gaza because it could no longer meet its payroll. External funding for the Hamas regime from Egypt had lessened after the fall of the Muslim Brotherhood regime. Iranian and Turkish funding had also fallen off. Hamas was forced to come to terms with its rival, Fatah. As a result, a Unity Government was formed, led by the Palestinian Authority and its President Mahmoud Abbas.

The cost of rebuilding Gaza was beyond the means of Hamas or the Palestinian Authority. To help rebuild after the war, The Popular International Committee to Support the Gaza Strip undertook a fundraising campaign to raise a billion $US. The Committee is a consortium of 50 organizations from 35 countries united in its goal of bringing relief from the blockade through such means as pressuring Israel to relax the blockade, pressuring Egypt into reopening its border, and delivering goods to Gaza.[15]

The Security Fence

In 2002 the Israeli government decided to build a tall fence as a security barrier in an attempt to keep violent Palestinians away from secure Israeli areas or the West Bank. Something similar had proven partially effective in Gaza. The initial proposal was to build along the Green Line, the border between the West Bank and Israel reached after the 1948 war. However, that would have walled out the thousands of Jews who live in settlements in the West Bank. Rather, the barrier's location follows Israeli security interests. As such,

The Security Fence in Israel

Photo: htp://commons.wikimedia.org/wiki/File:Israeli_West_Bank_Barrier.jpg?uselang=en-gb

---

[15]"1$ billion campaign to support Gaza Strip launched from Turkey," Middle East Monitor (Sept. 1, 2014). https://www.middleeastmonitor.com/news/europe/13852-1-billion-campaign-to-support-gaza-strip-launched-from-turkey.

it totally ignores the Palestinians needs to move from village to village, to access their fields or to visit relatives. If completed, the fence will eventually have run over one hundred kilometres, at an estimated cost of one million dollars (USD) per kilometre.

The Canadian Consortium on Human Security fieldworker cited in the insert box nicely sums up the two sides of the issue based on her interviews with Jews and with Palestinians in the West Bank village of Bil'in:

> The Israeli government describes the West Bank barrier—part concrete wall, part fence—as a temporary measure to prevent suicide bombers from crossing into Israel from the West Bank. Most Israelis in Jerusalem tell me that they feel safer with it in place, citing a decline in attacks in recent years. Palestinians, meanwhile, feel further isolated in an 'open air prison.' Moreover, the barrier does not follow the green line that separates Israel from territories occupied in 1967. The villagers of Bil'in complain that

---

Reflections of a Canadian Activist on the Palestinian Experience of the Security Barrier

Will took me to a house where villagers, along with Israeli and international peace activists, were... waiting for the demonstration to begin....

It did not take long to reach the barrier where the demonstrators began chanting slogans in Arabic, Hebrew and English at the Israel Defence Forces (IDF) stationed on the other side. We then moved on to where a hole had been made in the fence... and a few protesters proceeded to expand it. Civil disobedience, including such symbolic 'dismantling' of the barrier, is a common tactic at these demonstrations. Although the protesters were unarmed and essentially peaceful, a few youth... turned up to throw stones at the IDF.... I saw activists from the organised demonstration trying to stop them, concerned that this would only encourage the IDF to use greater force. For its part, the IDF, as usual, dispensed tear gas and rubber bullets, and a number of demonstrators were injured....

The IDF then unlocked a gate in the fence and charged through, chasing the protesters. As we fled, I saw a number of soldiers, perhaps... seize and begin beating Will.... He had... merely running from the army... a few days later, he remains in detention and will likely be deported."

Charmaine Stanley, "Notes from Israel and Palestine," *Canadian Consortium on Human Security* (2008). http://humansecurity.moonfruit.com/#/fieldnotestanley/4527999021.

---

they are losing nearly 60 percent of their land, including the olive groves that constitute their primary livelihood, to the barrier and the settlements built and expanded on the other side.[16]

The Old City's bazaar is lined with shops selling religious and other goods. Tourists are buying souvenirs in one shop, while local residents are buying food for their evening meal in the next. Strolling along the lane of shops, we pass from the Muslim Quarter into the Jewish Quarter without even noticing. When someone points this out, we retrace my steps to look for the dividing line. Nothing much changes, except in those shops selling religious objects such as crucifixes or Qurans. Then someone points to a strange grouping of tiles on the wall. It marks one of the Stations of

---

[16]*Ibid.*

> *the Cross. On Good Friday thousands of Christian pilgrims process along the route thought to have been taken by Jesus, stopping at the fourteen Stations of the Cross for special prayers. The route takes them right through this bazaar and ends at the Church of the Holy Sepulchre. Now we understand why this main shopping street is called Via Dolorosa, "Way of Sorrows."*

Religionization of the PLO and Hamas

The PLO was originally led by secular Muslims and its membership included a number of Christian Palestinians. Only later did it become more self-consciously a Muslim organization. Something similar happened with Hamas, except that Hamas did not involve Christians. This "religionization" of the Palestinian organizations has several possible explanations. One is that Palestinians became progressively more angry at the Christian world for its support of Israel. A very practical reason is that Palestinian groups needed to appeal to their Islamic neighbors for help. Yet another reason may be that the Palestinian movements have been caught up in the Islamic Resurgence that has been sweeping the world in the past few decades.

Rashid Kalida argues that Palestinian identity is not a recent phenomenon. As he sees it, there was a strong Palestinian identity before 1948 that was beaten down and almost defeated during the years when Palestine kept losing more and more territory to Israel. Now, in this era of Intifadas, Palestinian identity is strong again. He calls it the disappearance and redemption of Palestinian identity.[17]

ISSUE 3. CONTROL OF JERUSALEM'S OLD CITY AREA (TEMPLE MOUNT, OLD CITY GOVERNANCE)

Our third issue looks to a future, however distant it may be, when a Two-State Solution is under negotiation and some tentative agreement has been reached. There will need to be an agreement on how much land Israel will give up in exchange for peace. And some agreement on how much security Palestine is willing to guarantee Israel in exchange for the establishment of an independent Palestinian state. At that point this question must be addressed: Who is going to get control over Jerusalem's Old City area?

This is a major issue for both sides. The Jews want to maintain access to the Old City, partly because around 3,500 Jews live there, but mainly because Jews from Israel and elsewhere want to be able to pray at the Western Wall. The Palestinians want to maintain access for similar reasons. Around 33,000 Palestinians live there and others work in the Old City.

---

[17]Rashid K Khalidi. *Palestinian Identity: The Construction of Modern National Consciousness.* (New York: Columbia University Press, 1997), 177–209.

[18]For tourist's description of the stations, with photos, see http://landlopers.com/2011/04/03/walking-via-dolorosa-stations-cross-jerusalem-guide/

Map of the Old City, Jerusalem, showing the Four Quarters
Source: (WT-en) Jpatokal at English Wikivoyage [CC BY-SA 3.0 (http://creativecommons.org/licenses/by-sa/3.0)], via Wikimedia Commons

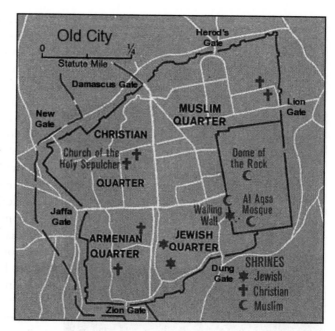

Palestinian Muslims, and all Muslims, want to be able to visit their holy sites there, especially the al-Aqsa Mosque and the Dome of the Rock. There are other parties for whom the control over the Old City is an issue. Several branches of Christianity have old and important churches or monasteries in the Old City. There are also the many sites sacred to Christians because of their connection with the life of Jesus. Then there are the interests of the Druze and other minorities. As if there were not enough complications, there is also the fact that the Old City is of major interest to so many around the world, regardless of their religious affiliation, as a historic site and tourist destination.

The Four Quarters, Residents, and Sites

Before looking at some proposed solutions to the problem of Old City governance, we need to appreciate that people of many religious communities live and shop there. There are many historic buildings and holy sites located there as well. They are organized here by religious tradition, but as one can see on the map in reality they are closely arranged and in some cases intermingle. By tradition the Old City is is divided into Four Quarters: Armenian, Christian, Jewish and Muslim. The Four Quarters are like small neighborhoods without any visible physical divisions, except for the wall surrounding the Old City. The division into the Four Quarters reflects centuries of historical realities rather than one recent, coherent plan. For example, there are two Christian holy sites located inside the Muslim Quarter, and the main shopping street runs through both the Jewish and Muslim quarters.

Christian Presence in the Old City
There are several branches of Christianity present in the Old City, and they do not necessarily get along very well. There are Roman Catholics, Greek Orthodox, and Protestant Christians here.

Church of the Holy Sepulchre. Note the ladder on the upper level, left in place after a dispute among the various Christian groups.
Photo: Michelle Morrison

The **Armenian Quarter** is the smallest of the four Quarters of the Old City, with approximately five hundred residents and students. The residents follow the Armenian branch of the Eastern Orthodox Church. They look to the Armenian Orthodox Patriarch for religious guidance. He also controls the land of the Armenian Quarter.

Christians share the **Christian Quarter**, with different groups having control or shared control of the Christian holy sites. The most important holy site here may be the Church of the Holy Sepulchre. It is said to be built in the region of Golgotha, or Calvary, where Jesus was crucified. As its name indicates, the church itself is built over the tomb of Jesus. Through the centuries as control of the Church changed, three different styles of small shrines were built over the tomb. Recent research has shown that the last two shrines were built surrounding and enclosing the previous one, like nesting dolls. The Church itself is a huge edifice built over the shrines and other sacred areas. Ownership and control of the Church has been controversial through the centuries. After many heated debates, not to mention fights, a status quo agreement was reached in the eighteenth century. It defines which areas are controlled by the various parties, including Eastern Orthodox, Armenian Apostolic, Coptic Orthodox, Syrian Orthodox, Ethiopian Orthodox and Roman Catholics. There are also areas designated as held in common.

Fights have often emerged between these stakeholders whenever there was the slightest hint that one of the other groups might be encroaching on their domain. It is difficult to make repairs because all the groups have to consent. One notorious dispute erupted over a ladder in the mid-nineteenth century. To make some repairs to a window sill, someone put a ladder up to the window. In the ensuing fracas the ladder was left under the window, where it can still be seen today. Disputes have broken out when someone left a door open or moved a chair to get out of the hot sun. When the Armenians undertook to celebrate their Palm Sunday in 2008, they pushed away and kicked a Greek priest they claimed was violating the "status quo" agreement by being in the area on their day to celebrate. When the police came to restore order, they were pummelled with palm fronds by the worshippers gathered for the celebration![19] One cannot help but wonder what Jesus would think of all this bickering in his name!

Jewish Presence in the Old City

Jews have lived in the **Jewish Quarter** of the Old City for centuries. During the 1948 War they had to flee, as Jordan (then called Transjordan) controlled the Old City. Since the 1967 war, Israel controls the Old City and life is bustling in the Jewish Quarter. There has been a drive to expand the Jewish Quarter, but of course that is quite contentious. By far the most holy site in the Jewish Quarter, or more precisely near the Jewish Quarter, is the Western Wall of the Temple Mount area. This wall was not part of the temple itself, but is part of the retaining wall build by King Herod to support the platform on which the temple stood. Since the destruction of the second Jewish Temple in A.D. 70,

Temple Mount or Haram Area

Photo: Derek Barker

---

[19]Sarah El Deeb, "Christians clash at Jesus' tomb on Orthodox Palm Sunday," *AP News* (April 20, 2008). http://apnews.excite.com/article/20080420/D905PU380.html

this is the closest Jews can get to praying at the temple itself. It has become a sacred site for Jews.

Muslim Presence in the Old City

The **Muslim Quarter** has the largest population, around 25,000, of the four quarters. Besides residences mostly occupied by Muslims, it has both mosques and some Jewish schools. Muslims access the Temple Mount through the Muslim Quarter.

The Temple Mount or al-Haram ash-Sharif

Jews revere the Temple Mount as the site of the first temple built by Solomon in the 900s B.C., later destroyed by the Babylonians. The second Temple, built in the 500s B.C., was later destroyed by the Romans. The theological belief is that God made his presence dwell on this site.

Muslims revere the same area, called al-Haram al-Qudsi Ash-Sharif, because it was here that the angel brought Muhammad during his night vision. The Dome of the Rock is thought to cover the very rocky outcrop from which Muhammad ascended on his white horse into heaven to talk with God and the earlier prophets. The Al-Aqsa Mosque, "Farthest Mosque," provides a large mosque for prayers on the Temple Mount.

Three Possible Models for Old City Governance

Given all the religious stakeholders in the Old City, what means of governance would work if and when Israel and Palestine come to peace terms? If Israel governs the Old City, how could the Muslims be assured of continued access? After all, the Israelis have occasionally limited Muslim access to the Temple Mount. Or, if Palestine were given control over the Old City, how could Jews or Christians be assured of continued access? Given the history of religious bickering in the Old City, what possible solution would pacify everyone?

There are also immigration and security issues. Who would have the authority to check passports or visas? Who would administer the police force? Would Jews ever accept a Palestinian police force or Palestinians ever accept an Israeli police force?

Several peace organizations have considered the long term governance issues for the Old City. Their various solutions tend to fall under one of three models: **Territorial Sovereignty**, **Special Regime** and **Hybrid**. All three models assume that East Jerusalem will be a part of Palestine and that West Jerusalem will be a part of Israel under some form of a Two-State Solution.

The Territorial Sovereignty model divides the Old City into an area of Israeli sovereignty and another area of Palestinian sovereignty. The advantage of this approach is that it would be similar, one assumes, to the way the rest of Jerusalem and surrounding territory would be divided between the two states. The disadvantage is that the shops, residences, and religious buildings of the Old City are so closely spaced and entangled that the plan seems unworkable.

The solution proposed by the Jerusalem Old City Initiative[20] is that a "Special Regime" be established to govern the Old City. There would be Palestinian and Israeli members involved in the administration of the Old City, but an internationally appointed agent who would serve as the main administrator over all aspects of the Old City, including the police. Access to the Old City and its holy sites, shopping areas, and residences would be guaranteed for all. There would be a special, multinational police force in charge of Old City security. One could enter the City with any nationality's passport or identity papers, but a security check of those exiting the Old City would make sure that people were exiting only into those areas in which they were entitled to enter. In other words, Israelis would exit through gates leading back into Israel. Palestinians would exit from gates leading back into Palestine. The advantage of the Special Regime model is that it keeps all parts of the Old City under multilateral control. That is, neither the Palestinians nor the Israelis would lose control or have to officially give up their claim to sovereignty over the Old City. This would defer rather than settle the question of which side has sovereignty over the Old City. A possible disadvantage is that this model involves a shared control whereas the distinct lines of control would be established elsewhere.

The third model calls for a hybrid solution to the problem. Under this model the two sides would have territorial sovereignty, but not in a way that establishes precise boundaries within the Old City. There would be some international involvement in governing the Old City, but not to the extent envisioned in the Special Regime model. The intent of this model is to draw upon the best parts of the other two models. The disadvantage of this model is that it may be unrealistic to expect that the two sides can cooperate enough to make the model work. [21]

Given the disputes that have erupted over such matters as rebuilding a stairway, it would seem overly optimistic to expect that the Territorial Sovereignty Model or Hybrid model could bring lasting peace to the Old City. The Special Regime model seems more realistic, at least for the first few years under a Two-State peace arrangement.

OVERVIEW AND THEORETICAL DISCUSSION

Our first issue discussed the way two very different groupings of right-wing Jewish parties have been quite active in shaping Israeli politics. The Haredic grouping includes the various Ultra-Orthodox organizations. They tend not to be Zionist, and some are anti-Zionist. Yet members of these groups have participated in the settlement movement which represents the current thrust of Zionism. Their political demands have to do mainly with the special privileges they enjoy as Jews who often choose a lifestyle of Talmudic study.

---

[20]The Jerusalem Old City Initiative is housed at the University of Windsor in Ontario, Canada. See web2. uwindsor.ca/wsgcms/Projects/JerusalemInitiative/indexTpl.php.

[21]For an excellent discussion of the three models see "Transcript for 'Is Peace Possible?' Chapter 4: Jerusalem", The Atlantic, Nov. 14, 2011. http://www.theatlantic.com/personal/archive/2011/11/transcript-for-is-peace-possible-chapter-4-jerusalem/248437/

Palestinian women in Gaza protesting the detention of their sons in Israeli prisons.
Photo: Muaamar al-Haddad.

The other right-wing group is the Religious Nationalists. They tend to be active Zionists and also active in the settlement movement. Their political influence in recent years has focused on advocacy for policies supportive of the settlements.

Our second issue dealt with the Palestinian parties, Fatah and Hamas. We saw that Hamas was formed during the First Intifada by Palestinians from Gaza who were totally frustrated with their situation. They felt their only solution to be a military one, with the goal of eliminating Israel. In effect, they hoped to turn the clock back before 1948. In contrast to Hamas, the PLO and Fatah have shown some willingness to live with Israel in a Two-State Solution.

We also saw that both the PLO and Hamas have moved from being more secular organizations to being ones with strong Islamic identities.

Our third issue dreamed of a day when peace might come to this troubled area of the world. As an important part of any acceptable and practical peace proposal, there must be some plan for the governance of Jerusalem's Old City. One such plan, authored by the Jerusalem Old City Initiative, calls for governance of the Old City by an internationally chosen Special Regime, with input from both the Israelis and the Palestinians, but beyond the direct control of either.

Theoretical Discussion

Zionists, Anti-Zionists, and Settlements

Jews moved to Israel for many reasons. Some were running for their lives from persecution in Europe. Some were looking to escape poverty. Still others were genuine Zionists who felt that it was God's will for them to return to their Promised Land. Many Haredic Jews were anti-Zionists because they thought that only the God's Messiah has the right to call Jews back to Israel, when he comes. We also suggested that even though the main Zionist immigration is long finished, Zionism continues in the form of the settlements that expand Jewish presence into former Palestinian areas of the West Bank. We saw that some Religious Nationalists have made the settlements their main cause.

We have seen that because of the traditional Jewish conception that the Messiah would come before the return of Jews to Israel, some Haredic Jews renounce Zionism and even maintain websites against Zionist concepts. However they live in modern Israel. For most Muslims this distinction is unimportant. The way many Muslims of the Middle East see it is that all Jews who have moved into the former Palestine area and those Jews around the world who support the modern state of Israel are Zionists. Because some of the groups of anti-Zionist Jews have participated in the settlement movement in the West Bank, further encroaching upon areas traditionally held by Palestinians, there is some validity to the Muslim tendency to lump all Jews together under the Zionist label. We might say that some Jews of modern Israel are theologically anti-Zionist but have nonetheless contributed to the Zionist dream of establishing a Jewish State in the Holy Land.

Marc Ellis, a contemporary Jewish theologian, argues passionately that God's covenant with the people of Israel has been called into question by the injustices against the Palestinians brought about by the creation and expansion of the modern state of Israel.[22] It is a very brave act for a Jewish writer to take this stance, but it is not so unusual for more neutral observers to be critical of the way Israeli Jews have treated the Palestinians. Before the end of political dominance by whites in South Africa, comparisons were made between the Palestinian camps of Gaza and the apartheid townships of South Africa.[23] Ellis suggests that the cycle of displacement and death in Palestine can only end when Jews realize that they have to share the land. The problem is that each side clings to a narrative that sees the land as exclusively theirs.[24]

Fundamentalism Theory

What would our theorists have to say about the religious actors in modern Israel? Let's start with the easiest one. Huntington's thesis about the new world order lining up along civilizational lines seems accurate here. Jews and Palestinians are contesting land and control in the former Palestine, with Western civilization mostly backing the Jewish side and the Islamic civilization backing the Palestinians. It does not seem to be an overstatement

---

[22]Marc H. Ellis, *O, Jerusalem! The Contested Future of the Jewish Covenant* (Minneapolis: Fortress Press, 1999).

[23]For a discussion from a legal standpoint, see www.abudis.net/applicability-of-apartheid-israel.htm

[24]*Ibid.*, 86.

to call the resulting struggle, with its series of ongoing wars, intifadas and seemingly endless peace conferences a "clash of civilizations." However, Western support for Israel is weakening, as evidenced by 2014 EU Parliament vote in favor of backing the concept of a Palestinian state in principle.

How about Ali's "clash of fundamentalisms" thesis? Does the situation in Israel and Palestine reflect American imperialism? Many Arabs would think it does.

Does Phares's "war of ideas" fit our data? Do we see jihadis against democracy advocates here, or is this more a fight for territory than a ideological conflict? Phares argues "that the Arab-Israeli conflict was transformed by regimes and organizations in a 'black hole' that overshadowed consideration of all other democratic transformations and human rights struggles in the region. These dominant establishments deliberately used the Arab-Israeli conflict as cover, behind which they suppressed civil rights and minorities' autonomies and, in the case of the Islamists, advanced the much larger goal of a restored caliphate."[25]

Herberg's pendulum thesis applies. There has been a swing toward a more religious identity by both the Jewish parties and the Palestinian PLO and Hamas organizations. There has been a resurgence in Islam as an important component in Palestinian identity.

Lawrence gives his view of several Jewish groups in his chapter "Fundamentalists in Defense of the Jewish Collectivity." Lawrence sees the Gush Emunim as a textbook example of religious fundamentalism. They take their allegiance to God and Torah as a higher authority than any allegiance to the state. They reject the values of modernity and downplay the role of women.[26] For similar reasons, Shahak and Mezvinsky also describe Gush Emunim as an example of religious fundamentalism. Its messianic ideology and pronouncements "...show the aim of Gush Emunim... is not limited to the strategic value of utilizing settlements to keep control of the Occupied Territories. The more important aim of Gush Emunim leaders is to create in their homogeneous settlements models of a new society. They hope this new society will spread until it finally absorbs the secular, traditional and Haredi Jewish population.... This identity will, they believe, be the religious, ethnocentric, anti-liberal and anti-universalist society ordered by God.... Gush Emunim leaders can tolerate democracy only so long as it helps to create the divine Jewish kingdom."[27]

Lawrence does not label Rabbi Kahane as a fundamentalist. Rather, Lawrence sees him as an activist and ideologue with an eccentric understanding of Jewish tradition and an extreme anti-Arab rhetoric.

It should be noted that there is a potential conflict between Palestinian nationalism and the rising tendency among Muslims to stress the oneness of the ummah, the Islamic community. Nationalism can be seen by some Muslims as a bad thing that goes against Quranic teachings.[28]

---

[25]Walid Phares, *The war of Ideas: Jihadism against Democracy*. (New York: Palgrave Macmillan. 2008), 126.

[26]Bruce Lawrence, *Defenders of God*.

[27]Israel Shahak and Norton Mezvinsky, *Jewish Fundamentalism in Israel*. (London: Ann Arbor: Pluto Press, New Edition), 83.

[28]Rashid K Khalidi, *Palestinian Identity: The Construction of Modern National Consciousness* (New York: Columbia University Press, 1997), 148.

Are Religion-based Land Claims to be Honored?

When it comes to the interface of religion and politics in Israel/Palestine, the elephant in the room is the Israeli claim to the land based upon a religious belief. Historically, land ownership was based on land settlement—who lived there—and the results of wars, treaties, or other land transfers negotiated between kings or sovereign powers. It was not common to lay claim to a tract of land on the basis that God had given it to a certain people. Zionism evolved from a movement calling upon Jews to move back to Zion, to gain some protection from periodic persecution in Christian Europe. Yet Zionism, led by such groups as Gush Emunim, took up the goal of occupying most or all of Palestine. Resentment of this has touched off wars and continuing anger among Muslims, and sympathy for the Palestinian plight seems to be growing, even among Christian Zionists in the United States, as we will discuss in a later chapter.

> *Time to pack up the souvenirs we bought in the shops along Via Dolorosa in the Old City. We take taxis to Ben Gurion Airport to catch our flight to Turkey. On the way to the airport, we pass miles of the security fence, a "Berlin Wall" of this era. Near the airport we have to pass through a security checkpoint where military personnel armed with machine guns look under our taxis for hidden explosives!*

STUDY QUESTIONS

1. How do the Heredic Jews compare with Salafi Muslims?
2. What were the motivations for creating the modern state of Israel, and did it fulfill those goals?
3. What are the bases for the conflicting claims over the lands of Israel/Palestine?
4. In what ways do religion and nationalism sometimes reinforce each other?
5. What groups lay claim to parts of the Jerusalem's Old City and how could a peaceful co-existence be managed?

FURTHER READING

Arian, Asher. *Politics in Israel: The Second Replublic.* Washington, D.C.: CQ Press, 2005. Good parties, elections, policies and other political topics.

Bickerton, Ian J and Klausner, Carla L. *A History of the Arba-Israeli Conflict.* Fifth edition. Upper Saddle River, New Jersey, Person Prentice Hall, 2007. A good source.

Ellis, Marc H. *O, Jerusalem! The Contested Future of the Jewish Covenant.* Minneapolis: Fortress Press, 1999. A Jewish theologian's call for a fair and peaceful sharing of the land between Jews and Palestinians.

Farsoun, Samih K. and Aruri, Naseer H. *Palestine and the Palestinians: A Social and Political History.* 2nd Ed. Boulder, Westview Press, 2006. Just what the title suggests.

Jamal, Amal. *The Palestinian National Movement: Politics of Contention, 1967–2005.* Bloomington: Indiana University Press, 2005. A good overview of almost a thirty year period.

Khalidi, Rashad. *Palestinian Identity: The Construction of Modern National Consciousness.* New York: Columbia University Press, 1997. Argues for the longstanding nature of Palestinian identity.

Levitt, Matthew. *Hamas: Politics, Charity, and Terrorism in the Service of Jihad.* New Haven, Yale University Press, 2006. A well-documented critical history of Hamas.

Lybarger, Loren D. *Identity and Religion in Palestine: The Struggle between Islamism and Secularism in the Occupied Territories.* Princeton and Oxford: Princeton University Press, 2007. Includes good case studies from several camps.

Murray, Michelle. "Jewish Traditions." In *A Concise Introduction to World Religions,* 3rd edition, pp. 92–106, edited by Willard G. Oxtoby, Roy C. Amore, Amir and Hussain. Toronto: Oxford University Press, 2015. A good, chapter length introduction to Judaism.

Najem, Tom. *Lebanon: The Politics of a Penetrated Society.* London: Routledge, 2012. A good recent account of the complexities of Lebanese politics.

Pappe, Ilan. *A History of Modern Palestine.* 2nd Ed. Cambridge: Cambridge University Press, 2006. A comprehensive history.

Qumsiyeh, Mazin B. *Sharing the Land of Canaan: Human Rights and the Israeli-Palestinian Struggle.* London: Pluto Press, 2004. Argues against a Two-State Solution, saying that a One-State Solution is the best way to protect the human rights of all.

Reinhart, Tanya. 2006. *The Road Map to Nowhere: Israel/Palestine since 2003.* London and New York: Verso. A critique of Israeli policies toward the Palestinians, with details about prisons, camps, motives and American influences.

Rougier, Bernard and Pascale Ghazaleh. 2007. *Everyday Jihad: The Rise of Militant Islam among Palestinians in Lebanon.* Boston: Harvard University Press.

Roy, Sara. *Hamas and Civil Society in Gaza: Engaging the Islamist Social Sector.* Princeton: Princeton University Press, 2013. A more recent treatment of Hamas in Gaza.

Shahak, Israel and Mezvinsky, Norton. *Jewish Fundamentalism in Israel.* New Edition. London and Ann Arbor: Pluto Press, 2004. A readable but somewhat dated treatment.

WEBSITES

web2.uwindsor.ca/wsgcms/Projects/JerusalemInitiative/indexTpl.php   Site of The Jerusalem Old City Initiative, hosted by the University of Windsor.

www.alqassam.ps/english/index.php?action   Official site of the Ezzedeen Al-Qassam Brigades.

www.chabad.org   Information on the beliefs and activities of Judaism from the point of view of the Chabad-Lubavitch tradition of Ultra-Orthodox Jews.

www.jewfac.org   Called "Judaism 101," this site offers comprehensive information on Judaism from an Orthodox perspective, but written by a Conservative Jew in the United States. Not much on politics here, however.

www.jewsagainstzionism.com/zionism/history.cfm   A brief history of Zionism from the Jewish non-Zionist viewpoint.

www.jerusalemites.org   A pro-Palestinian site run from Jordon.

www.mideastweb.org/palestianparties.htm   Lots of information, including a guide to the political parties of Palestine.

www.palestinefacts.org   A site with lots of information, seemingly from a pro-Jewish point of view.

www.palestinehistory.com   Gives a timeline of events from a Palestinian perspective.

www.palestine-info-co-uk/en/default.aspx   Site of the Palestinian Information Center (PIC), an independent Palestinian organization.

http://www.passia.org/palestine_facts/MAPS/images/jer_maps/old_city.html   A helpful map of the Old City.

KEY PEOPLE

Mahmoud Abbas   Known as **abu Masen**, he leads the PLO.

Yasser Arafat   Longstanding Chairman of the PLO until his death in 2004.

Baha'u'llah   Monotheistic prophet who founded the Baha'i religion.

Alfred Dreyfus   A French, Jewish soldier whose trial on false spying charges inspired the Zionist movement.

Rabbi Meir Kahane   A militant leader who founded the Jewish Defense League and the Kach party.

Salah al-Din, or **Saladin**   The Muslim leader who restored Islamic control to the Palestine area, ending the Crusades.

Baal Shem Tov, or **The Besht**   The title of an 18th century Jew who was very influential in shaping Hasidic Judaism.

GLOSSARY

Al-Aqsa Mosque   A large mosque on the Temple Mount , or Haram al-Sharif, in Jerusalem's Old City.

Ashkenazim   Jews tracing ancestry to Northern and Eastern Europe.

Baha'i   A monotheistic religion founded by Bahu'u'llah of Persia.

Balfour Declaration   Lord Balfour's statement in 1917 allowing more Jewish immigration to Israel.

Consociational Democracy   A power sharing system in which a fixed proportion of legislative seats and perhaps leadership offices are reserved for various ethnic or religious groups.

Crusades   A series of wars fought between Christians and Muslims for control of Palestine.

Dome of the Rock   A structure built of the Temple Mount rock from which Muhammad rose to heaven on his Night Journey.

Druze   A religious sect that combines Shi'i and ancient beliefs.

Fatah   A militant movement with the goal of restoring Palestinian control of Palestine.

ghetto   Originally, a small area of Venice in which Jews had to live in crowded conditions, by extension a crowded area in a city.

Gush Emunin   A former Israeli political organization that advocated for expanding Jewish settlements.

Halakha   A term for traditional Jewish law.

Hamas   The 'Islamic Resistance Movement', a militant Palestinian party

Haredim   Jews, sometimes called Ultra-Orthodox, who adhere strictly to the Torah.

Hasidim   A name for one form of the Haredim.

Holocaust   The mass killing of Jews under Nazi control during WW II.

Hybrid Model   A plan for administration of the Old City, drawing parts from the Sovereignty and Special Regime models.

Intifada   An "Uprising" of Palestinians against Jewish control.

Kach   Rabbi Kahane's far right Israeli party, now banned.

Knesset   The Israeli Parliament.

Maronite, Maronite Church   A Roman Catholic affiliated church tracing back to Syrian Saint Maron , now found mainly in Lebanon.

National Religious Party (NRP)   An Israeli party supported by the Religious Right.

One-State Policy   The concept that there should only be one state, whether Israeli or Palestinian, in the Israel/Palestine region.

PLO   The Palestinian Liberation Organization founded to liberate Palestine from Jewish occupation.

Right of Return   The concept that refugee Palestinians should be able to move back to their home.

Sephardim   Jews tracing ancestry to the Mediterranean region.

Shas   An Israeli party supported by many Ultra-Orthodox Jews

Sovereignty Model   A plan for dividing the Old City in Palestinian and Israeli control zones.

Special Regime Model   A plan for Old City governance by multilateral authority not controlled by any one faction.

Two-State Solution   A peace proposal of the type that calls for independent Israel and Palestine states.

Ultra-Orthodox Jews   Refers to various Heredi Jews who live a pious life and reject secularism.

West Bank   An area West and North of Jerusalem, between Israel and Jordan.

Yeshiva   A Jewish religious school.

Yiddish   A dialect of German traditionally spoken by many European Jews.

Zionism   The movement to encourage Jews to return to Zion, the Holy Land.

Chapter Seven

Europe

Islamic Voices in "Christian" Europe:
Turkey, France, the Netherlands

In this chapter you will learn about:

- the religious and political background of Turkey and selected European Union countries
- the religious barriers to Turkey's EU admission
- anti-immigration parties in France and elsewhere in EU
- the conflict between France's Laïcité tradition and religious freedom
- the conflict between freedom of expression and religious traditions in The Netherlands

Some readers may appreciate some background on religion and politics in Europe.

RELIGIOUS BACKGROUND: CATHOLICS, ORTHODOX, PROTESTANTS, MUSLIMS, AND JEWS IN EUROPE

Roman Catholicism came into Europe with the earliest spread of Christianity outside Palestine. After the death of Jesus, several of his apostles and the new convert Paul met in Jerusalem to determine the fate of the Jesus movement. There seems to have been a consensus that the movement should be spread abroad. However there was a sharp disagreement as to whether or not a non-Jewish convert first had to conform to Jewish law before becoming a Christian. This decision had very practical implications. For men,

253

it determined whether or not they had to undergo a painful circumcision operation. For both men and women, it determined whether or not they would have to conform to Jewish dietary restrictions. That is, to keep kosher. Normally, converts to Judaism, not those born into Judaism, have to undergo a baptism ritual. The Christians had already decided that all Christians, whether formerly Jewish or not, would have to be baptised. At the Jerusalem Conference Paul argued strongly that Christianity should not require conformity to Jewish law, meaning that getting circumcised or keeping kosher were not required. This would make it easier to bring gentiles into the movement.

James, the brother of Jesus,[1] led the argument for the other side, the "Judaizers." He held that converts must adhere to Jewish law as well as the tenets of the new faith. Paul's side won the argument. The conference also decided which disciples would head out to certain regions to spread the new gospel. Peter and Paul headed west. Paul's goal was to reach all the way to Gaul, modern France, to the Western reaches of the Roman Empire. He never made it that far. He did have success in Anatolia, now Turkey, and elsewhere around the Mediterranean. Peter made it to Rome, where he later came to be regarded as the First Pope, "Father," of Rome.

The theology of the Roman Catholic Church claimed that Peter was more important than the other disciples. Jesus had said Peter was the rock (Peter means rock) on which the church would be built. Peter was also more important, Catholics claimed, because Jesus had given him the keys to the kingdom. On the floor at the entrance to St. Peter's Basilica in Rome, there is a depiction of a large set of keys, the symbol of papal authority over who goes to heaven or hell.

A political realist might point to other reasons why the Church of Rome emerged as the church with supreme authority among Western Christians. For the first three hundred years the Christian church in Rome was alternately ignored or persecuted, depending on the Emperor of the period and whether or not that emperor needed a scapegoat for the Empire's problems.

In the early 300s Emperor Constantine switched from persecuting the Church to favoring it. His mother Helena was a very devout Christian, which must have had something to do with the change. After Constantine's conversion, a dispute arose among the Christian leaders in Egypt and they appealed to the Bishop of Rome to settle the dispute. The Bishop of Rome, with the backing of the new convert, Emperor Constantine, called a worldwide council in Nicaea to decide the matter. As presiding officer of the Council of Nicaea, with Constantine sitting near him, the supreme authority of the Roman Bishop over all other bishops was established. At least in the minds of the churches of the west.

---

[1]Note that Roman Catholics think of James as a relative rather than brother of Jesus. Otherwise, it would conflict with their doctrine that Mary was not only a virgin at the time of conceiving Jesus, but that she remained "ever virgin" throughout her life. Protestants, taking the Bible's own words in their more literal sense, believe that Jesus had sisters and a brother.

The Eastern Orthodox Church in Europe

The word *catholic* means "worldwide," and the name reflects the Roman Catholic doctrine that it is the sole true Christian Church. This claim has never been accepted by the **Orthodox Christian Church**. The governance of the Christian churches was organized along the lines of the two divisions of the Roman Empire. So, there was a tendency for the Eastern churches, those in the Eastern division of the Roman Empire, to distinguish themselves from the Western Church. They kept the use of Greek, the language of early Christianity and the New Testament. They read the early writers who wrote in Greek, the "Greek Fathers," whereas the Western churches had adopted Latin and read the "Latin Fathers." When their **Patriarchs**, the highest ranking officers, met, the Patriarch of Constantinople held the "supremacy of honor," as "first among equals." That meant he chaired the meeting, but unlike the Patriarch of Rome (the Pope), he was not considered supreme. In this way, the Patriarchs of the Eastern and Western halves of the Roman Empire were the top leaders, but only in the West was the leader given supreme and absolute authority.

At least in theory, the Eastern Orthodox and Roman Catholic Churches remained part of the same universal Church until the eleventh century, when they officially separated in what is termed the **Great Schism**. There have been efforts in the modern period to re-unite the two churches, but they cannot get around the issue of the supreme authority of the Pope. The Orthodox Church prefers to go its own way rather than accept that the Pope is their absolute boss.

The Orthodox Church is split into branches according to language and region. Besides the Armenian and Greek Orthodox Churches we discussed in regard to Jerusalem's Old City, there are Greek, Syrian, Russian, Serbian, Ukrainian, and other branches. Greece, Russia, and Eastern European countries tend to have a majority Orthodox population. Southern, Western, and Northern Europe were predominantly Roman Catholic until the **Protestant Reformation**.

The Protestant Churches

In the early 1500s some Roman Catholic priests became so outspoken in their protests against perceived abuses with their Church that they were condemned to death by the Church. One of them, Martin Luther, had the backing of his regional political leader, Frederick the Wise, the Elector of Saxony in Eastern Germany, one of seven who voted for a new Holy Roman Emperor. With this strong political support he was saved from being executed as ordered by the pope. Luther became a local hero who continued to preach and teach at Wittenberg University. He and other protesting priests and their followers became the **Protestants**. Several different Protestant Churches were started. First there was the Lutheran Church, followed by the Reformed Church led by John Calvin. Many others sprang up along the lines of countries or doctrines. The Church of England took a middle course. It bounced back and forth between being Protestant, first under Henry VIII, and then being Catholic. Finally it settled on being very similar to Catholicism in ritual and organization, but with some influence from Protestant doctrines and without recognizing the supremacy of the pope. The pope at the time sent the armies of Spain to kill Queen Elizabeth and restore Catholic rule, but the **Spanish Armada** did not succeed in conquering Britain.

As a result of the Protestant Reformation, the northern countries of Europe became predominantly Protestant, while the southern countries (Italy, Spain, France, Portugal and others) remained predominantly Catholic.

Muslims

Berber, or North African, Muslims conquered southern parts of the Iberian Peninsula starting in 711. They replaced the former rulers of the region, the Visigoths, a Germanic people. They formed a government and ruled over a region they called al-Andalus, which stretched from southern Spain up to and including parts of southern France. The new rulers were called Moors, meaning people from Morocco. They were part of the larger Islamic Empire ruled by the Umayyad Caliphs. At a decisive battle in 732, the Muslims were defeated in France, but remained in Spain and Portugal. Under Muslim control, the city of Cordoba became very prosperous, thanks to the introduction of irrigation and other technologies known to the Muslims.

Christian, Jewish, and Muslim leaders learned a lot from each other in this period. Mystical techniques, philosophy, alchemy, medicine, and other wisdoms of the time were mutually discussed and shared.

When Christians regained power in Iberia, the era ended badly for the Muslims. Muslims were expelled, along with Jews, by King Ferdinand and Queen Isabella in 1492, the same year that the ships they sponsored under Columbus' command reached the "New World."

Muslim armies also moved north of Arabia into Turkey and Eastern Europe. Muslim armies failed to take Constantinople in the 600s and early 700s, but the spread of Islam gradually weakened Orthodox Christianity in Turkey. Muslims eventually took Constantinople in 1453, renaming it Istanbul. Muslims had already taken control of other parts of Turkey. With Turkey as its base, the Ottoman Empire extended the territory ruled by the previous regime, the Seljuks, into Eastern and Central Europe, converting many local populations. Ottoman expansion halted when they lost the Great Turkish War in 1699 to a coalition of countries called the Holy League. As a result, the Ottoman Empire lost most of its holdings in Central Europe. Russia took control of many of those areas, including their Muslim populations. This explains the current tension between Russia and the Muslim population along its southern regions.

Jews

For most of the past five hundred years the religious population of Europe has been relatively stable, with Protestants, Catholics, Orthodox, and Muslims maintaining their majority status in various regions, even as political control shifted. The Jews, however, have been more mobile, often not by choice. Having been forced to leave Jerusalem in A.D. 70, a large percentage of those who moved to Europe did so by sailing on the Mediterranean to Iberia. There they were relatively free to practice their religion and various means of livelihood until their expulsion, along with Muslims, in 1492. Some were given a choice of converting to Christianity, moving, or being killed. All three choices were taken. But many who converted were killed later on the suspicion that their conversion was not sincere.

Many of the Jews expelled from Spain found their way to Poland, Germany, Russia, and Ukraine, where they adopted Yiddish or whatever it took to blend in with the Jewish communities already there. The next forced migration happened under the Third Reich. As Germany conquered Poland and other parts of East Europe, Hitler was able to apply his "Final Solution" to those regions as well. He often did so first by forcing the Jews into ghettos, which became overcrowded prisons, and from there they were forced into rail cars and transported to the death camps. A few Jews managed to escape, but over five million were killed in the death camps.

The other major Jewish migration evolved around the Zionist movement discussed in the previous chapter. From the late 1800s until the present, thousands of Jews have returned to Zion or Israel. Some did so because they were committed Zionists. Others because they felt threatened if they stayed in Europe. Some because they just dreamed of a better way of life.

POLITICAL BACKGROUND: TURKEY, EUROPEAN UNION

Turkey: Caught Between the European Union and the Islamic World

The modern state of Turkey dates from after the first World War, as a smaller replacement for the Ottoman Empire. After brief reviews of Turkey's modern history and of the gradual formation of the European Union, we will consider the role that religious and civilizational differences play behind the scenes as Turkey continues to seek admission to the EU.

STOPOVER IN TURKEY

> How exciting it is to arrive in Istanbul. The city built by Emperor Constantine was the capital of the western division of the Roman Empire. It became the capital of the Byzantine Empire, and was attack by Christians during Fourth Crusade.
>
> We arrive at Hagia Sophia, the Christian Church of "Holy Wisdom." It was the biggest and grandest church in the world when Emperor Justinian had it built in the sixth century. Legend has it that upon entering the grand church he proclaimed that

he had outdone Solomon. When the Muslim Mehmet the Conqueror took the city in 1453, he put dirt on his head in humility before entering the magnificent church. He turned it into a mosque and it remained a mosque until Kemal Ataturk made it a museum in 1935. Gazing at the huge dome, it is remarkable that such a structure could have been built without the use of high-strength modern materials.

Our next stop is the Blue Mosque, built by Sultan Ahmet I in the 1600s. He set out to build something as impressive as Justinian's church. The result is a huge and beautiful mosque, with space for thousands at prayer. We look for the piece of the black stone from the Ka'bah of Mecca that is set in the mihrab, the niche for orienting the prayers, but we are not allowed to get close enough to see it.

*Our next stop is the nearby Topkapi Palace, the home of **Ottoman** sultans for four centuries, before the last sultans built more western-style palaces. As we enter the first courtyard, it is rather surprising to see that a Christian church was part of this Ottoman palace. It is nice to be reminded of an era when Christianity and Islam were not antagonists.*

We buy a separate ticket to enter the Harem. Given our interest in the role of women in Islam, this should prove interesting. We learn that the Harem was actually like a small village. Young girls were brought here as slaves. Because Islam forbade holding other Muslims (or Christians and Jews) as slaves, the girls often came from non-Muslim areas of southern Russia and were taught Turkish and Islam. They were taught to read, write, sing, and recite poetry; as well as other matters that would please a male. It would be interesting to compare life in the Harem with the life of a geisha in traditional Japan. The sultans would come to be entertained by the girls after they had come of age. The sultan's mother was the head of the Harem, and besides the women, only eunuchs were allowed here. When the women grew older, they were often given their freedom and married to noblemen in the Empire. Many sultans did not have wives, only these concubines.

We are on the European side of Istanbul. We get onto the tram, ride it southeast through a tunnel under the Bosporus Strait and a few minutes later emerge on the Asian side of the same city. One city; two continents. And in many ways, one nation; two cultures.

Ancient Anatolia was the meeting and migration point between East and West. Modern Turkey is little different. In Huntington's terms, it is where the Western and the Islamic civilizations meet. Turkey is caught between the West and the Islamic world. Supporting its ties to the West are its membership in NATO and the Council of Europe, its application for membership in the European Union (EU), and its military which enforces secularism in government and tends to be pro-West. On the other hand, its largely Muslim population and their growing Islamic fervor support its ties to the Arab and Islamic world.

The Turkish language and culture arrived from farther East, from the region of what used to be called Turkistan but is now part of China. The Uyghurs of China are a Turkish people, and their area is the likely home and starting point of the Turks who migrated to Anatolia.

Young Turk Revolt and World War II

In 1908, two hundred disgruntled military personnel defected from the Ottoman army in protest of the Sultan's policies. This touched off a larger protest known as the Young Turk Revolt. The result was that a new political elite gained some power in the Empire.

A 1913 coup transferred real political power from the Sultan to a triumvirate of three high ranking officials known by the title Pasha. It was these officials, and not the Sultan, who moved toward an alliance with Germany.

The Ottoman Empire signed the Ottoman-German Alliance in 1914, which subsequently brought them into the war on the losing side. Some influential persons among the Ottoman elite had favored entering into an agreement with France rather than Germany, but this idea was overruled because France was allied with the Ottoman Empire's longstanding rival and enemy, the Russian Empire. Recall that it had been the Russian Empire that had taken over former Ottoman holdings in central Europe in 1699. Having sided with Germany, the Ottomans found themselves on the wrong side. The British took Baghdad in 1917 and, on the Palestine front, took Jerusalem in the same year. The Ottoman Empire had lost its Eastern province, Iraq, and much of its Western province, Palestine.

To make matters worse for the Ottomans, the Grand Sharif Hussein, head of the Arab nationalists, had entered into an agreement with the British. He had become disenchanted with the Ottoman rule and dreamed of uniting almost all of the Arab areas. There had long been a desire to restore Arab control over Arab lands. The British assigned a young captain named T. E. Lawrence to advise the Arabs on how best to organize resistance against the Ottomans. He soon learned that he first had to get the various Arab tribes to unite in the cause. His assurances that the British would support a united Arab state proved effective. He soon replaced his British uniform with Arab dress, learned to ride a camel well and to survive in the desert. He and his Arab band of raiders crossed a large desert area to make a surprise attack on an Ottoman-held city. They also kept blowing up the rail tracks the Ottomans needed as supply routes. His growing loyalty to the Arabs led to growing mistrust by the British of "Lawrence of Arabia," as he came to be called. The movie about him starring Peter O'Toole became a Hollywood blockbuster when released in 1962.

After the war ended, the British showed little interest in promoting a united Arab state, and Lawrence and his Arab fighters felt betrayed. The victorious allies met at the Palace of Versailles and divided up the conquered territory as the spoils of war. Historian Margaret MacMillan's book *Paris 1919: Six Months that Changed the World* documents the diplomacy that shaped the modern map of the Middle East.[2]

---

[2]Margaret MacMillan, *Paris 1919: Six Months that Changed the World.*

Kemal Ataturk

> We are in the Ataturk Museum in Istanbul. We stroll down a corridor lined with pictures from the Ataturk era. We spot a picture from Ataturk's era of female university students. It shows them dressed up in the latest European fashion, 1930s style. They have on fancy dresses cut just below the knees, and even fancier hats. To us it looks like an old fashioned Easter parade picture. The picture reveals what was good and bad about Ataturk's reforms. It shows that he realized that Turkey needed to imitate the West to pull itself out of poverty and backwardness. It also shows that he tried to move Turkey too far and too fast toward Western values. The dress of the girls would have been shocking and offensive to traditional Muslims.

The Turkish War of Independence (1919–23) was fought over whether or not Turkey would be totally sliced up and redistributed to the victorious allies, like the rest of the former Ottoman Empire. Mustafa Kemal emerged as the leader and forced the terms of the Treaty of Sevres to be replaced with those of the Treaty of Lausanne (1923). Kemal had negotiated a deal in which he would be allowed to establish an independent Turkey without undue interference, but with the promise that he would not seek to expand its borders beyond Turkey into places formerly held by the Ottoman Empire.

Kemal became leader of the new state of Turkey and came to be revered as the Ataturk, the "Father of the Turks." Kemal Ataturk established a secular state and turned to the West for models and help in developing his country. He built railways and other modern infrastructure. He took education out of the control of Islamic clerics and established a more European model of education for both females and males.

Turkey was a one-party state, under the Republican People's Party (RPK), led by Ataturk. A faction of the party split and formed the Progressive Republican Party (PRP) in 1924. This splinter party wanted less corruption. Religion only figured into the dispute in the sense that the PRP wanted a more gradual change away from traditional Islamic and toward Western culture. The opposition party was making inroads in several areas, but in 1925 the ruling RPK found either the excuse or the necessity, depending on your point of view, to impose a one-party state system when a Kurdish separatist movement began to take shape.

Kurdish Separatism and the AKP

The longing by some Kurds to form their own state embracing parts of Turkey and Iraq is a serious issue for both Turkey and Iraq, but it will not be one of our three issues because it is a conflict based on ethnic rather than religious issues. Unlike several other separatist movements, in this case the majority Turks and the minority Kurds belong to the same religious tradition, Sunni Islam.

The relationship between the Turkish central government and the Kurdish population of the mountainous regions of Eastern Turkey has never been good. The policy of modern Turkey has been to claim that the Kurds are not a distinct ethnic group. In fact the Kurds are a distinct group. The Kurdish language is part of the Indo-European family of languages, whereas the Turkish language belongs to a cluster of Central Asian languages often called the Altaic family. The culture of the Kurds is also distinct.

The **PKK,** from the Kurdish term for **Kurdistan Workers' Party**, is a party that has sometimes turned to militant tactics to advance its goal of a separate state for the Kurds in Turkey. Kurdish separatism has become a problematic issue in international relations. The United States has found itself caught between the proverbial rock and a hard place. On the one hand it wants to support Turkey as an important ally, a NATO member, and the closest thing there is in the Islamic Middle East to a pro-Western culture. To complicate matters, because it wants to hold Iraq together and not see it divide into Shi'i, Sunni and Kurdish states, the United States has an interest in discouraging the formation of an independent Kurdistan. On the other hand the American tradition of supporting freedom, self-determination, and democracy is called into question if the United States supports a Turkish government perceived to be suppressing its Kurdish population.[3] To some extent the United States' Iraq policy concerns are driving its policies toward Turkey.

The European Union (EU)

The European Union (EU) has grown out of a series of treaties and the admission of new members to the point where it now has twenty-seven member states, a Parliament, a currency (the Euro), borderless travel throughout much of Europe, a free trade zone and many other dimensions. It began with the formation of the European Coal and Steel Community in the early 1950s. This was expanded by the formation of the European Atomic Energy Community and the European Economic Community (the European Common Market) in 1958. Along the way new treaties added additional organizations, with the 1993 Maastricht Treaty being one of the most important in giving shape to the EU as we know it today.

ISSUE 1. EUROPEAN UNION ADMISSION OF TURKEY AND THE RELIGION FACTOR

Our first issue focuses on Turkey's application for EU membership. This is an issue for Turkey because, being caught between the Islamic and the European worlds, Turkey needs to have the matter decided one way or the other in a reasonable timeframe. The decision is crucial for Turkey because it will likely determine whether its future lies with forming close ties to Europe or to the Islamic Arab countries. It is an issue for the EU countries for several reasons to be discussed more in this section. In brief, many European leaders favor

---

[3]Irving Louis Horowitz, "The European Union, Turkish Limitations, and American Disinterest," *The Forum.* Vol. 5, Issue 4, Article 8 (2008): 1.

Statue of Mary in Turkey, near a small house where Mary is said to have lived after leaving Jerusalem following the crucifixion of her son Jesus.
Photo: Roy Amore

Turkey's admission for reasons of trade and international relations, whereas many EU citizens and some EU leaders fear Turkey's admission because they do not want Europe overrun with an Islamic culture, Turkish workers, or militants.

This issue brings to the forefront the way Turkey is caught between Islam and Europe on so many levels. On the broadest level, using Huntington's terms, Turkey straddles the Islamic and western civilizations. Christianity spread to Anatolia very quickly after its beginnings, and many of the churches founded or visited by Paul were in Anatolia. According to Turkish Christians, Mary, the mother of Jesus, moved to central Anatolia after the death of Jesus, and her home is now a sacred pilgrimage spot. Constantinople, the "City of Constantine," the first Christian Roman Emperor, became the home of Eastern Orthodox Christianity and the Byzantine Empire.

Before we look at the issue of EU membership, we need to review the role of religion and politics from the Ottoman days to the present, to gain some perspective on the complexities around the admission question.

Food on display in one style of Istanbul restaurant
Photo: Roy Amore

The Ottoman Empire and the West

We leave Istanbul for Turkey's central highlands, to see the more conservative side of the country. As we ride the bus into the highlands it gets cooler and dryer. Once in Konya, we head for the building where Mevlana taught. Mevlana, also known as Rumi, was a Sufi, a practitioner of a mystical form of Islam. The story is that one day while passing a shop, he heard a song being played on a reed flute. He stopped, then slowly began to twirl to the music. He danced himself into an ecstatic trance. He later wrote that a secret turning in us makes the universe turn. Head unaware of feet, and feet of head. Neither cares. They keep turning.

Rumi accepted students and trained them in music and his turning style of dance. They came to be known as "whirling darvishes." The practice had nearly died out here, but in the past few decades it has been revived as practitioners now come to Konya from all parts of the world for one week every year. They pray and dance to the music, twirling themselves into ecstatic devotion to God. Similar Sufi gatherings are held in North America and elsewhere annually.

Geographically, Turkey is where Europe and the Middle East meet. There are other metropolitan regions in the world that straddle two states or even two countries, but Istanbul straddles two continents! As the bridge between Europe and Asia, the region has been the meeting ground of European, Asian, and Middle Eastern peoples, ideas, and culture for thousands of years.

On the political level, the expansionary drive of the Ottomans brought them into direct conflict with Europe. Three times the Ottomans tried to take Vienna in the 1600s. They did rule Bulgaria for over a century, but their attempts to move into Ukraine and Poland brought them into conflict with Russia and Peter the Great.

In its glory years, the Ottoman Empire was the latter day successor to the Roman and Byzantine Empires, ruling over a racially, ethnically, and religiously pluralistic population spread over a vast territory. While medieval Europe lagged, Islamic civilization flourished. At one time, Islamic centers of learning were on the leading edge of science, math, philosophy and many other subjects. Other aspects of culture, such as art and architecture, also thrived under the patronage of the sultans. From its start in 1299 under Osman I, after whom we have the name Ottoman, it rose from being just one of many small states in Turkey to ruling over a huge empire stretching from parts of Europe and North Africa to Persia.

Bernard Lewis' book *What Went Wrong?* raises the question of why the Islamic Ottoman Empire was so advanced and mighty for so long, and then fell behind the West so badly. He argues that the underlying problem was the unwillingness of the Islamic culture to develop a scientific and technological culture. Whereas in its earlier days Islam had been quite open to science and technology, it later failed to keep pace with the intellectual and scientific advances of Europe. He also calls attention to the way in which Islamic culture for the most part kept women out of public life, and by so doing lost the productivity of half its population. He cites several firsthand accounts of Europe by visiting Muslims. Their comments reflect the culture shock they experienced at seeing women freely moving about in the streets, intermixing with men and participating in public discourse. One Muslim observer is amazed to see that even the emperor shows respect to women in public. "In this country I saw an extraordinary spectacle. Whenever the Emperor meets a woman in the street, if he is riding, he brings his horse to a standstill and lets her pass. If the Emperor is on foot and meets a woman, he stands in a posture of politeness. The woman greets the Emperor, who then takes his hat off his head to show respect for the women."[4]

Religion and Politics, Turkish Style

During the Ottoman period, Islam was officially the religion of the state, but other religions were well tolerated. Even though Islam from its beginning was a religion and a polity, with a Quran-based system of law, the Ottoman rulers tended to keep political policy superior to religious concerns. They maintained a group of clerics, who gave approval to the policies formulated by the rulers. Ultimate legal authority, in theory, was vested

---

[4]B. Lewis, *What Went Wrong? The Clash Between Islam and Modernity in the Middle East* (New York: Oxford University Press, 2002), 65, citing from E. Çelebi, *Seyabatname* (Istanbul).

in Islam. In practice, however, the rulers did what they thought best, within the general constraints of Islamic law.[5]

There were various Islamic brotherhoods who advocated for the establishment of a more strict Shariah system. In 1909, a year after the Young Turks took power, one such brotherhood rebelled in an effort to establish Shariah. The army put down the Shariah advocates and their leaders were hanged. From then on, the Shariah advocates of Turkey have remained an out-of-power but growing minority. The High Electoral Board, a committee of military leaders, is in charge of enforcing the secular approach that is the legacy of the Young Turks and Ataturk. That Board gets to decide who is eligible to run for office. It has in the past made certain Islamic parties or politicians ineligible for office on the grounds that the party or the candidate advocates a religious rather than secular state.

Erdogan, the AKP Party and the Shift Toward Islam

The resurgence of religion in general and of Islam in particular has brought about renewed pressure within Turkey for a return of more religious authority. The rise to power of Erdogan, despite the fears of the secularists, illustrates this.

Recep Tayyip Erdogan was raised in a poor family that lived in Istanbul from the time he was thirteen years old. He attended an Islamic school, where he excelled in academics as well as sports. He later became a professional soccer player. Based partly upon his fame from soccer, he was elected mayor of Istanbul.

Being too associated with Islamic political ideals for their liking, the military council banned Erdogan from holding political office. In 1999 he was convicted on a charge of inciting religious hatred and was jailed. His offense had been to have read a poem written by a nineteenth-century poet, Ziya Gökalp, who combined Islam and Turkish Nationalism during a public speech at a university. The poem contained the lines "The mosques are our barracks, the domes our helmets, the minarets our bayonets and the faithful our soldiers...." His party, the Justice and Development Party (AKP) was founded in 1999 out of a faction of the Welfare Party. It billed itself as a moderately conservative party in favor of sound economic development. It has strong Islamic roots, but claims not to be a religious party. To do otherwise would get it banned under Turkish law.

By the 2002 elections, Erdogan was no longer in prison but was still barred from holding office. Although he could not run for parliament himself, Erdogan led the AKP to a sweeping victory, winning 34 percent of the popular vote. His AKP formed the government, although he could not serve as Prime Minister. By 2003 the Election Board had a change of heart and allowed him to run for office. He won a seat in a bye-election and assumed the office of Prime Minister, which had been held by his designee. In the 2007 elections, the AKP increased its share of the popular vote to 46 percent, an impressive amount in a multiparty election.

Why did the High Electoral Board change its stance? One factor was that there was strong popular support for both the AKP and Erdogan. The military did not want an Islamic Revolution on its hands. For his part, Erdogan and his party had made some

---

[5]Andrew Mango. 1994. *Turkey: The Challenge of a New Role.* (Westport, Conn.: Praeger, 1928). 77.

commitments that reassured the council that he was not going to take Turkey toward an Islamic state. He pledged to support Turkey's bid for EU membership, as well as its continued NATO membership and, most importantly, to keep the concept of a secular state. Under his leadership, the government has allowed the United States to continue a military presence in Turkey. He extracted a considerable increase in American monetary assistance as the price for doing so. Another factor may have been that some EU members found the banning of a person from political candidacy to be incompatible with EU ideals.[6]

As one writer put it, Ataturk had banned religion from politics, but religion had become acceptable again.[7] The people of Turkey favor Islam and therefore they favor Islamic values in political decisions. Yet other Turks do not want a state controlled by clerics. Turkey has several different Shi'i groups, who are collectively known as Alevis, meaning the Party of Ali. The Alevis in Turkey favor a secular state because they like the protection that gives them against the Sunni clerics. Note that the Shi'i preference for a secular state is in sharp contrast to the goals of the Shi'i clerics in Iran whom we discussed in the Iran-Iraq chapter. It is a good reminder to avoid making sweeping statements about any religious tradition.

The Unending Application for EU Membership

Ataturk put Turkey on a pro-Western course after World War I. After the Second World War, it developed close ties with the United States as well as Europe.[8] The United States included its new ally, Turkey, in the Marshall Plan (1947) which brought much needed money to rebuild the economies of countries devastated by the war. With encouragement from the United States, Turkey joined NATO in 1952. It applied to be an associate member of European Community in 1957, and in 1987 it applied for membership in the European Union (when it was still named the European Economic Community). Turkey was given Associate Member status in 1963, and was officially put on a track for possible full membership in 1999. Several East European countries that applied long after Turkey have already been either admitted to the EU or put on a track leading to almost certain admission. Meanwhile, Turkey's admission process has been allowed to drag on and on, with no guarantee of it ever being approved. This raises many questions, including the two following ones.

Why Does Turkey Want to Join the EU?
Why does Turkey want to join the EU? The main motivation for Turkey to seek admission to the EU is economic. Yet there is more to it than just economic improvement. A Turkish official said in 2008 that EU membership would help in the economic, social, and political

---

[6]See for example the "European Commission: Strategy Paper and Report 2003." www.fifoost.org/EU/strategy_en_2002/node59.php.

[7]A. Mango, *Turkey: The Challenge of a New Role* (Westport, Conn.: Praeger, 1994), 80.

[8]Yasemin Çelik Levine, *Contemporary Turkish Foreign Policy* (Westport, Conn. Praeger, 1999), 98.

Bridge across the Bosphorus Strait, symoblizing the way that Turkey straddles Europe and Asia physically, culturally, and politically.

Photo: "Bosphorus" by Bertil Videt–Own work. Licensed under CC BY 2.5 via Wikimedia Commons - http://commons. wikimedia.org/wiki/File:Bosphorus.jpg#/media/File:Bosphorus.jpg

transformation of Turkey.[9] Also, there has been a longstanding rivalry between Turkey and Greece over Cyprus and other matters. One motivation may be that Turkey does not want to see Greece get the upper hand because both Greece and Cyprus are EU members already.[10] Yasemin Çelik points out that Turkey missed its opportunity to join when, in the early 1970s, it got cold feet about joining an EU predecessor. It thought it needed to keep tariffs to support its economy, whereas Greece went ahead with its application and joined the EC in 1975 despite its own concerns about the removal of tariffs.[11]

At the time of its application to the EU, the European countries were Turkey's largest trading partners. Its trade with its Arab neighbors was relatively small at the time, but has now increased dramatically. This change may alter Turkey's desire for EU membership if the process drags on too long. Or, if Turkey's request is eventually denied, the increase in trade with Arab countries may soften the economic blow for Turkey considerably. Turkey also wants more freedom for its workers to more freely move back and forth between their work in EU countries, especially Germany, and their home in Turkey. Germany's policy of allowing Turks in as "guest workers" rather than immigrants has been problematic for the workers because they were not allowed to stay in Germany. German industry needs the workers, but many German citizens object to having so many foreigners in the country. German policy on its Turkish workers has vacillated through the years. For example in 1973 Germany banned non-EU workers, but later had to soften that stance under pressure from its business sector.

[9]"EU needs Turkey to become a major power," *Turkish Daily News* (March 29, 2008).

[10]Levine, *Contemporary Turkish Foreign Policy*, 99.

[11]*Ibid.* 101–102.

Why Does the EU Not Want to Admit Turkey?

Here we will have to distinguish between the official reasons and the reasons the EU does not want to put in print.

Official Reasons for Delaying Membership. From the earliest application, the EU insisted that Turkey would have to undergo considerable economic progress and reform. It would have to bring itself up to EU standards before admission. Because the main motivation for applying in the first place was to raise its standard of living, this must have seemed like an unjust demand to Turkey. There was, however, some justification for the demand. The per capita income of Turkey was below the EU average, and its banking system and financial regulatory laws were not on par with the EU's. The other stated reasons included Turkey's political instability, arising out of its coup in 1980. Since then, Turkey has been more stable, politically.

Turkey's role in the Cyrus dispute was a stated area of concern. Turkey intervened militarily in 1974 to defend the Turkish Cypriots against perceived Greek dominance. Turkey helped set up an independent region of Cyprus called the Turkish Republic of North Cyprus. No other countries recognize it as an independent state. Greece objects to Turkey's military presence in Cyprus and, as an EU member, Greece insists on a resolution of the Cyprus situation before admitting Turkey to the EU.

Another objection is that Turkey is not really in Europe, at least most of it is not. This objection is probably the most defensible of all. But if this objecton is so definitive, why was Turkey not simply refused in the first place?

To meet the economic objection, Turkey undertook several economic reforms, and in fact has made some progress on raising its standard of living and drafting legislation that would be more acceptable to the EU. Whereas economic development has been held as a necessary precondition for Turkey's admission, the East European applicants, with similarly weak economies, have been fast-tracked into admission. Turkey finds this frustrating and unfair.

Turkey has become politically stable, so some progress has been made on one of the items. But Turkey has not come to an understanding with Greece about Cyprus.

Another stated reason is that a law passed in 2005 had made it illegal to insult Turkishness. This law has been used to convict Kurdish separatists and political dissidents, including Nobel laureate Orhan Pamuk. In support of the EU application, an attempt to soften these laws was made in 2008 when Article 301 of Turkey's penal code was altered such that it became an offense to denigrate the "Turkish nation" or its governmental institutions, rather than more vague and comprehensive "Turkishness." Turkish hard-liners objected that Turkey was just pandering to EU demands and was leaving the door open to Kurdish rebels. The opposition National Action Party reacted with a TV campaign with the slogan "Wake up Turkey! It is time for unity."[12]

---

[12]"Turkey under fire over laws banning insults to 'Turkishness'." *AP News* (2008). http://apnews.excite.com/article/20080421/D9062R800.html.

Unofficial Reasons for Delaying Membership. Besides the stated reasons, there are several other reasons that have emerged in interviews with EU officials, editorials, and public opinion polls. One of these is that Turkey's population is just too large. With over seventy million, it would become the second most populous EU country, after Germany. A closely related reason is that current EU members fear a large influx of Turkish immigrants if EU membership is approved. Historically, many Turks have moved to Germany, or other EU countries, as "guest workers," willing to take lower paying jobs. EU members worry that Turks will flock to EU countries in search of economic improvement.

Some Europeans fear that the role of women is not adequately protected in Turkey, although the status of women here is much more in line with European norms than in nearby Islamic countries. Turkey began the move toward political participation for women in 1908, with the adoption of the Second Constitution which called for the education of women. A group of women tried to enter Parliament as observers, without success but with international press coverage. By 1916 issues of special concern to women such as their status in marriage, divorce, and polygamous arrangements was seriously discussed in Parliament. Some Turkish writers also took up the cause. In Turkey's War of Independence (1919-23) women founded their own military units and fought in the ranks. One of these women soldiers was Halide Adivar, who later became a feminist novelist and a leader in the feminist movement.[13]

Another reason given is that Turkey is not culturally European. A very closely related reason is that Turkey is not Christian. As a former president of the European commission put it, the EU is a "Christian club."[14] Every time a Muslim publicly denounces the European way of life, the chance of Turkey's admission diminishes. The irony is, those who denounce the Western way of life are mainly doing so from the Salafi point of view, which is not that widely held in Turkey.

Popular opinion in the EU countries does not support admission of Turkey. It does vary widely by EU country. In a 2005 survey, the EU average was 36 percent for approval. The highest approval rate just over 50 percent, in Hungary. The United Kingdom was next most favorable with around 45 percent approving. Germany and France showed just over 20 percent approval. On the low end, Cyprus was around 16 percent, and only 10 percent of Austrians approved of the admission.[15] Austria and France have stated that in the case that the EU votes to admit Turkey, they would put the issue to a public referendum before signing. Given that the support in both countries is extremely low, a referendum favoring admission would surely fail.

The Reasons to Admit Turkey. With the official and unofficial objections to Turkeys' EU membership, the question naturally arises: What is in it for the EU? The most com-

---

[13]Emel Sonmez, "The Novelist Halide Edib Adivar and Turkish Feminism," *Die Welt des Islam.* New Series, Vol. 1/4, Issue 1/4 (1973), 81–115.

[14]"Turkey's EU Entry Talks," *BBC News* (Dec. 11, 2006). http://news.bbc.co.uk/1/hi/world/europe/4107919.stm

[15]*Ibid.*

mon reason given is that bringing Turkey into the EU would help it remain relatively secular and pro-West. This would give continental Europe some buffer between its states and those of more radical Muslim countries. A German official said in 2004 that Turkey's admission into the EU would in the long run be as important for Europe as D-Day.[16]

The request for admission has put EU member countries in a difficult position. If they admit Turkey, they fear they will have to cope with an influx of relatively unskilled workers and, perhaps with a rise of terrorist threats. If they do not admit Turkey, Turkey may move farther away from Ataturk's vision and toward a more anti-Western stance and alliance with the Arab countries.

STOPOVER IN PRAGUE

We arrive in Prague, in the Czech Republic, and change some money into Czech Koruna, or Crowns. The Republic is an EU member but the Czechs have resisted adopting the Euro. We have chosen to stop in Prague for several reasons. Prague was very important during the Thirty Years War. It was a Jewish center. And it is the home of Good King Wenceslas, Christian reformer Jan Hus, Charles IV and other famous Holy Roman Emperors, St. Agnes, as well as novelist Franz Kafka, astronomer Johannes Kepler and so many others. Besides the historical importance, there are many other reasons why we will enjoy Prague. It was one of the few East European cities not destroyed by bombs during the second World War, so the old town area, the Charles Bridge, and other old features are a tourist's delight. And we can enjoy great food and shopping at prices one will never see in the Euro zone.

We head first to the Old Town Square, to take a walking tour of the history of the interface of religion and politics, Prague style. Our next stop is Wenceslas Square, where we see a statue of the Good King looking down the boulevard. He was a tenth century prince who supported the then-new Christian religion among the Bohemians. He was killed by a group led by his brother, but was recognized as a Saint for his martyr's death and later miracles. The hymn about "Good King Wenceslas looking down on the feast of Stephen" became a Christian favorite.

Next we view the statue of local religious hero Jan Hus overlooking the Square.

Jan Hus, the Cooked Goose, and the Swan

Jan Hus was a young Catholic priest appointed in 1402 to preach in Prague's Bethlehem Chapel. Germans and their language had dominated the city previously. Now Czechs were numerous, so Hus was asked to preach in Czech. He drew huge crowds from the town's

---

[16]"Turkey EU Entry as Big as 'D-Day'," *BBC News* (October 20, 2004) http://news.bbc.co.uk/2/hi/europe/3758592.stm.

Painting of Jan Hus being burned at the stake for heresy.

Photo: "Spiezer Chronik Jan Hus 1485". Licensed under Public Domain via Wikimedia Commons - http://commons.wikimedia.org/wiki/File:Spiezer_Chronik_Jan_Hus_1485.jpg#mediaviewer/File:Spiezer_Chronik_Jan_Hus_1485.jpg

Czech population. The Roman Catholic Church was in a bad state at the time. There were two competing Popes, and the right to hold Church offices was commonly sold to the highest bidder. The Church seemed more interested in accumulating wealth than in helping the people. Hus started to preach about the need for sweeping reforms. A more radical reformer in England, named Wycliffe, had been advocating that the Church divest itself of its wealth and get back to the business of the gospel. The Catholic Church feared Hus was moving in that direction and had him taken to Germany for a church trial. He was found guilty and burned at the stake. After Hus's burning, his Czech backers rose up in arms against the German Catholics, touching off the Hussite War.

The word *Hus* means "goose" in Czech, and before dying on the fire in 1415, Hus is supposed to have issued a prophecy, saying that you are now roasting a goose, but God will raise up a swan whom you will not burn or roast, in one hundred years.[17] Just over one hundred years later, Luther demanded similar reforms, but was saved by Frederick the Wise from being put to death like Hus. Luther saw himself as that swan, and Lutherans made the swan a symbol, putting it on churches, weather vanes, and plates.

The Thirty Years War: Catholics against Protestants

We stroll slowly across the Charles Bridge, the site of the last battle of the war. Fortunately, this battle marked the end of major religious wars in Europe. That is, at

---

[17]Cited from the sermon at Luther's funeral. See http://beck.library.emory.edu/luther/luther_site/luther_text.html.

least, so far. As we cross the bridge, looking up we see the religious statues intended to make the townspeople more pious. Looking down we see many vendors, artists, and musicians vying for tourist money. Toward the Prague Castle side, there is a statue of the devil. Near it, an artist sets up his easel day after day, painting himself as the devil. He wears devil's horns, and leaves the impression that he is mildly insane. Is he faking that as part of his persona? Whatever the case, we cannot help but make a purchase.

The Thirty Years War was fought between Catholics and Protestants from 1618 to 1648. It was touched off when some irate Protestants threw two Catholic governors and their secretary out a Prague Castle window. The act is known as *Defenestration*, the term for throwing someone out a window. This defenestration was likely done in imitation of the first defenestration during the Hussite revolt. In this case, the Catholics survived because they landed in a dung pile. Later, Catholics said they were saved by angels!

The first major battle of the war took place on White Mountain near Praque in 1620. The armies of the Protestant nobility of the Czech regions fought against the imperial forces of the Catholic Holy Roman Emperor. The Thirty Years War took on many dimensions and spread throughout Europe, but at the start it was primarily a religious war. It pitted the traditional Catholic establishment against those recently converted to Protestantism, which was barely one hundred years old at the time.

Historical Persecution of Prague's Jews

The history of the Jewish Quarter in Prague is similar to that of other European cities. Jews were typically permitted to live only in small restricted areas of the city. As the population increased, those areas, the ghettos, became severely overcrowded.

There are old synagogues still standing in the Jewish Quarter. They now function as museums. One has a tiny cemetery, which reveals the way Jews were so

Crowded Jewish cemetary in Prague's old Jewish quarter.
Photo: Roy Amore

crowded for space in this ghetto. The cemetery only had room for a hundred or so graves, so they had to stack grave on top of grave and families had to share space.

Jews lived here for centuries, but not always in peace. One Crusader army came through here and persecuted the Jews in the process. Even when not being persecuted, Jews were often restricted in their occupations and were required to wear distinctive clothing. In 1389 the Christian clergy encouraged the looting of the Jewish Quarter. In the early 1700s Prague had the largest Jewish population in the world, but a ruler soon expelled the Jews. Some later returned, and Prague became a center of Zionism. Sadly, the majority of Prague's Jews were killed in Nazi death camps. Whatever one thinks about the Zionist move to Palestine, it is easy to see why so many wanted out of Europe.

ISSUE 2. FRANCE: BACKLASH, NATIONAL FRONT, BAN ON RELIGIOUS GARB

We land in Paris. We want to look at two forms taken by the backlash against immigrants in Europe. One is the National Front, a far-right party now moving toward the center and gaining in popularity. The other concerns the French law against wearing religious garb in public schools.

Anti-Immigration Parties, The National Front

The large number of immigrants in European cities has led to the creation of small but growing anti-immigration parties in most EU countries. We will discuss the main Dutch anti-immigration party later. We begin with the French party most associated with an anti-immigration stance.

Jean-Marie Le Pen and the NF Platform

Jean-Marie Le Pen was born in 1928 into a fisherman family. Orphaned at an early age, he studied law at the University of Paris, and then entered the Foreign Legion. Returning to France, he studied political science and at age twenty-eight became the youngest member of the National Assembly.

Trouble seems to have followed Le Pen around most of his life. He has been accused of participating in alcoholic brawls and of being complicit in military torture. He was once put in custody for alleged racist remarks. His political life was turbulent. He was beaten in the face while campaigning, his apartment was bombed, and he has been kicked out of political parties. Even his family has added to the controversy. His first wife posed for *Playboy* after their separation, allegedly to spite him. One of his daughters bolted to a rival party, but another now leads his party.

The **National Front**, or *Front National* in French **(FN)**, was formed in 1972 as a venue for an assortment of far-right groups. The founders were former members of the

> The Fair has come to town. It is September 1993, the late summer sun is shining and the various factions of the French far-right have gathered for a family day out. The National Front is holding its thirteenth annual Fete Blue Blanc Rouge.... The Party's youth wing... had its own stand and there was even a scout-like organisation for nationalist-minded children, complete with its own uniform that looked much like that worn by the Vichy malice during the Second World War.
>
> Jonathan Marcus, describing his field research in France.

Ordre Nouveau, a neo-fascist group, and Collaborationists—a term that in France means those who thought that German National Socialism (the Nazi Party) was a good polity. Its supporters also included former military officers who were still angry that France had pulled out of Algeria. There were also cultural and religious conservatives, including traditionalist Catholics, who refused to accept the Vatican II reforms of the Roman Catholic Church.

Despite the diversity of groups and political agendas, the party has been closely identified with Jean-Marie Le Pen, who moved the party away from its neo-fascist roots toward a more moderate conservatism that could potentially appeal to a broad base of voters. Le Pen contested the 1974 elections as a candidate for President on the National Front ticket, but he received very little support. However, by the 2002 elections, he finished a distinct second to Jacques Chirac. In the 2007 Presidential elections Le Pen finished a distant fourth. In the 2007 Assembly elections, the Front won no seats at all. The party had been weakened by internal rifts, and observers wondered if the FN party was on the way out.

Marine Le Pen Revitalizes the FN and Softens Its Anti-Immigration Stance

Jean-Marie Le Pen's youngest daughter, **Marine Le Pen**, is a lawyer who has long been active in her father's party. She succeeded him as its President in 2011. Since that time, she and the FN party have enjoyed a surge in popularity. She polled almost 18 percent, finishing third, in the 2012 presidential elections. In the run up to regional elections in 2015, she put an end to Front's anti-Semitic era when she publically criticized her father after he repeatedly uttered anti-Semitisms, such as dismissing the Holocaust's gas chambers as a (mere) "detail of history."[18] She announced that she would not support his candidacy to head the party's list in the regional elections. He then withdrew his name and backed the candidacy of his 25-year-old granddaughter, who is Marine Le Pen's niece.

Under her new leadership, the FN styles itself as conservative but not extremist. The Party is against corruption by political officials, against current immigration policies, and against a federated Europe. Marine Le Pen and the party want fewer immigrants, expulsion of illegal immigrants, a return to stricter secularism and a more traditional Francophone culture, and a reversal of the trend toward European political integration. The party insists it is not racist or anti-Muslim. Neither she nor other party leaders criticize Islam directly, in the manner of the Dutch politician Geert Wilders, which we will discuss in the next section. She did stir up controversy when she compared the closing

[18]http://www.bbc.com/news/world-europe-32282646

of some streets for Muslim prayers to the German occupation of France during World War II.

Despite the disclaimers, are Marine Le Pen and her Party against Islam itself? Is this a backlash against all immigrants or has it been made worse because the majority of recent immigrants are Muslims from North Africa? The answer needs to be set in the context of the French attitude toward foreign workers over the past century or more. France has a long history of bringing in large numbers of foreign workers to meet labor shortages at the low end of the pay scale. Although the French economy has needed these workers, they have not been well received. Even French speakers from Belgium brought in to work coal mines and steel plants were resented and looked down upon. Other European immigrants also were often seen as competing for jobs with French citizens, and as a threat to French culture. Whenever there was an economic downturn, working class French citizens objected strongly to the immigrant workers. For example, in the 1930s Polish mine workers were forced to return home after there were several violent incidents against them..

Even having the right religious identity did not guarantee acceptance. Some Catholic immigrants from Italy or Poland were criticized for being too religious because they came from cultures where Catholicism was still practiced more devoutly. It has been hard for immigrants to assimilate into French culture, regardless of religion or country of origin.

The National Front is against large-scale immigration, and because the recent immigrants are North African and Muslim, their anti-immigration stance takes on racist and anti-Islamic overtones, whether or not Marine Le Pen so intends.

Religious Garb

The Islamic Headscarf Affair
In 1989 three Muslim girls in France were told they could not wear their headscarves to school. When they refused, they were suspended from school. This touched off a feverish public debate in the French press and received international media coverage. The debate brought to the surface the anti-immigrant and anti-Islamic feelings of many French citizens. Those who favored a ban on headscarves pointed to the French concept of *laïcité*, "secularity," which is a French term for the separation of the religion and the state. At the request of an organization dedicating to racial harmony, the suspension was soon lifted. But the debate did not stop.

The decision to allow wearing headscarves was later supported in court. The debate hinged on the proper understanding of secularism in French law. The school principal took it to mean that no display of religious identity was allowed in a state school, whereas the proper interpretation was that no religious proselytizing or favoritism is allowed.

The heated public debate tended to polarize the mainstream French population and the North African immigrants. In an interview, Jean-Marie Le Pen mentioned how much the National Front had benefited from the Islamic headscarf affair, saying that it boosted

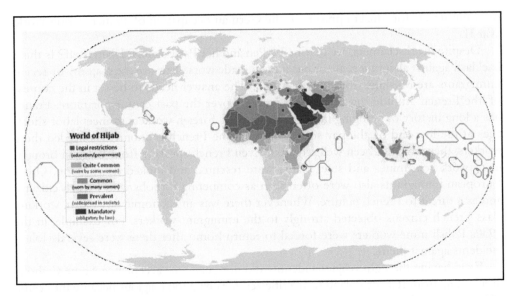

Map of the prevalence and legality of Hijab wearing worldwide. The red dots shows areas with some form of legal restrictions.
Map courtesy of Candelabra [Public domain], via Wikimedia Commons

the voter appeal of several of his candidates.[19] However, public opinion polls showed that most Muslims of France were actually in favor of banning headscarves in state schools.

Ban on Religious Garb

Growing out of the continuing controversy surrounding the wearing of Islamic headscarves in public schools, a broadly representative commission of twenty men and women was formed at the request of President Jacques Chirac in 2003. Referred to as "the Stasi Report" after the name of the Commission's chair, it attempted to clarify the practical implications of secularism in French public life. One of its positions was the principle that Jewish and Muslim holidays should be recognized, rather than just the Christian ones, as in current practice. It encouraged employers to allow employees to choose which religious holidays they want time off to celebrate. It recommended that school holidays reflect Christian, Jewish, and Muslim religious holidays. It recommended that special meals be made available for Muslims and Jews in cafeterias.

On the wearing of religious symbols in state schools, the report noted that consistency was essential. Either the symbols of all religions should be banned, or else none of them should be banned. One of the problems with the attempt to ban the wearing of Islamic headscarves was that in the past Jewish boys had been allowed to wear skull caps and

---

[19]Jonathan Marcus, *The national Front and French Politics: The Resistible Rise of Jean-Marie Le Pen* (New York: New York University Press, 1995), 8.

Christians had been allowed to wear large crucifixes. The report recommended that a law be passed banning the wearing of conspicuous symbols and garb in school, such as Jewish skull caps, Islamic headscarves, Sikh turbans, and large crucifixes. It suggested making exceptions for smaller, less conspicuous religious items.

President Chirac accepted most of the Report's recommendations, and signed a law on secularity and conspicuous religious symbols in schools in 2004. The law had the support of a majority of the French population. The law does not specify which religious symbols and garb are too conspicuous to be worn, but it was popularly perceived to be aimed primarily at banning Islamic headscarves. Besides Muslim girls, Sikh males who wear a turban were affected by the ban. The law is part of the regulations governing publicly-supported schools. It does not apply to universities, government offices, or any private sector institution. Nor does the law apply to religious institutions qualifying for government funding.

Headscarves and Women's Equality

Throughout the public debate, from the 1998 Islamic Headscarf Affair to the Stasi Commission Report, the headscarf has been, for some non-Muslims, a symbol of the women's inequality or suppression. The Stasi Report notes that some Muslim girls wear the headscarf because they want to, whereas others feel pressured by their parents or their peers. This is an issue where cultural perceptions differ widely. Although Muslims think of the need for women to dress modestly in public, many non-Muslim French think the headscarf and especially the veil go against the goal of gender equality for at least two reasons. One reason is that the very noticeable difference in Islamic dress codes for males and females suggests to some non-Muslims that women are not only different but inferior in status within Islam. A more defensible claim is that the whole concept underlying the need for women to dress modestly in public is based upon an old fashioned system, devised by males, which puts the onus on females to avoid provoking males into improper sexual acts. This raises the question of why should females be held responsible for the sins of males? In this line of thinking, if high school boys are getting too brazen in their sexual behavior, the parents and schools should correct the behavior of the boys rather than encourage the girls to cover up more.

The Cycle of Backlash, Social Barriers, Communal Identity, and Terrorism

The dynamics of immigrant communities work in a dysfunctional way in France. At first the North African Muslim immigrants tried to fit in socially, to assimilate into French society as much as possible without, of course, giving up their religion or their values. However, the backlash against them by some groups within France has led to social barriers being erected against them. The result is that some immigrant communities lose hope of ever being "French" and are turning away from the goal of fitting into French society. Instead, they are turning to their ethnic identity more than ever.[20] As researcher

---

[20]Fred Toner, "Multiculturalism in Debate: The Immigrant Presence as Social Catalyst in Contemporary France," in *France at the Dawn of the Twenty-First Century: Trends and Transformations,* ed. Marie-Christine Weidmann Koop (Birmingham: Summa Publications, 2000), 161.

Riva Kastoryano puts it, the immigrants begin to express political demands for the "right of difference."[21] This in turn will lead to even more backlash and barriers. It is a vicious cycle leading to a bad ending. The gangs of young immigrants burning cars and buildings around Paris in 2006 and 2007 are a manifestation of the trouble.

The 2015 killing of twelve people in the Paris office of the satirical magazine *Charlie Hebdo* by three Islamic terrorists reignited anti-immigration feelings. Political pundits quickly predicted that Marine Le Pen's party, and Europe's other right wing parties, would get a boost in support as a result of the horrific attack by home-grown French Muslims. The media immediately turned to Le Pen for interviews. She called for the restoration of the death penalty in France. Elsewhere in Europe, the media turned to the leaders of the other anti-immigration parties; such as the *Lega Nord* in Italy and the *U.K. Independence Party* in Great Britain.

Starting several months before the Paris attacks, a Germany-based group named *Perida* had been staging anti-Islamisation rallies in Dresden every Monday. The name Perida is an acronym based on the group's full name in German, which translates as "Patriotic Europeans Against the Islamisation of the West." Their Monday protests became larger and larger after the Paris attacks. Other Germans, who opposed the Islamophobia of Perida and feared it would just spark more attcks, organized rallies against Perida.

ISSUE 3. NETHERLANDS: BACKLASH, PARTIES, FILMS, CARTOONS

We take the very modern train from Paris to Amsterdam. From the train station we walk along a narrow street lined with restaurants and shops of every imaginable ethnic variety. We settle into a small hotel on a canal street. Cars park near the canal, but there are no guardrails for cars or pedestrians. It makes the canal more scenic, but we learn that some careless people do fall in sometimes.

Our third issue concerns other forms of the backlash taken by some Europeans against Muslims. We will deal with three of them: the Dutch right-wing anti-immigration parties, the making of films critical of radical Islam, and the repeated publication of cartoons offensive to Muslims. While discussing the issue, we will locate ourselves in The Netherlands, where the backlash films and film makers are a hot topic both in Parliament and in the popular press.

---

[21]Riva Kastoryano, *Negotiating Identities: States and Immigrants in France and Germany,* (Princeton: Princeton University Press, 2002), 182.

Dutch Anti-Immigration Parties

Pim Fortuyn, the leader of a Dutch anti-immigration party, was fatally shot just nine days before the 2002 elections by a non-Muslim man who said at his trial that he blamed Fortuyn for making Muslims the scapegoats for whatever was wrong in the country. His party, the **Pim Fortuyn List**, had been expected to do quite well in the elections, perhaps winning enough of the 150 seats in parliament to participate in a governing coalition. His platform mainly focused on anti-immigration concerns. He argued that The Netherlands had been too tolerant of immigrants. He had referred to Islam as a backward religion during the campaign. But his backers were not necessarily anti-Islam. Rather, they were working–class voters who lived in areas, such as the port city of Rotterdam, where the large numbers of immigrants living there had created a backlash against immigrants in general.

Dutch Tolerance and Salafi Rhetoric
Dutch society has been characterized by openness and permissiveness, and so the need to scrutinize radical groups or to restrict individual freedoms goes against Dutch norms.[22] Yet the rise of concern in the general public led the the Dutch Ministry of the Interior to publish a 2004 report, prepared by the Dutch intelligence service. The report had the provocative title, "From Dawa to Jihad." We might translate this as "from mission to holy struggle." The term *jihad* in Islam means struggle. This can apply to anything from stopping smoking to terrorist bombing, depending on which Muslim is using the term. The term *dawa* literally means "call," but has taken on an extended meaning of the mission to spread Islam. The report estimated that of the approximately one million Muslims in The Netherlands, 95 percent were moderates with no tendency toward violence. The 5 percent were said to be those Islamic groups or mosques who were especially against the Western way of life, and so Dutch citizens should not expect the potential for violence to lessen even if peace came to the Middle East.

The report mentioned that Salafist Islam, funded by Saudi money, has played an important role in fermenting anti-Western feeling. In the Saudi Arabia chapter, we discussed Salafi Islam and how the government had directed large amounts of money to the clerics to allow them to finance the spread of Islam, the *dawa*. In The Netherlands, we see the difference that has made.

The report warned that the Dutch society was not well-positioned to stop acts of terrorist violence, and that the moderate majority of Dutch Muslims were not able to stop it either. The report intended to calm concerns about the potential for Islamic terrorist violence by stressing that not more than 5 percent of Muslims in The Netherlands were against the Western way of life. This hardly reassured the public, because it implied that there were up to 50,000 potentially radical Muslims in Holland.

---

[22]Manfred Gerstenfeld, "Radical Islam in The Netherlands: A Case Study of a Failed European Policy." *Jerusalem Issue Brief* Vol. 4, No. 14, Jan. 2 (2005). http://www.jcpa.org/brief/brief004-14.htm.

Anti-Islamic Films

Dutch film makers have produced several films calling attention to the perceived extremes of some forms of Islam. The treatment of women in some Islamic countries has been one concern of these films. The terrorist killings supported by some Muslims have been another. The films have been quite controversial in The Netherlands and beyond. We will look at three of these filmmakers and the controversy and violence surrounding them.

The Murder of Theo van Gogh

A Muslim radical named Mohammed Boyeri murdered Dutch film maker Theo van Gogh on the streets of Amsterdam in 2004, setting off a wave of backlash fervor among non-Muslim Dutch. He was the great-grandnephew of the painter Vincent van Gogh. Many attempts to burn mosques and churches occurred in the following weeks. Van Gogh had made a film, called *Submission,* critical of the treatment of women in the Islamic world. He had received death threats, and then was killed by a Dutch citizen with Moroccan ancestry. Dutch society was outraged that a person was killed just because someone objected to the subject matter of this movie.

Mourners place flowers in memory of Theo van Gogh after his assassination.
Photo: Iijjccoo at nl.wikipedia [Public domain], from Wikimedia Commons

The incident pitted the values of secular pluralism against hard-line Islamic reactions to criticism. It turned out to be an omen of events to come.

Ayaan Hirsi Ali, Muslim Woman Turned Critic

Ayaan Hirsi Ali wrote the script for the van Gogh film *Submission*. She was born in Somalia, moved to other African countries, and later sought and received asylum in The Netherlands when she was 22 years old. She had run away from an arranged marriage to a man she feared. After arriving in Amsterdam she began to read widely, while working as a translator with Somali women seeking asylum. She earned a Masters degree in political science and published several articles and a book in Dutch.

After the 2001 attack on the World Trade Center Ayaan Hirsi Ali became critical of the way the Quran was used to justify both violence and the treatment of women. Her script for *Submission* and other writings brought her fame as a critic of Islamic practices concerning women. It also brought her threats and danger.

She was also active in Dutch politics. She was elected to the lower house of the Dutch parliament in 2003, but later had to resign when a scandal broke about the accuracy of the information she entered in her claim for asylum. Her critics called for the govern-

Ayaan Hirsi Ali speaking at St. Gallen Symposia in Switzerland, May 2011.
Photo: International Students' Committee (International Students' Committee) [CC BY-SA 3.0 (http://creativecommons.org/licenses/by-sa/3.0)], via Wikimedia Commons.

ment to revoke her Dutch citizenship. The controversy surrounding the matter led to the downfall of the governing cabinet in 2006.

Ayaan Hirsi Ali's international fame came after the release of *Submission* and the 2006 publication of a her book, *The Caged Virgin: A Muslim Woman's Cry for Reason*.[23] In both the book and the movie script, she laments the hatred and violence that have come into radical Islam. She detests the Islamic treatment of women in particular. She calls for a "Muslim enlightenment" leading to more equality for women in Islam and more tolerance by Muslims of other religions. Her 2007 book *Infidel* tells the story of her growing up in an oppressive culture and her move to Holland. She no longer considers herself a Muslim.

Her criticism of Islam has led to death threats against her by Islamic groups, including a threatening rap song. Her friend van Gogh was killed by a radical Muslim and her friend Pim Fortuyn by another radical, so she and the Dutch government took the threats seriously. She went into hiding for a while in Holland, and then moved to the United sstates to work for a think tank. She continues to publish about Islam, women, politics, and philosophy.

Wilders' Film Fitna *Draws Protests*

The reaction by Muslims around the world was quite critical after the release of Dutch political leader Geert Wilders' documentary film *Fitna* in early 2008. The film shows clips from interviews with radical Muslims interspersed with footage of violence and readings from the Quran. The point of view of the film is not that all Muslims are radical or violent, nor that Islam itself is a bad religion. But the way the film cites passages from the Quran seeming to support hatred or even violence against other religions is inflammatory. A spokesman for the Saudis said the film was full of errors and incorrect allegations that could lead to hatred against Muslims. An Indonesian Muslim called the film an insult to Islam hidden under the guise of freedom of speech.[24]

A group of concerned Dutch Muslims took the matter of the film's depiction of Muslims to court, but lost. The court ruled that Wilders' right of free speech allowed him to distribute a film critical of Islam or passages from the Quran. The Indonesian government sought to ban YouTube from their Internet service because it carried the film. It then decided to allow it when blocking the links to the film proved difficult and many Indonesians spoke out against government censorship. This did not necessarily imply they approved of the film itself.

Cartoons about Islam

A Danish newspaper printed a series of twelve satirical-style cartoons dealing with Islam and terrorism in September 2005. The context of the publication was an ongoing debate

---

[23]Ali, Ayaan Hirsi, *The Caged Virgin: A Muslim Woman's Cry for Reason* (London: Pocket Books, 2006)

[24]"Muslim nations condemn Dutch ani-Islam film." (March 28, 2008). www.euro-islam.info/spip/article. php3?id_article=2352.

in the Danish media concerning the way that some writers and artists had become afraid of drawing or writing anything critical of Islam for fear of being killed. Several examples were given of those who were practicing "self-censorship" out of fear of militant Islamic reprisals. The killing of Theo van Gogh the previous year was often mentioned in this debate. To contribute to the debate, the editor of a newspaper had invited twelve cartoonists to draw Muhammad as they see him. Not all drew Muhammad, but all dealt with Islam in some fashion. The most offensive one showed Muhammad with a bomb in his turban.

Many Muslims of Denmark found the cartoons offensive, and held some non-violent protests, but decided that it was better to not make a big deal out of them. Some Danish Muslims organizations, however, filed a complaint with the police stating that the publications of the cartoons violated a Danish blasphemy law under which it is illegal to disturb the public order by ridiculing the beliefs of some religion. Because the law had been used in cases offensive to Jews, the Muslims thought it should be used in the cartoon case as well. They had a good point.

Soon two Danish Imams who wanted to protest the cartoons more vigorously traveled to the Middle East, where they showed Muslim leaders a collection of the Danish cartoons, along with some other satirical art and other documents allegedly showing discrimination against Danish Muslims. An Egyptian newspaper picked up the story and published the cartoons in the context of condemning them as an insult to Islam. Ambassadors from ten Muslim countries protested to the Danish government about the cartoons. The Saudis recalled their ambassador to Denmark in protest.

The cartoons polarized the Islamic world and the Western world. It put traditional Islamic values in direct contrast to liberal Western values. To conservative Muslims, a government should intervene in such a case. It should prohibit the further publication of the cartoons and should arrest and possibly execute the cartoonist and the publisher. In Western values, the freedom of expression is an almost equally sacred principle. The Danish government was willing to apologize for the offense to Islam, but it was not willing to prosecute a cartoonist or a newspaper. As many as fifty other newspapers and websites republished the cartoons. Most claimed that they did so to affirm the value of free speech and the right of individuals to criticize a religion or anything else. Soon a few newspapers in other Western countries reprinted the cartoons, although at least one of the editors got fired for doing so.

Violence broke out during various protest demonstrations in Africa and the Middle East. Many of the protests targeted Denmark. Several people died during protests in Afghanistan, Nigeria and elsewhere. The Danish and Norwegian embassies were attacked in Syria.

Conservative Muslims complained that even with all of their free speech talk, the West would not have allowed cartoons like that to be published about Jesus and Christianity. And, they added, Muslims would not do that to Christianity. These claims led to the republication of various political style cartoons critical of Christians or Christianity. Some had originally been done by Westerners, others by Muslims.

A Muslim participated in one of the Unity Rallies, carrying a sign reading "They have stolen my religion" and "I am Charlie."

Photo: "Strasbourg-Rassemblement Charlie-11 janvier 2015 (5)" by Ji-Elle - Own work. Licenced under CC BY-SA 4.0 via Wikimedia Commons - http://commons.wikimedia.org/wiki/File:Strasbourg-Rassemblement_Charlie-11_janvier_2015_(5).jpg#mediaviewer/File:Strasbourg-Rassemblement_Charlie-11_janvier_2015_(5).jpg

After quieting down for a few years, an al-Qaeda spokesperson called for more reprisals against Denmark in early 2008, leading to the explosion of a bomb outside the Danish Embassy in Islamabad, Pakistan in June 2008. There is no way for anyone to put an end to the cartoon controversy. It continues to flare up from time to time, revealing the profound differences in underlying ideology.

The 2015 mass killings of the cartoonists and other workers at the Paris office of *Charlie Hebdo* continued the string of violence against the publications of cartoons severely critical of Islam. In reacting to the event, French President Francois Hollande emphasized that the French people should remain steadfast for freedom. Several moderate Muslim leaders denounced the killings. Some pointed out that even if the cartoons were considered to be libelous, the punishment for libel in Islamic law is not death.

Shortly after the January 2015 attacks on the office of *Charlie Hebdo*, a bomb explosion near a synagogue, and a deadly incident in a Jewish delicatessen, over 3 million people participated in "Unity Rallies" in Paris, in other French cities and throughout the world. Numerous world leaders attended the Rally in Paris, including Israeli Prime Minister Benjamin Netanyahu, Palestinian President Mahmoud Abbas, Jordan's King Abdullah II and many European leaders. Unity Rallies were also held in cities across Europe and North America. Many moderate Muslims participated in the rallies, holding signs such as "Not in Our Name" to denounce the violence.

The phrase *Je suis Charlie*, "I am Charlie," quickly emerged as a slogan expressing support for freedom of expression and post-enlightenment Western values.

Yet for some conservative Muslims any challenge to Islam is grounds for severe punishment. Just a few days after the terrorist attack on *Charlie Hebdo*, a blogger in Saudi Arabia named Raif Badawi was sentenced to a large fine, 10 years in jail, and weekly floggings of 20 lashes each over 50 weeks. Based on his blogs on a now-banned website, Liberal

Saudi Network, Badawi was convicted of cybercrime and insulting Islam. The floggings were carried out a very public way, in front of a mosque after Friday noon prayers.

OVERVIEW AND THEORETICAL DISCUSSION

Our first issue dealt with the way Turkey is caught between the European and Islamic worlds. It has been politically aligned with Europe since 1923. Yet it now finds its application for EU membership in limbo.

The second issue concerned the anti-immigration party and the religious garb law in France. We looked at the National Front as one example of the many anti-immigration, far-right parties in Europe. We saw that it is not overtly against African immigrants or Islam, but it champions the causes of non-immigrants over the policies of the ruling parties. Concerning the ban on religions garb, we saw that although most EU countries are secular in their outlook, France seems to be the most zealous about enforcing secularism in its public school system.

Our third issue dealt with the forms the anti-Islam backlash has taken in The Netherlands and Denmark. We discussed a Dutch anti-immigration party, whose leader was killed. We saw that various media have been openly critical of Islamic militancy and the alleged suppression of women in some Islamic countries. The release of films critical of the Islamic treatment of women has led to death and threats of death to those involved. The publication of a book by a former Muslim woman who is now an avid critic of the way some Muslims treat women has also led to death threats.

Theoretical Discussion: Minority Religious Rights vs. Secular Multiculturalism

The three issues of this chapter call attention to the differing worldviews of the largely secular European and the highly religious Islamic world. Besides the official reasons dealing with Turkey's relatively weak economy and unusual system of governance, there are the unofficial reasons for not admitting Turkey into the EU. Those reasons seem to come right out of Huntington's clash of civilizations theory. Many EU citizens and some EU leaders just feel that Turkey is not European enough. They worry about being overrun by workers who do not fit into the European culture.

The recent increase in headscarf wearing by Muslim school girls has led to an unending public controversy in France. With regard to the relationship of religion and politics, the crucial question concerns how to balance the religious freedoms of minority groups with traditional cultural norms of the majority. Normally, when a state styles itself as secularist, it intends to protect the rights of all religious groups without favoring any. Should there be limits to one's freedom to practice outmoded or controversial activities? Should there be limits to what one can or cannot wear in public places?

The cartoon controversy is symbolic of the conflicts between minority religious concerns and secular multiculturalism. Partly in response to previous militant Muslim attacks on artists and authors, a Danish newspaper touched off the great controversy when it published cartoons about Muhammad and Islam. The controversy has led to many deaths, mostly of Muslims caught up in protests in various Muslim countries. Tragically the wave of deaths spread all the way to Nigeria. Because the cartoons were originally published precisely to reaffirm the Western value of freedom of expression, this is a clear case of a clash between a secular Western value, freedom of expression, and the traditional religious value of safeguarding and protecting the sanctity of a prophet. In medieval Europe, someone might have been severely punished for painting Jesus in a defaming way, as John Hus was burned at the stake for seemingly lesser offense of suggesting that the Catholic Church was not using its money properly.

The troubling question of whether or not public media have the right to publish cartoons offensive to a conservative (Muslim) religious community again led to violence with the mass murder of people at the *Charlie Hebdo* magazine office in Paris. That satirical magazine had a long history of publishing severely critical stories and cartoons against the Catholic Church. As Islam became more prominent in French society, it made the editorial decision to treat Islam no better or no worse than Christianity. Yet from a traditional religious point of view, as taken by Muslims in this case, no amount of liberal talk about the freedom of the press can justify defaming the persons held in highest regard by that religion.

In post-Enlightenment Europe, should the values of artistic freedom outweigh religious sentiment? When *Charlie Hebdo* resumed publication after the deadly attack on its office, the cover of the new edition featured a cartoon of a Muslim holding a "Je Suis Charlie" sign, above which were words saying that all was forgiven. The edition quickly sold millions of copies, as people around the Western world bought it as an expression of solidary with the right to freedom of expression. The cover cartoon may have been intended as an expression of forgiveness, but radical Muslims quickly took offense and denounced the publication as yet another anti-Islamic cartoon. Many moderate Muslims also expressed regret that the pattern continued. The clash of secular values and conservative religious values was front page news.

> *We fly to North America next, to complete our round-the-world trip to understand the interface of religion and politics in the world's hot spots.*

STUDY QUESTIONS

1. What are the arguments for and against admission of Turkey into the European Union?

2. What are the historical and current reasons for France's relatively strict stance against "religious garb" in public places?

3. What are some of the planks in the party platform of Europe's rising right-wing political parties such as the Front National of France?

4. What are the issues concerning religious freedom, the arts, and conservative Islam in the Netherlands and elsewhere in Europe?

FURTHER READING

Ali, Ayaan Hirsi. *The Caged Virgin: A Muslim Woman's Cry for Reason.* London: Pocket Books, 2006. A former Muslim woman's criticism of Islamic treatment of women.

Ali, Ayaan Hirsi. *Infidel.* New York: Atria Paperback, 2007. The story of her life from childhood in Somalia to the murder of her friend Theo van Gogh.

Berluems-Stevelinck, C., Israel, J. and Meyjes, G. H. M. P., eds. *The Emergence of Tolerance in the Dutch Republic.* Leiden: Brill, 1997. Scholarly Essays.

Fourest, Caroline. *Marine Le Pen: Biographie.* Paris: Librairie Generale Francaise, 2012. A popular biography, for those who read French.

Levine, Yasemin Çelik. *Contemporary Turkish Foreign Policy.* Westport, Conn: Praeger, 1999. A good source for those interested in international relations.

Israeli, Raphael. *The Islamic Challenge in Europe.* Transaction Publishers, 2008. Warns of terrorist attacks throughout Europe.

Kastoryano, Riva. *Negotiating Identities: States and Immigrants in France and Germany.* Princeton: Princeton University Press, 2002. Compares the immigration patterns and issues in the two countries.

Koop, Marie-Christine Weidmann, ed. *France at the Dawn of the Twenty-First Century: Trends and Transformations.* Birmingham: Summa Publications, 2000. Essays by various scholars on many topics.

Lewis, Bernard. *What Went Wrong? The Clash Between Islam and Modernity in the Middle East.* New York: Oxford University Press. Paperback edition, 2003. New York: Harper. A scholar's explanation of why the Islamic world failed to modernize.

Mango, Andrew. *Turkey: The Challenge of a New Role.* Westport, Conn.: Praeger, 1994. A clearly written but now dated account.

Marcus, Jonathan. *The National Front and French Politics: The Resistible Rise of Jean-Marie Le Pen.* New York: New York University Press, 1995. A very readable account of Le Pen up to 1995.

Mastny, Vojtech and Nation, R. Craig, eds. *Turkey Between East and West: New Challenges for a Rising Regional Power.* Boulder: Westview Press, 1996. Various essays.

Tezcür, Güneş Murat. *Muslim Reformers in Iran and Turkey: The Paradox of Modernization.* Austin: University of Texas Press, 2010. Considers how moderation theory fits with the data on Muslim reformers as political actors.

WEBSITES

europa.eu/abc/history/index_en.htm   A brief history of the EU.

news.bbc.co.uk/2/hi/middle_east/4688602.stm   A *BBC News* timeline on the events surrounding publication of the cartoons.

ser.oxfordjournals.org/cgi/reprint/1/2/215.pdf   A journal article on right-wing, anti-immigration thought.

www.extremismus.com/texte/france_over.pdf   Information on France's anti-immigration movement.

www.humanityinaction.org/docs/Berghuijs__Chalker,_2002.pdf   On the rise of anti-Semitism in The Netherlands.

KEY PEOPLE

Ayaan Hirsi Ali A former Muslim and former Dutch politician who has been a leading critic of the treatment of females by some Muslim communities.

Mustafa Kemal Ataturk The secularist leader who created the modern state of Turkey out of part of the former Ottaman Empire.

Recep Tayyip Erdogan Former Prime Minister and now President of Turkey.

Pim Fortuyn Leader of a Dutch anti-immigration party who was assassinated.

Jean-Marie Le Pen The founder of the Front National in France.

Marine Le Pen Youngest daughter of Jean-Marie Le Pen who now leads the Front National party.

Theo van Gogh A Dutch film maker who was killed by a militant Muslim angry about his portrayal of Islam in his films.

Geert Wilders A Dutch politician and film maker whose controversial speeches and films have angered Muslims.

GLOSSARY

AKP The Justice and Development Party in Turkey, a moderate Islamic party led by Erdogan.

Alevis A Shi'i minority ethnic group in Turkey.

Catholicism, Roman The division of the Christian Churches that recognizes the authority of the Roman Popes.

Defenestration A term for the act of throwing someone out a window, as in the event that sparked the Thiry Years War..

EU, European Union A political and economic community of 28 states, and growing.

FN The **Front National**, or **National Front** a Right Wing French party now led by M. Le Pen.

Great Schism The eleventh-century break between the Roman and Orthodox Churches.

Laïcité The French term for secularism and the separation of religion and the state.

Orthodox Christian Church A group of churches that originated in the eastern part of the Roman Empire, as distinct from the Roman Catholic Church in the western part of the Empire.

Ottoman and Ottoman Empire A Turkish people and the empire they ruled from the region that is now known as Turkey.

Patriarchs Title for the leaders of the divisions of the Eastern Orthodox Churches.

Pim Fortuyn List An anti-immigration political party in The Netherlands from 2002–2006.

PKK The Kurdistan Worker's Party, a Kurdish separatist party of Turkey.

Protestant A adherent of one of the churches tracing its history to the Protestant Reformation.

Protestant Reformation A group of churches that broke away from Roman Catholicism in the early 1500s.

Chapter Eight

United States and Canada

The Increasing Role of Religion in Politics:
Social Activism, The Christian Right, and Islam

In this chapter you will learn about:

- Nigeria's Muslim-Christian tensions and Boko Haram
- the religious and political background of the United States and Canada
- the concept of the separation of religion and the state in the United States
- social and political activism among some liberal Christians
- the rise and concerns of fundamentalist Christianity in the United States
- the reason conservative Christians tend to be pro-Israel
- the similarities and differences between the United States and Canada
- the rise and development of the Nation of Islam
- the nature of Islam in North America[1]

> What you're doing is undermining the whole legal definition, the underpinnings of the institution of the family, and when that goes, everything goes with it, including the stability of the country... and the future of Western civilization.
>
> James Dobson on the effects of same-sex marriage.
>
> "Abolish Marriage: Let's Really Get the Government Out Of Our Bedrooms." In this revealing editorial, Michael Kinsley writes, "[The] solution is to end the insti-

---

[1]As cited in John C. Green, Mark J. Rozell, and Clyde Wilcox, Eds. 2006. *The Values Campaign? The Christian Right and the 2004 Elections.* Washington, D.C.: Georgetown Univeristy Press, p. 56.

tution of marriage, or rather, the solution is to end the institution of government monopoly on marriage. And yes, if three people want to get married, or one person wants to marry herself and someone else wants to conduct a ceremony and declare them married, let 'em. If you and your goverment aren't implicated, what do you care? If marriage were an entirely private affair, all the disputese over gay marriages would become irrelevant.

Michael Kinsley[2]

STOPOVER IN NIGERIA: A TORN STATE AND BOKO HARAM

We land at Nnamdi Azikiwe International Airport in Abuja, Nigeria. Heading downtown, we see a well-planned city that was built in the 1980s to be a more centrally-located capital, replacing the old capital, Lagos, on the southern seacoast. Along Independence Avenue we see the white, ultra-modern interdenominational National Christian Centre on one side and the Nigerian National Mosque with its golden dome and four minarets on the other. These two impressive structures remind us that Nigeria's large population of over 180 million is divided almost equally between Muslim and Christian.

Christian South versus Muslim North in Nigeria

In the past two centuries, most Nigerians have been converted to either Islam or Christianity. This religious division could lead to a future with a pluralistic democracy or else create unending conflict. So far, the latter seems to be the case. Most of the Muslims are in the north and are members of the Hausa (or Hausa-Fulani) group, who introduced Sunni Islam to the region. Most Christians are in the south and come from various ethnic groups, including the Yoruba and the Igbo, who were converted to Christianity during the colonial period. There have been numerous separatist movements, the most important of which led to the Biafran War (1967–1970) in which the Igbo sought unsuccessfully to form an independent state named Biafra.

Nigeria has good natural resources and oil reserves, but since gaining independence from Britain, political corruption and instability have kept most Nigerians from enjoying much benefit from the oil revenue.

Nigerian independence from the United Kingdom came in 1960. Unfortunately there has been considerable tension between the Christian south and the Muslim north ever since. There is no agreement about whether laws should be democratically determined or based on Shariah law. Starting in 1999, many states of the Muslim north began to govern themselves under Shariah. A limited use of Shariah goes back to the British period or

---

[2]*Washington Post*, OpEd, July 2003.

earlier. Under the influence of the Islamic resurgence movement, several northern states have moved to full Shariah law and are sentencing more strictly than in the past. For example, there has been an increased tendency for Shariah courts to impose the death penalty for adultery and the penalty of amputation of the right hand for theft.

Although these severe sentences have usually not been carried out, several of the cases involved young women perceived to be blameless victims by Nigerian Christians and the international community. This has led to protests and demonstrations.[3] For example, an Oprah Winfrey Show episode generated over a million emails about the case of Amina Lawal, a woman charged with adultery when she became pregnant after being divorced.[4]

Religion plays a big role in Nigerian politics because both Christian and Muslim Nigerians rank their religious identifications as more important than their identity as Nigerian or their tribal identity.[5]

There are Muslim minorities throughout the south and Christian minorities throughout the north. As we have seen in cases of religious minorities in other countries, Nigerian Muslims or Christians are at most risk if they are a minority in a mixed region. For example, in 2006, Muslims killed several Christians in Maiduguri in the northeast. A few days later, gangs of Igbo rioters killed several Muslims, burned Muslims shops, and burned the old mosque in the southern city Onitsha.[6]

The publications of the satirical cartoons in Denmark, as discussed in the Europe chapter, set off Muslim demonstrations and the killing of Christians in northern Nigeria. For example, sixteen people were killed during protests and violence in and around Maiduguri in 2006.[7] Some Christians in the south sought revenge against Muslims living in their areas, and the ensuing violence led to many deaths and arrests. Muslims claimed to be defending the honour of Prophet Muhammad, and Christians claimed to be revenging wrongful killings. It was another example of a cycle of violence touched off by strong religious identities.

As in other places troubled by violent extremists, peaceful leaders often arise to counter those who advocate for violence and intolerance. In the case of Nigeria, there are Christian and Muslim leaders who reject violence and work together for peace and understanding. Muslim Imam Muhammad Ashafa and Christian Pastor James Wuye are outstanding examples. They have turned from the religious-based militancy of their youths to

---

[3]For an example of the international coverage of the case of a woman charged with adultery, see www.bbc.co.uk/radio4/womanshour/2001_50_thu_05.shtml.

[4]See www.oprah.com/tows/pastshows/tows_2002/tows_past_20021004_b.jhtml.

[5]Based on a 2006 survey by Pew Forum. there are Muslim minorities throughout the south and Christian minorities throughout the north.

[6]Lydia Polgreen. 24 Feb. 2006. "Religion and politics a deadly mix in Nigeria." www.iht.com/articles/2006/02/23/news/lagos.php?page=1.

[7]19 Feb. 2006. "Nigeria cartoon protests kill 16." news.bbc.co.uk/2/hi/africa/4728616.stm.

co-found the Interfaith Mediation Centre, which has made process toward reconciliation between Muslims and Christians in Nigeria.[8]

Boko Haram's Anti-Western Extremism and an African Islamic State

Nigerian Muslims sometimes have drawn a sharp contrast between Islamic schools, with their Quran-based curriculum, and what they call the false or "fake" (boko in Hausa language) curriculum of Western style schools. This is the basis for interpreting the name Boko Haram as "Western Education is Forbidden (haram)." The organization's longer Arabic name refers to a commitment to the Sunnah and jihad.

Boko Haram was founded in 2002 by Islamists against western-style education. Its leaders are influenced by Wahhabi Islam. Starting as early as 2009, their goals included the establishment of an Islamic state based on Shariah. Recruiting for their movement may have been helped by the widespread poverty among the population of northeast Nigeria, making Boko Haram a means of employment and a hope for economic betterment for

Boko Harem poster

Photo: AK Rockefeller (Boko Haram) [CC BY-SA 2.0 (http://creativecommons.org/licenses/by-sa/2.0)], via Wikimedia Commons

---

[8]"Warriors and Brothers: Imam Muhammad Ashafa and Pastor James Wuye." In David Little. Ed. 2007. *Peacemakers in Action: Profiles in Conflict Resolution.* Cambridge: Cambridge University Press.

the region. The alleged corruption of some police, military and civil servants may also be a factor.

Boko Haram operates in Borno State in northeast Nigeria, but also in nearby states and across the border in Chad, Niger and Camaroon. Its fighters often cross into hilly border areas in Cameroon as a safe haven. The four African nations in which Boko Haram operates formed a cooperation task force to deal with the Boko Haram threat, but it did not prove to be effective. So in early 2015, as Boko Haram had gained strength enough to attack the Borno state capital, Maiduguri, the African Union agreed to form a West African Task Force consisting of 7,500 troops from Benin, Cameroon, Chad, and Niger to fight Boko Haram.

The means employed by Boko Haram have been violent to an extreme. Because it has such intense hatred for western education, Boko Haram has repeatedly attack non-Islamic schools, taking the boys and girls hostage. The boys are then trained as soldiers, and the girls are raped, killed, taken as wives, or sold as wives to raise money. The majority of the abductions have been Christians, and Boko Haram has sometimes returned Muslim girls. The abducted girls are forced to convert to Islam. Human Rights Watch has been critical of the Nigerian government's lack of security before the attacks and its failure to provide counselling or medical care for those girls who manage to escape.[9]

After nearly 300 girls were kidnapped from Chibok, Nigeria, in 2014, a social media campaign with the hashtag #BringBackOurGirls brought attention to their plight. Michelle Obama and others supported the campaign, but unfortunately it proved ineffective at either freeing the girls or stopping further attacks.

The Human Rights Watch's *World Report 2015* estimates that Boko Haram controls over 130 villages and towns in three northeastern Nigerian states and that it killed 3750 civilians in 2014 alone. It also estimates that over a million Nigerians have been displaced from their homes.[10]

In March 2015 Boko Haram's leadership pledged allegiance to the Islamic State, thus changing its affiliation from Al-Qaeda to ISIS.

The success of Boko Haram has been an embarrassment to both the Nigerian army and government. The army has been unable to keep many of its troops from deserting or keep its equipment and bases from falling into enemy hands. Former President Goodluck Jonathan's political strategy of pretending that Boko Haram had not taken control of large parts of the northeast lost credulity with each Boko Haram attack on schools and bases, thus setting the stage for his defeat in the 2015 elections.

Nigeria is an example of what Huntington terms a "Torn Country," meaning a state that is divided between two civilizations. We have seen a country torn between the western and the Islamic civilizations, with their very different notions of the basis of authority underlying the laws of the state.

[9]Mausi Segun, "Interview: Life After Escaping Boko Haram's Clutches" http://www.hrw.org/news/2014/10/27/interview-life-after-escaping-boko-harams-clutches.

[10]http://www.hrw.org/news/2015/01/29/nigeria-violence-mars-political-landscape

Our final destination is North America, where we first discuss the role played by both liberal and conservative Christians in politics as well as the increasing political presence of Muslims.

> *We arrive at Washington's Dulles International Airport, and head downtown to the National Mall area. We start at the Capitol Hill end and stroll along the Mall to take a fresh look at the interaction of religion and politics in the United States We spot museums, numerous monuments to former presidents, and several war memorials, but there is no church in the immediate area. Maybe there is some separation of religion and the state here? Yet there are major Christian churches of most the mainstream denominations nearby—Catholic, Baptist, Presbyterian, Episcopal, and others. The closest thing to an official state religious building is the Washington National Cathedral, which envisions itself promoting spiritual harmony and as a multi-faith venue for use by all for state occasions.*

RELIGION AND POLITICS: UNITED STATES AND CANADA

Separation of "Church and State" in the United States

The first amendment of the United States Constitution holds "Congress shall make no law respecting an establishment of religion, or prohibiting the free exercise thereof...." To grasp the meaning of this amendment to its original authors, one needs to understand what it means for a religion to be "established." Before the Enlightenment, it was common in Europe (and most other regions) for religion to be considered one of the functions of government. The nobility that ran the state saw it as part of their duty to set the religion of the state and to support it with both public and private funds. In Christianized Europe before the Protestant Reformation in the early sixteenth century, this meant that the state established either Roman Catholicism or Eastern Orthodoxy as the state religion. Churches were given tax-exempt status. Clergy were called upon to pray at public events as well as to officiate at baptisms, weddings, and funerals.

The Protestant Reformation, beginning in the sixteenth century, did not change this system at first. In Protestant areas, it just led to the governmental establishment of one of the various Protestant denominations. The old system of governments having an "established" religion was eventually undermined by Protestant and Enlightenment writers who tended to stress the individual nature of religious belief and practice rather than the old view that religion was part of the government structure in the broadest sense.

So, the First Amendment to the American Constitution meant, at the time at least, that the federal government should not officially support one particular denomination of Christianity in the manner of the Church of England or the Church of Scotland. The loophole, however, was that the federal constitution did not restrict the states from establishing a religion. States were free to favor one Protestant Christian denomination over others, and some did so.

In 1801 the Baptist Association of Danbury, Connecticut sent a letter to Thomas Jefferson, who had begun his presidency earlier that year, asking for clarification on this very matter. As a minority in Connecticut, the Baptists feared that the state might pass a law supporting other religious interests over their own. In fact, the Congregational Church, one of the Protestant denominations, had been enjoying tax support in Connecticut and would continue doing so until 1818. So the Baptists had some basis for their concern. Although they did not favor taxpayer support of any religion over its rivals, their main concern was for the protection of their religious liberty. It is important to note that the concept of the separation of religion and state was supported both by more secular citizens who did not want their tax dollars spent on religious institutions and by religious minorities who feared that restrictions might be placed on them by a religious majority.

Jefferson gave a carefully considered reply to the Baptists' request for clarification. His answer talked of how the First Amendment had been adopted by the whole of the American people, "thus building a "wall of separation" between church and the state.[11] So, the tradition of "separation of church and state" in the USA goes back to Jefferson's interpretation of the Federal Constitution in his letter rather than to a specific mention in the Constitution or a decision by the Supreme Court. The process of disestablishing religion (reversing legislation that favored one religion over others) worked its way through the various states, and was complete by the mid-nineteenth century. The system that evolved gave tax exempt status to religious properties and institutions, but did not transfer tax monies to religions. Later, we will discuss the "faith-based initiatives" widely used under the presidency of George W. Bush, which critics held to be a violation of the separation of church and state.

After the Civil War (1861–65), the Fourteenth Amendment defined citizenship so as to make sure that former slaves were citizens and to override the tendency of some former slave states to pass laws, referred to as "black codes," restricting the rights of former slaves. A subsequent series of Supreme Court decisions had the effect of applying the separation of religion and government to the states as well. This so-called separation of all religions from direct government support in the United States is commonly referred to as the "separation of church and state." Besides denying direct government funding of any particular religious group, it has meant that private religious schools do not receive government funding, at least not in a direct sense. The home school movement and various voucher programs have challenged that principle.

Protestant, Catholic, Jew: The Triple Melting Pot

Will Herberg's book *Protestant, Catholic, Jew* (1960) traces the religious history of the United States. He describes the waves of immigration by country of origin and religion. Approxi-

[11]Jefferson, Thomas, *Jefferson's Letter to the Danbury Baptists*, United States Library of Congress (January 1, 1802). www.loc.gov/loc/lcib/9806/danpre.html.

mately 75 percent of the first wave of immigrants was from England and Scotland, and so Protestantism, with its many denominations, became the mainstream religion of America. The waves of immigration after the War of Independence brought people from many other European countries, including Ireland, France, and Italy, where Roman Catholicism is predominant. The critical mass of Roman Catholics was then high enough in most cities to build churches and maintain Catholic identity. Herberg argued that whereas before Protestant Christianity was the only religion widely accepted as compatible with being an American, it gradually became acceptable for Americans to be either Protestant or Catholic. By the late 1800s and early 1900s, a third wave of immigration included many Jews from Germany, Russia and East Europe. As most Jews assimilated into American culture, being Jewish came to be seen as compatible with being American. However, becoming more normative in the United States did not mean that anti-Catholic or anti-Semitic sentiments had been completely eliminated.

Herberg argues that all three religions were shaped by the American experience, which grew out of the American frontier values of rugged individualism and being a self-made person. Herberg contends that what he terms the **American Way of Life** became the operative religion in America, meaning that the various forms of Protestantism, Catholicism, and Judaism had moved toward a common set of values such that it was hard to guess the religious identity of someone just from looking at their way of dressing or listening to their moral or political opinions. All three religions had been assimilated into what he called a "triple melting pot."[12] Later scholars, such as Robert Bellah, wrote of something similar to Herberg's American Way of Life, but preferred other terms for it such as **"Civil Religion."** Later we will deal with the numeric rise of Islam in North America, and in the Overview we will need to ask if Islam has become a fourth "American" religion, in Herberg's terms.

Religion and Government in Canada

The religious history of Canada differs markedly from that of the United States. Like the United States, the first wave of English-speaking immigrants in Canada was mostly Protestant. However, the French population of Upper Canada, now Quebec, was predominantly Catholic. During the period of French rule, immigrants to Upper Canada were supposed to be exclusively Roman Catholic. This may seem strange because in the Edict of Nantes in 1589 Henry IV of France had established basic rights for the Huguenots, the Protestants of France. Henry had himself been a Protestant before converting to Roman Catholicism as a condition for assuming the throne, famously saying "Paris is well worth a mass." In fact the early French settlers in Upper Canada had included both Roman Catholics and Huguenots.

Outside of Quebec there was religious diversity. Protestant denominations of Christianity predominated, but many early immigrants to Canada came from Catholic regions

---

[12]Will Herberg, *Protestant, Catholic, Jew: An Essay in American Religious Sociology* (Garden City: Doubleday, 1955), 6.

of Europe as well as Protestant or Orthodox regions. As a result, Catholicism became the dominant religion in Quebec and, alongside Protestantism, an important religion in the other provinces.

Canada did not follow the United States on the separation of church and state. John Webster Grant argues that the War of 1812 was a dividing point between the two countries.[13] Whereas the United States continued to separate itself from its European background, Canada continued to see value in its European heritage; religious and otherwise. Mark Noll suggests that the churches in Canada tended to be less independent minded, maintaining stronger ties with their European heritage. In the United States, a separation of church and state seemed the best approach, yet the Canadians tended to favor the protection of the rights of minority religions rather than a more strict separation of religion and politics. Noll concludes: "In a word, when we set Canadian religious history beside that of the United States, the chief contrast is between the Revolution that altered the shape of Christianity in the States and the Revolution that did not take place to the North."[14] Some provinces have publicly-funded religious school systems and adoption systems. In Ontario, for example, besides the non-denominational Public School system, there is the parallel Separate School system that runs elementary, middle, and high school education for Catholics. Catholic taxpayers become Separate School Supporters by opting to pay their education taxes to the Separate system rather than the public system. Each province governs its educational system, and there are many different approaches among the provinces. The new religious pluralism of Canada has brought about changes. For example, the Province of Quebec used to be known as a very pro-religion province, offering Roman Catholic instruction in its public school system. Yet that phased out in 2005.

Despite the very different histories, the percentage of Roman Catholics and of Protestants in the two countries was fairly similar according to Noll's estimates for the 1920s, which show Roman Catholics as 37 percent of the United States and 39 percent of the Canadian populations, while Protestants were 52 percent of the United States and 58 percent of the Canadian populations (see table). Besides the tensions between Protestants and Roman Catholics in both countries, the churches in the United States had to deal with the split between African American and predominantly white denominations, and the Canadian churches had to take the French-English split into account.

Rise of Fundamentalism in the United States and Canada

The first people to be called fundamentalists were ultra-conservative American Protestants in the early 1900s. The background was that Christian theological school professors were becoming increasingly divided into two camps.

---

[13]See John Webster Grant, *The Church in the Canadian Era* (Vancouver: Regent College Publishing, revised edition, 1998).

[14]Mark A. Noll, *A History of Christianity in the United States and Canada* (Grand Rapids: William B. Eerdmans Publishing Company, 1992), 161–62.

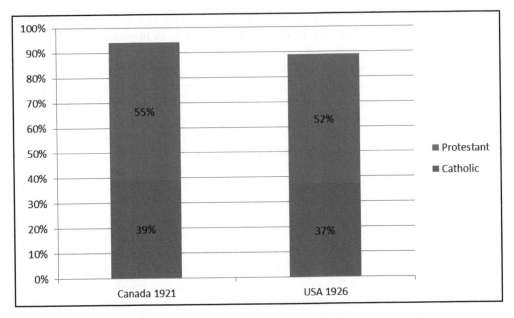

Note the similar proportions of Catholics and Protestants in the two countries.[15]

The more liberal camp had several traits in keeping with progressive thinkers of their era. For one, they tended to be open to modern science. Wherever the Bible seemed to be in blatant conflict with science, they tended to look to science for the facts and look to the Bible for the spiritual truths underlying the issue. For example, the Bible begins with the well-known story of God creating the world in six days and then resting on the seventh, the Sabbath. Taken literally, this conflicted with science in many ways. Darwin's theory of evolution suggested that the various species had evolved over millions of years, which hardly fit with the idea of God creating all the animals on a single day. So, the more liberal theologians were content to praise God as the Creator while not taking the Biblical account as the literal truth. A related liberal trait was to accept the relatively new approach to Biblical studies known as Biblical Criticism or Literary Criticism. This approach had been pioneered by German theologians and was making inroads in North America. The basic idea was to use the same literary and critical tools to understand the Bible as scholars would to understand other books. The liberals also tended to downplay the miracles in the Bible, preferring to think that the will of God could be worked without violating the laws of nature.[15]

The liberal camp got a boost when John D. Rockefeller endowed the Chicago Divinity School, which proceeded to staff itself with liberal minded scholars.

---

[15]Figures based on Mark A. Noll, A History of Christianiuty in the United States and Canada (Grand Rapids: Eerdmans, 1992), p. 463.

Some of the more conservative Christians were quite alarmed at these liberal developments in science and Biblical interpretation. They saw Darwinian evolution, Biblical Criticism and the rejection of miracles as a direct threat to the basics of Biblical faith. A group of these ultra conservatives met in Niagara in 1910. The meeting developed a list of the "fundamentals of the faith" and then later a series of tracts on the same topic. By 1920 another meeting was held, and a reporter described this new movement as "fundamentalism" due to the adherents' emphasis on the fundamentals of the faith as they saw them. Although the split between liberal and fundamentalist Christians played a significant role in the politics of many Protestant denominations, it did not play a major role in national party politics at the time.

The key traits of these fundamentalist Christians have not changed much since they were formulated in the 1910s and 1920s. The Protestant fundamentalist position is summed up in their phrase, the "inerrancy of scripture." The slogan means that the Biblical stories, such as the creation of everything in six days, are to be taken literally. Any scientific claims that there were species of animals that did not exist on earth for millions of years, and then came into existence later, therefore, has to be wrong. Similarly, any claim that humans evolved millions or billions of years after the creation of the earth must be wrong. The miracles of the Bible are to be taken as literal facts.

Fundamentalists also tended to be social conservatives, feeling that the traditional roles for women were the proper ones and that the male was supposed to be the head of the household. For a modern example of this, one website written from an evangelical Christian point of view advises that "Biblical dating" "begins (maybe) with the man approaching and going through the woman's father or family" and "is conducted under the authority of the woman's father or family or church."[16] Some studies in the United States have shown that both male and female conservative or fundamentalist Christians express more support for gender inequality than does the population at large. One study entitled "Gender and God's Word" analyzed the data more carefully by gender. It found that male and female conservative Christians tended to support gender role inequality for different reasons. For women who supported non-equal gender roles, the main determining factor seemed to be their individual belief that the Bible was the word of God. Whereas for men, the main determinant was belonging to a fundamentalist group.[17]

"Scopes Monkey Trial" (1925)

The attention of the nation focused on the conflict between liberal and literal interpretations of the Bible when the Scopes trial turned into a media circus. The trial arose after fundamentalist-minded Tennessee state legislators had passed a law making it illegal to teach evolution in public school science classes. The law had gone unchallenged until some of the leaders of the little town of Dayton, Tennessee got the idea that they could put their town

---

[16]www.pureintimacy.org/piArticles/A000000426.cfm.

[17]Charles W. Peek, George D. Lowe and L. Susan Williams, "Gender and God's Word: Another Look at Religious Fundamentalism and Sexism," *Social Forces* Vol. 69, No. 4, (June, 1991): 1205–1221.

Scopes Monkey Trial cartoon

on the map if they had a trial. They did so knowing that the American Civil Liberties Union had promised to defend anyone charged under the law. The local science teacher, John Scopes, agreed to play along. He was arrested for teaching evolution, and the trial began. Scopes later said that he did not think he had ever actually taught evolution, but the trial was not really about his guilt anyway. It was about the clash of two kinds of Protestant Christianity. In the interface of religion and politics, it was about whether humans should give final authority to science or scripture.

Scopes v. State soon got the popular name **"Scopes Monkey Trial"** because the issue that most caught the public's attention was whether or not humans evolved from primates. That concept was already widely accepted in scientific and liberal theological circles, but to conservative Christians it was considered an insult to human dignity and to the Creator. The majority of the people of Tennessee favored the fundamentalist side, whereas many—but by no means all—outsiders backed the liberal side. The prosecution was led by Democratic politician William Jennings Bryan, already famous as a three-time presidential candidate and a past Secretary of State. On the liberal side, the defense team was led by Clarence Darrow, an articulate agnostic from Chicago. Print and radio reporters flocked to Dayton for the trial, held outside under trees in the scorching summer heat of July 1925. During the trial, surprisingly little attention was given to whether or not the defendant had broken the law. It was the law itself that was on trial.

From a procedural point of view the trial took a strange twist when Darrow asked prosecution lawyer Bryan to take the witness stand as an expert in the Bible. Against the better judgement of his prosecution team, Bryan agreed to take the stand. Darrow then pressed Bryan hard with questions about apparent discrepancies in the Bible. Liberal theologians were already teaching that many passages in the Old Testament had been edited together from two or three sources, leading to numerous inconsistencies. For example, in one place it says that Noah took one pair of each kind of "clean" (edible) animals and one pair of each kind of unclean animals onto the ark. Yet in another place, it says that

Noah took seven pairs of the clean animals and one pair of the unclean ones.[18] How can you say the scripture is inerrant when it contradicts itself, Darrow demanded to be told. In the end, Bryan found himself agreeing that in places at least the Bible may need to be interpreted rather than taken literally. For example, perhaps the "days" in the six days of creation referred to "periods" rather than 24-hour days.

In another strange twist, Darrow, the defense lawyer, asked the jury to return a verdict of guilty. He wanted to appeal the case to the Tennessee Supreme Court. The jury complied and found Scopes guilty. The judge fined him $100, a sizable sum at the time. The Tennessee Supreme Court did hear the appeal and threw out the verdict on the technicality that the jury rather than the judge should have set the fine. The case was not tried again.[19] However, the divide in American opinion on the role and authority of Christian teachings in the public/political arena continues to define religion and politics in the United States.

The Bible Belt

There is a reason why conservative Christians, especially Baptists, are so strong in the south western states. As Will Herberg explains, before the Great Awakening—a period of religious revival among the American colonies beginning in the 1730s—most Protestant denominations were still connected to their European parent churches. Their clergy tended to be formally trained in seminaries located in large East coast cities. The Methodists and Baptists were more adapted to the American frontier, however. Many of their clergy were men recruited from the frontier who were comfortable travelling on horseback from small town to small town. These frontier preachers were willing to live on the hospitality of their host towns, foregoing the luxury of a settled life. So, the Methodist and Baptist denominations spread throughout the midwestern and southern states. The Baptists were especially strong in the south. Their strength there, and the conservative, Bible-based message they preached, created the social milieu known later as the Bible Belt because the regions with strong Protestant Fundementalist Christian cultures form a belt-like strip across a map of the United States.

As we will discuss below, their embrace of the Christian Right is one reason why the modern Republican Party has been able to count on the Bible Belt states as "red states." The use of blue as the color for Democratic states and red for Republican ones dates only to the 2000 Presidential elections. For those elections all the TV networks used that color scheme, following the lead of the colors on the party campaign ads and posters. Students of international politics will note that this modern American color scheme is the opposite of that used elsewhere. Red is commonly used as the color of the more left oriented parties. It is interesting that the generation of conservative American leaders who grew up hearing the anti-communist slogan "better dead than red" are now proudly using red as their party color.

---

[18]For the discrepancy in the number of animals to take on board the ark, contrast Genesis 6:20 and 7:2.

[11]For a good summary of the trial available on line, see www.law.umkc.edu/faculty/projects/ftrials/scopes/evolut.htm.

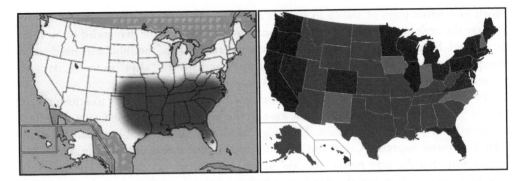

The map on the left shows the Bible Belt area of the United States, in the darker shadow. The right map shows the breakdown of red/blue states, shaded by the way each state voted in the five presidential elections of 1982–2008.

Source for the left map: http://commons.wikimedia.org/wiki/File:USA-Karte_mit_Bibelguertel.png?uselang=en-gb.
Source for the right map: Blank_US_Map.svg: User:Theshibboleth derivative work: Ninjatacoshell (Blank_US_Map.svg) [CC-BY-SA-3.0 (http://creativecommons.org/licenses/by-sa/3.0/) or GFDL (http://www.gnu.org/copyleft/fdl.html)], via Wikimedia Commons

The Social Gospel

'If ye love them that love you, what reward have ye?' declared Jesus; and in the logic of those words the whole social genius of the Christian religion is revealed. The transcendent perspective of religion makes all men our brothers and nullifies the division, by which nature, climate, geography and the accidents of history divide the human family. By this insight many religiously inspired idealists have transcended national, racial and class distinctions.[20]

—Reinhold Niebuhr

Detroit, Michigan was one of the centers of the **Social Gospel** Movement. Reinhold Niebuhr (1892–1971) was active in the Social Gospel movement, and his book *Leaves from the Notebook of a Tamed Cynic* describes his days as a social activist pastor in Detroit. He later became a famous theology professor of ethics at Union Theological Seminary in New York City. His book *Moral Man, Immoral Society*, appearing in 1932 during the Great Depression, argued that Christians are called to challenge the inhumane conditions in society. For those active in the Social Gospel in the 1930s and 1940s, those issues included the long hours and unsafe conditions in factories, the abject poverty of so many citizens, the lack of rights for women, and the discrimination against, and poverty amongst, African Americans.

The Social Gospel was primarily a Protestant movement. Walter Rauschenbusch (1861–1918), was a Baptist pastor in New York city's impoverished "Hell's Kitchen" area and later a theology professor. He is usually called the father of the Social Gospel movement, although there were others before him. In a widely used Bible study guide, he pointed out

---

[20]Reinhold Niebuhr. 1932, 1960. *Moral Man and Immoral Society: A Study in Ethics and Politics.* New York: Charles Scribner's Sons. 71–72.

that Jesus himself was quite against religion that did not lead to social improvement: "The opposition of Jesus was not, of course, against religion itself, but against religion as he found it.... He criticized the most earnest religious men of his day because their religion harmed men instead of helping them. It was unsocial, or anti-social." [21]

Social Gospel in Canada and Universal Health Care
The Social Gospel movement did not directly shape political parties or legislation in the United States, but in Canada the Social Gospel movement gave rise to Tommy Douglas, a Baptist minister turned politician who was a feisty fighter for health care and other benefits for all workers. Although he was a devout Christian, he was especially concerned with the alleviation of human suffering, seeing the church as a means of social change. He called for the "application of the gospel to social conditions."[22] He predicted, "The religion of tomorrow will be less concerned with the dogmas of theology and more concerned with the social welfare of humanity."[23] His reforms led to the creation of a political party in Saskatchewan, the Co-operative Commonwealth Federation (CCF). The CCF later united with the Canadian Labor Congress to form the **New Democratic Party** of Canada in 1961. The CBC (Canadian Broadcasting Corporation) ran a contest in 2004 in which they asked Canadians to nominate and then vote on the all-time greatest Canadian. The winner was Tommy Douglas, the man credited with bringing universal healthcare to Canada. In this context at least, Canadians seem to have appreciated the influence of religious convictions on the political process.

So, the Canadian version of the Social Gospel gave rise to the most liberal of Canada's mainstream parties, whereas the more conservative evangelical Christian movement underlies Canada's Progressive Conservative Party that later merged with today's Conservative Party.

ISSUE 1. POLITICIZED TOPICS: EVOLUTION, ABORTION, STEM CELL RESEARCH, BIRTH CONTROL, SAME-SEX-MARRIAGE

Evolution, Creation Science, Intelligent Design and the Creation Museum

The term *Christian Right* refers to a loosely defined movement of conservative or fundamentalist Christians who hold membership in or otherwise endorse one or more coalitions or organizations advocating for public policies to be based on conservative Christian val-

---

[21]Walter Rauschenbusch, *The Social Principles of Jesus* (1916), as cited in Robert T. Handy, *The Social Gospel in America 1870–1920* (New York: Oxford University Press, 1966), 372.

[22]Dave Margoshes, *Tommy Douglas: Building the New Society* (Montreal, XYZ Publishing, 1999), 30.

[23]Doris French Shackleton, *Tommy Douglas* (Toronto: McClelland and Stewart, 1975), 49.

ues. From the origins of the Protestant Fundamentalism movement in the early 1900s, the Christian Right in America has battled against the concept of evolution. Since that time, Darwinism has been one of the main dragons to be fought, but the approach of conservative Christians has changed through the decades. As we saw, the Tennessee legislature's attempt to ban the teaching of Darwinism led to the infamous "Scopes Monkey Trial." When that law was overturned by the Tennessee Supreme Court, the anti-evolutionists turned to a strategy of getting local school boards to refuse to adopt science textbooks that included a section on Darwinism and the theory of evolution. Publishers of high school science textbooks soon learned that it made good marketing sense to downplay or omit a discussion of evolution. They leave it for the teacher to introduce the topic or not, depending upon the religious stance of the teacher, the school board or the parents. A survey of 15 high school biology textbooks in 1987 found that only 6 textbooks gave a complete coverage of evolution; 4 textbooks discussed evolution among plants and animals, but avoided human evolution; 2 avoided the topic of evolution altogether; and 3 offered a balanced treatment of both evolution and creationism.[24] One source claims that 25 states now require that to be approved, if a science textbook mentions evolution is must also mention alternate theories to evolution.[25]

A 1968 Arkansas court ruling (Epperson v. Arkansas) held that laws banning the teaching of evolution violated the constitutional principle of the separation of church and state. Having been denied their first choice of banning the teaching of evolution, the creationists changed tactics. They decided to advance the idea that the Biblical concept of creation was itself a science deserving to be taught alongside of evolutionary theory. Foundations such as the Creation Research Society, the Institute for Creation Research and the Foundation for Thought and Ethics funded by Christian Right donors poured out booklets and textbooks giving equal time to **"Creation Science"** alongside "Evolutionary Science." The term "Creation Science" was used as a way of suggesting that the Biblical notion that God created the heavens and earth in a six day period only a few thousand years ago was a "scientific theory" in competition with the "theory" of evolution. A weakness, or at least a problem area, of Creation Science is that it not only has to attack the theory of the evolution of the species, it has to attack many other conclusions of modern science. To defend the Biblical notion that God created the world in six days, and only a few thousand years ago, Creation Science has to look for ways to refute the dating of the earth as billions of years old. Creation Science must ignore or refute the fossil evidence suggesting that species have arisen well after the formation of the earth, and that some species have become extinct. Many scientists objected that "Creationism" was a religious concept and not a result of any application of scientific experimentation or observation.

---

[24]Arthur Woodward and David L. Elliott, 1987, "Evolution and Creationism in High School Textbooks" *The American Biology Teacher* (Vol. 49, No. 3), 164–170.

[25]Rita Ciolli, "Book Banning and Revisions and Changes in Textbooks in America." www.aliciapatterson. org/APF0701/Ciolli/Ciolli.html

Other writers argue that the "theory" of evolution is now well documented and so well-accepted that it no longer should be considered a theory.

"Creation Science" failed to gain acceptance and was ruled to be religious in nature and therefore unconstitutional in the case of McLean v. Arkansas (1982), and the United States Supreme Court ruled against it in the case of Edwards v. Aguillard (1987). In response, concerned individuals and organizations of the Christian Right turned to the concept of "**Intelligent Design**." The idea is that the universe itself suggests that it had to have been designed by a supreme intelligence; that is, by God. Theologians quickly noted that the Intelligent Design concept is a modern name for one of the traditional philosophical arguments for the existence of God. Because it holds that the complexity and magnificence of the universe demonstrates that the universe has a purposeful End (*telos* in Greek), this approach was called the Teleological Argument. However, the philosophical arguments for God's existence used by traditional Christians traditionally were intended to enhance one's belief in God, and not to be a replacement for or equal to scientific inquiry.

The **Discovery Institute** was founded in Seattle in 1990 for the purpose of promoting the Intelligent Design concept. The Discovery Institute uses what it calls a "wedge strategy" to split the public confidence in mainstream science, splitting it like splitting a log with a wedge. Proponents of the Discovery Institute support "scholarship and writing that furthers the program of questioning the materialistic basis of science,"[26] weakening its appeal to make room for forms of "science" (such as Intelligent Design) that are not contrary to the teachings of the Bible as understood by conservative Protestant Christians. So far, the scientific community has reacted by saying that Intelligent Design is just a renaming of the old Creation Science idea, minus a specific reference to God.

The conservative Christians' struggle for influence in the school curriculum continues decades after the Scopes trial. In January 2009 the School Board of the state of Texas dropped a longstanding requirement that science teachers had to discuss the "strengths and weaknesses" of scientific theories. This was intended to give teachers the chance to downplay evolution, teaching it as a mere theory alongside other theories such as creationism. Having lost in their effort to force a classroom discussion of the weaknesses of evolution, conservatives on that Board succeeded in passing proposals to mandate teachers to "analyze and evaluate the sufficiency or insufficiency of natural selection to explain the complexity of the cell,"[27] thus undermining science in favor of belief in Intelligent Design.

The Creation Museum, Noah's Ark, and Young vs. Old Earth Creationism
In addition to efforts to shape high school science curricula and defend their position in courts of law, some Christian Right organizations have found ways to make their case in

---

[26]Philip E. Johnson, "How the Evolution Debate Can Be Won." Speech given at te 1999 *Reclaiming America For Christ Conference* called by D. James Kennedy of Coral Ridge Ministries.

[27]Michael Brick, "Defeat and Some Success for Some Texas Education Foes." *New York Times*, (March 26, 2009). http:www.nytimes.com/2009/03/27/education/27texas.html?scp=2&sq=evolution+theory+texas+school&st=nyt

an entertaining way in the court of public opinion. The **Answers in Genesis (AIG)** organization, for example, runs the Creation Museum in Petersburg, Kentucky. The Museum attracts over a quarter million visitors per year. It uses the engaging family entertainment style of a Disneyland complex to advance its position that the Genesis Biblical account is literally true and that God created the earth and all plants and animals in six days. Visitors see videos and engage with life-sized recreations of the Garden of Eden, complete with Adam, Eve and a snake. There is a large dinosaur display and a "Screaming Raptor Zip Line" experience.

AIG is also constructing a Noah's Ark exhibit in nearby Williamstown, Kentucky. The Ark, to be finished in 2016, will be a 510-foot long wooden structure with theme park style exhibits for tourist interaction as they walk through. The large size is based on AIG's interpretation of the Bible, but the size is also meant to counter any sceptic's claim that Noah's ark was not big enough to hold all the kinds of animals plus food for their voyage.

No matter how big the ark was, however, there remains the problem of showing all the planet's animals in one place and time. When an exhibit puts dinosaurs and giraffes

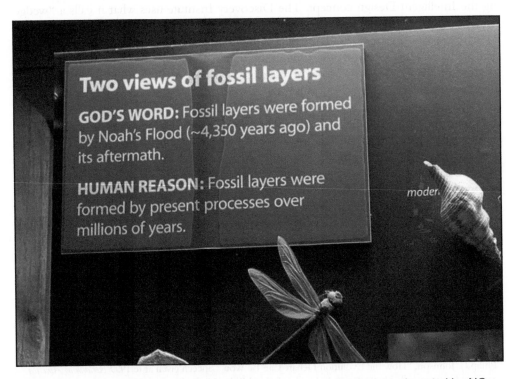

A sign at the Creation Science Museum contrasting the Young Earth view advocated by AIG with the standard scientific Old Earth view.
Photo: David Berkowitz from New York, NY, [CC BY 2.0 (http://creativecommons.org/licenses/by/2.0), via Wikimedia Commons.

together, for example, critics point out that giraffes and other large mammals didn't appear on earth until millions of years after the extinction of all dinosaurs (other than birds).

The earth age is a controversial one for some Jews and Christians who hold a strong Creationist viewpoint. The scientific consensus is that the earth is around 4.5 billion years old and the universe is over 13 billion years old, whereas the Book of Genesis has the whole universe and the earth created together, and much more recently.

Supporters of **Young Earth Creationism**, such as AIG, believe that the earth and the universe are less than 10,000 years old. The Book of Genesis does not contain any definitive date for the creation, but Jewish commentaries traditionally dated creation at around 5,000 to 6,000 years ago. This is reflected in the Jewish calendar. For example 2016 in the Western calendar corresponds to 5777 in the Jewish calendar. The ancient rabbis derived their various estimates of the year of creation by the genealogies in Genesis, which trace ancestry from Adam and Eve through to the patriarchs. Many Christian scholars have used the same approach.

There are two uncertainties in the calculations used by the Young Earth proponents as they read Genesis. This explains why the calculated date has varied. First, although the lifespan ages of some of the males in the genealogy are given, such as 969 years for Methuselah, one often has to guess how old each was when the son was born. If one estimates a typical generation as 20 versus 25 years, it makes a big difference in the date calculation. The second uncertainty is that some interpreters believe that some of the generations are missing from the genealogy list. Given these problems, the Young Earth Creationists are often content to say the earth and the universe is less than 10,000 years old, without being more specific.

The Young Earth Creationists are in direct conflict with the majority of the scientific community. Yet according to Gallup polls, about 4 of 10 Americans continue to believe that God created humans in the past 10,000 years, and in their present form.[28] This suggests that public funding for some scientific research may be in conflict with the beliefs of nearly half the population. The financial interests of Young Earth organizations may be adversely impacted as well. When AIG proposed to build its (Noah's) Ark Encounter Theme Park in Kentucky, it applied for and was led to expect $18 million in state tax incentives under the state's tourism promotion scheme. Some taxpayers objected on the grounds that it was really a religious endeavor, that it promotes the religiously-based idea that the earth is only around 6,000 years old, and that tax relief would violate the principle of separation of church and state. In December 2014 the state turned down the request for tax relief, apparently giving in to pressure from those who accept the scientific rather than the Young Earth viewpoint.

There are also **Old Earth Creationists.** They accept the scientific dating of the earth and universe, yet hold that both are the work of God. To do so, they interpret the six "days" of creation in Genesis in a figurative way. The Discovery Institute is an example of Old Earth Creationism.

---

[28]http://www.gallup.com/poll/170822/believe-creationist-view-human-origins.aspx

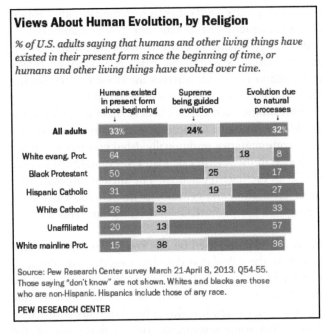

Views About Human Evolution, by Religion

% of U.S. adults saying that humans and other living things have existed in their present form since the beginning of time, or humans and other living things have evolved over time.

	Humans existed in present form since beginning	Supreme being guided evolution	Evolution due to natural processes
All adults	33%	24%	32%
White evang. Prot.	64	18	8
Black Protestant	50	25	17
Hispanic Catholic	31	19	27
White Catholic	26	33	33
Unaffiliated	20	13	57
White mainline Prot.	15	36	36

Source: Pew Research Center survey March 21-April 8, 2013. Q54-55. Those saying "don't know" are not shown. Whites and blacks are those who are non-Hispanic. Hispanics include those of any race.

PEW RESEARCH CENTER

Pew Research Center graph showing how religious affiliation impacts on acceptance of human evolution

Source: Pew Research Center (pew-research.org)

The interface of creationist religion and politics has occurred in several arenas. The effort to legislate against teaching evolution or for teaching Creationism/Intelligent Design, the strategy of taking control of school boards, the funding of court cases to defend Creationism, the founding of think tanks to promote Creation Science or Intelligent Design, and the construction of Creationist theme parks are serious attempts by conservative Christians to shape public policy in the United States. Because the percentage of Americans who believe in Creationism and the Young Earth is substantially higher than in any other Western country, these strategies have been effective.[29] Within the data for America, Republicans are more likely to hold Young Earth Creationist beliefs than are Democrats or Independents.[30]

We turn now to another key public policy concern of the Religious Right, abortion.

Abortion: A Concern of Many Religions

The idea that abortion is a form of murder and is therefore against God's will is widespread among religions. The Christian Right has made pro-life (their name for a stance against abortion) a defining issue. In the process it has found support from Roman Catholics, some moderate Protestants, as well as members of other faiths. A survey by the

---

[29]http://www.newscientist.com/article/dn9786-why-doesnt-america-believe-in-evolution.html#.VI9E1nuiWeI

[30]http://www.gallup.com/poll/155003/Hold-Creationist-View-Human-Origins.aspx

authors of *The Values Campaign?* found that 94 percent of those active for the Christian Right during the 2004 presidential campaign favored abortion restrictions.[31]

Prior to 1973, many states had laws restricting abortions, but in that year the Supreme Court heard the case of a Texas women who wanted an abortion even though Texas law allowed an abortion only if the woman's life was endangered. Her name used in court was Jane Roe. In ***Roe v. Wade***, the court ruled that under the Fourteenth Amendment, as interpreted by the court, state or local laws restricting a woman's right to privacy were null and void because a woman's right to privacy allowed her to abort until the time of the baby's viability. The Fourteenth Amendment says nothing specifically about abortion, but the court's interpretation relied upon the clause "No State shall make or enforce any law which shall abridge the privileges or immunities of citizens of the United States; nor shall any State deprive any person of life, liberty, or property, without due process of law." It held that the "due process" clause inferred a woman's right to abort a fetus up until the time that it became viable. Thus the court permitted a woman to choose an abortion during the first trimester, but allowed states to restrict but not prohibit abortions during the second trimester. It allowed states to prohibit abortions during the third trimester, when the baby would be viable.

The *Roe v. Wade* ruling meant that laws in forty-six states restricting abortion before the third trimester were struck down. Since Americans were then and still are divided fairly evenly on the abortion issue, the *Roe v. Wade* decision angered about half the population. Most, but not all of those upset by the ruling were religious persons who blamed the court for *making* legislation rather than just *interpreting* it. Commenting on *Roe v. Wade* in the *Yale Law Journal*, John Hart Ely denounces this kind of court decision: "It is bad because it is bad constitutional law, or rather because it is not constitutional law and gives almost no sense of an obligation to try to be."[32] Anti-abortionists longed for a more conservative court. This, perhaps more than any other issue, helped politicize the Christian Right. The legacy of *Roe v. Wade* continues among the Christian Right. Republican presidents tend to appoint "strict constructionists" to the Supreme Court, meaning judges who only interpret the laws passed by legislatures rather than reading their own views into their rulings. As President George W. Bush expressed it, "I don't believe in liberal, activist judges, I believe in strict constructionists."[33] Ninety-eight percent of those active in the Christian Right movement during the 2004 elections were in favor of the position "judges should only interpret the law."[34]

---

[31]John C. Green, Mark J. Rozell, and Clyde Wilcox, ed.s, *The Values Campaign? The Christian Right and the 2004 Elections.* (Washington, D. C.: Georgetown University Press. 2006), 36–38.

[32]John Hart Ely, "The Wages of Crying Wolf: A Comment on Roe v. Wade," *The Yale Law Journal* Vol. 82, No. 5 (1973): 947.

[33]Lee Epstein and Jeffrey A. Segal, *Advice and Consent: the Politics of Judicial Appointments* . (New York: Oxford University Press, 2005), 60.

[34]Green, et al, *The Values Campaign?* 37.

Some anti-abortionists have turned to violence and terrorist tactics to change public policy on abortion to conform to their religious principles. For example, Randall Terry has been arrested repeatedly for his alleged role in disrupting or bombing abortion clinics. He founded the organization Operation Rescue, now known as Operation Rescue/Operation Save America. There is a similar organization now using the original name. These groups use civil disobedience tactics to disrupt abortion clinics. They have managed to get some clinics to close by repeated disruptions and publicity. The Army of God organization is much more militant. It holds that violence against those involved with abortion is justified. Army of God militant Paul Hill, a Presbyterian minister until he was excommunicated in 1993, killed abortion doctor John Britton and a security guard in 1995. He was found guilty and executed under Florida law in 2003. He is looked upon as a martyr to the cause by his supporters. John Salvi, another Army of God member with a Roman Catholic background, was convicted of killing two women and wounding others when he ambushed an abortion clinic in Massachusetts. The Ku Klux Klan puts a racist spin on the abortion issue. It condemns abortion for whites, but helps fund abortion clinics in African American neighborhoods.

Stem Cell Research: A Concern of Many Anti-Abortionists

One study found that faith-based voter behavior was particularly strong among those interested in the issue of **stem cell research**.[35] Embryonic stem cell research involves the extraction of stem cells from embryos only a few days old for the purpose of deriving new cures to several illnesses. The reason for using these cells is that they still have the potential to develop into any kind of cell. Therefore, the possibility exists for finding a way to cultivate stem cells that might be usable for transplant into humans. The embryos used are ones left over from fertility clinics and they would have otherwise have been discarded. At fertility clinics, it is normal procedure to cultivate more embryos than needed, and then discard the unused ones. Anti-abortionist advocates have seized on embryonic stem cell research as a form of abortion. President George W. Bush backed this position, In 2001 he froze federal funding to any research project involving new lines of stem cells. President Obama, using an executive order, reversed this policy shortly after taking office in 2009.

Having been stopped from developing new stem cell lines under George W. Bush, United States researchers looked for new approaches, such as extracting cells from the embryos without harming them, or by using cells from umbilical cords.

Canada did not follow the United States in this decision. The Canadian Institute of Health Research published guidelines in 2002 allowing the use of embryonic stem cells for research as long as they are leftovers from *in vitro* fertilization and are used with permission. Unlike the United Kingdom and South Korea, Canada did rule out the cloning

---

[35]Barbara Norrander and Jan Norrander. "Stem Cell Research and the 2004 Election" in *A Matter of Faith: Religion in the 2004 Presidential Election,* ed. David E. Campbell (Washington, D.C.: The Brookings Institute, 2007), 142 ff.

of embryos solely for research. One of the Canadian successes has been in transplanting stem cells into persons suffering from Parkinson's disease. Canadian and other scientists are also working on alternate, less objectionable ways to get stem cells. One promising way is to use the "adult stem cells" already found in the brain.[36] If scientists can find ways to accomplish their goals of developing new medical treatments without using any cells from unused fertility clinic embryos, then "stem cell research" ceases to be a public policy issue for religious conservatives.

Birth Control and Sex Education

The Roman Catholic Church's longstanding ruling against using artificial birth control devices is well known, but according to surveys, that restriction is not followed by many North American Catholics. Actually, religious objection to birth control found its way into a series of nineteenth-century legislation referred to as the Comstock Laws. The 1873 federal version of these laws made it illegal to distribute birth control, abortion and other birth control methods considered lewd via the United States Postal Service. Many states followed this with similar laws at the state level. Later court challenges restricted the nature of materials considered too obscene to be mailed. An 1879 Connecticut law, largely unenforced, banned the use of any kind of birth control drug or device, which meant that clinics such as Planned Parenthood were engaging in illegal counselling and distribution of birth control means. In the 1960s the law was deliberately challenged. Estelle Griswold, the Executive Director of Planned Parenthood, was found guilty of violating the old statute. The ban was upheld on appeal at the state level. Yet in 1965 the United States Supreme court ruling in *Griswold v. Connecticut* struck down the state law, reversing the decision on the grounds that the Constitution implied a right to privacy for married couples. In 1972 the Supreme Court broadened the application of the privacy argument to cover unmarried couples as well.

The practice of birth control by abortion remains extremely controversial and the Christian Right has strongly opposed it. The Christian Right denounces the legalization of "morning after" birth control pills and medications such as RU486 that provide a high enough level of hormones to prevent the formation of a placenta. Because the Christian Right defines "life" as beginning with conception, they believe even a fertilized egg is a life to be protected. Thus, they oppose these drugs, asserting that their use amounts to abortion. Such pills have been commonly used in Europe since their introduction in France in 1999. Although they are available by prescription, there has been great resistance to them by religious conservatives in the United States. A group of conservative legislators with a strong anti-abortionist stance introduced the Schoolchildren's Protection Act[37] in the United States House of Representatives in 2009. The bill, if it had passed, would have

---

[36] Brian Bergman, "Canada Is in the Vanguard of Stem Cell Research," *MacLean's Magazine* (May 30, 2005). www.thecanadianencyclopedia.com/index.cfm?PgNm=TCE&Params=M1ARTM0012779.

[37] The bill was referred to as HR 2458.

withheld federal funds from schools that make "emergency contraception," pills available to be taken after sexual intercourse to prevent pregnancy.[38]

Another birth control-related concern has to do with sex education in schools. Many liberal Americans, as reflected in the positions of organizations such as the American Psychological Association and the American Medical Association, tend to support the idea that their children should be getting information on the biology of sex in schools, including information on how to avoid unwanted pregnancies. This approach leads to a "comprehensive" sex education curriculum, with students introduced to various aspects of biology and sexuality appropriate to their age levels. With the strong support of religious lobbying groups, the United States Congress included funding for "abstinence only" programs in the Social Security Act of 1996, in an attachment known as "Title V, Section 510 Abstinence Education Programs." This meant that funding could only go to sex education programs that did not advocate any means of birth control other than sexual abstinence. At the time, proponents of the Title V expected the programs to reduce the rate of premarital sex and unwanted teenage pregnancies. Some critics predicted that using only the "abstinence-only" approach would lead to less knowledge among teens of how to prevent sexually transmitted diseases and unwanted pregnancies. One provision of the Act called for a follow up study to determine the program's effectiveness. That study, published in 2007, offered the following summary: "Findings indicate that youth in the program group were no more likely than control group youth to have abstained from sex and, among those who reported having had sex, they had similar numbers of sexual partners and had initiated sex at the same mean age. Contrary to concerns raised by some critics of the Title V, Section 510 abstinence funding, however, program group youth were no more likely to have engaged in unprotected sex than control group youth."[39]

In a 1999 study in the United States, 58 percent of high school principals reported that their schools followed the comprehensive approach, while 34 percent described their school's approach as abstinence-only.[40] Just over half of the principals surveyed reported that religious leaders were either "very involved" (15 percent) or "somewhat involved" (36 percent) in the process of setting the school curriculum.[41]

The Christian Right, with its stress on the family, prefers to leave sex education to the parents. It favors the approach known as "abstinence only" until marriage. The abstinence only approach often encourages young persons to take a virginity pledge, promising to remain a virgin until marriage. A study published in the journal *Pediatrics* in 2008 found that, on average, teens who had taken the virginity pledge were no more likely to avoid premarital sex than others, and were less likely to use birth control protection when they did engage in premarital sexual activity. It did note, however, that conservative religious

---

[38]www.govtrack.us/congress/bill.xpd?bill=h111–2458.

[39]See http://aspe.hhs.gov/hsp/abstinence07/index.cfm.

[40]www.kff.org/youthhivstds/1560-PressReleasesexed.cfm.

[41]www.kff.org/youthhivstds/loader.cfm?url=/commonspot/security/getfile.cfm&PageID=13531

teens, including ones who have taken the virginity pledge, do tend to have their first sexual experience at a much later age, at age 21 compared to 17 for others.[42]

The Christian Right is particularly against school-based education about birth control devices on the grounds that it might promote premarital sex and abortions. Liberal critics counter that the Christian Right has it backwards. They argue that if one wants to reduce the number of abortions, one should promote sex education and make birth control devices available in schools. However, this argument does not convince many Christian conservatives because their abstinence only policy wants to eliminate both abortions and premarital sex. One public opinion poll showed the 81 percent of Americans prefer that schools combine the two approaches, teach abstinence as a goal while also providing education about how to prevent unplanned pregnancy and sexually transmitted diseases.[43]

Same-Sex Marriage, the 2004 U.S. Elections, and the Right to Refuse Service

The authors of the essay "Saving Marriage by Banning Marriage: The Christian Right Finds a New Issue in 2004"[44] argue that, leading up to the 2004 presidential campaign, the Religious Right was short on fresh issues to aid in their recruitment of volunteers and donations, and that they benefited from the same-sex marriage issue.

The same-sex marriage issue was the first new issue with significant public appeal since the debate over inclusion of gays in the military in early 1993. The same-sex marriage issue presented several opportunities to the Christian Right movement. Unlike other issues on the Christian Right agenda, the opposition to same-sex marriage issue attracted majority support in 2004. In some states, popular opposition to same-sex marriage was overwhelming.[45]

The authors suggest that the same-sex marriage issue quickly became the top item for the Christian Right in the 2004 campaign. It allowed them to form new coalitions across religious and racial lines, and it led to new state organizations. It rallied conservative religious voters in some states where they had not been a significant factor before. Yet post-election analysis indicates that this may not have been a decisive factor in the election of George W. Bush over Al. Gore.[46]

The Massachusetts Supreme Court ruled in 2003 that legislation banning same-sex marriage was unconstitutional, so same-sex civil marriages became legal in the state in 2004. Connecticut did the same in 2008, and in 2009 Iowa and Vermont did as well, all because of court rulings rather than political supports. Voters in Maine intervened in an

---

[42]www.cnn.com/2008/HEALTH/12/30/virginity.pledges/index.html?iref=storysearch.

[43]www.kff.org/womenshealth/loader.cfm?url=/commonspot/security/getfile.cfm&PageID=14903.

[44]Clyde Wilcox, Linda M. Megolla, and David Beer. "Saving marriage by Banning marriage: The Christian Right Finds a New Issue in 2004," in *The Values Campaign?*, ed. Green et al.

[45]*Ibid.*, 58.

[46]http://journals.cambridge.org/action/displayAbstract?fromPage=online&aid=296249.

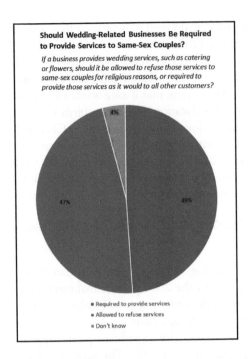

Should Wedding-Related Businesses Be Required to Provide Services to Same-Sex Couples?

If a business provides wedding services, such as catering or flowers, should it be allowed to refuse those services to same-sex couples for religious reasons, or required to provide those services as it would to all other customers?

4%
47%
49%

■ Required to provide services
■ Allowed to refuse services
■ Don't know

Pew Research Center graphic showing how evenly split Americans are on the matter of providing services for same-sex marriages.

effort to stop same-sex civil marriages in 2009. The California Supreme Court forced the legalization of same-sex marriage in May 2008. Proposition 8, passed by California voters the following November, limited marriage to opposite-sex couples. A challenge to the ban on same-sex marriage was filed in federal court and succeeded. Arguments grounded in strongly-held religious convictions may be heard on both sides of the debate. Those against same-sex marriage appeal to Biblical passages and traditions in which marriage is always between a man and a woman. Proponents of same-sex marriage argue that it is a matter of fairness, equality and basic human rights. The courts have tended to give more weight to the human rights and fairness arguments. The California Supreme Court, for example, held that discrimination on the basis of sexual orientation is no more permitted than discrimination on the basis of race or gender.[47] Besides the religious-based concerns, there are serious financial and public policy implications, such as insurance and employee benefit coverage, or spousal involvement in critical decisions involving hospital care.

Can someone who does not approve of same-sex marriage refuse to provide services to such a marriage on religious grounds? For example, should a member of the clergy be able to refuse to conduct the ceremony? Should it be public policy that a caterer, formal attire provider, or flower provider be allowed to refuse to provide that service for a same-sex marriage? A Pew Research poll in 2014 showed United States residents to be almost evenly split on the matter of providing services.[48]

[47]www.latimes.com/news/la-me-gay-marriage17-2008may17,0,7229587.story.

[48]http://www.pewresearch.org/fact-tank/2014/09/22/5-takeaways-about-religion-and-politics-before-the-midterms/

A wave of "Religious Freedom" bills and laws swept through many conservative states in 2015. A 1993 federal law, the Religious Freedom Restoration Act, was intended to protect minority religious persons from undue infringement on their religious practices. In 1997 the Supreme Court ruled that the federal law did not apply to states, so various states undertook to pass their own legislation. As with the federal law, the official intent of the legislation was to safeguard the rights of citizens to practice their religious traditions. Critics of the state versions of religious freedom laws pointed out that in the more than two decades since the federal law passed, gay rights had increased and some states had legalized same-sex marriages. So, rather than protecting the rights of religious minorities, critics feared that the real intent of the new laws was to allow persons or businesses to refuse services to same-sex weddings on religious grounds.

The Indiana religious freedom law received the most attention. On the positive side, conservatives in other states including Arkansas and Michigan soon initiated or renewed their support for similar laws. On the negative side, liberal supporters of gay rights soon brought both moral and economic pressure on the State of Indiana and its governor, Mike Pence. The economic pressure included announcements by numerous businesses and sport organizations that they would no longer do business or hold sports events in the state if it continued to discriminate against gays and lesbians. Gov. Pence attempted to soften the potential economic blow to his state by calling a press conference in which he declared that the law was not discriminatory in intent or practice, but critics did not accept this defense of the law because the freedom to refuse services seemed be the flip side of discrimination. Their fears were supported when the Indiana legislators had defeated amendments to the law that would have made it clear that the law did not override anti-discrimination concerns.

The fact that Gov. Pence was a possible Republican nominee for the 2016 Presidential Election brought media attention to his support of the law. Republican presidential hopefuls had to clarify their positions.

In June 2015 the US Supreme Court ruled, based on the equal protection clause in the 14th amendment, that same-sex couples could not be denied this fundamental right. Social conservatives and states-rights advocates objected strongly. Conservative states began exploring ways to avoid making the change, while public opinion polls showed majority support for the decision.

Anglican Church in Canada Split over Same-Sex Marriage

The issue of homosexuality has played a big role in church politics as well as in government politics. All of the attention given to the topics of homosexual rights and same-sex marriage in the political and court arenas has forced religious organizations to debate or make controversial decisions on whether or not to recognize same-sex marriage or ordain gay or lesbian clergy. In this case, politics and public policy have spilled over into organized religions. The **Anglican Communion**, the worldwide network of Anglican Churches, has been particularly hard hit by controversy over homosexuality.

Historically, the Church of England spread to the numerous British colonies, where it formed national churches with "Anglican" in their names. The Anglican Church of the United States was renamed the Episcopal Church to distance itself from England during the War of Independence. For decades there was a family of Anglican Churches, known as the worldwide Anglican Communion, under the leadership of its senior bishop, the Archbishop of Canterbury. However, the world Anglican movement split in two mainly over the issue of whether or not the Church should bless same-sex marriages and ordain persons openly living in a same-sex relationship. In 2008, James Packer, a best-selling conservative Anglican theologian, officially resigned from membership in the Vancouver Diocese. He was protesting because its head, Bishop Michael Ingham, and other bishops had taken a stance allowing rituals blessing same-sex marriages. Parker called this stance "arguably heretical." Earlier that year, several Anglican congregations broke away from the Anglican Church of Canada to form the Anglican Network of Canada, recognizing a South African Bishop as their spiritual head and adhering to the position that the Bible considers homosexuality a sin. The Anglican Church of Canada refused to endorse same-sex blessings during a heated meeting in 2007, but some local divisions of that Church do endorse such blessings.[49]

The worldwide Anglican Church has experienced other defections over the issue of blessing same-sex marriages. Two African bishops started a break-away network of Anglican congregations opposed to same-sex blessings and the ordination of gay clergy. Known as the Anglican Mission in the Americas, several United States and Canadian congregations are now affiliated with this conservative organization.

ISSUE 2. THE CHRISTIAN RIGHT IN POLITICS: MORAL MAJORITY, CHRISTIAN COALITION, FAITH-BASED INITIATIVES, SUPPORT FOR ISRAEL, CANADA

"There's the religious absolutism of the Christian Right, a movement that gained traction on the undeniably difficult issue of abortion, but which soon flowered into something much broader; a movement that insists not only that Christianity is America's dominant faith, but that a particular, fundamentalist brand of that faith should drive public policy, overriding any alternative source of understanding, whether the writings of liberal theologians, the finds of the National Academy of Sciences, or the words of Thomas Jefferson."

—Barack Obama[50]

---

[49]Douglas Todd. "Evangelical wades into Anglican fray." *The Vancouver Sun* (April 26, 2008). communities. canada.com/vancouversun/blogs/thesearch/archive/2008/04/26/top-evangelical-theologian-leaves-anglican-church-of-canada.aspx.

[50]Barack Obama, *The Audacity of Hope:.*(New York: Random House. 2006), 38.

The Christian Right Goes Political

Now we will discuss the increasing role of the Christian Right in party politics as a way of shaping public policy around abortion, same-sex marriage, and their other concerns.

Historically, Americans did not form political parties along religious lines. Unlike many European countries, the United States did not have a "Christian Democratic" or other religion-based party. Christian Democratic parties in Europe had grown partly out of Pope Leo XIII's 1891 encyclical *Renum Novarum* ("Of New Things") which embraced the cause of the poor working classes and laid down a "Christian" middle ground between communism and unregulated capitalism. The Catholic encyclical did not carry so much political weight in the predominantly Protestant United States, where all major parties drew support from a majority Christian base and the idea of separating religion and politics made it seem inappropriate to name a party after any religion. This changed, beginning with the rise of consciously Christian third parties in the 1970s and continuing with the absorption of the Christian Right movement into the Republican Party by 2000.

The Moral Majority

The **Moral Majority** organization was founded in 1979 in part by the Reverend Jerry Falwell, a televangelist and a prominent pastor of a Baptist megachurch (one with a very large congregation) in Virginia. The name reflected the organization's belief that the policies it lobbied for were consistent with the moral beliefs of the majority of Americans. The movement was rooted in conservative, Protestant Christianity of the type that critics might call fundamentalist but that followers call Evangelical. The term *evangelical* derives from the Greek word for *gospel*, so all Christians could be called evangelical in the sense of believing in the gospel. But in the modern North American context, Christians who self-identify as Evangelicals tend to believe in the inerrancy of the Bible, the need for a personal conversion experience (becoming a "reborn" Christian), and the mission of spreading Christianity at home and abroad. As a group, they tend to be socially as well as religiously conservative. The Moral Majority grew out of Protestantism and was based in the Bible Belt states of the southern United States. The Moral Majority was intended to include Catholics and Jews who shared its political agenda. Falwell remained a Baptist pastor, but in founding the organization he consciously deviated from the Baptist tradition of keeping religion and politics separate.

The Moral Majority's various political action committees lobbied at the state and federal levels for laws it deemed important. At its zenith, it had over a million supporters, including many elected Republicans and Democrats. Under the leadership of Falwell, it took a strong anti-abortion stance and condemned homosexuality as being against Biblical teachings and against the norms of family life. It lobbied against the passage of the proposed (but never ratified) Equal Rights Amendment, which would have given women constitutionally guaranteed equal rights, because the Moral Majority favored a more traditional view of the role of the woman in family life. It found the women's liberation movement to be in conflict with its version of the traditional, ideal family with the male as the head of the family and the wife as the nurturer of the children. Its lobby, along with several others (including some labor unions), contributed to the failure of the effort to gain ratification by enough states to pass.

Announcing that the Moral Majority had achieved its goals, the organization was dissolved by Jerry Falwall in 1989. It is credited with bringing the Christian Right into the political process, and with paving the way for the Christian Coalition.

The Christian Coalition of America

The Reverend Pat Robertson was a candidate in the Republican presidential primary in 1988, but lost to George H. W. Bush, who went on to win the election. After his unsuccessful bid for the presidency, Robertson founded the Christian Coalition, Inc., later renamed the **Christian Coalition of America** (CCA). Like the Moral Majority, it was not a political party. Its main mission was to shape laws and public policy through various means, especially finding and supporting candidates who agreed with its agenda. This was a somewhat different approach. It was based upon the observation that lobbying elected officials might not be as effective as getting the right candidates elected in the first place. So, the Coalition worked to get conservative Christians nominated and elected to public office at all levels. It published **voter guides** critical of incumbents who had not voted in ways favored by the Coalition. As we will discuss, these guides were very effective for their target audience. The Coalition peaked in the mid-1990s. It is no longer a major influence on American politics, although its spirit lives on in the broader movement known as the new Christian Right.

Successful Partnership with the Republican Party

The Reverend Pat Robertson had stated publicly that his goal was "to elect a pro-family Congress by 1994 and a pro-family president by 2000."[51] With the help of the Christian Right in state elections in 1994, the Republican Party did in fact retain control of both houses of Congress for the first time in four decades. George W. Bush rode a pro-family agenda to a slim victory in 2000. This was a big achievement for both the Republican Party and the Christian Right. One of the strengths of the movement is that it can use existing churches as its bases. Rather than having to recruit a base of party supporters, rent a headquarters and pay for publicity, the Christian Right has been able to use both the people and the buildings of the churches. It is a political movement anchored in a particular kind of faith, but not limited to a specific denomination. The unofficial home base of the movement, however, is the Southern Baptists, a very large branch of Protestantism.

Voter Guides

One of the successful tactics of the Christian Right has been the use of **voter guides**. These guides usually rate each candidate in the local, state, or federal race according to their position on a variety of issues important to the Christian Right. For example, on the abor-

---

[51]Green et al, *The Christian Right in American Politics*, 2.

tion issue, the candidate will have a checkmark under either pro-life or pro-choice. This approach leaves little room for the nuances of political debate. Nor does the candidate have any input into the way he or she is ranked. The result is a voter guide that greatly favors the religiously conservative candidates. Millions and millions of these voter guides are distributed during elections in shopping malls, street corners, and especially in churches. The churches occasionally have been challenged for doing this on the basis that, as tax exempt religious institutions, they legally are not allowed to actively campaign for a particular party. The churches get around this potential problem by handing out voter guides that do not specifically promote a political party, but only list the positions of individual candidates. Another way around the potential mixing of religion and politics is for the voter guides to be handed out to the members on the edge of church property as they leave the service. Still, some critics feel that the promotion of voter guides by churches crosses a line and mixes religion and politics too much.

A voter guide distributed by the Family Research Council in 2012.
Source: http://downloads.frcaction.org/EF/EF12F14.pdf

Do voter guides work? A 1996 survey found that 20 percent of Americans reported that voter guides had influenced their voting decision. But this percentage was dramatically higher among conservative Protestants, with 48 percent reporting that they had been influenced by Christian conservative organizations in their voting decisions. By way of comparison, the figure was 21 percent of persons who self-identified as liberal Protestants and 28 percent of those identifying as Catholics.[52] The Christian Right has not always been successful, and their approach has varied from state to state. Sometimes they have followed a confrontational approach, demanding that they have a veto over the Republican Party's candidate. Other Christian Right organizations have adopted a consolidation strategy in which they work with the party to achieve the nomination of the best candidate possible from their point of view. Some research suggests that the Christian Right has been much more successful where it has used the consolidation rather than confrontational strategy.[53]

Faith-Based Initiatives

During the 2000 Presidential campaign George W. Bush put great emphasis on **"faith-based initiatives."** The concept was to channel government funding to religious and social organizations. Rather than directly funding programs intended to help the poor or disadvantaged, advocates argued that existing faith-based organizations, such as churches and church related institutions, could do the job more efficiently because they already had a base and infrastructure. They would also do it better because they knew their communities well.

As the authors of the book *Of Little Faith: The Politics of George W. Bush's Faith-Based Initiatives* write, during the campaign period "the potential political support was bipartisan, broad-based, and reflective of a variety of points on the political spectrum."[54] After Bush won the election, the faith-based initiatives bills failed to gain support in Congress, especially in the Senate. One difficult issue concerned the control of hiring in faith-based organizations (FBOs). Would religious groups be required to follow the usual government guidelines when staffing their projects, which prohibited hiring on the basis of religious affiliation? Or could they insist on hiring someone of the faith and denomination of the organization? Another issue had to do with whether or not faith-based organizations were really all that cost-efficient as a means of helping the poor. Proponents had assumed that faith-based initiatives would be more cost-effective, yet there was no way to prove that in advance of trying it. Then there was the difficult task of defining what "faith-based" meant. Would all faiths be eligible? What if bogus organizations were created to take advantage of the opportunity? What rules would apply? Finally, members of both sides of the House began to question whether the proposed

---

[52]Mark D. Regnerus, David Sikkink, Christian Smith. 1999. "Source Voting with the Christian Right: Contextual and Individual Patterns of Electoral Influence." *Social Forces*, vol. 77, 1384–1386.

[53]Green et al, *The Christian Right in American Politics*, 3.

[54]Amy E. Black, Douglas L. Koopman, and David K. Ryden, *Of Little Faith: The Politics of George W. Bush's Faith-Based Initiatives* (Washington, D.C.: Georgetown University Press, 2004), 265.

legislation might take the country down the slippery slope leading to the non-separation of "church and state." Partisan politics was also a factor. Bush had just barely won the election—depending on how one treated the infamous "hanging chads" of the ballots in the predominately Democratic areas of Florida—and so the Democrats did not want to let the Bush White House look good in its faith-based endeavors. Regardless of the outcome, the gap separating religion and politics had been closed a little.

Charitable Choice and Executive Orders
Ultimately, Congress did not enact any faith-based initiatives, but that was not the end of the story. The Bush White House put its faith-based initiatives into effect by two means. One was to use existing legislation. During the Clinton era, provisions were added to several bills allowing for "charitable choice," a concept that would allow federal or state administrators to channel funds to religious organizations without the restrictions previously used. However, the charitable choice legislation had been passed without much debate and had hardly been used or even known by politicians or funding administrators. So, the Bush White House was able to use that legislation to move forward its concept of faith-based initiatives. The other way was by executive order, a form of presidential degree used frequently by the George W. Bush White House. By issuing a series of executive orders, President Bush was able to create or expand several faith-based programs.[55] The result was that most branches of the government no longer needed to avoid funding organizations with direct or explicit religious identities.

Did the faith-based projects work well or not? That is the question addressed in the book *Charitable Choice at Work: Evaluating Faith-Based Job Programs in the States* by Sheila Kennedy and Wolfgang Bielefeld. Its authors first call our attention to the problem of definition. It is not clear how precisely to say whether or not a certain group is a FBO. Does it depend on the personal faith of the workers? If so, the term would encompass many programs funded through the years. Does it mainly depend on whether or not the funding is housed in a church or other religious building? That was the criterion typically used by previous federal administrations, whether Democrat or Republican, the "charitable choice" provisions had the effect of removing that barrier. Or is the crucial thing that makes a program 'faith-based' the inclusion of some religious component? One expert who was called upon to make suggestions for implementing the programs found that the federal administrators themselves held a wide range of ideas about the goals of the programs. The range went from those who just wanted to "level the playing field" for faith-based applicants to those who made the "faith-factor" the central concern.[56]

Supporters of the programs point to the way in which money has been channelled to some groups that would not have previously received funding. Critics say it blurs the

---

[55]See Appendix C "Executive Orders Affecting Faith-Based Policies, 2001–2002" in Black et al, *Of Little Faith*. 297–308.

[56]Sheila Suess Kennedy and Wolfgang Bielefeld, *Charitable Choice at Work: Evaluating Faith-Based Job Programs in the States* (Washington, D.C.: Georgetown University Press, 2006), 174–175.

separation of church and state while not accomplishing anything very new. Before the Bush administration used charitable choice and executive orders to fund FBOs, large amounts of funding went to the Salvation Army, Catholic Charities, and other religious based groups judged to be helping the impoverished. The real difference under the Bush administration was that more religious organizations were able to qualify for funding. However, that change does not seem to have made a measurable difference in alleviating poverty, as hoped by proponents, nor in undermining the separation of church and state, as feared by critics.

The Obama White House continued to allow funding to flow to faith-based organizations, while making some administrative changes under the new title "White House Office of Faith-Based and Neighborhood Partnerships."[57] The new focus was providing information to organizations on the various funding opportunities which would best match their objectives.

Faith-based Initiatives in Canada

The controversy over funding for faith-based initiatives erupted in Canada in March 2010 when a proposal for public funding for a multimillion-dollar youth recreation center in Winnipeg, Manitoba came under attack by politicians and critics of mixing religion and public projects. The project's supporters, led by Winnipeg Mayor Sam Katz, assured the public that the organization receiving the funding, Youth for Christ (YFC), was not going to attempt to convert the youth. New Democratic Party Member of Parliament (MP) Pat Martin criticized the plan to use large amounts of funding funds for a project operated by what he termed a "fundamentalist group." Martin asked, "What if the group was called Youth for Allah?"[58] Other critics also doubted that YFC was not out to convert youth to their version of Christianity, quoting from the organization's mission statement: "To impact every young person in Canada with the person, work and teachings of Jesus Christ and discipling them into the Church."[59] The YFC website expresses pride in being a faith-based organization, but affirms that it welcomes all youth into its programs and does not coerce them to become Christian.[60] The project did receive over six million dollars (Canadian) in municipal and federal funding, but controversy continued when the YFC refused to provide a detailed accounting of its services.[61]

Religion and Voter Behavior in Presidential Elections

Although the Republican Party has become closely aligned with the Christian Right, that has not meant that most Christians vote Republican. Most Christians who identify themselves as Evangelicals do vote Republican. Yet moderate and liberal Christians, whatever

---

[57] See http://www.whitehouse.gov/administration/eop/ofbnp

[58] http://www.cbc.ca/canada/manitoba/story/2010/02/18/mb-pat-martin-christian-facility-winnipeg.html#

[59] http://yfccanada.com/ourvisionc1.php.

[60] https://yfccanada.org/

[61] www.cbd.ca/canada/manitoba/youth-for-christ-not-obligated-to-justify-programs/.2649045

their party affiliation, tend not to make the religious profile of a candidate a decisive factor in their decision. Several studies of voter behavior have confirmed a strong correlation between being a Christian Evangelical and voting Republican in recent elections. However, this strong correlation applies only to white Evangelicals. African Americans show a strong preference for the Democratic Party, and while most are members of an evangelical church, their preference for Democrats seems to trump their evangelical membership. One voter behavior researcher writes, "Even when just looking at African Americans, the relationship between membership in an evangelical church and voting Republican remains negative."[62] However, in the 2004 presidential elections there was enough of a shift among African American Evangelicals toward voting Republican to help George W. Bush carry the crucial states of Ohio, Florida, and Wisconsin. Compared to Al Gore in 2000, John Kerry received around 20 percent less of the African American evangelical vote.[63]

When researchers look at the broader correlation between all Christians, not just Evangelicals, the waters become quite muddy for anyone trying to use religion as a predictor of voter behavior. Diana Forster notes, "The most striking aspect of the comparison of the coefficients across all religions is the sheer lack of any significant coefficients for the denominational measures."[64] One researcher found significant differences between the 2000 and 2004 presidential races: "In 2000, mainline Protestants, evangelical Protestants, black Protestants and Catholics were all at least marginally more likely to vote for Bush than those who claimed no religion; yet, in 2004, the signs for all of the coefficients are switched, indicating that Christians were more likely to vote for Kerry than those who claimed no religion."[65] The explanation for the weakening role of religion in 2004 voter behavior may be that for many voters, their stance on the Iraq war trumped their religion. "In the relatively peaceful climate of the 2000 election, religiosity exerted a powerful impact on presidential vote choice; however, in 2004, religious concerns appear to have been displaced by the saliency of the war in Iraq. I conclude by suggesting that the increased importance of foreign policy in presidential elections has resulted in at least a temporary decline in the influence of religion...."[66]

A series of polls taken by NBC News during the Congressional elections of 2006, 2010 and 2014 found that among Republican voters, the percentage of those who identified as white Evangelicals or born again Christians rose from 70 to 78 percent over those eight years. The data indicates that the close alliance between white Christian Evangelicals and the Republican Party is getting even stronger.[67]

---

[62]Brad Lockerbie, "Religion and Voting in the 2004 election: A Question of Black and White." (2007). www.allacademic.com/meta/p143604_index.html.

[63]www.alternet.org/story/21096/.

[64]A. Diana Forster, "Religion, Voting Behavior, and Electoral Context in Contemporary U.S. Presidential Elections." (2008), 9. www.allacademic.com/meta/p212260_index.html.

[65]Ibid., 9.

[66]Ibid., 2.

[67]See http://www.pewforum.org/2014/11/05/how-the-faithful-voted-2014-preliminary-analysis/pf_14-11-

324 • CHAPTER 8

Support for Israel and Christian Zionism

According to a 2013 BBC poll, the majority of citizens of all countries except the United States (and Israel) are critical in their views of Israel's "influence in the world." Participants were asked to choose, for each country in the survey, if it had a mainly positive or mainly negative influence in the world." 51 percent of Americans said Israel had a mainly positive influence compared to 32 percent who said negative, with the rest undecided. Among Canadians, the results showed only 25 percent "positive" and 57 percent "negative." Globally, the average was 20 percent "positive" and 52 percent "negative."[68] Why do people in the United States have so much more positive feelings toward Israel than do those in other countries?

One reason may be that the strong pro-Israel stance of the Christian Right has greatly influenced public opinion and perhaps foreign policy in the United States. **Pastor John Hagee** is the leader of **Christians United for Israel**, the largest of the pro-Israel groups which collectively form the **Christian Zionist** movement in the United States. Pastor Hagee is influential in the Republican Party, is popular as a speaker to Jewish groups and has publicly denounced President Obama as being anti-Israel.

Christian Zionist organizations and churches often organize tours to "The Holy Land." When these Christian Zionists visit Israel, their belief that God is active in modern Israel is reinforced by the thrill of seeing the Biblical sites and by the interpretative commentary provided by the Christian Zionist tour guides. For example, when asked about the meaning of "the Green Line," one Christian Zionist tour guide explained it as a reference to how Israeli Jews had brought green crops to the formerly arid desert, rather than explaining it as the demarcation line drawn in green ink on the map of Israel/Palestine during the 1949 Armistice Agreements.[69]

Millenarian Movements as Political Actors
To understand another reason why the Christian Right in the United States has been strongly pro-Israel, we need to consider the role that millenarianism plays in the history of conservative Christianity in the United States. The last book of the New Testament, known under the titles *Revelations* and *The Apocalypse*, talks of a coming era when Christ will return to earth and rule for a thousand years (a millennium), with the help of a select group of his faithful followers. The time just before the Second Coming, as it is called, will be marked by apocalyptic upheavals such as earthquakes, fires, volcanoes, pestilence and other earth-shaking events. Inspired by this prophecy, many Christians through the centuries have envisioned that they were living in the last days, just before the coming mil-

---

05_faithfulvotes-01/

[68]http://www.worldpublicopinion.org/pipa/2013%20Country%20Rating%20Poll.pdf

[69]Based on a paper "'It is what it is': Rhetoric of Legitimation and Authentic Identity Construction on a Christian Zionist Tour of Israel" presented by Sean Durbin at the 2014 meeting of the American Academy of Religion.

lennium rule by Christ. Believing the end of the current era was near, they were especially zealous in their commitment to their religious beliefs.

The term **millenarian** is used, in its broadest sense, to describe any religious group whose members expect an "end of the world" scenario to occur in the near future, and who consequently develop into a fervent social, religious, or political movement. As James Rinehart writes in *Apocalyptic Faith and Political Violence: Prophets of Terror*, "researchers have come to view the phenomenon in increasingly secular as well as behavioral terms—as a response to massive upheaval such as that engendered by natural disasters, socioeconomic disturbance, or the disorientation resulting from the collision of highly different cultures."[70]

The history of the millenarian movements among American Protestants stretches over the past two centuries. In the 1800s a visionary Protestant named **William Miller** prophesied that the events of the Second Coming of Christ would begin sometime within the year beginning March 21, 1843, based upon his imaginative reading of the Biblical books of *Daniel* and *Revelations*. The numerous Americans who had believed him are known as Millerites, and they belonged to various denominations of Protestantism. When March 21, 1844 passed without the Advent, another Millerite recalculated the date as October 22, 1844, which bought the Millerites seven more months of time. However, the Millerites experienced what was called the Great Disappointment when that 1844 date also passed without any sign of the Advent of Christ. Yet the millenarian fervor did not die out. Soon Ellen White, one of Miller's followers, founded the Seventh-Day Adventists church. Similarly, another believer named Charles Russell founded the Jehovah's Witnesses organization—*Jehovah* being the name for God in the King James translation of the Bible used by Protestants at the time.

Many Protestant Christians, especially but not exclusively Baptists, continue to expect the Second Coming of Christ soon, perhaps within their lifetimes. Based upon their reading of the Apostle Paul's *First Epistle to the Thessalonians*, they hope to be alive for *The Rapture*—a time when Christ is expected to hover in the clouds above the earth. At that time, it is believed, a select number of believers will be "caught up" into the sky to join Christ in his reign. The Rapture concept has been popularized by books such as Hal Lindsey's popular *The Late, Great Planet Earth* (1970) and Tim LaHaye's series of *Left Behind* books, which fictionalize the Rapture and Tribulation events. Based on the results of various polls, between 30 and 55 percent of Americans believe in The Rapture.

The Perceived Connection between Modern Israel, the Third Temple and the Second Coming
Most Americans who believe in The Rapture also believe that God unfolds his plan for history in stages, which are called **dispensations**. For example, **Dispensationalists** believe that God's plan for the ancient Israelites is found in the Old Testament, which was followed by the New Testament Dispensation. The Dispensations can be further broken down by time periods. The time in the Garden of Eden, before The Fall, is the Dispen-

---

[70]James F. Rinehart, *Apocalyptic Faith and Political Violence: Prophets of Terror* (New York: Palgrave MacMillan, 2006), 3).

sation of Innocence, for example. The time from Moses to Christ is the Mosaic Law Dispensation, and so on. The sixth and current Dispensation of Grace began with Christ, and it will end with the seventh and last Dispensation, the Millennial Kingdom. Based upon their reading of the Hebrew Biblical books of *Daniel* and *Ezekiel* as well as *Revelations*, Dispensationalists became convinced that the Second Coming of Christ would not take place until the return of Jews to Jerusalem and the rebuilding of the Jewish Temple. The political event of the founding of the modern state of Israel in 1948 was therefore taken as a great religious event. The restoration of Jewish control of Israel would, they expected, soon lead to the rebuilding of the Temple and set the stage for the return of Christ. Many Evangelicals held a Dispensationalist understanding and therefore saw modern Israel as proof that God was continuing to act in the world to unfold a divine plan.

The decisive victory by Israel in the Six Day War in 1967 led to Jewish control of East Jerusalem and the Temple Mount area. This was seen as yet another encouraging sign for the building of the third temple. The first temple, built by Solomon, had been destroyed during the Babylonian captivity in 586 B.C. The second temple, completed around 515 B.C., was destroyed by the Romans in A.D. 70. An insurmountable obstacle to building a third temple, however, is that the Temple Mount has two structures sacred to Muslims: The Dome of the Rock and Al-Aqsa Mosque. Any attempt to tear down those structures and establish Jewish dominance on the Temple Mount would likely touch off a major war, but such a war could be seen by Dispensationalists as the prophesied Armageddon War associated with the End Days.

The influence of Christian Zionists may have peaked during the presidency of George W. Bush. During that era most Americans who self-identified as evangelical Christians were strong supporters of Israel. The organization Christians United for Israel (CUFI) provides strong leadership to the pro-Israel Evangelicals. However, there are indications that younger Evangelicals are turning away from, or at least questioning, the pro-Israel stance. A Pew Research Center survey in 2011 found that only 30 percent of Evangelical leaders expressed strong support for Israel, with almost half that many sympathizing with the Palestinians. In contrast to the pro-Israel position of CUFI, the Telos Group is an organization of Evangelicals who strive for a peaceful, Two-State Solution for Israel and Palestine.[71] An increasing awareness of the suffering of ordinary Palestinians seems to be at the heart of its shift from pro-Israel to a more neutral position among Evangelicals. It remains to be seen if this shift among Evangelicals will have any impact on the United States' international relations.

The Christian Right in Canada

The Christian Right in Canada is centered in the Western provinces, especially Alberta, the home of the Reform Party that has morphed into the Canadian Alliance Party, and then, along with the Progressive Conservative Party, into the Conservative Party.

---

[71]http://www.washingtonsblog.com/2014/07/israel-losing-support-biggest-ally-evangelical-christians.html.

Concerns of the Canadian Christian Right

The main concerns of the Christian Right in Canada are the same as those in the United States. Topping the list are its stances against abortion and same-sex marriage. The Campaign Life Coalition, usually shortened to Campaign Life, was founded in the 1970s in Ontario. Its main concern was with abortion. Its strategy included getting pro-life candidates nominated and elected, regardless of their political party affiliation. However, some Campaign Life members were involved in forming a pro-life political party in 1987, the Family Coalition Party (FCP). The FCP has never won an election, but did the best in the 1990 elections when it received the support of about 10 percent of the voters in some elections it contested. The FCP sees the family rather than the individual as the basic social unit. Put in terms of Bruce Lawrence's thought, we could say that the FCP is a reaction to modernity's emphasis on individualism.

The Christian Right was in shock in 2005 with the passage of Bill C38 legalizing same-sex marriage in Canada. It motivated the Coalition Life and related organizations to take action against the perceived threat to traditional marriage. They became much more active both as candidates for office and as advocates of conservative public policy agendas. By 2008 approximately seventy members of the ruling Conservative government were conservative Christians. Prayer breakfasts and prayer meetings, common meeting points for the Christian Right and politicians in the United States, had become commonplace in Ottawa. Prime Minister Stephen Harper, as a member of an evangelical congregation, was supportive.

Behind the scenes, close ties have developed between Christian Right leaders of the United States and Canada. Many of the Christian Right organizations of the United States gave rise to Canadian organizations. For example, the Focus on the Family organization gave rise to the Focus on the Family Canada and its subdivision, the Institute for Marriage and the Family. A former associate of Prime Minister Stephen Harper, Dave Quist, is its Executive Director.

Another common cause among conservative Christians on both sides of the border is a fervent support for modern Israel. Many conservative Canadian Christians, like their American counterparts, believe that the role of the Jews in Israel is somehow tied to the second coming of Christ. They therefore wish their government to strongly support Israel. The Harper government was the first to withhold funds from Palestine after Hamas swept the Palestinian elections of 2006. In that same year two thousand Evangelicals and political leaders attended a meeting at Canada Christian College to hear United States evangelist John Hagee urge Christians to rally support for Israel.[72] The pro-Israel voice of several million conservative Christians in Canada has more political weight than that of the 350,000 Jews of Canada. Although it remains under the public's radar, as long as the Conservatives are in power, the Christian Right has considerable influence over both domestic and foreign policy in Canada.

---

[72]Marci McDonald. "Jesus in the House: Is the Religious Right Taking over Stephen Harper's Government?," *The Walrus* (October 2006), 46.

Evaluating the Christian Right

In their book *The Christian Right in American Politics* the editors conclude by asking whether or not the politicization of the Christian Right has been good or bad for democracy in the United States. Those who think it has been good for democracy point to the way it has brought many new persons into political activism. Those who are critical of the movement point out that the new politicos are not learning to associate with other groups, in the classic democratic manner. However, the movement may have largely overcome this problem. By moving from the strategy of running as a third, Christian party to becoming one stream of the Republican Party, the movement has had to learn to compromise and advance its goals more effectively. The 2008 presidential race was a good illustration of this. John McCain quickly became the front runner in the Republican Primaries. However, he did not have the profile desired by the Christian Right, so they quickly promoted Mike Huckabee as their candidate of choice. Huckabee did well in the Bible Belt states, but had no hope of overcoming McCain's lead in delegate votes. When Huckabee withdrew, the Christian Right did not risk marginalizing itself by running a third party candidate.

One of the patterns we have seen in our travels to the hot spots of the world is that conservative or fundamentalist religious actors firmly believe that they follow a higher authority than the authority of their nation state. The certitude that they are on God's side has been both the strength and the weakness of the Christian Right in politics. It is a strong motivation to get active and to get out the vote—Republican campaign strategist Karl Rove used this to get George W. Bush elected twice. The weakness is that it makes it difficult for the Christian right to compromise with other political groups. "Individuals bent on doing God's work are unlikely to find common ground with those who oppose them."[73]

ISSUE 3. THE RISE OF ISLAM IN THE UNITED STATES AND CANADA: NATION OF ISLAM, GROWTH OF ISLAM

Our third issue concerns the implication for politics and public policy arising from the significant increase in the Muslim population of the United States and Canada over the past decades. For some non-Muslims, this is an issue of accommodation. Schools and work places are being asked to schedule Muslim prayer times and to provide a place for prayers. Public holidays have traditionally reflected the wishes of the Christian majority, but now public policy may need to accommodate Islamic holidays as well. For Muslims the issue is that the increase in their numbers and the media attention on Islamic terrorism have put Islam and Muslims in the spotlight. We will discuss the nature of the Islamic population in North America, including both traditional Islam as well as the rise of the Nation of Islam and its offshoots among the African American population.

---

[73]Green et al, *The Christian Right in American Politics*, 278.

Brief History of Islam in America

The history of Islam in North America reaches back to Colonial times. An unknown number of the slaves brought to the United States on slave ships may have been Muslims at the time of their capture in Africa. Scholars trying to estimate the percentage of Muslim slaves take into account that many slaves were captured in non-Muslim regions of Africa, whereas a large percentage of those from the Senegal and Gambia regions may have been Muslim.[74]

Although Islam did not become widespread in the colonial period, waves of immigration from Islamic countries beginning from around 1800 brought a Muslim presence to the United States and Canada. There was a wave of immigration after the end of World War II, and another beginning in 1967. By then, Muslim immigrants were coming from nearly every Islamic country, especially in the Middle East, South Asia, and Africa.[75]

There are three main streams of Islam in North America. Besides the Sunnis and the Shi'is , there is the unique phenomenon popularly known as the Black Muslims. We will focus on their very interesting history.

The Nation of Islam (NOI) and the American Muslim Mission

The first Islamic movement among African Americans was the Moorish Science Temple founded in 1913 by Noble Drew Ali. He thought of Christianity as the proper religion for light skinned, European peoples and Islam as the proper religion for darker people. If each group followed its destined religion, there would be peace on earth, he imagined.[76]

The **Universal Negro Improvement Association** founded by Marcus Garvey in the 1920s had as many as four million followers at its peak. Garvey held that the only real solution to the poverty and oppression among people of African descent was to establish their own nation, their own manufacturing operations, and their own institutions. His dream was to do this in Liberia in Northern Africa, but the government of Liberia did not welcome his movement. The Garveyites were not Muslim, but his very popular effort to unite and improve the lot of all African Americans would later inspire the Nation of Islam (NOI) movement.

Wallace D. Fard emerged as a public figure in Detroit in 1930. There are several versions of the story of his background. He is thought to have been the offspring of a white mother and a Muslim father, but the country of his father's origin is debated. Whatever his parentage, he was convinced that the African Americans had to unite to improve their lot,

---

[74]Michael A. Gomez, *Exchanging our Country Marks: The Transformation of African Identity in the Colonial and Antebellum South, 1526-1830* (Chapel Hill: University of North Carolina Press, 1998).

[75]For a brief account of the waves of immigration and countries of origin, see www.islamfortoday.com/america11.htm.

[76]C. E. Lincoln, *The Black Muslims in America* (Grand Rapids: Eerdmans, 1994), 56.

[77]Louis Farrakhan, Muhammad Speaks (January 31, 1964) 8, as cited in Lee, *Nation of Islam.*

and that Islam was the means to accomplish that end. His followers now use an Islamic spelling of his name, Farad.

Fard's version of Islam was not at all consistent with traditional Islam. Besides differences in style of worship and the notion of black supremacy, a paramount difference evolved out of his first encounter with the young man who would become his key disciple, Elijah Poole. The young Elijah Poole had felt called to a religious mission, but did not think of it as a Christian one. He had dropped out of church attendance before his fateful 1923 meeting with Fard in Detroit. Like John the Baptist announcing the importance of Jesus or The Bab announcing the prophecy of Baha'u'llah, the young Elijah saw Fard in the same manner:

> "Hurry and join unto your own kind. The time of this world is at hand."
> Louis Farrakhan[76]

> when I got to him I shaked [sic] my hands with him and told him that I recognized who he is and he held his head down close to my face and he said to me, "Yes, Brother." I said to him: "You are that one we read in the Bible that he would come in the last day under the name Jesus."... Finally he said; "Yes, I am the one that you have been looking for in the last two thousand years."[78]

Following this encounter with Elijah Poole, Fard allowed his followers to think of him as Allah or as the return of Jesus. This meant that his version of Islam was at odds with the strict monotheism of traditional Islam. Fard was so impressed with Elijah Poole that he authorized him to teach Islam with his blessing. Poole later changed his name to **Elijah Muhammad**, and he quickly became Fard's favorite disciple.

Fard's **Nation of Islam** (NOI) movement quickly came to the attention of the authorities in Detroit. There was a rumor that he had promised life in heaven for anyone who killed four whites. He is known to have been quite critical of whites and he is said to have preached that anyone who killed four devils would go to heaven. It may be that he was referring to the killing of the four beasts mentioned in the Book of Revelation in the New Testament, but regardless, some of his followers took him literally and a few whites may have been killed under his influence.

He had previously been arrested in 1926 and convicted on drug charges. After another arrest in 1933, Fard was expelled from Detroit and fell out of contact with his followers. Elijah Muhammad, the former Elijah Poole, took over the leadership of the movement, but it soon divided into many factions. Some factions were quite hostile to Elijah Muham-

---

[78]Hatim A. Sahib, "The Nation of Islam." (Master's Thesis: University of Chicago, 1951), 91-92, as cited in Martha Lee, *The Nation of Islam: An American Millenarian Movement* (Syracuse: Syracuse University Press, 1996), 23.

mad, and he left Detroit in 1935. He settled in Washington, D.C., where he preached his version of Islam under the name Elijah Rasool.[79]

Elijah moved to Chicago in 1942 and attempted to rent a place for regular meetings, but potential landlords were pressured into refusing to rent to him. He and several of his followers were put in jail for refusing to register for the draft. The black supremacy rhetoric and the refusal to serve in the military clearly threatened the status quo, leading to instances of harassment and arrest by officials. His wife, Clara, directed the organization while he was in jail. After the end of the Second World War he was released from jail and the movement began to flourish. Their numbers quickly grew and they were able to buy a building to use as a temple.

The Distinctive Theology of the Nation of Islam
The theology of the Nation of Islam was developed by Fard, Elijah Muhammad, and other early leaders, all of whom were more familiar with the Bible than the Quran. This, combined with their concept of black supremacy, led to a distinctive theology

Elijah Muhummad
Photo: FBI (FBI Primer) [Public domain], via Wikimedia Commons

from that of either mainstream Christianity or Sunni Islam. For example, the Nation of Islam teaches that God is not a spiritual being but rather a material or earthly entity as known through Fard. Given Islam's strong denunciation of the sin of "association," meaning the mistake of associating any human, planet or idol with God, the Nation of Islam's claim that Fard was Allah is considered grossly heretical.

The Nation of Islam also teaches that the black race has been chosen by Allah. It tells a story unknown to either Christianity or Islam about an evil person named Yakub who lived in Egypt over 6,000 years ago. It teaches that humans had already been on the earth for millions of years and that they were all black and all lived in harmony as one tribe called Shabazz. Yakub rebelled and moved to an island where he created a white race by killing all dark babies. Eventually, the evil white race returned to Egypt and subjugated the blacks. Yakub and his white race brought oppression and disunity to humankind. The

---

[79]Lee, *Nation of Islam*, 26.

whites are the bad race, the devils. They were driven out of Arabia and went to Europe. God sent Moses to try to redeem them, but that effort failed.

Now the blacks need to undergo a "resurrection," meaning they need to develop a self-understanding of themselves as the proud members of the original Shabazz people who once had a great and peaceful society.

The Nation of Islam is a **millenarian** movement, as Martha Lee has argued.[80] In the Nation of Islam's version of history, the rule by whites has lasted over six thousand years and is about to come to an end. The Nation of Islam thought that the First World War was to have been the beginning of this End.

The inspiration for the belief in the End Time came from the Biblical book Ezekiel, also a favorite among millenarian Christians. The End Time will see the destruction of the white race by the Mother of Planes, a huge aircraft base in the sky inspired by the Biblical prophet Ezekiel's vision of a great wheel of light in the northern sky. The "Fall of America" is to be expected soon. In fact, Elijah Muhammad originally prophesied that Fall to occur in 1965 and 1966. When that failed to occur, the End Time became vaguer and less literal in the Nation of Islam's thought.

The Nation of Islam is an economic movement as well. It advocates self-sufficiency as an alternative to poverty for African Americans. It also teaches a strict, disciplined way of life. It follows the Islamic prohibition against eating pork and drinking alcohol, but Elijah Muhammad also thought the traditional southern diet of the African Americans was unhealthy. He called it "slave food."

Elijah Muhammad demanded a large amount of territory in which the blacks could live a separate social and economic existence. To accommodate this goal would have been a political impossibility. It would have required laws forcing non-African Americans off lands somewhere in the United States to make room sufficient territory for approximately 10 percent of the population. This demand was never seriously considered by Congress and now has been downplayed by the Nation of Islam.

Malcolm X Turns to Sunni Islam

Malcolm Little's background contributed to his distrust of white people. The family story was that his Jamaican grandmother had been raped by a white man, leading to the birth of his fair-skinned mother. His uncle had been lynched, and three of his brothers had been killed by whites. His father was an active Garveyite and often received threats from whites. When Malcolm's father was found dead, having been apparently run over by a street car, the coroner ruled it a suicide. However, the Little family believed he had been killed by the Black Legion, a white supremacist group.

Later, Malcolm moved to Boston, where he became involved with criminals. While imprisoned for theft, he read about the Nation of Islam. After release from prison in 1952, he became a key disciple of Elijah Muhammad. He was told to drop his "slave

---

[80]Lee, *The Nation of Islam.* 3.

Malcolm X and Martin Luther King, Jr.
Photo: "MLK and Malcolm X USNWR cropped". By Marion S. Trikosko, *U.S. News & World Report* [Public domain], via Wikimedia Commons.

name." Like other converts, he was given the temporary name X to symbolize the absence of an African name.

Malcolm X's leadership of the Harlem and other NOI temples in the Eastern United States was very successful in gaining new converts. His eloquence brought him national attention as an advocate for Black Power. He came to symbolize the black defiance of white racism in America.

Despite his success as a leader in the movement, Malcolm X became alienated from it. He became critical of Elijah Muhammad for violating the Nation of Islam's strict rule against adultery. And his remarks after the assassination of President John F. Kennedy, saying that the chickens had come home to roost,[81] caused him to be rebuked by Elijah Muhammad. In 1964 he broke away from NOI and founded Muslim Mosque, Inc. He had

---

[81]"Malcolm X Scores USA and Kennedy." *New York Times* (December 2, 1963), 21.

become aware of the great differences between the Nation of Islam's understanding of Islam and that of traditional Islam. Under the influence of some Muslims, he converted to Sunni Islam and made the pilgrimage to Mecca. It was a life-changing event, for he saw that Islam was not an exclusively black person's religion as he had been taught by the Nation of Islam. He returned to the United States and taught a non-racist understanding of Islam, changing his name to El Hajj Malik El-Shabazz.

Malik, the former Malcolm X, had received threats from the members of Nation of Islam, and in 1965 he was assassinated while giving a speech in New York. Three members of the Nation of Islam were convicted of the murder, but suspicions remain as to whether outsiders were involved, partly based on remarks found in his *Autobiography* about previous attempts on his life in which he says he no longer thinks it is the Muslims (Nation of Islam members).[82]

NOI has been bolstered by loans and donations from Middle Eastern and African countries, starting with a three million dollar loan from Libya in 1972. NOI purchased temples with these funds. It also purchased a bank and started other enterprises intended to make blacks more financially independent and affluent. Yet the organization had trouble managing its new financial empire, and by the late 1970s it had a multimillion dollar deficit.

The early 1970s also saw a softening of NOI's attitude toward whites and an increased willingness to work with other black organizations. The movement was moving toward the mainstream.

Wallace Muhammad Reforms and Renames the Movement
Elijah Muhammad, known as the Messenger, died in 1975 and the leadership passed to his seventh son, Wallace, who took NOI further toward the mainstream. He made the organization's membership and financial records less secretive, and he redefined the idea that whites were devils. In his thought, the "devil" was a mental attitude rather than a characteristic of all whites.[83] Wallace Muhammad withdrew the demand for a large territory, as the home of a state for blacks. He helped put NOI on a sound financial basis, establishing a better relationship with the banking and political leaders of Chicago. He renamed the temples, calling each one a Masjid, the Arabic word for mosque. This, combined with more emphasis on studying the Quran, moved NOI closer to Sunni Islam.

Having moved away from most of the theologically distinctive claims made by Fard and his father, Wallace changed the organization's name to the World Community of al-Islam in the West, or WCIW. If the story ended there, NOI would no longer be crucial to our topic, but it did not end there. Louis Farrakhan brought NOI back into politics in a heated way.

---

[82]See Lee, *Nation of Islam.* 44, and www.trutv.com/library/crime/terrorists_spies/assassins/malcolm_x/5.html

[83]Lee, *Nation of Islam.* 63.

Louis Farrakhan Restores the Nation of Islam and Turns Political

Minister Louis had been one of the leaders in the NOI from its early days. He had initially accepted the leadership of Wallace, but the reforms Wallace instituted went too far for him. He broke with WCIW in 1978 and founded a new organization intending to recapture the doctrine and discipline of the old Nation of Islam. He restored the original name, reinstituted the Savior's Day festival which had been the most popular annual event for members. Returning to NOI's past, and his charismatic leadership, attracted a large number of members to his new form of the NOI.

The Million Man March. Farrakhan drew national attention when he organized the "Million Man March" on Washington, D.C. in 1995. The march was a combined effort by many African American organizations, and most of the participants had a Christian background. But as the main organizer, Farrakhan set the agenda. As Dennis Walker writes:

> The March was an Islamizing event. A range of Muslim sects were allowed to appear before the multitude and recite the Qur'an in Arabic on a basis of equality with the Christian and black Jewish clerics whom Farrakhan had inducted. It was a recognition in public space of Islam as part of the being of blacks that had had no precedent. Farrakhan led the multitude through chanting of "as-Salamu 'Alaykum," the Arabic greeting of "Peace be Upon You" between Muslims that also recurs in Islamic ritual prayer.[85]

The march was criticized in advance by some for potentially causing trouble or for seeming, by its title and leadership, to downplay the role of African American women, but large numbers of African Americans participated in the march. A second march to Washington was held ten years later. One of the objections to Farrakhan playing the role of leader of all African Americans is that his remarks were sometimes racist. His favorable comments about Hitler made him seem anti-Jewish, but he denies those charges.

It was a big shift for NOI to get involved in politics at all. The Nation of Islam had begun as a millenarian movement expecting the imminent "Fall of America." Fard and Elijah Muhammad thought NOI members should have only minimal contact with the government, which was in effect considered to be the enemy of blacks and of God. Based on that principle, they had even gone to jail for refusing to register for the draft. But in 1994, Farrakhan decided to become politically active and stage the march. Having made this decision, he quickly grew in stature from being an organization leader to being a national leader of black Americans and bringing Islam into a more influential role.

---

[84]Louis Farrakhan, *Muhammad Speaks* (January 31, 1964) 8, as cited in Lee, *Nation of Islam, An American Millenarian Movement.* Syracuse: Syracuse University Press, 1996

[85]Dennis Walker, *Islam and the Search for African-American Nationhood: Elijah Muhammad, Louis Farrakhan and the Nation of Islam* (Atlanta: Clarity Press. 2005), 508.

Nation of Islam leader Louis Farrakhan
Source: United States government public domain file

But all is not well for the Nation of Islam. Vibert White's book *Inside the Nation of Islam* is quite critical of Farrakhan's handling of its money. After describing how the NOI puts great pressure on its members, most of whom have very modest incomes, to donate substantial sums to the organization, White describes the way that monies donated by members or gifted by Libya and others finds its way to mansions, farms and other luxuries for the various members of the Farrakhan family. He laments the fact that so many struggling black-owned businesses have been stuck with unpaid bills for their services. He describes Farrakhan's plan to build an expensive mansion in Michigan at the same time as the NOI's own operations were badly in debt. He wonders what happened to all the money raised in the Million Man March. He concludes about the 1995 march:

The Million Man March was a success for Farrakhan and his Nation; however, both in the planning of the event and in the aftermath, confusion, antagonism, and financial mismanagement corrupted the Million Man March, transforming its image from having been a totally successful historical spectacle into a mass gathering filled with many lingering questions.[86]

Moving the Nation of Islam toward Sunni Islam

Farrakhan has moved the Nation of Islam toward the Islamic mainstream by encouraging Islamic-style daily prayers and the study of the Quran. His courting of Libya's Muammar Gaddafi and other African leaders for money and support necessitated his acceptance of Sunni beliefs. The most difficult change that he had to make was to drop the traditional NOI theology that saw Fard as Allah and Elijah Muhammad as his Messenger. In a 1997

---

[86]Vilbert L. White, Jr., *Inside the Nation of Islam: A Historical and Personal Testimony by a Black Muslim* (Gainesville: University Press of Florida Press, 2001), 159.

conference, Farrakhan publicly affirmed Muhammad was the last and greatest prophet of Allah, thus moving NOI theology into a space acceptable to Sunni (and Shi'i) Muslims.[87]

The Growth of Sunni and Shi'i Islam in North America

The growth of Islam in the United States and Canada has been quite dramatic. There are now mosques in most cities, and membership in those mosques is diverse in terms of country of ancestry, skin color or mother tongue. According to a 2001 study entitled "The Mosque in America: A National Portrait" Islam is growing at an impressive rate through immigration, large families and conversion. The study confirmed the pattern of ethnic diversity among mosques. It found that on average the background of mosque members was 33 percent South Asian, 30 percent African American, and 25 percent Arab. It found that only 7 percent of mosques are attended by only one ethnic group.[88] Mosques are much more ethnically diverse than most churches or synagogues.

By one count there were 2106 mosques in America in 2011, up from 1209 mosques just 11 years earlier. The report found that the average mosque gains sixteen new members per year by conversion.[89] Estimates by Pew Research made in 2010 put the Muslim population in the United States at between 2 and 3 million, just under 1 percent of the total population.[90] Perhaps fifteen percent are Shi'i Muslims. (The differences between Shi'i and Sunni Islam were discussed in earlier chapters.)

The rapid growth in new mosques and expansion of existing mosques has led to numerous re-zoning controversies, whether caused by the usual zoning concerns or by Islamophobic reactions.[91] The most controversial of all was the high rise building proposed for 51 Park Place in lower Manhattan. The site was so near the former World Trade Center that parts of one of the planes that hit the Trade Center landed in and near the building. The proposal did not seem controversial at first for several reasons. The existing building was already serving as residences for many Muslims and it housed a Muslim prayer room. The proposal was to replace the old building with a 13-story condominium complex that would include a large prayer room as well as a Muslim community center, along the lines of a Jewish community center. That is, the proposal was to replace an old building with a new, larger one with enhanced facilities for area Muslims as well as an interfaith area. Nevertheless, a heated controversy arose in 2010 when critics labeled the

---

[87]Dennis Walker, *Islam and the Search for African-American Nationhood: Elijah Muhammad, Louis Farrakhan and the Nation of Islam* (Atlanta: Clarity Press, 2005), 495.

[88]*Ibid.*

[89] Ihsan Bagby, Paul M. Perl, and Bryuan T. Froehle. "The Mosque in America: A National Portrait" (Washington, D.C.: Council on American-Islamic Relations, April 26, 2001), 6. www.cair.com/portals/0/ pdf/the_mosque_in_america_a_national_portrait.pdf

[90]www.Pewresearch.org/daily-number/americas-muslim-population-2030/.

[91]Figures according to the Pew Research Center. For an interactive map of the zoning controversies, see http://www.pewforum.org/2012/09/27/controversies-over-mosques-and-islamic-centers-across-the-u-s-2/.

project a "ground zero mosque," thus making it seem that the former site of the World Trade Center or an adjacent site was to become the location of a mosque. The distinction between a mosque and a prayer space was largely lost in the debate, as was the fact that the proposed building was not actually visible from the ground zero memorial area. Also lost in the debate was the fact that the Muslim cleric who headed the prayer space, and planned to head the new space, was a Sufi Muslim who has a long track record of promoting interfaith dialogue and religious harmony.

Various polls taken around the time of the controversy showed the majority of Americans opposed the proposed "ground zero mosque," and the proposal has been largely withdrawn, to be replaced with more modest plans. There remains a concern that the widespread backlash against the proposal will play into the hands of extremist Muslims who may point to the event as proof that Americans are anti-Islam. Such accusations fuel the recruitment efforts of ISIS and other extremist groups.

Based on the 2001 Census, Statistics Canada reported that the number of Muslims in Canada had more than doubled since the 1991 census, from 253,300 to 579,600. In that ten year period, Muslims rose from one percent to two percent of the population. By 2011 the census reported over a million Muslims in Canada, about 3.2 percent of the population. The percentage of other non-Christian adherents had grown as well. Hindus increased by nearly as much, with Sikhs and Buddhists making impressive gains as well. By comparison, the number of Jews remained fairly constant. Roman Catholics increased slightly, while Protestant numbers fell.[92] The growth continues. Pew Research estimated the Canadian Muslim population at 940,000, or 2.8 percent in 2010.[93]

The Controversy over Shariah Arbitration in Ontario

A big controversy occurred in Ontario, Canada starting in the Fall 2003. It began when Dr. Syed Mumtaz Ali announced that he was opening an Islamic Institute of Civil Justice to establish a Shariah Court in Ontario. His plan was to engage in the arbitration of family law and inheritance matters based on Shariah, Islamic law. When the press picked up the story, the public got the impression that something new was being introduced by the government. In fact, under Ontario law as it existed at that time, individuals could mutually agree to arbitrate a dispute, divorce, or other matters under any law they wished. It could have been Jewish Law, Roman Catholic Canon Law, or the laws of England. It did not matter as long as the parties agreed.

The media hype around the issue raised fears that all of the perceived excesses and injustices in Shariah law cases would be introduced into Canada. People worried about the legalization of polygamy, because Islamic law allows a man to marry up to four wives. They worried about the legalization of female genital mutilation, as practiced on young girls in some African Islamic countries. Mostly, they worried about Taliban- or Saudi Arabian-style

---

[92]www12.statcan.ca/english/census01/Products/Analytic/companion/rel/canada.cfm.

[93]www.pewforum.org/2011/01/27/table-muslim-population-by-country/.

discrimination against females. Numerous womens' organizations rallied against the perceived introduction of Shariah into Ontario. Muslims themselves were divided on the issue.

The government had to respond to the huge public outcry. The chief of staff of the Ontario Attorney General's Office reports that they had never received so many letters and emails from the public, and they were almost all against the perceived introduction of Shariah.[94] The office was also flooded with requests for media interviews from around the world, including from Al Jazeera network so popular among Arab speakers. The government's first step was to ask Marion Boyd, a former Attorney General and former Minister for Women's Issues, to do a formal review of past practices and to make recommendations.

Boyd's report, entitled "Dispute Resolution in Family Law: Protection Choice, Promoting Inclusion," recommended keeping the current law, thus allowing for faith-based arbitrations. Ms. Boyd cited the fact that she had found no Ontario cases in which any faith-based arbitrations had proven problematic in terms of generally accepted norms as established in law. However, the report also called for the introduction of some government regulations on such arbitrations. Mainly, she called for the inclusion of protections to ensure that all decisions were within the general parameters of Ontario law. She also called for each person seeking such arbitration to seek independent legal advice and to get the decision in writing. Her report pointed out the need to protect an individual's rights and interests even if they are a part of a religious group and turn to faith-based arbitration. She wrote, "If the state allows cultural groups complete freedom to define family and inheritance matters those groups may trample on the rights of individuals within the group and may discriminate in ways that are unacceptable to Canadian society."[95] This was to address the public fear that Muslim women would be coerced into terms of settlement that they did not really want or that went against the Canadian Charter of Rights and Freedoms.[96]

Critics quickly pointed out that the Boyd Commission did not have access to data about previous faith-based arbitrations because the terms of settlement were not usually a matter of public record. Many women's organizations were critical of the Boyd Report because they did not think it addressed the problem of females being coerced into unfair, unwanted or abusive agreements. Their concerns gained widespread support, and an International Day of Protest was held in September 2005. Five days later the Premier of Ontario, Dalton McGinty, put an end to the public debate when he announced that his government would no longer allow faith-based arbitration, thus going completely against the recommendations of the Boyd Report. In a rare moment of solidarity, some Jewish and Islamic leaders held a joint press conference denouncing the decision.

---

[94]This is based on a talk given about the Shariah law controversy given at the University of Windsor by Mr. Adam M. Bodek.

[95]Marion Boyd, "Dispute Resolution in Family Law: Protection Choice, Promoting Inclusion," (Ministry of the Attorney General, 2004), 3.

[96]For an Executive Summary of the Boyd Report, see www.attorneygeneral.jus.gov.on.ca/english/about/pubs/boyd/executivesummary.pdf.

Since 2005, no official faith-based arbitration is permissible in Ontario. Some observers have suggested that this just places the whole matter out of the public view. With no reporting or public scrutiny, there is no possibility for the government to intervene in extreme cases where the rights of an individual may have been violated.

OVERVIEW AND THEORETICAL DISCUSSION

In our first issue we focused on the concerns and agenda the Christian Right has had with regard to public policy and the public arena. That agenda includes a stance against evolution, abortion, birth control, stem cell research, and same-sex marriage. Edward J. Larson, an historian and lawyer who has written on the Scopes Trial, makes some interesting points about the conflict between fundamentalists and evolutionary science. One point is that the public controversy has centered almost exclusively in the sphere of high school education, and not at universities or in the arena of scientific discourse.[97]

The second issue concerned the growing effectiveness and political maturity of the Christian Right, as it shifted from being apolitical to independent political activism, and finally to being a key component of the Republican Party. A transition has occurred in American Party politics, such that it is now the case that Americans who consider themselves Evangelical Christians are most likely to vote Republican and to identify with the public policy values of the Christian Right. The conflict between secular science and the Christian Right plays out in the public arena in such ways as research funding, tax incentives, and high school science curricula.

In the third issue we discussed the history and growth of Islam in North America. Besides the numerical growth of the Muslim population, we saw how the Nation of Islam has moved from its roots as a religion for African Americans toward a more orthodox, Sunni form of Islamic belief and practice.

Theoretical Discussion

The Role of Religion in American Exceptionalism Theory
The phrase "American Exceptionalism" is used by theorists to refer to the belief among Americans that there are things that are both unique and outstanding about the United States. The concept runs from the time of the Puritans and the Founding Fathers through to the contemporary period. The Puritans conceived of their society as a "City on a Hill," meaning that they saw themselves as a beacon of a new way of democratic and moral life. After touring America in the mid–1800s, the French social critic Alexis de Tocqueville wrote of America as *exceptional* in terms of its Puritan ideals, its relation to

---

[97]http://www.pewforum.org/2005/12/05/the-biology-wars-the-religion-science-and-education-controversy/

the land, the way it drew upon European values without being bound to them and many other ways.

Religion has played a key role in shaping American Exceptionalism in several of its forms. From the Colonial era there was a sense that America was playing a special role in God's plan. The related concepts that America has a "manifest destiny" or that it represents the "kingdom of God in America" are also instructive about the perceived connection between God and nation in American understanding. Although every nation state has reasons to take pride in its people, customs and cultures, Americans from Puritan New England to the present tend to take normal cultural pride to a higher, religious dimension.

During our travels we have seen that America is not the only country that mixes religion and nationalism. We saw that Hindu Nationalists take pride in being the homeland of the high Vedic culture. In Sri Lanka we noted that Sinhalese think of their island as the "Bulwark of Buddhism." State Shinto stressed that the gods created the Japanese islands first, and that the emperors were descended from the goddess. And we noted that the House of Saud takes pride in being the protectors of Islam's two most holy cities. But American Exceptionalism takes on a political dimension that seems to go beyond that of most nations.

The foremost theorist about American Exceptionalism was the late Seymour Martin Lipset, who thought American Exceptionalism could be summed up in the way that Americans understand liberty, egalitarianism, individualism, populism, and *laissez faire*—the idea that government should have only minimal influence in economic and business affairs.

More recently Stephen Brooks, author of *American Exceptionalism in the Age of Obama*, calls our attention to the variety of understandings of American Exceptionalism that are expressed among Americans.[98] Brooks writes that one approach sees America as exceptional in the sense of being a bastion of democracy and freedom. Another sees America in terms of superlatives—having the best economy, military, influence, freedom of opportunity, and so forth. That is, one approach stresses America's exceptional set of values, while the other focuses on exceptional outcomes. For President George W. Bush and others who talk proudly about the American mission to spread "Freedom" throughout the world, that term is used to capture the American Exceptionalist pride in the unique values that America is thought to represent. That one word, Freedom, expresses the certainty that United States alone embodies the values that can make the world a better place. But when Americans express their appreciation of some good accomplishments with the phrases such as "only in America," they are celebrating American Exceptionalism in terms of what Brooks calls "values" and "superlatives."

Richard Hughes's book *Christian America and the Kingdom of God* notes that 'the notion of Christian America and the notion of the kingdom of God are polar opposites whose values could not be further apart. This means that the idea of Christian America is in every key respect an oxymoron—essentially a contradiction in terms—when measured

---

[98] Stephen Brooks, *American Exceptionalism in the Age of Obama* (New York and London: Routledge, 2013), 1-17.

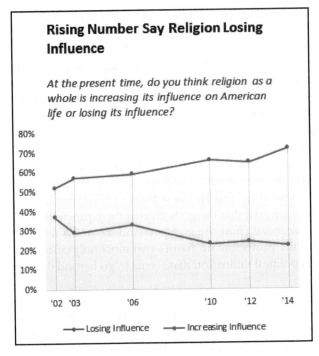

Rising Number Say Religion Losing Influence

At the present time, do you think religion as a whole is increasing its influence on American life or losing its influence?

Losing Influence —— Increasing Influence

A Pew Research Center graph indicating the growing percentage of Americans who feel that religion is losing influence on public life, and most of those lament the loss.

by the most sacred document of the Christian tradition: the Bible itself."[99] His point is that although many American Christians think of the United States as a Christian nation, or even as the kingdom of God on earth, in Biblical terms no earthly nation would ever qualify for or be thought worthy of such a title. Hughes uses Christian thought to refute the nationalistic claims of the Christian Right. Drawing upon the historical record of such practices as slavery, broken treaties with Indian tribes, state-sanctioned torture, and racial discrimination, Hughes draws attention to examples of quite un-Christian behavior by America. He acknowledges that the Christian Right is a powerful political force in America, and then challenges conservative Christians to rethink what it might mean to apply what the Bible really teaches to political behavior.

Has Islam Become the Fourth American Religion?

We discussed how decades ago Herberg claimed that first Protestants, then Catholics and then Jews became accepted into the mainstream of what he termed "The American Way of Life," but should Islam now be added to this list? There are several reasons favoring adding Islam. For the first time a Muslim, Keith Ellison, was elected to the United States Congress in 2006, and his Minnesota constituency is not predominantly Muslim. It is a heavily Democratic district, but he emerged victorious from a hotly contested Democratic primary. Minnesota voters clearly did not see his religion as un-American. A few states have also elected a Muslim to their state legislatures. Ellison converted to Sunni Islam from Roman Catholicism while he was a university student in his native Detroit. Ellison cooperated with Farrakhan on organizing the Million Man March, but he is not a Nation

---

[99]Richard T. Hughes, *Christian America and the Kingdom of God.* (Champaign: University of Illinois Press. 2009. Kindle Edition, 222–224.

of Islam follower, and he has distanced himself from the anti-Jewish remarks associated with Farrakhan and some of his followers.

Another reason is that the critical mass of Muslims is now in place. By 2007 or earlier, the Muslim population had surpassed the Jewish population in the United States. Like the Jewish population, the Muslim population is concentrated in cities. For Muslims, those cities are New York, Los Angeles, Chicago and greater Detroit.

Given the numbers of Muslims in the United States and the way in which most of them have adapted themselves to American culture, it would have been almost automatic to add Muslims as the fourth mainstream religion in America if it were not for Islamic-based terrorism. The 2001 attacks on the World Trade Center and the Pentagon, the various failed terrorist plots, and the fact that the nightly news often has coverage of Islamic terrorist activities somewhere in the world work against the full acceptance of Islam into the North American mainstream.

Public attention often focuses on the concern non-Muslims have arising from acts of terrorism committed by radicalized Muslims, but news reports of terrorist attacks by extremist Muslims impacts the daily lives of all American Muslims. How concerned are American Muslims about the negative repercussions of extremism on themselves? According to a Pew Research Center survey conducted in 2011, ten years after the attack on the World Trade Center and Pentagon, 60 percent of Muslim Americans said they were either "very concerned" or "somewhat concerned" about Islamic extremism. When Muslim Americans in that survey were asked about how much support there was for extremism among Muslim Americans, 21 percent reported either a "great deal" or "fair amount" of support, whereas a majority of 64 percent reported either "not much" or "none at all." When asked if United States Muslim leaders had spoken out enough against extremists, 48 percent of American Muslims said the leaders had not, and 34 percent said they had.[100] In the years after that 2011 survey, the internet messages by ISIS challenging American Muslims to commit terrorist acts may have raised the level of concern even higher among American Muslims.

The controversial activist Pamela Geller and the organization she leads, the American Freedom Defense Initiative, planned an event intended to affirm the right of free expression to be held in Garland, Texas in May, 2015. The event was to feature cartoonists making drawings about Islam, to reaffirm the freedom of expression. Besides cartoonists, several notable speakers were in attendance, including Geert Wilders, the anti-Islam, Dutch politician discussed in the previous chapter. As the event was getting started, two Muslim extremists launched an attack, but they were killed outside the venue by a policeman. One of the extremists had just posted on Twitter that both he and the other attacker had pledged allegiance to the ISIS leader. ISIS later claimed responsibility for the attack and continued to call for attacks on Americans. Ten years after the publication of cartoons

---

[100]"Growth in Alienation or Support for Extremism", Pew Research Center, 2011. http://www.people-press.org/2011/08/ 30/muslim-americans-no-signs-of-growth-in-alienation-or-support-for-extremism/. See pewresearch.org for the latest survey updates.

about Islam in Denmark, the violence arising from the conflicting values of freedom of artistic expression versus protecting the sanctity of the Prophet Muhammad had made its way onto American soil.

To become a fourth religion in The American Way of Life, as Herberg used that term, Islam would not only have to be accepted into the North American cultural landscape by non-Muslims, but many Muslims would themselves have to adopt North American cultural values. That seems to be happening, but it may be too soon to know how assimilated into the cultural norms of the United States or Canada the majority of its Muslim citizens have or will become.

Religions on the Rise and the Pendulum Theory

Herberg's pendulum theory seems to apply in the United States. Evangelical Christian churches are on the rise in terms of adherents, church attendance and media outlets. Their political influence grew to new heights under the two terms of the George W. Bush presidency. Meanwhile the non-evangelical Christian churches have remained fairly constant in numbers and in political influence, although the latter is hard to assess.

In Canada, membership in evangelical churches is also growing while non-evangelical churches struggle with aging congregations and diminishing resources. The Christian Right is not as numerically strong, but it has managed to gain some political leverage through its strong presence among both the elected representatives and the constituencies of the Conservative Party.

Islam is also on the rise in North America. Through immigration, conversion and birth rates Islam has grown in both the United States and Canada. In the United States, both the Sunnis and the Nation of Islam have been very successful at gaining converts to Islam. The slow but meaningful movement of the Nation of Islam's leaders toward more orthodox Sunni Islam means that the two main streams of American Islam may be expected to work more closely together to influence the political process in the future.

In conclusion, we have seen that the upswing of religious fervor in the United States has led to an increase in religious influence in the political realm. A similar pattern may be emerging in Canada under a Conservative government led by Stephen Harper. Meanwhile, the increase in the numbers of Muslims in North America will likely continue, positioning them to play a larger role in the political process in the near future.

STUDY QUESTIONS

1. How and why have Creationists influenced school science curricula?
2. Why are many conservative American Christians also Zionists?

---

[101]http://www.pewforum.org/2014/09/22/public-sees-religions-influence-waning-2/pr_14-09-22_religionpolitics-01/

3. What are some of the differences between Canadians and Americans regarding religion and politics?

4. What public policy concerns does the Christian Right have?

5. What does the term "young earth" mean and why do people hold to that view?

FURTHER READING

Abdul-Ghafur, Saleemah. Ed. *Living Islam Out Loud.* Boston: Beacon Press, 2005. An anthology by and for American Muslim Women.

Black, Amy E., Douglas L. Koopman, and David K. Ryden. *Of Little Faith: The Politics of George W. Bush's Faith-Based Initiatives.* Washington D.C.: Georgetown University Press, 2004. A good review of the issues enriched by many interviews conducted by the authors.

Brooks, Stephen. *American Exceptionalism in the Age of Obama.* New York and London: Routledge, 2013.

Campbell, David E. ed. *A Matter of Faith? Religion in the 2004 Election.* Washington, D.C.: Brookings Institute, 2007. Good detail on the subject.

Dart, Ron. *Canadian Christian Zionism: A Tangled Tale.* Dewdney: Synaxis Press, 2014. On the complex relationship between Christians and Israel.

Hughes, Richard T. *Christian America and the Kingdom of God.* Champaign: University of Illinois Press, 2009. Challenges American Christians to rethink the "Christian America" notion.

Gomez, Michael A. *Black Crescent: the Experience and Legacy of African Muslims in the Americas.* Cambridge: Cambridge University Press, 2005. History of African Muslims throughout the Americas.

Green, John C., Rozell, Mark J., and Wilcox, Clyde, eds. *The Christian Right in American Politics: Marching to the Millennium.* Washington, D. C.: Georgetown University Press, 2003. Essays giving state-by-state studies on the Christian Right from 1980 to 2000.

Green, John C., Rozell, Mark J., and Wilcox, Clyde, ed.s. *The Values Campaign? The Christian Right and the 2004 Elections.* Washington, D. C.: Georgetown University Press, 2006. Essays giving overviews and state-by-state studies on the Christian Right in the 2004 elections.

Gutiérrez, Gustavo. *A Theology of Liberation: History, Politics, Salvation.* Maryknoll, N.Y.: Orbis Books, 1988. A revised edition of one of the classics in Liberation Theology, the Latin American parallel to the Social Gospel movement.

Herberg, Will. *Protestant, Catholic, Jew: An Essay in American Religious Sociology.* New York: Anchor Books, 1955, 1983. A classical book in the sociology of religion field documenting the way Protestants, then Catholics and then Jews became accepted into the American Way of Life.

Jackson, Sherman A. *Islam and the Blackamerican: Looking toward the Third Resurrection.* New York: Oxford University Press, 2005. Good source for the relations of African American and Middle Eastern Muslims in America.

Kennedy. Sheila Suess, and Wolfgang Bielefeld. *Charitable Choice at Work: Evaluating Faith-Based Job Programs in the States.* Washington, D.C.: Georgetown University Press, 2006. A non-partisan evaluation of the successes and failures of the charitable choice programs.

Kepel, Gilles. *Allah in the West: Islamic Movements in America and Europe.* Stanford: Stanford University Press, 1997. A good but dated source.

Lee, Martha F. *The Nation of Islam: An American Millenarian Movement.* Syracuse: Syracuse University Press, 1996. A description of the movement based on field work among the Chicago leaders.

Lilla, Mark. *The Stillborn God: Religion, Politics, and the Modern West.* New York: Alfred A. Knopf, 2007. Traces the intellectual history of the humanist challenge to religious-based authority.

Pipes, Daniel. *Militant Islam Reaches America*. New York: W. W. Norton and Company, 2002. An attempt at an objective account of militant Islam and American politics.

Raza, Raheel. *Their Jihad… Not My Jihad: A Muslim Canadian Woman Speaks Out*. Ingersoll: Basileia Books, 2005.. A Canadian feminist Muslim distances herself from the Jihadis.

Walker, Dennis. *Islam and the Search for African-American Nationhood: Elijah Muhammad, Louis Farrakhan and the Nation of Islam*. Atlanta: Clarity Press, 2005. Introduction to the Nation of Islam.

White, Vilbert L. Jr. *Inside the Nation of Islam: A Historical and Personal Testimony by a Black Muslim*. Gainesville: University Press of Florida, 2001. An account made more interesting because it is written by someone involved in the movement and organizing the 1995 Million Man March.

Wilcox, Clyde, and Carin Larson. *Onward Christian Soldiers: The Religious Right in American Politics*, 3rd edition. Boulder: Westview Press, 2006. Great information on the topic.

WEBSITES

ava.publicreligion.org   Interactive maps on topics in the United States.

news.bbc.co.uk/2/hi/africa/country_profiles/1064557.stm   BBC News country profile on Nigeria.

news.bbc.co.uk/2/hi/africa/country_profiles/1072592.stm   BBC News country profile on Somalia.

www.cc.org   Site of the Christian Coalition of America.

www.cddwestafrica.org/index/php   Website of the Center for Democracy and Development, a Nigeria based group promoting better democracy and poverty relief in West Africa.

www.cufi.org   Site of Christians United for Israel.

www.discovery.org   The site of the Discovery Institute, an advocate for Intelligent Design.

www.finalcall.com   The official news site of the Nation of Islam.

www.muslimsinamerica.org   Has interesting pictures and stories reflecting the history of Muslim in America.

www.politicalresources.net/canada/canada.htm   Links to articles and information on Canada's political parties and related topics.

www.telosgroup.org   Site of the Telos Group

KEY PEOPLE

The Rev. Jerry Falwell   A Christian pastor who founded the Moral Majority.

Wallace Fard or **Farad**   Founder of the Nation of Islam.

Louis Farrakhan   Current leader of the Nation of Islam.

Pastor John Hagee   Chairman of Christians United for Israel.

William Miller   A prophet who predicted the Advent of Christ would take place by 1844.

Elijah Muhammad   An early convert and subsequent leader of the Nation of Islam.

The Rev. Pat Robertson   A Christian pastor who founded The Christian Coalition.

Malcom X   A leader/author who turned from the Nation of Islam to Sunni Islam.

GLOSSARY

American Exceptionalism A term for the idea that the United States is unique in its democratic freedom ideals, or its accomplishments, or both.

Anglican Communion The network of Anglican Churches worldwide.

Answers in Genesis (AIG) A Creationist Christian ministry organization that operates theme parks in Kentucky promoting a Young Earth point of view.

Bible Belt Nickname for a belt-like strip of Christian conservative states stretching across the southeast of the USA.

Christian Coalition of America An organization advocating positions of the Christian Right in politics.

Christian Right A collective name used for conservative Christian organizations active in politics.

Christian Zionism, Christian Zionists A term for those Christians who support Zionism as a sign of the Second Coming of Christ.

Christians United for Israel A Christian Zionist organization.

Civil Religion A term referring to the religious and moral values of a nation as expressed through public rituals and customs.

Creation Science The concept that the belief in divine creation can be defended as a kind of science.

Discovery Institute An organization that promotes Old Earth Creationism.

Dispensationalists Christians who believe God's plan is dispensed in stages.

End Time or **Eschaton** The expected end of the current social order, as part of God's plan.

Faith-based initiatives A plan to deliver social programs through religious organizations.

Intelligent Design The belief that the order of the world suggests that it was the work of a intelligent designer; that is, a divine creator.

Millenarian A person or group who believes that the end of the current social order is coming soon.

Million Man March A 1995 gathering of African American men in Washington D.C. to advocate for African American issues.

Moral Majority A lobbying group advocating Christian Right issues.

New Democractic Party A left-leaning Canadian political party.

Old Earth Creationism A Creationist theological stance that accepts the scientific claim that the earth and universe are billions of years old.

Roe v. Wade A 1973 United States Supreme Court Case in which the ruling was more permissive for abortion.

Social Gospel A social activism movement mostly by liberal Christians.

stem cell research An innovative branch of medical research opposed by many in the Christian Right, mostly out of fear that it might promote abortion.

Voter Guide A comparative listing or rating of candidates' positions, usually distributed by the Christian Right.

Young Earth Creationism A Jewish and Christian theological stance that accepts the Genesis as proof that the universe and the earth are less than 10,000 years old.

Chapter Nine

The Big Picture

OVERVIEW: THE MANY VARIATIONS OF THE RELIGION AND POLITICS INTERFACE

We have visited the hot spots from Japan to North America where religion and politics are interfacing. Our first major stop was China, where we found an officially atheistic government that wants to discourage religion and control organized religion. The Chinese model for the interface of religion and politics is that the government insists on approving the appointment of all religious leaders and arrests any religious leader thought to be a threat to the government or its policies. The religions try to stay under the government's radar and not be perceived as a threat. The government recognizes five religions officially: Daoism, Buddhism, Islam, Catholicism, and Protestantism. The government's fear that Catholic loyalty to the papacy might undermine its own authority has driven many Chinese Catholics into an underground Catholic Church still loyal to the papacy. Similarly, the government's excessive control over Protestants has given rise to the growing House Church movement. As for the Muslims, the government does not interfere too much with the Hui Muslims, who are well assimilated into Han society. However, the situation is quite different with the Uyghur Muslims, whose separatist movements have led to strong countermeasures by the government. The Tibetan Buddhist minority also feels that the government has overly restricted both the Tibetan religion and Tibetan culture. Protests for more regional autonomy by the Uyghur and Tibetan minorities have been met with severe government crackdowns.

Our stopover in Thailand revealed a model in which the king must be a Buddhist, and the king's ritual changing of the robes on the Emerald Buddha image symbolizes the subservience of politics to religious authority. Despite the official and symbolic links between Buddhism and politics, the Thai parliament is relatively free of direct religious influence, and the Buddhist organizations are relatively free of direct political meddling. The Thai model of the religion and politics interface has worked reasonably well for the Thai Buddhist majority, but not for the ethnic Malay Muslims in the South, who have not received their fair share of government assistance.

In Sri Lanka we saw a nation still trying to heal the wounds of a civil war between Tamil separatists who were mostly Hindus and the government forces backed by the majority Sinhalese Buddhist population. We saw that the Tamil demands had touched off a Buddhist Nationalist movement that has influenced government policies. The Buddhist Nationalist movement led to the formation of a National Heritage Party that once elected monks to seats in parliament and remains a staunchly nationalist voice in parliament. A small but militant number of Sinhalese Buddhists have recently become hostile toward other religions.

The Maoist rebel movement in Nepal has led the Maoist party to a position of strength. The Maoists have forced the unpopular king to resign, putting an end to a longstanding and formerly respected monarchy. As the head of a coalition of parties, the Maoists now have formed the government. The Maoist party is not against religion, in the Marxist fashion, but was against the monarchy and the exploitation of the masses by the higher castes.

In India we saw the world's largest democracy and a secular state. Yet there are problems arising from the religious sphere. One problem is that the traditional high caste discrimination against the Dalits has led to a controversial affirmative action program, but has not done much to alleviate the poverty of millions of India's Dalits. Another problem is that India's Muslims continue to feel dominated by the Hindu majority. The tension between Muslims and Hindus has been highest, we saw, when the Hindu Nationalists have been in power as they now are. One of the troubling issues is what to do about the site of the former Babri Mosque in Ayodhya. Should the Hindus be allowed to build a Ram temple there, or should the Muslims get to restore the Babri Mosque? Either political decision will touch off riots by the losing side.

Our travels to Saudi Arabia revealed yet another model for the interface of religion and politics. The House of Saud and the House of the Shaykh have been supporting each other since the mid-1700s. This partnership between a strictly conservative group of Salafi clerics and an ambitious monarchy started humbly but took on major significance after the discovery of massive amounts of oil in Saudi Arabia. To appease the Salafis, the Saudi government has given a significant portion of the oil revenues to fund overseas Islamic institutions. This has led to the building of mosques, staffed by Salafi Imams and backed by Salafi publications, throughout the world. The Shi'i minority in the oil rich eastern part of Saudi Arabia has been discriminated against for centuries by the Salafi faction within Sunni Islam, but they are now trying to assert their rights within Saudi politics. The rise of Shi'i political power in Iraq and Iran is playing a role in raising their expectations while also raising the fears of the Saudi royalty.

We saw a modern theocracy at work in Iran. There is an elected parliament, but a head cleric is the Supreme Leader. Working through a series of councils of other clerics, he maintains an absolute veto power over all government decisions. No candidate, no political party and no legislation can proceed without the approval of the appropriate clerics. We also saw that the influence of the Shi'i Muslims of Iran has spread throughout the Middle East, especially into Iraq and Lebanon. Whereas Shi'i Islam has been out of political power for much of its existence, it is now on the rise. The spread of Shi'i money, weapons and influence is profoundly shaping Iraqi politics as Iraq struggles to find a way for Sunni, Shi'i and Kurd Muslims to govern themselves peacefully and effectively.

Lebanon provides a very different model, Consociational Democracy, for the interface of religion and politics. Maronite Christians dominated Lebanese politics before the current power sharing agreement came into effect. Political power sharing, Lebanese style, means that each of the Maronite Christian, Sunni Muslim and Shi'i Muslim communities get a fixed number of seats in parliament and places in the civil service. Also, each political position from the President on down through civil service appointments is reserved for one of the three religious communities. This system of religious power sharing has kept the peace, but lately the Shi'i Hezbollah faction is demanding a bigger slice of the political pie.

Israel provides a different model of the influence of religion on politics, one involving invoking religious authority for possessing land. The Zionist claim to the territory is based upon a promise said to have been made by God to the Israeli people. In practical terms, it was the discrimination, pogroms, and holocaust in Europe that drove so many Jews to migrate to Palestine. Yet the theological claim to the territory remains quite important, especially for the more conservative Jews. The Palestinian resistance to Jewish territorial expansion has taken several forms. The PLO began as a rather secular organization, with participation of both Christian and Muslim Palestinians, but it has moved toward the Islamic camp while still having Palestinian Christian support. Hamas, on the other hand, began as an Islamic organization committed to restoring Palestinian rule over Palestine. As a Nationalist movement, it is somewhat out of step with the pan-Islamic goals that have emerged among many militant Islamic groups.

Our stop in Turkey let us see a model that is the polar opposite of the Iranian one. Whereas in Iran, a council of clerics makes sure that all legislation and policy is religiously acceptable, in Turkey a council of military leaders makes sure that all legislation and policy is not too religious. The insistence upon maintaining a secular form of government goes back to the days of Kemal Ataturk, but the majority of the Muslims in Turkey today seem to want more Islamic influence upon the government. Ironically, the majority of Muslims in Iran seem to want less religious influence on their government. We saw that Turkey's quest for entry into the European Union has been stalled in part because many current EU member states fear being overwhelmed by Islamic immigration or influence.

France revealed a government somewhat obsessed with keeping its school system secular. To do so, France has banned the wearing of large symbols of religious identity. This ban seems to be mainly aimed at prohibiting Muslim girls from wearing headscarves to public schools, but it applies to all religions. We noted that most EU countries have a right wing, anti-immigration party. The French right wing party, the Front National, has gained in popularity under the leadership of Marine Le Pen and in an era of increasing Islamic terrorism such as the attack on the staff of *Charlie Hebdo* in January 2015.

The clash between secular Western culture and conservative Islamic culture got our attention during our stop in The Netherlands. We saw that the insistence of one newspaper in Denmark on giving cartoonists a free forum for the publication of cartoons about Islam, whether critical or not, led to a cartoon controversy that played into the hands of Islamic conservatives from Nigeria to the Philippines. A film critical of Islamic extremists made by a Dutch politician has touched off a new round of confrontation between those who advocate the freedom of expression and those who hold that Islam should not be subject to public criticism.

In North America we saw the legacy of the Social Gospel. It helped with the labour movement in both Canada and the United States, and it led to the public health and other social services systems in Canada. We saw that the Christian Right in the United States was initially not very effective in politics, but that all changed when its members became an important component of the Republican Party, helping to elect George W. Bush twice. The Christian Right in Canada has also come into a position of influence through the Conservative Party, which has roots in evangelical Christianity. The Nation of Islam in the United States has been quite successful in recruiting members from among the African American population. It originally avoided politics, on the belief that the American political system was an evil one destined for self-destruction, but more recently the NOI has helped organize political marches to Washington. The NOI is also developing a better relationship with Sunni Islam. The United States model is to idealize the "separation of church and state" while at the same time accommodating considerable religious influence upon the political agenda.

THEORETICAL DISCUSSION

The Islamic Revival and Other Pendulum Swings

One theory that we have considered is the state of religiosity in a particular nation does not necessarily remain constant. On the contrary, it often seems to swing like a pendulum. For example, in a particular decade or even larger time frame, religiosity in a country may be waning. Rather than stopping at a neutral position, it often overswings toward secularism. Once quite overextended, it starts swinging back toward the religious side, and overextends in that direction. That is, the extent of religious influence on politics tends to cycle when seen on a long time scale.

These swings in religiosity are relevant to understanding shifts in a population's view of the proper role of religion in politics. When the pendulum swings far to the religion side, public support grows for the state to be governed by religious values and moral principles.

Conversely, when the pendulum is far to the secular side, the more religious-minded citizens begin to feel alienated from the state. They may start private, religious-based schools to educate their children into their religious worldview. Or they may withdraw into communities separated from the mainstream way of life.

Europe remains predominantly secular, while China provides the best example of a pendulum that has begun to swing from the secular toward the religious side. The government of China remains staunchly secular, while tolerating religious organizations as long as they submit to governmental controls. And yet there is a strong religious revival happening in China. Ethnic minorities, such as the Uyghurs and Tibetans, are looking more strongly to their Muslim or Buddhist identities for support. And the majority Han Chinese are more and more rediscovering their ancestral traditions or, especially, turning to evangelical forms of Protestantism or to Catholicism.

In India, a reaction by some conservative Hindus against secularism, Muslim activism and Christian missionizing has helped spawn a Hindu Nationalist movement that wants to rebuild the Ram Temple, rewrite school history curricula, and counter the demands made by some Muslim groups. Nehru's goal of having a secular state, while accommodating all religions, has slowly given way to a system in which various political parties tend to promise support to a particular religion to gain votes.

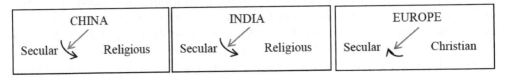

In the United States, the Christian Right has emerged as an influential political force, thereby swinging the pendulum more toward the side of religious influence on politics and public policy. Despite the official separation of church and state, there is significant religious influence on public policy issues such as abortion, stem cell research, high school curricula, and same-sex marriages.

The Islamic Revival is, however, by far the most important example of the swing toward more religious involvement in the political process. The 1979 Islamic Revolution brought a conservative form of Shi'i Islam in Iran, establishing a theocracy in the modern era. More recently, Shi'i political assertiveness has spread into Iraq, Syria, Jordan, and beyond. Among Sunnis, the various Brotherhood movements, ranging all the way from North Africa to China, are becoming more united behind the idea of establishing Muslim states strictly governed by Shariah. Meanwhile, the most militant group, ISIS, has carved out a sizable 'Islamic State' under its control.

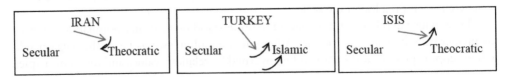

The One Truth versus Many Truths

One of the many things that complicate the interface of religion and politics is that so many religions hold very strongly to the notion that their religious tradition is the one and only true religion. This stance is typical of the religions that arose in the Middle East, including Judaism, Christianity and Islam. If the religious leaders and the majority of the citizens firmly believe that their religion is the absolute truth, it becomes easier to make religious law the basis of state law and to justify mistreatment of followers of other religions.

On the other hand, the idea that there are many paths leading to the top of the mountain is a common position taken by religions originating in India, such as Hinduism and Buddhism. For example, during his 2008 trip to the United States, right at the height of his being blamed by the Chinese government for protests in China as it was about to host the Olympics, the Dalai Lama said, "As you know, I always believed since all different traditions have the same potential to bring inner peace, inner value... it is important to keep one's own tradition."[1]

Fundamentalists, Secularists, and the Moderates on the Basis of Authority

A radical dispute over the basis of authority lies at the heart of the interface of religion and politics. If we surveyed all humans with the question "Where religion and society conflict, do you follow religious teachings or other social norms?" and graphed the results, we would likely get a continuum of answers ranging from extreme secularism to extreme religious authority. Yet most persons would likely fall somewhere in the mid-range of that graph.

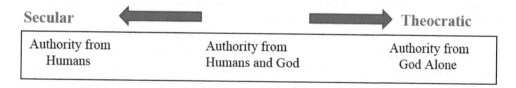

Secular		Theocratic
Authority from Humans	Authority from Humans and God	Authority from God Alone

Fundamentalist on the Basis of Authority
At the far right of our graph are those who mistrust any social norms, political laws, or scientific views that conflict with the teachings of their religious tradition. These are the self-styled "true believers" and they refuse to reinterpret their religious teachings to accommodate new knowledge or new social norms. As one fundamentalist Christian put it, "democracy is the cause of all world problems... humans are under the law of God, and thus they CANNOT do anything they want or speak anything they wish to speak... democ-

---

[1]Tenzin Norbu, *Ocean of Compassion: A Guide to the Life of Universal Loving* (Bloomington: WestBow Press, 2012), xvii.

racy ultimately started with Satan... we can't rule ourselves. God must rule us."[2] Islamists would concur, holding that the Shariah based on the Quran and other Islamic documents has authority over any contravening laws humans might legislate. When ancient Hebrews asked Samuel to appoint a human king, the conservative Hebrews favored the older system in which God was thought to be their king.

Secularists on the Basis of Authority

At the far left of our graph are those who put their trust in science, humanism, and the values of modernity. For them, no religious or social norm of the past is too sacred to be rethought or replaced. They are secularists, although they may very well hold spiritual beliefs and traditions.

Secularists are generally opposed to the mixing of religion and politics. They point out that religion has been the cause of, or at least an exacerbating factor in, most wars. They see no way in which a modern, pluralistic nation with citizens of many religions could ever successfully accommodate all of their many holidays, school curriculum demands, dietary restrictions, dress codes, or moral teachings. So they think that best solution is to move public education, public holidays, public policy, and politics far away from religious control.

Middle Ground

Then there are the many moderates who fall somewhere in the middle of the graph. On the one hand moderates tend to think that there should be some limits on the interface of religion and politics. They have confidence in science and are open to new social norms. They resist religion-based denunciations of such things as stem cell research or same-sex marriage. On the other hand, they may find spirituality or an association with an organized religious group to be a very valuable part of their lives. They may even be quite religious personally, but they are fairly tolerant of other religions or of secular values. They may say they believe in a Creator God and they may also say they believe in modern science. Moderates may also favor some government support for religious traditions, such as public displays at major religious festivals. They manage to keep a foot in both camps. Those who are affiliated with a religion may find themselves criticized by that religion's more fundamentalist members as not being "reborn Christians" or "good Muslims" or "pious Jews," and so on. Those who are committed secularists may criticize them for bringing religion too much into politics, the school curriculum, or public funding of science. Yet moderates want the best of both the religious and the secular worlds. When it comes to vote, moderates may reject a candidate who seems too religiously conservative as well as one who seems overly critical of religion.

Moderate versus Militant Fundamentalism

Whether they are Hindus, Buddhists, Muslims, Christians, or Jews, most fundamentalists we have encountered are not militants. They may be zealous in their spirituality. They may

---

[2]From "Christian Fundamentalism Exposed." www.sullivan-county.com/news

be quite missionary. They may dress in a traditional way and follow religious law such as the Torah or Shariah in their personal life, and they may wish that everyone did the same. But they do not attack those with other beliefs and practices. They are moderates and not militant extremists. They form the vast majority of fundamentalists among any of the religions we have discussed.

Yet there is a minority of fundamentalists among all of the religions who do turn to violence to enforce their way of life or punish those who they feel are breaking God's law. These are the Christians who bomb abortion clinics, attack homosexuals, or push foreign-looking people in front of trains. These are the Buddhists who burn Muslim shops. These are the Muslims who behead foreigners, bomb hotels, or fly planes into buildings. These are the Hindus who randomly attack Muslim homes and shops in revenge for some incident in another city. These are the people around the world who commit acts of terrorism in the name of some religion.

MIXING OF RELIGION AND POLITICS: GOOD OR BAD?

We have travelled to many of the world's hot spots in search of an understanding of the interface of religion and politics. Now that we are on our way home, we can think about our initial question about mixing religion and politics: Good or Bad?

The answer to the question seems to come down to what one sees as the final basis of authority. Those who think that ultimate authority is based on religious revelation and tradition, not on science, reasoning, public norms, or democratic processes, want politics to conform to religious truth as they understand it. So they are pleased when their version of religion gets influence over politics. The trouble for them is that in every country we visited, there are several interpretations of religious truth, even among those of the same religious tradition.

Those who see religious teachings as just the wisdom of humans a long time ago, and not really based on the word of God or having ultimate authority over every aspect of life, favor the separation of religion and politics. For them, mixing religion and politics is definitely a mistake.

Those in the middle tend to think the two should not normally mix but that there should be a system of checks and balances. They want religion to check major political wrongs. They want a religious or moral voice publically criticizing corruption or unjust practices by the political and business elites. They prefer a world in which someone like Gandhi, Martin Luther King, Jr. or the Dalai Lama can appeal for a radical change in the political status quo in the name of higher moral or religious principles. They may also feel that there are times when political authorities have to put a check on religious groups who may be violating widely accepted social norms.

We have seen that there are so many variations that it now seems simplistic to say that religion and politics should never mix. Maybe we need to pose the question in a more complex way: Under what circumstances should religion interfere in politics, and under what circumstances should a government interfere in religious matters?

We began this book with this question: Is the mixing of religion and politics good or bad?

A Zen master once told a student, who was being too dependent on the master for guidance, that if there is anything to take hold of, you must take hold of it for yourself. In that spirit, we end the book with this reply: You must decide for yourself.

Index